D0907799

A MASSIVE SEASON

*

SIRK'S NOTEBOOK CHRONICLES THE 2008 COLUMBUS CREW

WADE,

THANK YOU FOR THE AWESOME MLS: CUP
PHOTOS. THEY MADE THE BOOK FEEL COMPLETE
TO ME. YOUR SHOT OF FRANKIE AND THE
THIRD GOAL IS ONE OF MY FAVORITES.

Steve
Sirk

*

BY

STEVE SIRK

This book is dedicated to the memory of anyone who loved the Columbus Crew but did not grace this world long enough to witness the team's Massive accomplishment on November 23, 2008. This includes, but is sadly not limited to:

Crew founder Lamar Hunt (d. December 13, 2006)

Former Crew coach Tom Fitzgerald (d. December 4, 2004)

Crew fans Marlane Berlat (d. March 17, 2001) and Jim Nelson (d. March 18, 2008)

And my mother, Jeanne Kraft (d. June 19, 2006)

TABLES OF CONTENTS

I took "Table of Contents" literally and created actual tables for the contents. But since this is America, I did not create a "single table." Sorry, Eurosnobs.

A Forward's Foreword, by Dante Washington............................*i*

Preface & Acknowledgements...*vii*

SECTION I: THE WAY WE WERE

Massive	3
Sirk's Notebook: Bring out Your Dead	11
Flick's 2005 Crew Obituary	16
My First Game of the Sigi Era	17
Sigi's (De)Press(ed) Conference	21
Supporters	23
Curses	24
Signs of Life	28

SECTION II: THE REGULAR SEASON

Media Day	35
The Ridiculous Press Release	39
Sirk's Notebook: Crew 2, Toronto 0 (March 29, 2008)	41
Myth: Toronto Invented Columbus	54
Road Work: New York 2, Columbus 0 (April 5, 2008)	59
Sirk's Notebook: Crew 4, Chivas USA 3 (April 12, 2008)	60
Road Work: Crew 2, D.C. United 1 (April 17, 2008)	75
Sirk's Notebook: Crew 1, Houston 0 (April 26, 2008)	76
Sirk's Notebook: Crew 2, Kansas City 1 (May 3, 2008)	89
Road Work: Crew 3, San Jose 2 (May 10, 2008)	101
Road Work: Crew 0, Toronto 0 (May 17, 2008)	102
Sirk's Notebook: New England 1, Crew 0 (May 24, 2008)	103
The Incidents, Part I: The YouTube Video	115
U.S. Open Cup: Crew 2, Salt Lake 0 (May 27, 2008)	119
Road Work: Chivas USA 2, Crew 0 (May 31, 2008)	120
Sirk's Notebook: San Jose 2, Crew 0 (June 7, 2008)	121
U.S. Open Cup: Chicago 3, Crew 2 (OT) (June 11, 2008)	133

SECTION II: THE REGULAR SEASON CON'T

Road Work: Crew 3, Kansas City 0 (June 14, 2008)	134
Road Work: Crew 3, Los Angeles 3 (June 21, 2008)	135
Sirk's Notebook: Crew 2, Colorado 1 (June 28, 2008)	136
Sirk's Notebook: Crew 2, Chicago 2 (July 5, 2008)	149
Road Work: Salt Lake 2, Crew 0 (July 12, 2008)	160
Sirk's Notebook: Crew 3, Kansas City 3 (July 17, 2008)	161
The Incidents, Part II: West Ham United and the Importance of Diction	175
Road Work: Crew 2, Colorado 0 (July 27, 2008)	177
Road Work: Houston 2, Crew 0 (August 2, 2008)	178
Sirk's Notebook: Oughton's Intro-Dunc-tions (2008)	179
Oughton's Re-intro-Dunc-tions (2006 & 2007)	185
Sirk's Notebook: Crew 2, Dallas 1 (August 16, 2008)	192
Sirk's Notebook: Crew 3, Salt Lake 0 (August 23, 2008)	207
Road Work: Crew 2, Dallas 1 (August 30, 2008)	223
Sirk's Notebook: Crew 4, New England 0 (September 6, 2008)	224
Road Work: Crew 1, Toronto 1 (September 13, 2008)	242
The Incidents, Part III: A Scare in the Air	243
Sirk's Notebook: Crew 3, New York 1 (September 18, 2008)	251
Road Work: Crew 1, New England 0 (September 27, 2008)	270
The Incidents, Part IV: (Not) Leaving (For) Las Vegas	271
Sirk's Notebook: Crew 1, Los Angeles 0 (October 4, 2008)	278
Frankie Hejduk: Tailgating Captain	295
Road Work: Crew 2, Chicago 2 (October 12, 2008)	296
Road Work: New York 3, Crew 1 (October 18, 2008)	297
Sirk's Notebook: Crew 1, D.C. United 0 (October 26, 2008)	298
Bonus Crew-D.C. Notebook Blog	307
2008 Columbus Crew Team Award Winners	312

SECTION III: THE PLAYOFFS

Road Work: Crew 1, Kansas City 1 (November 1, 2008)	321
Sirk's Notebook: Crew 2, Kansas City 0 (November 8, 2008)	322
Sirk's ECF Notebook: Crew 2, Chicago 1 (November 13, 2008)	334
The Awkwardness Amidst the Joy	354

SECTION III: THE PLAYOFFS CON'T

Playoff Beards: BC vs. Gaven	359
LA Blog: Greetings from the Golden State	360
LA Blog: Friday Morning Notes	364
LA Blog: Friday Afternoon Notes	367
LA Blog: Dwight	370
LA Blog: Moffat & Lenhart's Celebrity Sighting	372
LA Blog: A Brief Chat with Dan Hunt	374
LA Blog: Some Gibberish about Saturday	375
A "Flick On" About MLS Cup Eve	378
LA Blog: It's Here	379
Wyatt's Winning Ways	380
Sirk's MLS Cup Notebook: Columbus Crew 3, New York Red Bulls 1	381
Crew Blog: The Big Nasty Fan Club	421
Crew Blog: Haircuts	422
Two More Awesome MLS Cup Photos	425
2008 Major League Soccer Standings	426
2008 Columbus Crew Final Stats	427
2008 ColumbusCrew Individual MLS Honors	428

SECTION IV: THE JOYOUS AFTERMATH

Airport Adulation	431
Crew Blog: Meeting with the Guv	433
Champions Way & Championship Row	435
Championship Bling	436
The Champs Visit the White House	438
From Those Who Had Come Before…	441
A Picture is Worth a Lifetime of Words	452

A Forward's Foreword
By Dante Washington

There are not many people that have had a relationship with the Columbus Crew like the one that I have been fortunate to have. As a player, ex-player, then player, then ex-player, then player again, then ex-player again, and now broadcast analyst, I've experienced a full range of emotions – from the frustration of near-misses and the anger of being let go, to the pride and joy of the 2002 U.S. Open Cup and 2008 MLS Cup championship.

Although I am from Maryland, my relationship with Ohio started many moons ago with a soccer tournament in Centerville. I do not remember much from the trip other than not winning the whole thing and driving there in a rented Buick Century. My mother must have loved the trip because she bought a Buick Century shortly after we got home. It turned out to be a lemon. Great job, Mom!

I returned to Ohio again in 1992 for a U.S. Olympic Qualification match in the Columbus suburb of Dublin. Coming from a soccer-rich area in Maryland, I had no idea that 10,000+ people in OHIO would come watch a soccer game! The atmosphere was great, as it was our only sell-out, and we won handily.

In 1996, I joined the Crew for the first time after being convinced to play professionally by the late Tom Fitzgerald. Fitz was instrumental in my career after playing for him with the National "B" Team. Sadly, this trip to Columbus was merely a pit-stop, as I was traded one month later to Dallas. (Me for my Olympic roommate Brad Friedel. Good trade.) It was a huge shock to me because I did not want to leave Columbus. It was also a huge shock to Fitz, who did not expect Dallas to pick me from the list of players they could choose from. Fitz promised that if he ever had the chance to bring me back, he would.

True to his word, Fitz brought me back to Columbus before the 2000 season. During my longest tenure, from 2000-2003, I began to bleed Black & Gold. I enjoyed my most success as a pro and developed a serious affection for the area. I had great personal success in 2000, we won the Open Cup in 2002, and I had a locker room full of stellar teammates. I felt comfortable here, and Columbus began to feel like home. (Columb-US, Columb-IA. Coincidence?) Plus, we were averaging 17,000 fans a game in the first soccer-specific stadium, the team was having success, and people around town knew and supported us. I felt like I was a part of the community. I truly felt like I was playing for my city.

But, as all good things come to an end, I left in 2003, returned in 2004, and then left again early in 2005, retiring at the end of that season. Then in 2007, General Manager Mark McCullers opened the door for me to once again become a part of the Crew family by hiring me as a broadcast analyst.

As a part of the broadcast team for the 2008 championship season with Dwight Burgess, I saw the evolution of this once-in-a-lifetime experience. I do not think that we will ever see something like this again. This is not to say that the Crew will never again win MLS Cup, but there were myriad scenarios that occurred during the season that were extremely rare and made the season so unique. The many moving parts of the team all beautifully came together.

The 2008 Crew had the ingredients of a successful team: talented youth, talented veterans, cohesion, great coaching staff, and luck.

A perfect example of the 2008 Crew's talented youth is Robbie Rogers, who was named to the MLS Best XI at the age of 21. And it's hard to count a 22-year-old like Eddie Gaven as "young talent" because he has been in the league for so long. Maybe he should be called a "young veteran."

The Crew also had talented "old" veterans like league MVP Guillermo Barros Schelotto and team captain Frankie Hejduk. Guille is a Boca Juniors legend who truly makes his teammates better, and Frankie's motor never stops running. I guess when you weigh 140 pounds, you can run all day. Having played in the Bundesliga and in two World Cups, Frankie's reputation precedes him. But it is not just what Frankie brings on the field, but off the field. He can bring the comic relief, or he can say the things that need to be said. And another important veteran was Alejandro Moreno. Not only did he play a pivotal role in the Crew's offense, but he has won three MLS Cups, which speaks for itself. Add in Duncan Oughton (who I have seen blossom into the consummate professional), Ezra Hendrickson, and Stefani Miglioranzi to the mix, and right there you have well over 30 years of professional playing experience!

The 2008 Crew also had incredible team cohesion. When you have guys that are in it for the team, the team is always better. This was a team that if a player was out there for 8 minutes, 30 minutes, or 90 minutes, each player was going to bust his butt to fulfill his role. They did it time and time again.

A part of this team cohesion was the undying support of the fans. The decision to put a stage in the North End was the catalyst for the

Nordecke. It seemed like all of the stars aligned. As the section grew, it carried over onto the field, and then Sigi and the players did a great job of reciprocating that love. They let the fans know that they fired them up when things were good and picked them up when things were down. Every successful team needs the support of the fans.

The Crew also had an experienced and knowledgeable coaching staff. The staff consisted of head coach Sigi Schmid, assistant coaches (and former Crew players) Mike Lapper and Robert Warzycha, and goalkeeper coach Vadim Kirilov. I didn't really know Sigi before he came to Columbus. It's easy to look at his accomplishments and tell that the man can coach. He's won multiple championships at both the collegiate and professional levels. He clearly knows what he's doing and put together a great staff.

As I got to know him better, I saw that he had a good grasp on the goals he wanted to achieve, and then would tell the team exactly how they were going to get there. And then they did it. Going into the season, I doubt there were more than a few people in Columbus who thought he knew what he was doing, but he proved them wrong. And hats off to the Hunts for sticking with him. Sigi finally found the right ingredients. People don't realize how hard it is to coach in MLS since you don't have an open checkbook like other leagues.

And then there was luck. Every championship team needs it. I think back to that last game of the season. D.C. United hit every square inch of the left post, but couldn't buy a goal. Then Brad Evans hits that same goal post from 30 yards away and it goes in. That game kept D.C. out of the playoffs and got New York in. Then New York benefitted from a whole bunch of goalposts in the playoffs just to get to MLS Cup. And then their luck ran out against the Crew.

However, the Crew was not just a lucky team. I firmly believe that you make your own luck. The 2008 Crew could not be deterred in any way. If you put two in on them, they would just go out and get three. The team found a way to get results and often in convincing ways. Just when you thought the wheels were going to fall off, they found a way to pull it out and get a positive result. This all culminated with me standing on the field of the Home Depot Center looking at the screen reading "2008 MLS Champions: The Columbus Crew." On many personal levels, it was a true pleasure to see it all happen and to be there for the final whistle.

I remember looking at the screen and seeing MLS Cup champions along with our logo, and I kept thinking, "Something's going to happen." Like, Don Garber was going to say that there was some kind of mistake, and then a Red Bulls logo would go up on the screen instead. But that didn't happen. We really made it to the top of the mountain.

A lot of the current players said that the win was also for all of the older Crew players who came before, and it's great that those guys felt that way. There were a lot of players who experienced near misses and a lot guys who worked hard to put them where they are today. But that's how it goes. The torch is always passed on to someone else. Someday in the future, some new group of Crew players is going to talk about trying to put another star on the crest to build on what this group of players has done.

A constant through all of my years in Columbus, and also of the championship season of 2008, has been Steve Sirk's Notebook. Often giving a "different perspective", the Notebook takes you into the locker room and the mind of the team as it has done for many years. Through the comical Notebook, Sirk has chronicled many of my comments and emotions through the years. He was my link to you, the fans, on a weekly basis. As players, win or lose, my teammates and I were able to let our personalities show. This was therapeutic after a loss and icing on the cake after a win.

Just like on the field, the torch gets passed from guys like me, Duncan, and Brian Dunseth. Duncan transcends both eras, but now we have characters like Adam Moffat and Danny O'Rourke. I'm glad Sirk hired a Scottish translator to get all those funny Moffat quotes, and I love that Danny will always have a go at Duncan. As many of you know, I appreciate anyone that will have a go at Duncan.

One of the things that lets players show their personality is not talking about soccer. We always talk about soccer, so it's great when Danny talks about his fashion style compared to Duncan's, or when Moffat talks about corn hole or bagpipe music, or when Sirk conducts serious investigations into such important topics as team beard-growing competitions or why Will Hesmer was suddenly going by "William." And only Sirk would create a team-wide process to name Duncan's post-retirement pub, or cover the Crew's fantasy football league as if it were a real sport. (Note to Danny O'Rourke—it's not.)

When we leave the stadium, we all know the outcome of a game and what transpired. There are countless media outlets for that. But there is only one Notebook.

I am sure that Sirk considers it a miracle that you are holding this book in your hands. Being a Browns and Indians fan, he has grown accustomed to disappointment. But thanks to the incredible story of the

A MASSIVE SEASON

2008 Columbus Crew, he has learned firsthand that there is light at the end of the tunnel, even if the dark tunnel for a Cleveland fan like him was very, very long.

The Crew is not like my mother's old Buick Century. We might be yellow in color, but we're sure no lemon.

DANTE WASHINGTON
Columbus, Ohio
June 2009

Preface & Acknowledgements

Let me start by stating that this is a book for Columbus Crew fans. I do not mean to dissuade others who may be looking for a season-long scrapbook about an MLS team, as other MLS fans may very well enjoy it, but the Notebooks (and therefore this book) were not written with non-Crew fans in mind. This is why I intentionally declined to lure a wider reading audience by subtitling the book:

"A Massive Season: The Year **THE BECKHAM EXPERIMENT** Came to Columbus and Becks Answered Questions Asked **BY GRANT WAHL**"

That, and what the lawyers told me.

I did not set out to write a book about the 2008 Crew season. I did not partake in secret dinners with players, coaches, and staff, tucking away little tidbits of information as I furtively worked to share an insider's account of the 2008 Columbus Crew. Rather, the Notebooks came home to TheCrew.com in 2008, and I just went about doing what I've done for most of the decade. By the end of the championship season, people started making comments about anthologizing my output from the 2008 season. Crew PR Director Dave Stephany casually mentioned that he was going to destroy acres of Amazonian rainforest by printing out each Notebook and putting them in a binder so he would have his own printed record of the season, and several readers emailed asking if I was going to publish all the Notebooks in book form. Based on overwhelming evidence that the demand could possibly approach double digits, I thought "what the hell" and rolled with it. I mean, a club only wins its first championship one time, right?

Had I just stuck to the Notebooks, this book would have been about 230-240 pages long. As you can see, it's about twice that length. A collection of Notebooks seemed incomplete, especially since I only do them for home games. Plus, the Notebooks are still available on the Crew's website if you want to save some money and read them in their not as toilet-friendly web form. Wanting the book to be more than just reprints of the Notebook, I went back and wrote up one-page recaps of all of the road games. Then I decided footnote commentary for the Notebooks might be a good idea. Then I wrote some new essays here and there. Then I decided it might be fun to pull out a few scraps that showed how dismal things were before the Massive Season. Then I decided to throw in some pictures, which ended up being way more pictures than I ever intended. Then I thought it might be fun to catch up with some former Crew players. And so on and so on. Again, I rolled with the "you'll never get a second chance to chronicle a first Crew championship" mantra, so I just tried to make this the type of enormous scrapbook that I would enjoy as a Crew fan. I hope you will too.

A season's worth of oddball reportage and the creation of a book require much more help than I can offer myself. There are plenty of people who assisted me throughout the 2008 season and in the creation of this book, so it's only fair that they share in some of the blame.

Dave Stephany did the impossible when he convinced me to commit to a full season's worth of Notebooks for TheCrew.com, despite the fact that I went to lunch with him for the sole purpose of getting the both of us a free expense account lunch at Chili's[1] before I turned him down. I was actually planning to take 2008 off from the Notebook. I am dead serious. My mind was 99% made up. But Dave's enthusiasm sparked my enthusiasm, and next thing I knew, I agreed to rejoin the Crew. I cursed Dave's name the whole way back to my office. In retrospect, I may have been wrong to do that. I finally told him this story in the Crew's champagne soaked locker room at the Home Depot Center, except that time I thanked him for talking me aboard against my wishes. I should also thank Dave for being a joy to work with, sticking to his word about non-interference, and for editorially helping me out when some of the stuff I turn in contains glaring errors or makes no sense whatsoever.

Crew President & GM Mark McCullers likes to use the term "Crew family" a lot, but I have been a firsthand beneficiary of this mantra. Whether it is Mark himself, or staff members such as Brian Bliss, Chad Schroeder, Scott DeBolt, Jason Smith or anyone else associated with the front office, I have certainly been made to feel like a member of the Crew family and not some idiot in the corner who writes stupid articles for the website. So I offer a big thank you to the Crew organization, top to bottom, both for 2008 and for their help in making this book a reality. The photo rights alone were an enormously big contribution, as were the stock away game quotes and the text from the 2008 Crew awards ceremony.

Over the years, I have always maintained that the Notebook would not exist without the help of the players, and that is perfectly true once again. First, I offer a very special thank you to Notebook Hall of Famer Duncan Oughton for a lifetime material in just eight seasons, including many quality

---

[1] In the immortal words of "The Office" boss Michael Scott: "Chili's is the new golf course."

additions in 2008. I think it was pretty obvious from my MLS Cup writings that out of all the players, I was happiest to see Duncan be crowned a champion. Also, thanks to Danny O'Rourke, Adam Moffat, William Hesmer, Steven Lenhart, Jason Garey, Andy Gruenebaum, and Frankie Hejduk, who have been kind enough to let me bother them whenever the mood strikes, and often play along with whatever stupid idea I have at the time. And thanks to Stefani Miglioranzi for following through on my stupid request for a photo of the Redondo Beach In-N-Out Burger. After being traded to the Galaxy, he was the only person I knew who lived in LA. But it's almost unfair to single anyone out because from top to bottom, the 2008 Crew had one of the friendliest and most accessible locker rooms that I have ever seen. As a whole, this team answered intelligent questions honestly, unintelligent questions gracefully, and silly questions with a knowing smile. One of the longstanding goals of the Notebook has been to bring the fans a little closer to the players by spotlighting their personalities and revealing some of the locker room hijinks. If the players lacked personalities or the willingness to show those personalities beyond standard postgame fare, I would be dead in the water. So a big thank you to the guys for trusting me and letting me occasionally barge into their world so that I may share tiny slices of it with you.

Like anyone remotely associated with the team side of the operation, I owe an enormous debt of gratitude to team administrator Tucker Walther. If the Crew had borrowed the concept of the National Debt Clock and had installed a Tucker Debt Clock upon his arrival in Columbus, it too would need to be replaced because it ran out of digits. His superhuman helpfulness always makes my job easier than it would be otherwise and I am but one of hundreds to have sincerely made that claim over the years. Other members of the team staff who deserve their share of thanks include Jason Mathews, Skylar "Paco" Richards, Steve Tashjian, Rusty Wummel, and Dr. J—a.k.a. "Dr. Scott Johnson." What an entertaining group.

It would be borderline criminal not to give a tip of the cap to Shawn Mitchell of the Columbus Dispatch and Craig Merz of MLSnet.com. Not only are they true professionals who do excellent work, but as friendly and trusted colleagues, they have also directly and indirectly contributed quality material to the Notebooks. Some of it is obvious. I mean, I am convinced that Merz works up Notebook-worthy conversation material in advance of our pregame chats. But some of it is not so obvious, as I have greatly benefited from the abundance of leftover crumbs generated by Shawn's and Craig's more astute observations and interview questions. Also, Merz gets an extra special thank you for being my primary chauffeur in Los Angeles and for letting me mooch free breakfast at his hotel.

Additionally, other media members have also been of immense help. Columbus Alive's Chris DeVille seemed to specialize in unearthing absurd Adam Moffat nuggets that I could then explore in even more absurdist detail. The Dispatch's Michael Arace deserves thanks, not just for causing me to weep in despair over his command of the language, but also for using the polarizing term "Fighting Canaries", which he then changed into "Massive Canaries", which therefore inspired my derivative creation of "Massive Bananas." Thanks to radio man Neil Sika for letting me crash in the booth sometimes and, more importantly, for using "Massive Bananas" on the air. Dwight Burgess should be thanked simply for being Dwight Burgess. If you asked him, he would agree, and if you knew him, you would understand. Since 1998, Dwight has been a helpful and hilarious part of my Crew world, and 2008 was no different. And while chatting with Katie Witham would brighten most anyone's day, I consider myself fortunate that she is good humored enough to let me catalog some of her blonder moments.

Notebook Hall of Famers turned broadcasters Dante Washington and Brian Dunseth continue to be valued friends and dependable co-conspirators. The always generous and versatile Dunseth shows up several times in this book in many different roles—broadcaster, player, chick magnet, think tank member, celebrity hobnobber, backseat driver, In-N-Out Burger photographer— while Dante did me the tremendous honor of writing the foreword. Dante was the first Crew player to truly "get it" when it came to the Notebook, so it was very important to me that he be involved in this project. He's the original Notebook Hall of Famer for a reason, and I am glad he came back for a fourth tour of Crew duty so he could be aboard for this magical championship ride. Crew Stadium is always more fun when Dante is around.

A few other ex-Crew men also helped out a bit. Nelson Akwari graciously provided personal updates throughout the Charleston Battery's run to the 2008 U.S. Open Cup final, going so far as to send one update from the library after his laptop computer melted down. And the former Indiana University trio of Crew Originals—Brian Maisonneuve, Mike Clark, and Todd Yeagley— provided momentum for a last second addition to this book. You'll see it at the end. And an extra special thanks to Mais for being a delight to cover when I first started out as a clueless, untrained, 23-year-old novice reporter freelancing the "Maisonneuve beat" for the Michigan Soccer News in 1998. I will never forget that within minutes of our introduction, he handed me a piece of paper with his home number on it, and told me to call him anytime I needed anything. Had he been a jerk, I might have decided I was in over my head and quit.

My friend Stephanie Morgan did a masterful job of stitching together dozens and dozens of separate documents into one properly numbered manuscript that could be shipped to the printer. She also redid all of the photos after I formatted them incorrectly. Had she not undertaken such a monotonous and soul-crushing task, you would not be holding this book in your hands because I would have hung myself.

Mike Flickinger (aka "my good buddy Flick") was kind enough to share two pieces of his own writing, plus he gave me a disc full of photos that he placed in his mailbox for me to pick up...while simultaneously setting his lawn sprinkler to bombard the mailbox with water. Good times. Notorious Big Soccer blogger Bill Archer kindly agreed to let me print excerpts of some of our private correspondence, as I felt his story of wanting to hire a witch doctor in 2007 was too good not to share as a prelude to the Massive Season. Matt Rolf was an invaluable source of writerly inspiration, feedback, and commiseration, plus he has designed and hosted the book's official website at www.sirkbook.com. And my friend Rob Jones subtly contributed with his encouragement, entrepreneurial enthusiasm, and shared wariness of the toy matinee.

Despite my initial intentions, this book contains a lot of photographs, mainly due to my fondness for these people and their efforts. I would like to stress that this book contains substandard reproductions of top-notch work, so please understand that any loss in quality is mine and mine alone. These started as crisp, vibrant, color pictures worthy of glossy photo paper, yet have been reduced to resized grayscale reproductions on normal print paper.

Greg Bartram contributed many excellent pictures to this tome. All of Greg's best shots are licensed through Getty Images, but the Crew had the ability to reassign any unused photos to a schmuck like me, so I thank them for doing so. Greg did yeoman's work in tediously digging through his archives and cross-referencing to ensure that I was only given the leftover shots that weren't sent to Getty. Thankfully, Greg has some good leftovers. To see Greg's best shots, please visit www.gettyimages.com and search by his name or the Crew. There are plenty of great photos available for purchase. Also, please visit www.betterimage.com if you are in need of Greg's local professional photography services.

Sam Fahmi was another treasured photo contributor. Sam is the official photographer of the Nordecke, so you'll notice that many of the excellent crowd shots bear his name. This book contains a number of Sam's photos that I love, but most crucially, he provided the only shots available to me of Chad Marshall's historic goal over Brian McBride in the Eastern Conference final. Both Bartram and Jay LaPrete had breathtaking shots, but those were property of Getty Imgages and the Associated Press, respectively. Sam came through with a tremendous time-lapse four-photo sequence captured from behind the goal. This book would have been lacking without it.

To see all of Sam's work, please visit his archives at www.flickr.com/photos/studio79.

One of the problems about doing this book after the fact is that I was not aware I was doing a book when everything went down. As a result of having no known agenda, I was hurting for photos from MLS Cup until the fine folks at Yellow Card Journalism came to the rescue. Over the past decade, Andy Mead and his merry band of shutterbugs have done a tremendous job shooting major soccer events all across the USA, and even the world. Through the graciousness of Mead and Wade Jackson, I was able to include YCJ photos from MLS Cup weekend. Mead also landed the cover shot. For more of their drool-worthy work, please visit www.ycjphoto.com.

Apart from these main contributors, I received photographic help from many others. Allison Andrews of www.SoccerCityUSA.com in Portland, Oregon, kindly provided a photo of Nas Kabourous that she shot during Hollywood United's ("famous" to me / "infamous" to her) U.S. Open Cup upset of the Portland Timbers. The book also features photos contributed by the following friends, fans, players, and staff: Mike Flickinger, Neil Sika, Adam Moffat, Steven Lenhart, Stefani Miglioranzi, Brian Dunseth, Tucker Walther, Jason Mathews, Dave Stephany, Andy Zartman, Mike Blankley, Kerri Jones, Janet Handler, and the late Jim Nelson. Thanks to all.

There are plenty of people who have helped during and even before this dozen-year journey of pro sports writing. My dad, Steve (but not Senior), was convinced that I would write a novel, but he will have to settle for this book instead. Also, he deserves all the credit in the world for rolling with the punches when I shattered his dream of being a Little League coach by stating that I wanted to play soccer instead of baseball. He learned about the sport, took me to Cleveland Force games, and never looked back. My mother, Jeanne, was also an avid sports fan who took me to many professional soccer games. She even attended the 1994 World Cup final through a friend who won the ticket lottery. Had Mom amended her will so that I would inherit her ticket, I would probably be rotting in prison today. She was also a large source of my sense of humor. And my life-long friend Jeff Pesek convinced me to play soccer when we were in first grade, which was truly a life-altering sales job. Not bad for a six-year-old.

I owe former Crew GM Jim Smith a debt of gratitude for his support during my first stint with the team. He encouraged me to write whatever I wanted and was extremely tolerant of what that entailed. I was lucky in that the Notebook would not have become what it did without his willingness to roll the dice like that. Former Crew PR guy Jeff Wuerth also deserves a lot of thanks for his patience as I learned the ropes around the press box and locker room in those early days when I clearly had no clue what I was doing. (By patience, I mean yelling at me instead of revoking my press pass.) And former Crew webmaster Shane Murphy was an excellent partner in crime. Besides, if he hadn't written such good game stories, I wouldn't have been forced to come up with something else like the Notebook.

Then there's the long list of other people that I have worked for, worked with, or received substantial help from over the years. This list of people includes Lee Smith, Scott Tann, Mark Montri, Walt Wheeler, Rich Fidler, Kristine "Hoolie" Fidler, Andy "The Nefarious Numbers Runner Known as Zman" Zartman, Jamie Fellrath, Alan Plum, Matt Bernhardt, Dr. Chuck Pearson, Andreas Stanescu, Mike Cornell, Chris Gallutia, Marlon Morris, Steve Thayer, Doug Allton, Dave Weissman, Barry McBride, Arthur B. Bietz, Jay Meno, Kori Stenzel, Scot Sedley, Jason Vestfals, Brian Guilfoos, Bob Cole, Dustin Scheurmann, plus many others I may be regrettably overlooking. All of the readers who have written in over the years are also deserving of my gratitude, and I want to give a special shout out to Thomas Luebke of Dortmund, Germany, who decided to follow the Crew in 2008 because their color scheme matched that of his beloved Borussia Dortmund. Our correspondence throughout the year is permanently intertwined with my memory of the Massive Season.

And finally, this whole journey would not have been possible without an old college friend named Abrahm Shearer. Back in Shively Hall on the campus of Ohio University, I used to write some goofy pieces solely for the amusement of my friends. I even wrote a silly piece or two for the school newspaper on nothing more than a lark. For some reason, Abrahm filed this away. In 1997, he gave me my first paying writing gig, paying me $20.00 to pen an article for his little Grand Rapids soccer 'zine, The Soccer Scoop. And most importantly, upon meeting Bob Cole, the publisher of the Michigan Soccer News, Abrahm talked me up, then called me out of the blue to put me in touch with Bob about covering the Crew for the MSN. Shortly thereafter, I suddenly had my first press pass, despite never even having considered being a writer nor having the slightest clue what I was doing as a reporter. I've improved only marginally since then, but the rest is history.

Looking back, I think it's funny that the groundwork for this book is largely the result of two random phone calls placed a decade apart— one from Abrahm Shearer in late 1997 and one from Dave Stephany in early 2008. It just goes to show that "luck" is more than what you know or who you know. It's also if they call, if you pick up the phone, and if you let them talk you into doing something you weren't otherwise planning to do on your own.[2]

STEVE SIRK
Dublin, Ohio
August 2009

---

[2] That's 100% true. It's not just me. For example, Sigi Schmid knows a lot about coaching soccer and knows a lot of people in the professional soccer community. That's all well and good, but it's only part of the equation. Beyond that, Mark McCullers called Sigi, Sigi answered the call, and a short while later, Sigi found himself packing his luggage in Manhattan Beach and moving to Columbus Freakin' Ohio. See what I mean? (In my warped mind, I always pictured Sigi's first reaction to getting the call from the Crew to mirror Lou Brown's when he got the call to manage the Cleveland Indians in "Major League.")

SECTION I:

*

THE WAY WE WERE

*

Before proceeding to the Massive Season, I thought it might be "fun" to put things in perspective by looking back at a few things leading up the Crew's championship run. So we'll look at Columbus' inferiority complex and the word "massive", a blistering Notebook excerpt from 2005, Flick's obituary for the 2005 Crew team, a Notebook excerpt from my first game during the Sigi era, a surreal Sigi press conference from 2006, a look at the supporters from the home finale in 2006, the time Bill Archer got in touch with me about hiring a witch doctor in 2007, and some Notebook excerpts that indicated that this group of Crew players was exhibiting signs of life and could be the group to restore pride in the club.

The Way We Were, Pt. I
Massive

The word "massive" will play a prominent role in this book. The word has become so ubiquitous that it I didn't think twice about using it in the title.

The term started out as a self-deprecating joke. Former Crew supporter culture kingpin Zak Bernardo[3] watched with great amusement in 2003 when Manchester City signed Kevin Keegan to be their manager, and the term "massive club" was thrown around willy-nilly to describe the success-starved club that lives in the shadow of Manchester United's colossal trophy case. If ever there was a gag to be appropriated for Columbus and the Crew, the "massive" angle was it. The city suffers from bigger-city disrespect (real or imagined), the Crew are certainly not a glamour club in MLS circles, and one can even argue that the very existence of the Crew was the result of Columbus' small-town insecurity.

Outside of the Buckeye State, newspapers refer to Columbus by many names, such as:

   * "Columbus, Ohio"
   * "Columbus, OH"
   * "Columbus (OH)"
   * "Columbus (Ohio)"
   * "Columbus, Oh."

While "Cleveland" and "Cincinnati", sans annotation, are commonly assumed to refer to the cities in Ohio, and not Tennessee and Iowa, respectively, Columbus needs that little extra description so that a metro area of 1.7 million people isn't mistaken for any of the other 17 Columbuses in the U.S., who have a combined population of about 312,000. That's fewer than 20,000 inhabitants per "other" Columbus, yet if one doesn't append "Ohio" to the end, the average person's first thought is assumed to be, "Columbus, North Dakota?"

---

[3] Zak was the leader of the V-Army supporter group and was the foremost proponent of the "rowdier" supporter culture seen in the Nordecke today. He was a little ahead of his time in Columbus, for better and worse.

And it's not like Columbus has traditionally received much respect from within the state. For centuries, Cleveland has been Ohio's largest population and economic center, while Cincinnati has been the unquestioned counterweight at the other end of the state. Meanwhile, Columbus was a slightly overgrown university/government town. It was a place for college football games, civics class field trips, and the perfect spot for a pee break when driving between Ohio's bonafide big league cities.

As Columbus began to grow, it began to have big league aspirations of its own. Long a "junk sports" graveyard—I think Columbus has fielded a pro team in every possible activity, save for badminton and jai alai—Columbus wanted to use big-time sports to put itself on the map. In 1987, the city made a run at acquiring the St. Louis Cardinals NFL team, hoping that pro football would transform Columbus from a flat, nondescript, Midwestern government seat in the middle of frickin' nowhere to something entirely more respected and glamorous, matching the metamorphosis experienced three years earlier by...um...Indianapolis.

Unable to land the Cardinals, thus failing to become "the next Indianapolis", Columbus would welcome a destined-to-fail spring-league football team to pass the time until the city's next big chance. The Ohio Glory (surely short for the "Columbus, Ohio, Glory") spent the spring of 1992 representing Columbus in the clumsily named World League of American Football. The Ohio Glory might as well have been named the Ohio Bobcats, as they sucked at football and went 1-9 on the year, finishing dead last. They were outscored 230-132 on the year. The league folded after the season, but Columbus was one of the few bright spots, averaging an announced attendance of 30,891 per game.

Just two years later, Columbus would get another shot by applying for—what the hell, why not?— a soccer team. Typically home to minor league teams or offbeat sports, this was a chance for Columbus to join a top national league on the ground floor. If soccer finally took off in America, Columbus would be *in*. And this league had "Major League" in its title!

So Columbus was one of 22 cities that applied for entry into Major League Soccer, surely joining Louisville, Raleigh-Durham, and Tulsa in the "shyeah, right" pile next to Alan Rothenberg's paper shredder. But then a funny thing happened. Thanks in large part to a local grocery store chain, Columbus was the first and only applicant to meet Major League Soccer's minimum requirement for season ticket deposits. And so it was that on June 15, 1994, MLS announced that Columbus (Ohio) had earned a charter membership, thus putting the "minor league" in Major League Soccer.

4

Central Ohio was abuzz with the news. A flurry of questions followed from the excited populace. Would the league fold before it ever played a game? Could the local team survive on an average attendance of 302 disheveled foreigners trying to barter their way into the stadium with a battered hand-drawn cart full of chickens and goats? And what impact would the estrogen-soaked tears of dainty, effeminate soccer pansies have on the quality of the Ohio Stadium playing surface come football season?

To the surprise of many, this much-maligned sport fared well in this much-maligned city. The Crew averaged 18,950 fans in their inaugural season, causing many sports talk radio types to suggest that supporting the team could lead to Columbus getting a *real* sports team. The idea was that if Columbus showed someone like, say, Lamar Hunt, that they would come out to watch *soccer*, imagine what would happen if Columbus got a team in a *real* sport! Even in success, the Crew were viewed, by a segment of the community, as the hamster that needed to be tended to so that the town could prove it could care for the puppy that it really wanted.[4]

Being a Crew fan in those early days was a lot of fun. The team played exciting soccer, was a championship contender, and boasted a roster full of good guys that were easy to root for. That's not even mentioning Crew Stadium, which was the first major soccer-specific stadium in America and a source of great pride. Despite all this, the indignities and inferiority-feeding setbacks piled up quickly. Apart from the usual league blathering about how important it is to having a winning team in places like New York and Los Angeles, or the run of the mill cow-intensive insults lobbed by opposing fans, here are but a few of my favorite examples:

- In 1996, defender Paul Caligiuri sued MLS, claiming that the league had originally promised to assign him to the Los Angeles Galaxy, but then assigned him to the Crew instead. As a result, the league

---

[4] And it worked, as the Crew and Lamar Hunt played a pivotal role in laying the groundwork for the NHL's Columbus Blue Jackets. Of course, the Crew have become an integral part of the community in their own right, and have given the city an international appeal and reputation that no other American sport could have done. The name "Columbus" generates fearful shivers in Mexico City and incoherent ranting in Toronto. Columbus jerseys have been spotted from Argentina to Italy. Columbus is known in England for Brad Friedel, Stern John and Brian McBride. I receive emails from places like Ireland and Germany. The Dispatch's Aaron Portzline blogged in 2008 that he got into a cab in Atlanta, and the Ethiopian cabbie asked where he was from. When Aaron said Columbus, the Ethiopian's first words were "Columbus Crew." I would venture to say that Columbus' global awareness has increased immensely due to the existence of the Crew.

unilaterally transferred Caligiuri to Los Angeles for the 1997 season. Caligiuri maintained that he simply wanted what he was promised to him, but to Crew fans, he became The Man Who Sued MLS To Get Out of Columbus.

- In May of 1997, Columbus voters soundly rejected a sales tax that would have built a new hockey arena and soccer stadium. Opponents charged that the measure amounted to nothing more than "a soccer sucker tax."

- In October of 1997, D.C. United head coach Bruce Arena, never one to bite his acid tongue, disparaged the Crew's game day experience. "They play music during the game," he told the Washington Post. "It's a circus. But it's probably very good entertainment for Middle America." (The Crew responded by hiring clowns, jugglers, and other circus performers for United's next visit.)

- In February of 1998, the Crew were once again rebuffed at the ballot box, as Lamar Hunt failed in a bid to build a stadium in suburban Dublin. Residents were simultaneously concerned that nobody goes to see soccer and therefore the stadium would be nothing more than an empty white elephant, and also that the traffic jams caused by 50,000 soccer hooligans would be a major inconvenience.

- In October of 1998, on the day before the deciding game three in the Eastern Conference Finals, referee Noel Kenny opened up about his need to personally protect D.C. United playmaker Marco Etcheverry, whom Kenny also declared to be the best player in the league. "When he gets tackled, he does not like it," Kenny told the USA Today. "I need to be close to make sure that he gets a fair shake." (Despite citing the idealistic notion that there were 21 other players who deserved to get a fair shake, the Crew were unsuccessful in their attempt to get a new referee assigned to the game. Perhaps psyched out before they even set foot on the field, the Crew lost 3-0.)

- Also in October of 1998, the Crew were forced to play the U.S. Open Cup Final against Chicago in front of a hostile crowd of 20,000. In Chicago. The game had originally been scheduled for a neutral site in Virginia Beach, but had to be postponed due to Hurricane Bonnie. The USSF then decided, in the interest of unfairness, to make it a Fire home game. The Crew lobbied to have the game played in Indianapolis, equidistant between both sets of fans, but instead, the Fire were given home field advantage. Naturally, Chicago won 2-1 in overtime.

- In 1999, the Crew lost in the conference finals for the third consecutive year to those arrogant, dirty, evil bastards from D.C. United.

- When English Premier League side Newcastle United came to the U.S. to play in D.C. and then Columbus in 2000, I couldn't help but crack up when English newspaper reporter Jason Mellor decreed, in print, that the Magpies had departed D.C. for "Columbus, an all together less fashionable part of the United States." (That quote remains my Big Soccer signature to this very day.)

- After second-place finishes in 1997, 1998, 1999, 2001 and 2002, the Crew finally broke through with a first-place finish in the Eastern Conference. Not only that, but they captured the Supporters' Shield for having the league's best record. Only the Crew could produce the league's best team and have it nitpicked to death by fans of lower-standing teams. The 2004 Crew had the fewest points of any team to ever win the Shield, finishing with more draws than wins. The team's cautious, safety-first, play-not-to-lose soccer caused much consternation amongst fans of all stripes. Worst of all, the kvetching gained legitimacy when the Crew lost a playoff series to a 4th place New England team, capped by a nightmarish Halloween night when the Crew missed two penalty kicks on their home field.

Again, there were lots of great times, but Crew fans were never far from reminders that their team, their city, or their sport weren't quite good enough.

By the middle of the decade, things weren't going so well in Crewville. The team, once a perennial contender full of familiar faces, had fallen on hard times. As the club's performance fell of a cliff, attendance began to decline. These were dark times indeed.

It was in these dark times that Zak's "massive" joke really began to pick up steam. What could possibly be more "massive" than a small-market last-place team that fans around the league made fun of?

Crew fans laughed away their frustration by embracing the massive concept. Suddenly, on Crew message boards, the Crew fans found themselves in the middle of every major European transfer. Inevitably, the player would back out because Columbus was "too massive", so the player would opt to sign where there would be less pressure to perform, such as, say, Real Madrid.

One of my favorite gags is when it was decided that the Crew were so massive that they would start their own television network to keep up with the pent-up demand for Crew content. My good buddy Flick took to creating occasional channel listings. Here is a sample of the programming that was available…

Tonight on CrewTV (check your local listings)

8:00— "I'm Coming After You, Ripken!"; Stephen Herdsman's Pain-Free Soccer.[5]

8:30— Fair Play Soccer, with Mark Williams.[6]

9:00— Ricci Greenwood's Real-Time Soccer.[7]

9:07— Great Crew Away Victories When Trailing at the Half.[8]

9:08— Ye Olde Crew Workshoppe: Five-Minute Trophy Case.[9]

9:13— Foundation of a Dynasty: The Crew's 2003 SuperDraft.[10]

---

[5] Herdsman played for the Crew from 2004-2005. He was lightning fast…when healthy. He appeared in just 15 out of 60 games over his two seasons in Columbus.

[6] Williams was one of the most ridiculous blunders in Crew history. They traded away popular central defender Brian Dunseth in August 2003 so they could replace him with Williams. The Northern Irish international did not have the fitness to keep up in MLS. He played in 5 matches in his Crew career, and not only committed 16 fouls, but earned a yellow card in all 5 matches. (This caused Flick to declare, "At last, some consistency in the back!") Most memorably, in an event that perfectly summarizes his Crew career, Williams literally tore the jersey off of D.C. United's Thiago Martins after Martins ran right past him. If you don't account for the inevitable suspensions, Williams' stats prorated to 96 fouls and 30 cautions over a 30 games season. Quality!

[7] Ricci Greenwood made one seven-minute appearance with the Crew in 1996. It was the only MLS action of his career. He has become a cult figure in Crew lore over the years, mainly because who among us wouldn't kill to wear the colors for seven minutes and have our name in the record book forever?

[8] When Flick did these TV listings, the Crew had never won a road game when trailing at the half. They were, like, 0-3,287,308-1, or something like that.

[9] They needed to quickly whip up something in which to display the 2002 U.S. Open Cup.

[10] This draft produced Diego Walsh, Michael Ritch, Guy Abrahamson, and Jake Traeger. Abrahamson never made it, and the remaining trio combined for 2 goals and 31 appearances. All were gone by the end of the 2004 season.

9:30— Real World: Crew Generation Adidas.[11]

10:00— "I Gave My Love A Cherry...": Kyle Martino Live in Concert.[12]

11:00— Jon Busch's Serenity and Soccer.[13]

11:30— Frank Klopas: Crew For Life.[14]

12:00— Sucking Down Sausage: The History of Buck-A-Brat Night.[15]

A funny thing happened in 2008. What had long been a self-deprecating in-joke amongst the Crew's most ardent fans suddenly morphed into a widely-accepted expression of Crew Pride. The word "massive" was everywhere. The Nordecke chanted "We are massive!", and one of the more recognizable banners in the section reads "Be Massive, my friend." Dwight Burgess, as he had done in the past on the radio, started working the term into TV broadcasts. The word was sprawled across the cover of Columbus

---

[11] A re-imagining of the hit MTV show, but with the Crew's young "Generation Adidas" players.

[12] As Martino's career began to progress below expectations, Crew fans latched on to the fact he played guitar. His acoustic guitar became the lightning rod for the fans' frustration.

[13] Sure, all goalkeepers are insane, but no Crew keeper has been as intensely competitive as Jon Busch. (At least outwardly.) Flick used to ask me if they hung a straightjacket in his locker. Buschie's competitive fire was that of a million suns, and it was obvious to see on the field. He delivered one of my all-time favorite quotes after the Crew had squandered a late lead. He was clearly agitated, and was asked what the Crew needed to do differently to hold the lead. He replied, "We need to rip out their throats and shove it down their throat." (Busch is not insane in real life. In fact, his Crew career and now post-Crew resurgence with the Fire have both involved him plugging away in the face of long odds. He was an undersized minor league journeyman before winning a job with the Crew, and he came back from a pair of ACL tears to win the Fire job. If we could all be so determined to succeed as Jon Busch...but between the pipes, the guy is certifiably nuts.)

[14] The Crew acquired Klopas on October 30, 1997, after the conclusion of the 1997 season. The Crew then traded Klopas to the Chicago Fire on February 19, 1998, before the start of the 1998 season. That means Klopas was Crew property for 3.5 months during the 1997-98 offseason. (Naturally, Klopas scored the golden goal game-winner for Chicago against Columbus in the 1998 U.S. Open Cup final.)

[15] This joke speaks for itself, but it was also a set-up for another joke Crew TV program that I am not going to print here. Use your imagination.

Alive. Dispatch columnist Michael Arace picked up on the us-against-the-world, nobody-likes-us-but-we-don't-care origins of the joke and began using the term in his Crew columns. And when the Crew won it all, the Columbus Dispatch's sports page headline read simply: MASSIVE!

As the term seeped into the mainstream, I couldn't help but wonder what Zak Bernardo thought of the popularity of his silly joke. Due to a rift with the organization a few years prior, Zak had stopped coming to Crew games and stopped posting on the Big Soccer message boards.

My friend Matt Rolf has dubbed Zak to be "the Syd Barrett of Crew supporters." Like Barrett, who founded Pink Floyd and burned out before the band found mainstream success, Zak laid the foundation for a success of his own, then became a sought-after recluse once it all took off without him. Just as occasional news snippets would leak out about Barrett's mundane post-Floyd life, Crew fans receive occasional offhand updates about Zak through mutual friends. ("Zak's doing well. He's really into the Cincinnati Reds these days.") And like Syd, Zak prefers not to go back to that specific time in his life, ignoring the Crew just as Barrett had ignored the Floyd.

Still, I wondered if he was in any way amused to see his joke going on to mainstream success. My attempts to contact him went without answer.

"I called him on MLS Cup Sunday to see if he was watching the game," said a mutual friend, Scot Sedley. "He said he didn't even know it was on."

If Zak Bernardo is indeed the Syd Barrett of Crew supporter culture, then 2008 was Massive's "Dark Side of the Moon." It was unfathomable success intertwined with a legendary absence.

Shine on, Zak. How we wish you were here.

The Way We Were, Pt. II
Sirk's Notebook: Bring out Your Dead

Score: Kansas City 4, Columbus 0
Match date: May 14, 2005
Attendance: 9,620
Crew's record afterward: Beyond repair.

"If the fans don't want to come out to the ballpark, you can't stop 'em."
-- Yogi Berra

Even the world's foremost practitioners of professional turd-polishing would be hard-pressed to add a fly-resistant sheen to the soft-serve stink pile that was the Crew's 4-0 loss to the Kansas City Wizards. The Tasmanian Devil himself would not be able to provide the amount of spin necessary to penetrate the rock-hard reality of Saturday night's debacle.

Never in my life did I think I would describe a regular season crowd at Crew Stadium as "Wizardly", "Earthquakian" or "Fusionesque." But with an announced crowd of 9,260, with an in-house crowd of maybe 2/3 that amount, it looked like Miami redux. The fans who didn't leave after a 0-3 halftime performance booed in the rare event that they felt the dull twinge of any emotion at all.

This, my friends, is it. The nadir.

If George and Jeb had been forced to watch the videotape of this game, even those sons of Bushes would agree that some persistent vegetative states aren't worthy of emergency feeding-tube legislation.[16] To avoid sitting through the rest of the Crew's performance, Dubya would probably grin and say "sanctity of life, my ass" while seeking out some pretzels on which to choke himself to death.

The game tied for the worst home defeat in Crew history. You'd have to take the Way Back Machine all the way to Timo's March To Oblivion in 1996 to find another 4-0 home loss. Suffice it to say, that's not the Tenth Season tie-in anybody was hoping for. After the Crew's 3-0 season opening win over Los Angeles, which is looking flukier than a fat-guy/hot-chick sitcom marriage, the Crew have lost five of six, being outscored 14-2 in the process.

---

[16] This was written when the Terry Schiavo case was all over the news.

Yes, 14-2.

Just look at those numbers. Stare at them. Soak them in. That's this many (two full hands of fingers, then flashing four more) compared top this many (holding up two fingers.) (Choose the fingers that feel right for you.) (Even if it's one on each hand.)

After a woeful home loss on April 30, for which I was mercifully absent, the Crew came out the next week at RFK and picked dandelions and chased butterflies until they were down 2-0 a scant nine minutes into the game. Afterward, goalkeeper Jon Busch said the flat start was all mentality, and that the Crew shouldn't be losing games in the first ten minutes.

So this week, those first ten minutes were really good. It was the other 80 that were horrific. The Wizards seemingly scored at will after a persistent stream of odd-man rushes. And by odd-man rushes, I mean there were more defenders than attackers. There is no acceptable explanation for any of it.

Last week, Busch said that he hoped the D.C. game would be the catalyst that got the team "pissed off" enough to play to its potential. So much for that. While both the 2004 and 2005 Crew squads have gotten off to bad starts, I have noticed one crucial difference between the two squads:

Last year's team truly believed in itself.

As the losses mounted, every player spoke evangelically about the turnaround that was to come. Coach Greg Andrulis spoke with fervor when insisting that the talent was there and that the turnaround was imminent, and the players spoke every bit as fervently. Personally, I thought they were all a bit nuts, but one couldn't help but feel the depth and strength of their resolve and their belief in themselves. Ultimately, they were right, and the team went on to win the Supporters Shield.

But then game the playoff flameout known as The Penalty Kicks. And it's been all down hill from there.

The same spark isn't there this year. Sometimes the players will say the talent is there, or that the turnaround is coming, but there's no glimmer in their eyes. Telemarketers reading off of a script deliver their message with more élan. In the event that All The Right Things are being said, it has come across as more of a wistful lamentation than a heartfelt declaration.

Nobody will flat out say it, with loose lips sinking leaky ships and whatnot, but body language and demeanor alone can tell even the most emotionally dense individual, such as myself, that happiness is in short supply these days. It's the Great Fun Famine of 2005. Andrulis is keeping a stiff upper lip and a square jaw, even going on the offensive and doing some newspaper sniping, but he nevertheless looks weary. The players appear to bicker on the field, and seem distant and sullen in the locker room. Granted, losing does this to teams, but not to this extent. Last year, everyone insisted there was light at the end of the tunnel. This year, it feels like not only is there no light, but there's not even an oncoming train to end it all. Just a long, dark, infinite tunnel.

I hope I am wrong. It is killing me to write these words. But I didn't even have the heart to carry on gathering material for a proper notebook. Sure, I took notes about mascot soccer. I could tell you that the mascots lined up in a 2-1-1, with the eagle in goal, the koala and tiger on defense, the ostrich manning the midfield, and Crew Cat running up top. I could tell you that the kids from Groveport employed the (12)-(12)-(12) formation, whereby all twelve kids followed the ball wherever it went. I could tell you the kids won 3-0, despite the fact that, as Dwight Burgess and I analyzed, the mascots had a better team on paper. The eagle gave them aerial superiority, the tiger is a ferocious tackler, the ostrich can run all day, the koala is a cute distraction for little kids, and Crew Cat is Crew Mutha Effin' Cat, the best striker in the mascot soccer business.

But none of that seems important now.

Well, not that it was ever important to anyone but an idiot like me, but you know what I mean.

What's important is that Crew Stadium was practically empty. The few fans in attendance ranged from surly to apathetic. Walking around the concourse after the game, I did not spot one smile. Not ONE smile. I don't know why I decided to count, but I did. I was hoping that even if the game gave the fans nothing to smile about, they would at least be in a healthy frame of mind to enjoy a joke with a friend, a hug from a lover, or a small child's antics. But in a quarter-lap of the concourse, not a single person, male or female, young or old, soccer fan or casual night out, cracked a smile within my range of vision. I don't know why they would have, but it still sucked to count all the way up to zero, as if I were adding up the ticket revenues from the night's walk-up sales.

While Andrulis has long had his detractors, this is the first time I really recall such in-stadium hostility toward the team itself. And the players heard it loud and clear. Contrary to the talk in the papers, Busch's pipe has remained open.

"They deserved to boo," he said, when asked if it sucked to hear the team booed off the field at halftime and at the end of the game. "They paid their money to come to the game. If I was paying whatever they pay for a ticket, and I saw a performance like that, I would boo too. That's their right when they buy a ticket. They work hard all week to afford a ticket to come see us play a game on the weekend. That's part of the game, you know? It doesn't bother me. (In the sense that he's not mad at the fans for booing.) Playing in Columbus is great. I could never imagine playing anywhere else. If that's what they want to do, then they should. I mean, if that's the worst that they are doing to us right now, then God forbid."

(Busch and Blue Jackets goaltender Marc Denis are the two most stand-up guys in Columbus sports when it comes to giving interviews after every game, good or bad, and then answering questions honestly from their heart. It must be a goalie thing.)

I am hard-pressed to come up with a similar juncture in Crew history. Oddly enough, I am getting the vibe of another of my favorite disasters, the Cleveland Browns. Right now, it feels like the Bill Belichick era. The team is not playing well. The hardcore fans are becoming angrily alienated from the front office and the coach. The players don't look to be enjoying their work. The crowds are down. Fan apathy is as contagious as a yawn. The 1994 Browns and 2004 Crew playoff teams were whispered to have been smoke and mirrors successes, before flaming out in the postseason against the Steelers and Revolution, respectively. The follow-up seasons are both heading down the same brutal path. Hell, the splashy off-season acquisitions of proven temperamental offensive weapons Ante Razov and Andre Rison are working out about as well the other. And their names are kinda similar. How weird.

So maybe the Crew will move to Baltimore later this year.

Okay, that's not going to happen, but Saturday's game had a special feel. It's hard to describe, but it was in the air. It was the type of game that everybody will tell their grandchildren that they never bought a ticket to, even though 9,260 people will be lying. And fewer will be lying when they say they had a ticket but didn't go. And even fewer than that will be lying when they say that they went but didn't stay until the end.

But for those who were there, you know you felt it. It had the feel of the 0-0 Miami game in 2001, only with four goals allowed. The 4-0 embarrassment will be an infamous game in Crew history, for like the Miami game of yesteryear, it made it official: Welcome to Flatline City. Bring out your dead!

Oh, it could be worse. They could lose the next game 8-0. They could lose 17 in a row. Jeffrey Dahmer taught us that there are many ways to violate a corpse, but that is beside the point. Once you're dead, you're dead. Any atrocities committed beyond that point are merely fodder for Thomas Harris novels.

I do not relish committing doom and gloom to the potentially-printed page, but the buzzards are circling over Crew Stadium. Some of them are surely getting sucked into jet engines. Nevertheless, it is imperative that the useful organs be salvaged before the franchise's carcass is picked clean.

Given the dismal psychological state of Crew Soccer Nation, and the erosion of passion across the board, the time has come for GM Mark McCullers and Hunt Sports Group to play Dr. Frankenstein. They need to identify the salvageable organs, find replacements for the rest, and then get to work on stitching and bolting it all back together.

Then some day in the future, after some frightfully stormy nights in the laboratory, Crew fans may eventually hear those magic words:

It's alive. It's alive! IT'S ALIVE!!!

Questions? Comments? Zoloft? Feel free to write at sirk65@yahoo.com

15

The Way We Were, Pt. III
Flick's 2005 Crew Obituary

Once the 2005 Crew were mathematically eliminated from the playoff contention in mid-August, my good buddy Flick emailed me the following obituary notice.

CREW 2005 Columbus Crew died August 14, 2005, at Giants Stadium in New Jersey from lack of offense among other ailments. The 2005 Crew appeared on this earth November 1, 2004, though the seeds of its life were planted much earlier, perhaps most notably the day the 2003 Columbus Crew passed. The 2005 Crew are preceded in death by its predecessor, the 2004 Columbus Crew (cause of death – flameout), as well as Jeff Cunningham of Colorado, Ante Razov of New York, Greg Andrulis of Miamisburg, and 2005 CD Chivas USA of Los Angeles with one of its cousins, 2005 Real Salt Lake of Utah, suffering and near death. The 2005 Crew are survived by its HSG brothers, 2005 Kansas City of Missouri and 2005 FC Dallas (Burn) of Dallas. Additionally, the 2005 Crew are survived by its cousins, the 2005 MLS clubs throughout the country that are good enough to get the necessary points to earn or at least challenge for playoff spots beyond mid-August.

The 2005 Crew enjoyed entertaining its family, as evidenced by its .500 record at home. Never wanting to overstay its welcome at its family's houses, the 2005 Crew is winless on the road. The 2005 Crew believed in giving back to its community, perhaps best demonstrated by its (-13) goal differential.

Public visitation is scheduled for COLUMBUS CREW STADIUM on August 20, September 17, September 21, and October 1, with internment services scheduled immediately after the October viewing. Internment will be in the history books and the media guides of MLS and the Columbus Crew. A reception featuring the finest in grilled meat and cold beverages will precede each viewing, weather permitting, just as the 2005 Crew would have wanted. The organization suggests that in lieu of flowers, donations be made in the form of season or individual game tickets to help the lagging attendance.

The Way We Were, Pt. IV
My First Game of the Sigi Era
Notebook Excerpt: Crew 1, Galaxy 1 (July 23, 2006)

After a family-related absence that simultaneously seemed eternal and nowhere near long enough, it was finally time to come back to Columbus. I needed to get reacquainted with my normal life. Surely I could find solace in the familiar comfort of my usual summer companion-- the Columbus Crew.

Well...had I spent four years growing a beard, spearing fish, and talking to a volleyball on a deserted island, I still could not have been more disoriented upon reacquainting myself with the Crew. New coach. New players. New uniforms. New beat writer. New PA guy. New Autograph Alley. About the only things that weren't new were the dismal home record, the last-place standing, and the "Bring out your dead!" guy clanging his bell outside the trainer's room.[17]

During my hiatus, I learned that soccer is damn near impossible to follow from a distance, especially when it is the 500th thing on your mind. It's not like baseball, where the box score can recreate the game. A soccer box score is mostly meaningless, especially when the names in the lineup might as well have been picked out of the phone book. Newspaper and internet accounts can only paint so much of a story. The gnashing of virtual teeth on message boards can only convey the general emotion. One of the great and frustrating things about soccer is that it is largely open to interpretation. It is not uncommon for two people who have watched the exact same game to have two entirely different opinions about everything. In some respects, soccer is more music than sport.

My first attempts at following the Crew again were fairly disastrous:

- I attended the DC United game, but spent most of the time chatting with people I hadn't seen in months. Since it was Star Wars Day at the stadium, my good buddy Flick and I attempted to cast the movie from the Crew's starting lineup. We only got as far as casting Richie Kotschau as Han Solo and Joseph Ngwenya as Jar-Jar Binks. (And Kei Kamara may not look like a Star Wars character, but his name sounds like one.) (That didn't count though.)

---

[17] I would like to point out that even though they appear just pages apart, over a full year went by between my "bring out your dead" jokes.

- I watched the away rematch at RFK and tried to figure out who the hell was even on the team. Was this really my Crew anymore? Like, who the hell is Noah Palmer, and did he grow a mullet specifically because he would be playing his home games on the Ohio state fairgrounds? (Have the Crew even had a player with an honest-to-goodness mullet before?) Is Bisaku the name of a new player, or was Bill McDermott struggling in an attempt reminisce about Ubusuku Abukusumo? And who is Jacob Thomas, and is he trying to make #7 the official Crew uniform number for fast bald-headed white guys? [18]

- I listened to parts of the home loss to the Red Bulls on the radio. Dwight Burgess has been subjected to more Crew soccer than anyone on earth over the past 10+ years, and I think it's finally getting to him. He's probably pricing out ass-to-scalp follicle transplants, just so he can have some hair to pull out while repeatedly using phrases like "bad giveaway" and "unforced turnover" and "yes, you heard me correctly, that shot resulted in a throw-in."

Even though all evidence, be it statistical or anecdotal, seemed to indicate that the Crew stink worse than Matthew McConaughey's non-deodorized B.O.,[19] I was paradoxically determined to have fun AND pay attention to Saturday's game against the Galaxy. To that end, I decided to watch the game with Dwight as he did his radio call. Not only did I figure it might be informative, but I also wanted to be there in the event he finally snapped and pulled a Harry Doyle from "Major League"...

Dwight: "...and one shot on goal for the Crew. That's it? One goddamn shot?"

Katie: "Coach, you can't say 'goddamn' on the radio!"

Dwight: "It doesn't matter. Nobody's listening anyway. The Crew postgame show is brought to you by....Christ, I can't find it. To hell with it."

---

[18] Matt Kmosko also wore #7.

[19] That was an inside joke for Kristen Lavric, who told me that day that she had read an interview where McConaughey stated he does not wear deodorant.

We were also joined by Crew GM Mark McCullers, who assured me that the Crew have been saving their best soccer for my return. What great news for me, even if the season has sucked thus far for the rest of you.

I mentioned my delight over the fact that the Crew were wearing their traditional banana kits. "Mark, I have no idea who half these people are, but at least they look like the Crew today."

McCullers said that the afternoon's banana kits were his doing, and I was quick to thank him on behalf of Crew fans everywhere.

"Look," I said, "I know quibbling about uniform selection sounds stupid, but you guys have completely turned this roster over. It feels like we've gone from the '95 Browns to the '99 Browns, but without a 3-year hiatus in between. The bond with the players isn't there yet, but like the Browns unis, the banana kits---"

"---give the fans something to hold on to," said McCullers, completing my thought before I could say it. Nodding his head, he continued, "The all-yellow gives the fans something traditional that they can relate to and bond with."

I considered asking him to sign a blood oath that the Crew would wear the banana kits for the rest of the year, but opted not to since he obviously gets it and nobody in the booth had a knife and a scroll of yellowed parchment.

The game easily surpassed my lowered expectations. The Crew played a very entertaining first half, even getting one of those whatchamacallits...goals. With LA's outside backs auditioning for roles as hotel doormen, the Crew had plenty of crossing chances. One of them bounced off Eddie Gaven's head and went into the net in the 9th minute.

Having nearly doubled their typical home offensive output, the only question was whether or not the Crew could make the goal hold up. Naturally, they could not. LA's Peter Vagenas scored on a bad deflection in the 14th minute. But at least the Crew had a lead for a little over four minutes, right? It's a start.

Anyway, the point is that I actually had fun at Saturday's game. Maybe it's because I miss it. Maybe it's because I have not been beaten down by the failures of the season like most of my friends, who are so worn down that they can only look at the Crew through turd-colored glasses.

I guess I just have to look at the 2006 Crew like the 2003 Indians. Most of the familiar names have been replaced by anonymous young guys, the play on the field is underwhelming and impotent, and it may not be a whole lot of fun to watch at times. But that's how rebuilding works.

I remember watching the 2003 Indians and being thoroughly unimpressed by scrubs like Coco Crisp, Travis Hafner, and Brandon Phillips. Crisp was some banjo-hitting outfielder who got picked off base nearly every time he got on. Hafner was a lug who didn't hit for power or average. Phillips swung from his heels and rarely made contact, which is exactly what you want from a smallish middle infielder. I remember being excited by the play of Jody Gerut, whose mediocre-to-decent batting stats towered over those of his teammates.

It's funny to look back and imagine ever feeling that way about those players. Since that time, the trade of Crisp nearly caused a fan revolt, Hafner is one of the top five hitters in all of baseball, and Brandon Phillips is playing at near All-Star quality, even if it's for the Reds. Jody Gerut is a footnote.[20]

The 2006 Crew may very well suck, and they may be agonizing to watch, but hopefully some of these guys will become as beloved as Hafner and Crisp became in Cleveland. And hopefully the Crew won't let their Brandon Phillips go. And even if some of these guys fade out like Jody Gerut, maybe they will provide a modicum of entertainment in the interim.

As a baseball junkie, I got through the infinite disinterested tedium of the 2003 Indians season. As soccer junkies, we can get through the 2006 Crew season.

---

[20] Jody Gerut.

The Way We Were, Pt V:
Sigi's (De)Press(ed) Conference

Notebook excerpt from August 19, 2006, after the Crew's 2-1 loss to second-year Real Salt Lake on August 16.

Let's see....a 2-1 loss to a team that had won three prior road games in its existence. Former Crew lightning rod Jeff Cunningham assisted on the game winner in the 90th minute. Crew coach Sigi Schmid said his team has no character and seems incapable of making decisions on the field. Then he wondered if he should resign.

But hey, at least nobody in the parking lot peed in my car's open sun roof.

I have been to some awkward Crew press conferences before. I was there when Fitz blew up at the Washington press corps in the bowels of RFK Stadium.[21] I was there for Fitz's Nixonesque display of darty-eyed defiance after the 0-0 draw with Miami in 2000.[22] I was there for all those weird interview sessions that commenced moments after Greg Andrulis finished picking pink slips out of his hair.[23]

And then there was Wednesday night, when one of the most successful coaches in NCAA and MLS history sounded as if he were composing a suicide note.

"I feel sorry for the fans," Schmid glumly said. "I've never felt this way. Maybe it's me. Maybe I need to step away. Maybe I need to resign.

---

[21] Those of you who remember Fitz know what a monumental occasion this was. Fitz was the most personable, laid back, affable guy. On this particular day, the Crew had lost a playoff game to D.C. United, extending their dreaded RFK Jinx to 0-12 all-time. Washington reporters kept grilling him on the Jinx, one question after another. It was almost like they were playing a game to see if they could make him snap. When it was suggested that the press finally move on to another topic, the next question was, "Do you ever think about the fact that you've never won here?" Fitz had had enough. After sharing a few choice words about how he'd have to be an idiot not to think about it, he then stormed off the podium. Good for him. They were being jerks to a guy who didn't deserve it.

[22] There's nothing more depressingly awkward than the press conferences where a good guy coach has reached the end of his tenure, but hasn't quite been fired yet. I've gone through this with Fitz, Andrulis, and Gerard Gallant of the Blue Jackets, and I know of others who went through it with Romeo Crennel of the Browns. Not good times.

[23] See previous footnote.

Maybe they need somebody else because obviously I'm not getting the job done. And I've never had that feeling with any team I've ever coached, but right now I have that feeling with this team and that's something I've got to wrestle with."

When it was over, I remember looking around the room and thinking, "Someone's going to take Sigi's belt from him before he heads back to the solitude of his office, right?"

It was sitting in this press conference that made me realize the magnitude of the Crew's terrible season. A successful coach with a decades-long track record was being reduced to rubble before my eyes.

I don't think I found a way to summarize this realization as succinctly as a BigSoccer poster named HuntKop, who wrote, "Interesting how this club can make even the most seemingly self-assured people crumble. That's our Crew!"

Thankfully, Sigi has come to his senses, apparently after his wife beat him over the head with a rolling pin the moment he walked in the door or something like that.[24] Good for you, Valerie Schmid. And hopefully good for all of us too.[25]

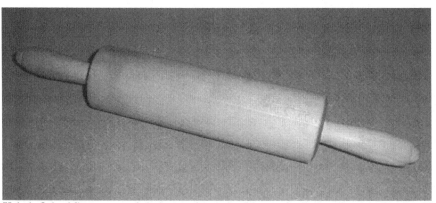

Valerie Schmid's weapon of choice, as determined by my fertile imagination. So what if she didn't LITERALLY beat Sigi over the head with a rolling pin? The bottom line is that her "stern scolding" had joyous long-term implications for Crew fans.
(Photo by Kerri Jones)

---

[24] In the August 18, 2006, Columbus Dispatch, Shawn Mitchell wrote that Sigi received "a stern scolding from his wife, Valerie" after she learned of his comments. I just liked the cartoon visual of her beating him over the head with a rolling pin, even if it was just a scolding.

[25] Wow. One can't say enough about Valerie's verbal scolding. Any championship relies on countless displays of unsung heroism, and now we know that that can include spousal chastisement from two years prior.

The Way We Were, Pt. VI
Supporters

When marveling at the size, energy, and passion of the Nordecke, remember that the building those groups has taken a lot of work by a lot of good people. To give you some idea of how far the Crew supporters have come, I now turn it over to "Hard Hat Mike" Blankley.

"As you know, until 2008, the 'hardcore' Columbus supporters were a pretty small group," he says. "In the torrential downpour that accompanied the last home game on the 2006 season, there were literally 15 of us standing in the old North End, defying Mother Nature and singing the Crew to a win over FC Dallas. Comparing then and now is like night and day. Some of us that remember those dark days find ourselves looking around in the middle of our matches now, amazed at what we see. It's even harder to hold back a tear or two when one of your friends, who stood next to you in that downpour in September of 2006, looks around as well then puts his arm around you and says, 'Thanks for helping create this.'"

Crew President and General Manager Mark McCullers (center) invited supporters onto the field to pose for a picture after these hardy few had sung and chanted their way through a torrential downpour on September 30, 2006. The Crew beat FC Dallas, 3-1, that night. A year and a half later, this group would number 1,000-2,000 on most game days. (Photo courtesy of Mike Blankley)

The Way We Were, Pt. VII:
Curses

Quality people or not, the Crew got off to a miserable start in 2007. They won only one of their first ten matches, holding a dreadful 1-4-5 record. On the heels of the 2005 and 2006 nightmare seasons, a 1-4-5 start was almost too much to bear. Something needed to be done.

Fortunately, notorious Big Soccer blogger Bill Archer is a man of action. One June 15, 2007, I received an email from Bill that laid out a definitive plan to right the Columbus ship:

Sirk,

So what the f*** is with the Crew? One goddamn win? The team must be ready to kill themselves.

I am working on a project that I will bring you and a friend or two of your choice in on if and when I can get it lined up. Basically, it involves hiring a real, live Indian shaman to come and remove the curse from the stadium. (There must be one, right? What other explanation is there?) I know someone who is into all that New Age jazz and he says there's a woman around Dayton someplace, supposedly at least part Indian, who cleanses stuff, chases demons and curses, etc.. Might cost 100 bucks or so, and worth every penny. It'll cost you guys my bar tab afterwards.

I'll give you first whack at the narrative. Think Flick would like to do the PBP?

Later,
Bill

This was my kind of idea, so I wrote him back the next night, June 16, after the Crew "improved" their record to 1-4-6:

U-Town Billy,

I am totally in for the curse removal. Just make sure it's not 7/7/07 vs. RSL, as I will be at a wedding.[26]

I have not yet talked to Flick or Zman, but I am sure they would be happy to participate. Flick, so he can provide a list of grievances that need to be rectified, and Zman because he'll be hyped to participate in any type of ridiculous ritual. He has a natural thirst for these types of things.

While I have not mentioned it to Flick or Z, I did mention it to Dante when we talked on the phone at halftime tonight. He said something about the Crew being cursed, and I told him that mum's the word, but...

He was dying. He told me to keep him in the loop. He said if you collect $5 apiece from Crew fans to defray the costs, you'd more than cover the tab. He surmised that some how, some way, this shaman is probably a distant relative of Ansil Elcock.[27]

Later,
Sirk

On the afternoon of June 20, before the Crew's home match against Kansas City, Bill sent me an update.

Hey,

FYI, I'm still working on the curse thing - these spiritualists aren't exactly good at getting back to you. She needs a booker or a secretary or a phone that gets answered.[28]

Later,
Billy

---

[26] Rob and Kerri.

[27] For those who weren't around, Ansil Elcock was a gap-toothed Trinidadian goofball from the Crew's early teams. Dante's joke was probably more truth than fiction.

[28] I suggested that she needs to hire the "WE GOT ONE!" lady from Ghostbusters.

That night, the Crew snapped their seven-game winless streak and won for only the second time in 12 matches. Eddie Gaven and Stefani Miglioranzi scored as the Crew topped the Wizards, 2-1.

Three nights later, after flying across the country to the West Coast, the Crew knocked off the Galaxy in a 3-2 thriller.[29] Chad Marshall, Ned Grabavoy, and Alejandro Moreno found the net for Columbus.

I got another email from Bill on June 28.

Hey,

I'm very bummed about the curse deal - the broad finally gets back to me when the team is on a two game winning streak. It would have been a classic, and the best part would have been if we had done it when I wanted to, everyone would be crediting *us* with the turnaround.

Later,
Bill

For good measure, on June 30, the Crew picked up a 1-0 home victory over New York, with Kei Kamara doing the honors. After collecting just one win in two-and-a-half months, the Crew rattled off three wins in the span of ten days. There was no longer any need for a Native American shaman lady to perform some sort of exorcism ritual to chase the demons away from Crew Stadium. It would have been pointless. Right?

In hindsight, the answer was yes, it would have been pointless...but not for the obvious reasons. Let us chew on some numbers...

---

[29] The night of Rob's bachelor party. I won money at poker despite being glued to the Crew game instead of the poker game. The diversion probably helped since I don't actually know how to play poker. I just do random things until people grudgingly shove chips in my direction for reasons I cannot comprehend.

The Crew's record in the Sigi Era *before* Bill Archer undertook steps to hire a Native American shaman lady to eradicate paranormal sources of misery and misfortune from Crew Stadium:

9-19-15

The Crew's record (including playoffs) in the Sigi Era *after* Bill Archer undertook steps to hire a Native American shaman lady to eradicate paranormal sources of misery and misfortune from Crew Stadium:

28-14-10

(Plus a Supporters' Shield and an MLS Cup championship.)

It would have been pointless to follow through with the ritual because we had already accrued the benefits. The numbers clearly show that the *very thought* of Bill Archer hiring a Native American shaman lady to give Crew Stadium a ritualistic mystical enema caused the accursed demons of despair to proactively vacate the premises.

Well done, Bill. You completely altered the destiny of our beloved Crew, plus you didn't even have to spend your hundred bucks. Those who say "you can't get something for nothing" have obviously never contemplated a shaman's services.

The Way We Were, Pt. VIII
Signs of Life

In looking back at some of my writing over the past few seasons, not only did I unearth a lot of doom and gloom, but I also discovered a few nuggets that pointed to the better days to come. Here are some of those snippets…

Why Duncan is Captain (9/2/06)

Given the general mood amongst the players that the team is building cohesion and is turning the corner, I asked Duncan if he has noticed a change in the team since finally breaking the winless streak. What followed was an impassioned monologue that I will now print in its entirety.

"The first game against New York felt like a good battle, and then these two New England games have been more of the same. I think the guys are realizing that we need to pick it up. If we don't, we're not going to be in the playoffs, which means we might not be back next year playing in front of these amazing fans. Maybe it's a bit late, but it might not be too late. It's not over. If we win the rest of our home games, we can make something happen.

"I've been around a while, so I know what the passion is like here. When I came in, there were guys like Brian Maisonneuve, Brian McBride, Mike Clark, and Dante Washington, and we need to honor what those guys left behind. It's good to remember them and they way the played the game in a Crew shirt.

"I think when you turn a team over like this, it's hard because everyone is getting to know each other. It can take some time to come together. The initial tendency when you get all new guys is that people say, 'Wow this is nice' or 'I'm happy to be here,' but we need to stress that that's not good enough in Columbus. Those guys in the past I just mentioned always stressed that we're professionals who have been brought here to win games. So we need to honor what they built, and I think this group is coming to realize that if we start winning games, we will get incredible support. Even tonight, the fans that were here were outstanding. At the beginning of the game, we could hear the New England fans in their corner, and it was, like, 'Wow. I don't like that one bit.' It's been a tough year, but when we rewarded the fans tonight, it got very loud. They generated a lot of good noise, which definitely boosts you when you're going in for a tackle. It was nice to get the 12th man behind us and pushing us toward three points."

And on a Serious Note... (4/7/07)

Last year sucked. Both personally and Crew-wise, it sucked. I missed the first half of the season to be with my family as we all pulled together to make sure Mom was supported and cared for at home during her final battles with cancer. After a four-year fight, cancer finally won on June 19, claiming Mom at the age of 52.

When I finally came back to Columbus in July and tried to get back in the swing of things, the Crew were already in shambles. They were in last place, the roster had been completely turned over to players I didn't know, and the fans had long stopped giving a crap. It was nearly impossible to half-heartedly stumble into that mess mid-way through the season.

That's why I am excited for this season. The whispers are nothing but positive.

The whispers have suggested that this team is really bonding. A collection of strangers a year ago, they are now friends and trusted teammates. There is a better understanding between players and coaches. The guys like playing here and want to be a part of the community...no more aging vets just passing through; no more "major market" primadonnas like Ante Razov or Tony Sanneh.

Anyone who reads my gibberish surely remembers Duncan Oughton's impassioned speech last year about what it means to play in Columbus and how the new generation needs to honor McBride, Maisonneuve, Clark, Washington, and the guys who came before. Whispers abound that the "new" Crew gets it. They want it. They are happy here and want to win over the community. They want to restore some luster to the badge and add some hardware to the trophy case.

There just seems to be a resurgence of Crew Pride, for lack of a better term. Surely it helps to have a leader like Oughton, who is a living bridge between the "original" Crew and the current squad. It helps to have longtime players like Robert Warzycha and Mike Lapper on the coaching staff. It helps to add another player, Dante Washington, in the broadcast booth.

But there are subtle cosmetic things too. The locker room got a fresh coat of paint, and in the locker area, the white has been replaced with gold to offset the black lockers. It is now truly a Black & Gold locker room. There is also a wall with five or so glass cases, each containing a game ball from a historic Crew Stadium event, such as the inaugural game or the 2000 All-Star game. The hallway leading from the locker room to the entrance tunnel now has four frames on the wall. There is a portrait of Lamar Hunt, a large collage of supporter photos, as well as framed game jerseys worn by Stern John and Thomas Dooley.

Both tangibly and intangibly, the locker room seems different this year. I still don't know half the guys in that locker room, and they sure as heck don't know me, but now I am looking forward to getting acquainted with them. I have always intended for the Notebook to be a place where the players can let their guard down and let their personalities shine through. We all know that over the years, players like Dante, Duncan, Dunseth, Cunningham, Busch, etc., have been regulars in this space. Who's next? Hell if I know.

But the whispers insist that this is a great group of guys. And they want to play for you. And they want your support. And they want to make you proud. After a few fractious years, it appears that a new core is in place, and they, as much as anyone, want to restore the bond between players, fans, and club.

I have no idea how the 2007 Crew will fare, but if the whispers are correct, win or lose, they will be *your* Columbus Crew once more.

I am looking forward to the journey.

No Hellhole for Danny (4/19/07)

Getting back to the subject of making Columbus a tough place to play, I asked O'Rourke, as a local kid, if he remembered the dream of legendary Crew goofball Ansil Elcock, the cackling Trinidadian who dreamed of turning Columbus into a "hellhole."

"Um, that has never crossed my mind," said a stunned and perplexed O'Rourke. "I would like to make it a tough place to play…but I don't know about a hellhole. I grew up here, so I'd kinda like to think that it's a pretty nice city. I don't want it to be a hellhole— just a tough place to play that's not a hellhole."

Cue up Sister Sledge (4/28/07)

Crew coach Sigi Schmid: "Before the game, Frankie gathered everyone and was saying 'We're a family! We're a family! Let's go out there and fight for each other like a family!' It's that sort of mentality that is getting ingrained with our team. As long as these guys maintain that fighting spirit, we will be in every game."

The Offensive Prowess Of Danny O'Rourke (7/22/07)

As a defensive midfielder, Danny O'Rourke gets called many things. A "destroyer"...a "destructor"...a "butcher"...a "pillager"...a "vandal"...a "meatheaded defiler of the beautiful game, and studs-up raper of more talented men."

Most of these descriptions are not complimentary. Well, unless one is a defensive midfielder. But even Danny prefers to put a red-meat American spin on it, whereby he is a combination of a free safety and middle linebacker in football. When he steps on the field, Danny O is Troy Polamalu without the Diana Ross wig; he's Ray Lewis without the Elaine Benes dance routines after every tackle.

But why can't people ever focus on the beautiful side of Danny's game? Everyone talks about his bone-crunching tackles, but nobody has ever taken a moment to admire the offensive prowess of Danny O'Rourke. Until now.

Every good offensive-minded player has a signature move. Frankie Hejduk has his step-over dribble. Alejandro Moreno posts up like a basketball player in the paint. Ned Grabavoy runs directly through the legs of much taller defenders.

But what of our man Danny O? Does he have a signature move? Of course he does! When Danny receives the ball in traffic with two opponents nearby, his first touch gets him around the first opponent. His second touch is a slide tackle that preemptively wins the ball from the second opponent. With one guy in his rear view mirror, and a second guy writhing on the ground holding his shins, our man Danny can then pop up to his feet and calmly play a square ball to an outside back.

I asked Danny about his highly successful evasive-fist-touch/slide-tackle-second-touch move.

"I'm getting my stats up," he explained. "I get paid per tackle. Since I never score any goals or assists, I need to get my stats up by making tackles on defense AND on offense. When you see me do that, I'm just padding my stats."

Near the very end of Sunday's game, Danny decided to put on a show. He ventured deep into the offensive third, near the Hosers' end line.

"I reached into my bag of tricks since we were up 2-0," he said. "I played forward for so long when I was growing up, but I forgot all the moves."

His forgetfulness came with a price tag. While trying to remember a dazzling move from his U-11 days, Danny got cracked across the shins by

Tyrone Marshall-- who is a destroyer, destructor, butcher, pillager, and vandal. The hard foul dropped O'Rourke to the turf with a thud.

"I finally got a taste of my own medicine," he said with a smile. "But you know what? I liked it. My medicine tastes *good!*"

Guille Learns English (7/22/07)

Although he spoke through an interpreter when a dozen reporters crowded around him, which is completely understandable, I've heard that Guille has been making phenomenal progress in learning English.

Once the press chat was over, Guille started speaking in English to teammates and locker room staff. He wasn't perfect, and it took him a little bit to understand some things, but he was definitely eager to work on it.

"He's been doing a great job," said one front office staffer, when I asked about Guille's rumored progress. "I think he takes three classes per week, and he really works at it. I think he's such a confident person that he knows he will get the hang of it and is not ashamed to make mistakes. Over the years, you see some guys who are nervous, or are afraid that they will look stupid if they say something wrong, but that's not how he is. He carries a notebook around and is always making notes after he has conversations in English. He wants to make sure he understands, and wants to make sure he corrects any mistakes. He's serious about it. It really shows you what type of person he is."

It was fun going back and finding these clips. So many little clues were there. Duncan's role as the soul, Frankie's role as the heart, the team's desire to make Crew Stadium a tough place to play and to restore pride to the organization, Danny's ability to laugh at his reputation, and Guille's confident determination to succeed at everything. All of these traits would play a pivotal role in the Massive Season.

Speaking of 2008, let's get on to the good stuff, shall we?

SECTION II:

*

THE REGULAR SEASON

*

Media Day

The Columbus Crew held their annual media day on Tuesday, March 25, 2008. It's the club's first chance to get its spin out there while plying the media with free food and gifts. It's a day for salesmanship. The general manager typically gives a speech about how business is improving, the coach typically gives a speech about how the team is coming together now that the right pieces are in place, and the players typically speak about how this is a good group that has a chance to do special things. And then there's the awkward mayoral speech and photo op. It's the same thing every year, down to the part where there are infinitely more media there on media day than on any other day of the season. I mentioned the free food, right?

2008's media day was no different. Crew GM Mark McCullers was bullish on the Crew's business. Sigi Schmid was confident he had the pieces in place. The players felt that they were going to surprise a lot of people who weren't taking them seriously. Mayor Coleman said encouraging things like, "We've got to get this team from Toronto defeated on this here Saturday!" A lot of rarely-seen media types gorged on chicken, pasta, and cookies. All in all, it was a great success.

At one point in the afternoon, I sidled up to Crew PR Director Dave Stephany, who was already engaged in a conversation with another reporter. The guy asked Stephany how he honestly felt the Crew would do in 2008.

"I think we're a playoff team," Stephany declared. "I think we'll definitely make the playoffs, and once we're in, anything can happen."

Pouncing on a pause in the conversation, I added, "And if you can't trust the team's PR guy, who can you trust?"

On that day, I honestly had no idea what to make of the Crew's chances in 2008. On one hand, I saw Dave's point. Despite a lot of bad breaks, the 2007 team narrowly missed the playoffs. Nobody thought that that the 2007 team was particularly good, but the truth was that with even average luck, it was a lower-rung playoff team. Assuming the 2008 team had even average luck, the playoffs seemed like a possibility. But the team was hard to figure. Media day focused on the positive, but there were also many question marks.

Starting at the top, head coach Sigi Schmid was in the final year of his contract, and there was considerable doubt as to whether he would survive that long. With a long and successful career at UCLA, and an equally impressive stint with the Los Angeles Galaxy, Schmid was thought to be a high-profile championship-caliber hired gun brought in for 2006 to resurrect a Crew club that had lost its way. However, in two years, Schmid's remolding of the club had produced very little in the way of results, and rumors were persistent that a hot start was a prerequisite for keeping his job. Schmid had succeeded everywhere he had gone, and he was very open about how his struggles in Columbus were foreign and flummoxing to him. But in 2008, he believed that he had finally put the pieces in place.

On the forward line, Schmid was counting on a big year from Boca Juniors legend Guillermo Barros Schelotto. Signed part way through the 2007 season, Schelotto scored 5 goals and added 11 assists while learning the MLS game and undergoing the mutual adaptation process with his teammates. Now that Guille was a familiar and comfortable presence in the Crew's lineup, Schmid envisioned even bigger things from the Argentine. Also, Schmid said he expected 10-15 goals out of Alejandro Moreno, the Crew's bulldozing, bulletproof holding forward. Moreno had tallied 7 goals and 7 assists while playing off of Schelotto after a 2007 trade brought him from Houston to Columbus, so Schmid certainly had reason for optimism.

Behind the forwards, Schmid liked his revamped midfield. On the left wing, he envisioned speedy youngster Robbie Rogers scoring 5-10 goals. The 20-year-old had scored 3 goals in 10 games in 2007, despite missing time with the U.S. team for the FIFA U-20 World Cup. On the right wing, Schmid was counting on the further blossoming of 21-year-old Eddie Gaven. In the middle, he saw the midfield anchored by former D.C. United stalwart Brian Carroll, whom Schmid had acquired in an expansion draft trade with San Jose, and by an unknown 21-year-old Scottish terror named Adam Moffat, who played hard from box to box and reportedly had a long-range shot unlike anything Crew fans had ever seen.

The back line was to be anchored by team captain and World Cup veteran Frankie Hejduk. Schmid liked his center back combo of the towering Chad Marshall and the newly-converted Danny O'Rourke, a player Schmid felt had the speed and tenacity to complement Marshall. The left back slot was still a work in progress, but the Crew had just signed an Argentine named Gino Padula, who had trialed with the team during their preseason trip to Europe. He was reportedly a smooth and calm presence who could play the ball out of the back.

And in goal, Schmid was counting on the emergence of William Hesmer as a bonafide #1 keeper. After missing the first part of the 2007 season due to injury, Hesmer got the first extended playing time of his career, and Schmid was confident that Hesmer would build off of that for an even better 2008.

Listening to Schmid, one couldn't help but feel optimistic. But that's how these things work, right? At the start of every season, any team can say "If this, this, this, and this happens, then we're going to be a good team."

There's always the flip side to that argument, though. What if the opposite happens? From the pessimists view…

Forwards: The Crew were counting on a magical season from a 35-year-old and expecting 10-15 goals from a guy who had never scored more than 8 in his career.

Midfield: Robbie Rogers had played all of 10 games, and you never know with young players, especially since he could miss significant time with the summer Olympics. Eddie Gaven had been good but unspectacular, and some considered him to have regressed since his teen years with the MetroStars. Brian Carroll was left exposed in the expansion draft, so of course that's the type of guy you want to anchor your midfield. And who the hell is Adam Moffat? So in addition to an expansion draft castoff, the central midfield is being built around a guy who spent 2007 playing in the freakin' 3rd division with the Cleveland City Stars. Excellent.

Defense: Okay, even though he's not getting any younger, Frankie's still the man. But the rest? Yeesh. Where to start? Did Sigi forget that Chad Marshall missed most of 2007 with concussion-related issues and could be just one bump away from calling it a career? He's a great player, but not one to count on making it through the season. This had Ross Paule, Part II, written all over it. And, um, Danny O'Rourke as a center back? The guy is a mauler. Putting this guy in the penalty area is like putting your pit bull in a fenced-in daycare center. Something bad is going to happen, and when it does, there is going to be a terrible price to pay. And as for Gino Padula, the guy had played 12 combined games in the previous three seasons in lower-division European soccer. That's right— an average of four games per year! For second and third division teams! Clearly, he's the answer at left back.

Goalkeepers: Both Hesmer and Andy Gruenebaum had shown to be decent MLS keepers in limited action, but neither had been mistaken for Pat Onstad. Besides, considering that neither of their career totals equaled so much as a single MLS season's worth of appearances, that's a lot of inexperience to be banking on.

Add it all up, and this team will challenge the 1999 MetroStars and the 2001 Tampa Bay Mutiny for the title of "Worst. MLS Team. Ever."

Of course, the rosy coach's scenario and the worst case scenario are worlds apart, and the truth is that any season can be expected to fall somewhere in the middle. A few optimistic projections pan out, a few bad things happen, and then some unexpected and unanticipated developments can move things up or down from there.

In the end, I decided that if the 35-year-old Schelotto and the oft-concussed Marshall stayed healthy, yeah, I would agree with Dave Stephany that this was a playoff team. If either one missed significant time, they might miss the cut. And if both went down, the season would be lost.

One thought that never crossed my mind that day—and how could it have?—was that Sigi Schmid was an oracle and that his media day speech was pure prophecy.

Columbus Mayor Michael Coleman, a longtime friend of the Crew, delivers his famous "We've got to get this team from Toronto defeated on this here Saturday" speech at Media Day on Tuesday, March 25, 2008. Coleman's exhortations would be rewarded, but nothing could be as eerily prescient as Sigi Schmid's view of (and expectations for) his 2008 Crew team. (Photo by Greg Bartram / Columbus Crew)

The Ridiculous Press Release

In the weeks leading up to the season, Crew PR Director Dave Stephany kept pestering me for a quote for a press release. I thought it was completely absurd to issue a press release about my return to the team's official website, but in addition to informing the Crew's fan base, I think Dave thought it was just the right amount of absurd to be befitting of the Notebook. After putting it off for weeks, I eventually relented and gave him a quote. I figured it was going to happen anyway, and if that's the case, a good Dante Washington joke is a terrible thing to waste.

I reprint this press release here not out of any sort of ego trip—I was thoroughly embarrassed by it at the time—but because it was one of the silliest things I have ever been a part of, and yet, by the end of the year, it was so far down on the list of unbelievable stuff I witnessed in 2008. It was a surreal start to what would become a surreal season.

For the record, despite the press release, I did not wake up the next morning to find Dom Tiberi, Bob Hunter, and Larry Larson camped out on my front walk. It's funny to imagine how quickly they hit the delete button when this sucker landed in their inbox to coincide with the publication of 2008's first Notebook.

Here's what the Crew sent out. Seriously. I am not making this up.

Steve Sirk returns with Crew column

Column highlights club's lighter side and personalities at TheCrew.com

03/31/2008 4:04 PM   Columbus Crew Media Relations

COLUMBUS, Ohio - The Columbus Crew announced today that Steve Sirk and the popular "Notebook" column he has authored after home matches for the last eight years return to TheCrew.com this season after a four-year hiatus.[30] Sirk has covered the Crew since 1998 for a variety of outlets, including TheCrew.com from 1999-2003.

---

[30] I wish I had thought to suggest that Dave include the standard player signing boilerplate, "Per club and league policy, no further terms of the deal were disclosed."

"It is a pleasure to welcome Sirk back to TheCrew.com," said Crew communications director Dave Stephany. "To its many devotees, his Notebook column has become part of the club's fabric and lore by creating and developing - in his own witty, entertaining style - a rich universe and cast of characters that helps illuminate our players' personalities. I look forward to enjoying his unique perspective and clever observations - and the laughs that come with them - throughout the season."

Sirk enters his 11th season covering the Crew overall, having started in 1998 as a Michigan Soccer News correspondent. He then spent most of the next five seasons writing for TheCrew.com, joining the club's official site midway through the historic 1999 season and continuing through the end of the 2003 season. It was during that tenure that the Notebook column was born and built a loyal and devoted readership.

"They say you can't go home again, but when it comes to the Crew, Dante Washington has proven that you can come home again and again and again," Sirk said, tongue in cheek. "I am happy to be returning to TheCrew.com for a second stint, and like Dante, I look forward to returning many more times in the future, if necessary."

A "Notebook Hall of Famer," as Sirk has designated him, Washington played for the Crew in 1996, 2000-02, and 2004, and became a Crew television analyst in 2007. Washington is joined in the Notebook Hall of Fame by current Crew midfielder Duncan Oughton and former defender Brian Dunseth.

Sirk is also writing an alumni profile entitled "Where Are They Now?" in each of the four issues of "FreeKick" magazine, the official game program of Major League Soccer. Longtime Crew midfielder Brian Maisonneuve is featured in the first issue.

Founded by American sports pioneer Lamar Hunt, the Columbus Crew is Ohio's Major League Soccer club, anchoring a diverse sports and entertainment enterprise. One of the league's Charter Members and U.S. Open Cup champion in 2002, it opened its 13th season overall and 10th in first-of-its-kind Columbus Crew Stadium on Saturday, March 29.

Sirk's Notebook: Crew 2, Toronto 0

Match date: Saturday, March 29, 2008

Scoring:

26: CLB Moffat 1 (Carroll 1)

76: CLB Moreno 1 (Gaven 1)

Attendance: 13,843

Crew's record afterward: 1-0-0

Internet message boards buzzed with boastful activity. Newspaper articles forewarned of the coming invasion. All that was missing was some modern-day Paul Revere taking a midnight gallop down High Street while shouting "The Hosers are coming! The Hosers are coming!"

In Central Ohio, one of the major storylines surrounding First Kick 2008 was the fact that approximately 2,300 Ontarians had descended upon Crew Stadium, making it the largest infestation of Canadians Columbus has endured since...well...the 2007 NHL Entry Draft. In fact, this show of support from the Toronto FC faithful probably even dwarfed the mass border crossing that occurred when Doug MacLean hired every man, woman, and child of Prince Edward Island to work for the Blue Jackets[31]. Like they say, all records are made to be broken.

Nevertheless, with the help of their own supporters, the Crew shrugged off the bussed-in Maple Menace and dispatched of Toronto FC by the score of 2-0. Adam Moffat gave the Crew a 1-0 lead in the 26th minute, and then Alejandro Moreno buried the Hosers with a counter-attack goal from a wonderful Eddie Gaven feed in the 76th minute.

What follows is a collection of notes, quotes, stories, and general stupidity from my notebook...and since the fan angle seems to be getting the most play, we'll start with a bunch of stuff relating to the fans.

The Fans (Part I: The Maple Menace)

Toronto fans will be the first to tell you how great they are, which is a shame, because so many others would compliment them if they could get a word in edgewise. And let's face it—Saturday's show was amazing. From the upper deck, their tailgate looked like a swarm of fire ants attacking a brewery. Inside the stadium, the show was even more impressive. They filled the entire south end, plus nearly three full sections in the upper deck. They sang songs,

---

[31] MacLean's organization was jokingly referred to as "The PEI Mafia."

they chanted, they waved flags, they batted balloons, they threw streamers and they made themselves the stars of the show before kickoff.

According to my good buddy Flick, his seat neighbor in section 107, a guy named Nate, looked around the stadium and sardonically turned the tables by saying, "Man, look at all those yellow shirts. This is by far the most fans we have ever brought to an away game."

Even Crew coach Sigi Schmid was effusive in his praise. "I think what Toronto did maybe takes the league to a next level," he said. "Maybe D.C.'s fans will say, 'Hey, we're pretty good. We're going to travel.' Then maybe our fans say, 'Hey, maybe we can bring 300 to Chicago.' It's just going to make the league better, and the atmosphere today was tremendous."

The Fans (Part II: Streaming Guille)

In one of the more comical events of the afternoon, the Toronto fans took to showering Guillermo Barros Schelotto with streamers as he lined up for a corner kick in the 39th minute.

Ooh. Streamers. Schelotto has spent his entire career playing before criminally raucous crowds in Argentina. Until the stuff being thrown at him has been lit on fire, I doubt Guille would even notice.

That's probably why it started raining smoke bombs in the second half.

"It was a very good show," said Schelotto afterward. "Toronto brought a lot of fans and smoke bombs and pyrotechnics. It obviously doesn't compare to Argentina, but for MLS, it was very exciting."

The Fans (Part III: Columbus Streams Back)

One of the best moments of the afternoon occurred in the 42nd minute. Just three minutes after Guille was showered in streamers at the Toronto end, Todd Dunivant lined up to take a corner kick just a few feet from the Crew's supporter sections. Dunivant was nearly mummified in black and gold streamers as Crew fans leaned over the railing and filled his ears with insults.

The rest of the stadium gave the supporters a large round of applause for their efforts. In the locker room, Frankie Hejduk savored that historic moment. "I think this was the first time our fans have actually thrown stuff at the opposing team, which is a good thing. That's how it's done all over the world."

[NOTE: Players are of course concerned for their safety. I get the general impression that they have no problems with harmless objects like streamers and confetti, but none of their remarks should be construed as a license to throw objects that can cause injury, such as rocks, coins, batteries, firecrackers, toasters, claw hammers, horseshoes (individual), rotary telephones, anvils, refrigerators, horseshoes (attached to a horse), live lobsters "liberated" from the tank at your local seafood establishment, running chain saws, rabid raccoons, rival fans that have been doused in cheap cologne and set on fire, etc.][32]

The Fans (Part IV: Victory To Columbus)

The players could not say enough about the support of the Hudson Street Hooligans, Crew Union, La Turbina, and whatever other brands of Crew-supporting souls banded together in the northeast corner. The supporters turned what could have been an embarrassing moment into one of their finest hours. They defended Crew Stadium as if it were the Alamo, except if Santa Ana were Canadian, and if the good guys won despite being vastly outnumbered. It was a heroic performance.

"I thought it was great how our fans stepped up to the challenge," said Schmid. "I know (some of them) were disappointed about the stage going in, but with all of them sitting together in the corner, I thought it was tremendous. To see all that black and gold, and all the flags, I thought it was great."

"It was an awesome atmosphere," said Crew goalkeeper William Hesmer. "Our fans rose to the challenge. Honestly, when I was at the stage end, I had a harder time hearing, and the back line had a harder time hearing me. So I think our fans were even louder than their fans."

"Our section over in the corner responded to all the hype over the Toronto fans," said Crew defender Danny O'Rourke. "Don't get me wrong—the Toronto fans were great. But we got a couple goals to reward our fans and they were really into it. It was great. Hopefully we can grow a big old army in that corner."

Alejandro Moreno made a beeline to the corner after scoring his goal. After the match, the Crew went to the corner as a team.

"We wanted to make a point to show them that we appreciate what they do," said O'Rourke. "We felt bad that the stage went in and took their turf away, so we wanted to make a point of thanking them. They put on a show today."

---

[32] Okay, so this wouldn't work out so well by May. It was worth a shot, right?

Frankie Hejduk summed it all up thusly: "As players, it makes us proud of this team and proud of this city when the fans are as loud as they were today."

Okay, on to some soccer…

The Moffat Rocket

The Crew took a 1-0 lead in the 26th minute when Adam Moffat chested down a Brian Carroll re-start pass, took a controlling touch, and then skipped a net-seeking missile past Hoser goalie Brian Edwards from 25 yards away. Schmid had often mentioned this aspect of Moffat's game, and the 21-year-old made him look like a genius on opening day.

"I've been practicing striking the ball in case I get some space and can have a shot," said Moffat. "I was fortunate that it found the back of the net."

Okay, that was much too modest, especially since it happened right in front of that maple-waving mass of booze-addled Ontarians. Nailing the sweet spot and then silencing the self-congratulatory cacophony of those crocked Canucks[33] deserves a little more than "I was fortunate." Surely Moffat had something a little juicer to say.

"When I hit it, I knew it was a good strike," he said, when pressed further. "Sometimes you just know. It's a great feeling. Anytime I score, it's a surprise to me. (The Toronto fans) were loud. They've got great fans. But as soon as it hit the net…nothing.[34]"

Ah, that's a little better.

---

[33] I swear that this was the only time that Dave Stephany and I clashed in terms of content. I used the term "Canucks" but Dave insisted it had to be edited to "Canadians" because "Canucks" was an offensive term. I was baffled by his point of view, considering the existence of the Vancouver Canucks, or Canuck Place Children's Hospice, or the fact that Canada's "Uncle Sam"-type character is named "Johnny Canuck." However, after doing some research, the term originated as a pejorative used against French-Canadian loggers in the Northeast United States, although it has since been co-opted into everyday usage and has become the Canadian equivalent of "Yankee." However, I read that the term can still be used in a pejorative manner along the U.S.-Quebec border. Not so coincidentally, Dave grew up in Vermont, very close to the Quebec border. I suddenly understood his previously puzzling position that the innocuous term "Canuck" was somehow offensive. The article had long been published, but Dave and I were happy that we learned something, so I thought I would share it with you too. For the book, I have restored the text to read "crocked Canucks", the way I originally intended. If you live along the Vermont-Quebec border and are offended by this change, let the record show that Dave Stephany fought the good fight for you.

[34] More on this in a bit, but the oft-told "TFC took over Crew Stadium" legend that exists in MLS lore has forgotten or erased just how quiet the TFC fans were for most of the game.

Another reporter mentioned that Moffat has now scored a goal in two of his three official appearances with the Crew (the other being the friendly vs. Tecos UAG in November). "I like to think it's part of my game, gettin' some goals," Moffat said, "but I don't know if I can make it three."

No pressure, Adam, but if there's a bouncing ball on the New York half of the field next week, you might want to have a go, just in case.

Adam Moffat unleashed his famous Moffat Rocket to give the Crew a 1-0 lead on March 29, 2008. It was both the Crew's and league's first goal of 2008. (Photo by Greg Bartam / Columbus Crew)

The Penalty Kick

Few things alter the complexion of a game like a saved penalty kick. The emotional swings that take place from the whistle & point to the saved shot are almost incalculable. Let's take a look at what transpired in the 44th and 45th minutes in the words of some of those who were involved.

First, Crew defender Danny O'Rourke was whistled for the penalty. He strangely leaped into the air and impeded the dribble of Toronto striker Jeff Cunningham. It was practically a basketball foul, as if Cunningham gave a shot fake and then drove to the lane, colliding with the airborne O'Rourke. O'Rourke, however, wasn't so sure. "I'd like to see a replay," he said. "I thought it was shoulder to shoulder, and I know I hit the ball with my thigh or shin. I was shocked when he called the penalty." Surely the shock would have subsided after seeing a replay, but nevertheless, the Crew protested the call to no avail.

Next up, Toronto striker Collin Samuel collected the ball. One might have thought that 96-goal man Cunningham would have grabbed the ball to convert the penalty he earned, especially playing in the stadium he christened with its first ever goal. However, TFC coach John Carver explained the process. "We spoke about it (Friday)," said Carver. "I said who wants to take the penalties, and Sammy said he did. If a player has that confidence, then I am fine with it."

With Samuel setting the ball on the spot, it was time for Crew goalie William Hesmer to shine...with an assist from Frankie Hejduk, who held a brief conference with Hesmer before the shot was taken.

"Frankie came up to me and said, 'I have no idea where he is going, but I just want to get into his head and make him think'," Hesmer revealed. "Who knows? Maybe it worked. He did look a little bit timid before he took it."

Samuel's penalty was so weak that it might as well have been hit with Tony Sanneh's purse on a chilly October night[35]. Hesmer dove to his left and made the save. "Normally I'll make up my mind to dive one way or the other," said Hesmer, "but this time I held for a moment, and then I actually over-dove it and gave up a rebound. Thankfully Moffat was there to come on over and bang it out of there."

Ah, yes. Mr. Moffat. Again.

As Samuel momentarily froze in terror over what had transpired, Moffat outraced him to the rebound and launched it over the crossbar a split second before Samuel could tuck the tap-in home.

Moffat said that the goal-saving clearance was nothing more than old-fashioned fundamentals. "It's something I've been taught since I was younger," he explained. "You start the same distance he is from the penalty spot, and when he starts running, you start running. If you do that, you're going to be the first one there. He was a bit casual, so I managed to get my foot in there and clear it away."

Schmid said the whole sequence was huge. "Those are the types of plays that change games," he said. "It's something that gives your team confidence and really gets the fans going."

For Carver, it was time to seek a new volunteer. "At halftime, I asked who wants to take the next penalty, and Cunningham said 'I'll take it.' So we'll work our way through the team."

---

[35] October 31, 2004. I used to be a lot more bitter about this than I am now. But let's not kid ourselves—given the circumstances, I will always be a little bitter about it.

And what of dear Danny O'Rourke, who, without benefit of replay, was unsure of his penalty? Did he feel any vindication by the save and clearance?

He cracked a mischievous smile. "The ball never lies[36]."

The Fans (Part V: Hey, Hey, Good-Bye)

When Alejandro Moreno buried his counterattack goal in the 76th minute, he finished off both Toronto FC and their fans. Whereas Toronto had been controlling the second half up to that point, Moreno's goal devastated them. The Hosers spent the final 14 minutes aimlessly wandering around the field like 11 lost toddlers looking for their moms at the mall.

Up in the stands, the south end was silent, except for the pitter patter of Canadian tears. Meanwhile, the stadium echoed with Crew supporters' chants of "USA! USA!" and "Nah-nah-nah-nah, hey, hey, goodbye!"

"As many fans as they had, we shut them down," said Hejduk. "We shut them up a bit. I was actually smiling on the field late in the game when we had a throw-in or certain bits of possession. Normally I'm very intense and very into the game, but I think I had a couple smirks out there. In the past, we haven't killed off some games that we should have, but we did it today. I think some of that is because of the fans and the atmosphere."

The Maple Menace fills the south stands. This picture would look a lot more impressive if it were in color instead of black and white. Not only would sea of red wow you, but that smoke bomb sailing toward the field in the right side of the picture would stand out a lot more. (Photo by Greg Bartram / Columbus Crew)

---

[36] Well, except for when it does. (Both for better and for worse.)

Trillium Cup

Earlier in the week it was announced that the Crew and Hosers would be competing annually for the Trillium Cup, which is named after some kind of politically-honored flower that grows in both Ohio and Ontario.

After Saturday, the botanical rivalry doesn't feel nearly as manufactured as it did in the lead-up to the season. The Crew were selling it hard, but on media day, Columbus Mayor Michael Coleman took the sales job to a whole 'nother...planet.

"I don't like Toronto," said Mayor Coleman. "We need to get them defeated this here Saturday and take this rivalry to a whole new level. I have been to Toronto many times, and I don't like Columbus being beat by Toronto; Columbus has to beat Toronto on every occasion. This is going to be a terrific rivalry. I know that our team, our players, our coach are going to send Toronto where they belong— back across the border! We're used to beating teams across borders. First Michigan-Ohio State; now Toronto-Columbus!"

Coleman wasn't just shooting off at the mouth though. He engaged in one of those non-monetary mayoral bets with Toronto mayor David Miller. The mayor of the losing city agreed to wear the other team's jersey at a photo shoot.

Scoreboard: Coleman.

That means that the next time Toronto's mayor cuts the ribbon at the dedication ceremony for a new hockey rink, beer factory, or moose brothel, he'll be doing so while wearing the glorious gold jersey of the Columbus Crew.

"Mean Guy" of the Game Award

During the fan forum held on March 19, Hejduk stated that the 2008 Crew needed to play like a bunch of "mean guys[37]." As someone who can smell a cheap column gimmick a mile away, I eagerly asked Frankie who was this week's "Mean Guy" Of The Game.

"I think the whole team was one big mean guy today," said Hejduk. "I can't single anyone out. I thanked the team after the game because I challenged them to be mean guys, even though the word I actually used was (a naughty equivalent of 'mean guys.') As a team, we were mean today, and

---

[37] Not the actual word. Not by a long shot.

that's what we need to do week in and week out. Every guy on this team worked his ass off this week, and that's what we need. If I can single somebody out as a 'mean guy of the game', then we're not getting it done. We need every single guy, every single week."

That's good stuff. But so much for the cheap, season-long column gimmick.

Dear Media, Stop asking about Danny Dichio

Members of the Toronto media wanted to know if Danny Dichio was going to start for the Hosers next week in D.C., at which point TFC coach John Carver had had enough.

"I am not going to give anything away because people will hear this interview," said Carver. "I will go away now, and I'll analyze it, and then think about it. I want to set the record straight about Dichio. Dichio is going to have a large part to play for this club. He hadn't started today's game because I thought the pace of the other two lads could cause some problems, and it did. So let's forget about these things. Let's not go personal with Danny Dichio and ask why isn't Danny involved, why isn't he playing, and will he start in the next game. Danny's got a big part to play in this."

The Fans (Part VI: Why MLS Is Cool)

As TFC was coming off the field, young Crew fans crowded around the tunnel while hurling the tried and true insults of the adolescent mind....."Canada sucks! Toronto sucks! You guys suck!" etc. (Actually, according to William Hesmer, this was also the sophistication of the insults he received from the adult Torontonians, but that's not important for this anecdote.)

As Jeff Cunningham jogged toward the tunnel, the kids' tune changed slightly when confronted with the presence of the Crew's all-time goal scoring co-leader. "Toronto sucks! But Jeff, you're still cool!"

Cunningham stopped running and said, "I'm still cool?" Despite a tough and emotionally-charged loss, Cunningham plastered a smile on his face and gamely signed autographs for the young Crew fans before resuming his sprint to the locker room.

Home games before tax day

Crew GM Mark McCullers is a staunch believer that the Crew should not host any games before Tax Day on April 15. A quick look at the kick-off conditions for the last three openers seems to reinforce McCullers' point:

04/07/2007: Cloudy and 30 degrees.
04/15/2006: Sunny and 70 degrees.
04/02/2005: Rain and 37 degrees.

Considering that the Crew were opening their home schedule in March this year, Saturday's sunny skies and 46-degree temperatures had to be considered a blessing.

"We got really lucky," McCullers said while walking the field before the game. "This is as beautiful as you could hope for in March, and we're sitting squarely between two fronts right now. A day or two either way and it would have been miserable. I think the sunshine is a good omen[38]. Ohio weather is hit or miss this time of year, and we were long overdue for a hit."

Nostra-Dant-us

Crew away-game television analyst Dante Washington had a brilliant day in terms of on-the-spot predictions while watching the game from the upper deck. In the 26th minute, Brian Carroll's aerial pass found Adam Moffat in the open field. As Moffat chested the ball into the acres of open space, Dante said "Goal" before Moffat even took his second controlling touch and uncorked the 25-yard laser that gave the Crew the lead. ("It's what he does," Dante offered after the high-fives had subsided.)

Later in the half, when the Hosers were awarded a penalty, Dante was relieved that Samuel was taking the penalty instead of Cunningham. "Samuel ran and grabbed the ball, and that's just crazy," he said. "He's going to miss. He's cold. He hasn't been involved in the game. Will's going to save it."

From Dante's mouth to Hesmer's hands.

Tucker's prediction

Dante wasn't the only one in the prediction game. Crew team administrator Tucker Walther confidently told me before the game that he was expecting the Crew to win "three or four to nothing."

Since the final score was 2-0, I asked if I should put him down as 50% right or 67% percent right.

"You should put me down as 100% right," he said. "The guys won. They got a shutout. And all of my goal predictions come with a built-in plus-

---

[38] Reading this a year later, all I can say is "wow."

minus of one goal. Since the guys scored two goals, it was within the plus-minus."

Yes, but Tucker said "three or four", not just "three."

"The actual pick was 3-0," he explained. "The 'or four' was just to demonstrate the plus-minus system[39]. I didn't feel like I had to say 'three or four or two to nothing' since I thought you'd be smart enough to figure it out."

Okay. Fine. If Chris Bradley can make temperature predictions on the nightly news based upon a "Three Degree Guarantee", I suppose Tucker can make soccer predictions as the "Within One Score Guarantor."

DP Eddie

Eddie Gaven is entering his sixth MLS season, so sometimes it is easy to forget that he is only 21 years old and therefore still serves as the shy, soft-spoken, picked-upon kid brother to many of his teammates. (Along with Robbie Rogers, of course.)

The latest example occurred on media day. Fresh off a stint with the U.S. Olympic team, including a stoppage-time, game-winning goal from the penalty spot, Gaven's Crew teammates have teased him that he will be the Crew's high-priced Designated Player under the so-called Beckham Rule. To that end, Gaven has been given the nickname "DP Eddie."

When Gaven was called upon to do a TV interview, the team was immediately abuzz with chatter about DP Eddie soaking up the limelight and basking in the media's ever-present glow. Duncan Oughton, naturally, took it to another level by acting out what he imagined to be a typical DP Eddie television interview:

Duncan as interviewer: "Eddie, what does football mean to you?"

Duncan as DP Eddie: "What does football mean to me? I'll show you." (He reached into his pocket, pulled out an imaginary wallet, grabbed an imaginary wad of cash, and then created an imaginary two-handed fan-out of $100 bills.) "THIS is what football means to me."

Interior decorating

During the Metapan pre-season friendly, Dwight Burgess, Dante and I did a quality control check on one of the suites. ("Yep! Heater's working!") Inside the suite was a framed picture of Oughton in action. Dante looked at the picture and shook his head in dismay.

---

[39] Tucker can spin a web of B.S. with the best of them.

"That is the worst piece of interior decorating I have ever seen," Dante lamented.

Upon learning of Dante's comment, Oughton waved it off. "Dante miraculously comes up with these witty quips when I am a safe distance away," he scoffed. "He should be a man about it, but the big fella will not say them to my face because he knows the retaliation will be immense."

In the end, Duncan conceded it was strange that suite holders would be subjected to his likeness. "Maybe they are behind on their payments and they don't get a better picture until they pay up."

Farewell, Jim

Saturday's official attendance was 13,843. Sadly, it should have been 13,844. On March 12, the Crew community lost a dear friend in Jim Nelson. Eleven days earlier, Jim went for a walk. He slipped on some ice and hit his head. He fell into a coma and never came back. I have given up trying to make sense of the senseless.

Some of you have met Jim, and those who have know that he was always a friendly presence at Crew events. The post-game scene in the tent seemed strange without him. I would occasionally chat with Jim after games. The best time to do so was after losses. Losses can be frustrating as a fan, and even more so as a journalist. Traipsing around a sullen locker room is never fun. But a quick chat with Jim could always be counted on to boost one's spirits. He'd be disappointed in the Crew's loss, but after a few jokes and a few doses of "we'll-get-'em-next-time…unless-we-don't," one couldn't help but chuckle at the patent absurdity of letting a soccer match sour one's disposition.

For those who never met Jim, if you own a Crew license plate for your car, or if you see one on the road, those plates were Jim's baby. He organized the petition drive and did all of the paperwork to make those license plates a reality. So every time you see a Crew license plate on the road, give a nod to Jim.

Gosh, it was this time last year that I was on a roll with Jim regarding content here in the Notebook. During the first Notebook of the season, I had made some sort of comment about the Katie Witham Stalker Club, in reference to those who admire the Columbus Sports Network reporter. Jim sent me an email saying that just because he grabbed her and tried to carry her away, it didn't make him a stalker. He attached a photo of himself carrying a smiling Katie.

The next home game, I had printed a comment from my good buddy Flick regarding a banner that read, "Brad Evans Down on the Pitch." It was clearly a play on the Bob Evans jingle, but Flick joked that "it's almost like that person is rooting for an injury. If Evans blows out his knee, the person who made that sign is going to look like a (jerk.)"

The day the comment was published, I got an email from, who else, Jim Nelson. See, Jim made and hung most of the banners displayed around Crew Stadium. "No, I'm not rooting for an injury," he wrote. "Geez…I think this team has had enough to last a few seasons into the future!"

When I talked to him in the tent after the next game, we joked that I had him under constant surveillance, which is how I was "unwittingly" coming up with Nelson-related Notebook topics.

Okay, I am babbling now. But I felt Jim deserved a section of the Notebook. He was a great ambassador for the team and a friend to every fan. He will be missed.

Rest in peace, Jim. I'd ask you to put in a good word with the soccer gods, but between a sunny day in March and a saved penalty, it looks like you were already on it. Thanks.

Jim Nelson, circa 2006, attempting to kidnap a smiling Katie Witham.
(Photo courtesy of Jim Nelson)

Questions? Comments? Played high school soccer with me and randomly picked me out of a stadium crowd after 16 years?[40] Feel free to write at sirk65@yahoo.com

---

[40] Joe Brkic did just that as Dante and I watched the game from the upper deck.

Myth: Toronto Invented Columbus

The Nordecke figured prominently in that season-opening Notebook and their support would become a recurring theme throughout the season. In 2008, the Northeast corner of Crew Stadium transformed into one of the loudest and liveliest supporter sections in all of MLS, and easily surpassed any prior supporter efforts in Columbus history. The team fed off the fans, the fans fed off the team, and the symbiosis carried both to unparalleled heights.

It was a great story. Unfortunately, it's a great story that often gets buried beneath a maple-flavored myth. This myth has been told so often that many in the MLS community naively treat the fiction as fact.

I'd tell you the myth myself, but there's a man who tells it much better than I do, so I will defer to him. Ladies and gentleman, here's MLS Commissioner Don Garber...

- "On opening day, Toronto brought down 2,000 fans and overwhelmed the local Crew fans. In response, Crew supporters went from a few hundred to almost 2,000 of their own." – MLS Cup press conference on November 21, 2008.

By the start of the 2009 season, Garber began attributing the myth to people in Columbus...

- "I've heard stories from people in Columbus that their supporter's group, which continues to grow, was really berthed out of the fact Toronto fans came into their stadium and really almost dominated them during the opening game last year." – The National Post (Canada), March 24, 2009.

What's funny is that in reviewing what I wrote at the time, the popular legend could not have been further from the truth. Toronto brought large numbers, yes, but they did nothing to dominate the proceedings. In fact, a lot of the talk was about how relatively little noise they made in comparison to the Nordecke. (Which contained more than "a few hundred" people, by the way.) Adam Moffat took great delight in how his goal silenced the Maple Menace for the rest of the afternoon.

Did Toronto play a role in the Nordecke's success? Certainly. But the real story is much more complicated than that, and it's nothing at all like the myth.

Unlike with the Screaming Eagles and La Barra Brava in D.C., or with Section 8 in Chicago, the Crew never really got off to a great start in terms of establishing a large and effective supporter's group. This is not to discount the efforts of Matt Bernhardt and Contractors S.C. at Ohio Stadium, nor those Wrecking Crew dudes, nor Zak Bernardo and V-Army. It's just that Crew supporter groups were usually a small and fractious lot, and successful growth was rarely sustained before the next fracture occurred.

By the end of 2007, the Crew had three distinctly different supporter groups spread across the north end of the stadium. Crew Soccer Union consisted of mostly 30-somethings, some of whom were survivors of the various supporter group factions over the previous decade. Hudson Street Hooligans was the group for the rowdy college set. And then there was La Turbina Amarilla (The Yellow Engine), the Crew's Hispanic support section.

When the Crew decided to erect a concert stage in the north end of the stadium after the 2007 season, it meant that many of the supporters were displaced from their traditional sections. It was a blessing in disguise.

Mike Blankley, aka "Hard Hat Mike", has become the de facto spokesman for the Nordecke. He is but one of many leaders amongst the three main supporter groups, but his propensity to speak thoughtfully, intelligently, and soberly has made him the go-to guy when the media wishes to speak about the Nordecke. He describes the section as "one big dysfunctional family."

While the concert stage was the first non-Toronto factor in the birth of the Nordecke, the three groups and the Crew's front office were the second factor. Historically, the Crew's front office has had a tenuous relationship with supporter groups, but there was a sea change from within, and working with the supporters became a priority. That work began as soon as the 2007 season ended.

"Before Christmas, we were talking about how to work this new area that we were creating," said Blankley. "There was meeting after meeting between Chris Keeney of the front office; myself, Kevin McCullough and John Clem of Crew Union; Grant Thurmond and Jon Winland of Hudson Street Hooligans; and Miriam Ponce and other members of La Turbina Amarilla. We outlined a plan for meshing these three unique groups. It took much time and patience to work out who would be where, what the ground rules would be, and how to fill it up."

With the Crew front office and all three supporter groups working together for quite possibly the first time ever, things were off to a good start. And then it got better.

"Once the 2008 schedule was released, we knew we had some work on our hands," said Blankley.

This is the point where fact and fiction collide. Like many myths, the "Toronto Invented Columbus" tall tale has some basis in reality. I'll let Blankley explain...

"Toronto definitely played a part in the formation of the Nordecke as we know it today," he said. "As soon as the 2008 schedule was released in December of 2007, the trolling of the Big Soccer forums began. TFC fans poured onto our boards telling us how they were bringing so many people and how Crew Stadium would finally see what it's like to have a good loud crowd. Honestly, had they not said a word and had they worked out their trip logistics on their own message boards, we wouldn't have had a clue. Their own hubris was their undoing."

The Toronto hubris turned the upcoming visit into a full-blown media story, as the newspapers in each city repeatedly featured and trumpeted the Hosers' impending arrival.

"We now had a rallying cry," said Blankley. "We had an invasion on our hands. Repel the Canadian hordes! And Columbus didn't disappoint. We had people we had never seen before standing next to us cheering."

Toronto's role in creating the Nordecke wasn't confined to rallying cries and pre-game chatter. No, the fact that a thousand-plus people in the Nordecke held their own against the much-hyped 2,300 fans from Canada gave the group its swagger. I watched the game near midfield on the west side, about equidistant from the two groups. After all, I thought the fans were going to be the story, not a game between two teams nobody picked to go anywhere. As a result, I was more focused on the fan battle. From my equidistant perch, the Nordecke was the winner in the volume department. The Crew's 2-0 victory surely had a lot to do with that.

It was a stark contrast to all those times in the past when the Chicago Fire would bring several hundred fans and shout down Crew Stadium. Fire fans jokingly referred to Crew Stadium as "Fire House East." They had good reason to do so, since they usually came out on top on the field and in the stands.

But March 28, 2008, was different. For the first time ever, the Crew supporters had banded together to outperform a large and organized band of visitors. In fact, it was a historic band of visitors, as Toronto brought the largest contingent of traveling fans in MLS history. The Nordecke successfully countered a record traveling party.

The Crew took care of business on the field while the Nordecke took care of business off the field. The team's performance helped the Nordecke win the battle of the voices, and the team gushed over the Nordecke's performance and how it helped them on the field to open the season with a victory.

The positive feedback loop had been established.

Did Toronto play a role in helping the Nordecke to become what it is today?

Yes. I don't think anyone honestly claims that the Nordecke would have been such a first day sensation had the Crew been scheduled to play Colorado or some other random team. The 2,300 Toronto fans played a large role in the Nordecke's smashing debut. But it wasn't because Toronto fans "overwhelmed" and "dominated" a Nordecke consisting of "a few hundred" people.

That's the myth. It's 100% tall tale fiction.

The truth is that the Hosers' defeat on the field and in the stands was the perfect launching pad for something that fate and hard work had put together in the offseason.

Let's put it this way…the legend, as espoused by Garber and others, says that Mr. Toronto was the muscular bully who kicked sand in the face of the 98-pound weakling, Mr. Nordecke, who then hit the gym so he could eventually become ripped and hold his own.

The truth is that the Mr. Nordecke was already in the gym, and when Mr. Toronto spent months talking about how he was going to kick sand in the Mr. Nordecke's face, Mr. Nordecke was up for the challenge. And not only did Mr. Nordecke reverse the script and kick sand in Mr. Toronto's face, Mr. Nordecke walked off with Mr. Toronto's willing girlfriend. And then on November 23, she gave birth to a baby that looked like this…

(Photo by Tucker Walther)

....and everyone knew who the daddy was.[41]

---

[41] Okay, that may be the most tortured, strained, nonsensical and overwrought analogy ever. But what the hell. It was fun anyway.

Road Work: New York 2, Crew 0

Match date: Saturday, April 5, 2008
Scoring:
1: NY van den Bergh 1 (Ubiparapovic 1)
8: NY Goldthwaite 1 (Angel 1, van den Bergh 1)
Attendance: 17,119
Crew's record afterward: 1-1-0

RETROACTIVE RECAP

The Crew's first road game of the year pretty much ended before it began. The Red Bulls scored 46 seconds into the game when Dave van den Bergh's skidding turf shot eluded William Hesmer. Kevin Goldthwaite tapped home another goal in the 8th minute. The Crew did much better from that point, but such is often the case when an opponent has a two-goal lead.

Hesmer ran his penalty save streak to two in a row. Danny O'Rourke was whistled for a penalty on Oscar Etcheverry. Red Bulls ace Juan Pablo Angel went to the upper right corner with his penalty, but Hesmer extended and tipped the ball over the crossbar.

QUOTES

Sigi Schmid: "I just thought we didn't play well in the early part of the game. Part of it is the field, because it is a very matted-down turf. It's not a stand up turf, so it plays very quick. They watered it beforehand so it was very slick. It contributed (to the first goal) because we didn't give ourselves a chance to get used to the field before we started to play balls we shouldn't have been trying to play. That's our fault and we just didn't manage the game well in the first 10-15 minutes. If we manage the game well there, I think we're OK today."

Alejandro Moreno: "Obviously, this was not the start that we wanted. When you allow two goals in the first eight minutes, it makes it very difficult. At times, when we put the ball down and tried to play we were decent. We created some opportunities, but chasing the game after the eighth minute makes it very difficult."

Frankie Hejduk: "We win as a team and we lose as a team and obviously tonight, we lost as a team. It's a team; it's nobody's fault; we can't look too much into it. We think of it for the next couple hours and then we work for next week on Monday."

Sirk's Notebook: Crew 4, Chivas USA 3

Match Date: Saturday, April 12, 2008

Scoring:

26: CLB Schelotto 1 (pk)

33: CHV Kljestan 2 (Savage 1, Bornstein 1)

35: CLB Moreno 2 (Schelotto 1)

71: CLB Rogers 1 (Schelotto 2, Moreno 1)

72: CHV Marsch 1 (Nagamura 1)

78: CHV Nagamura 1 (Kljestan 2)

82: CLB Rogers 2 (O'Rourke 1)

Attendance: 6,733

Crew's record afterward: 2-1-0

Saturday's Crew–Chivas USA match was so lights out that, well, the lights went out. And that was before the teams lit up the scoreboard in a thrilling 4-3 Crew victory.

Sometimes the soccer gods smile on the hardiest fans and this was one of those special nights where those who craved the warmth and comfort of home were the ones left out in the cold. The Crew put forth a riveting display of attractive and attacking soccer, the likes of which has long been desired and all but forgotten in these parts. The purposeful and intelligent movement… the insightful passing… the composed finishing… the long-range missiles… the diving headers, heel flicks, and other flashes of style… it was a beautiful thing to watch. For those who braved the cold, windy and wet elements, it was impossible to tell where the shivers of frigidity ended and the shivers of delight began.

That's not to say the Crew played a perfect game. But they played a fun game. And they won. After years of ho-hum un-fun, they won fun, so well done.[42] What's not to love about that?

So for those who saw it in person, and for those deservedly kicking themselves that they didn't, here is the usual collection of notes, quotes, and general stupidity from my notebook…

---

[42] I grew up feasting on Jim Ingraham's coverage of the Cleveland Indians in the Lake County News-Herald. The footnoted sentence strikes me as the type of goofy thing that Ingraham might write. Hooray for influences!

All Aboard the Great Goalercoaster

All of the goals in the match occurred in two distinct windows of action that saw momentum flip one way, flop the other way, and then flip back again.

In the first nine-minute window, the Crew took a 1-0 lead on a Guillermo Barros Schelotto penalty kick in the 26th minute. Then Chivas tied the game on an unbelievable bender from Sasha Kljestan in the 33rd minute. Then the Crew reclaimed the lead in the 35th minute on an Alejandro Moreno finish.

In the second 11-minute window, the Crew capped an impressive 20-minute display of attacking soccer with a Robbie Rogers goal in the 71st minute to go up 3-1. Before the Crew were even out of celebration mode, Chivas halved the lead on a Jessie Marsch goal in the 72nd minute. And then, horror of horrors, Paulo Nagamura tied the game at 3-3 in the 78th minute. But then Rogers answered with the game-winner in the 82nd minute.

And then, for good measure, Chivas received back-to-back ejections in the 83rd and 84th minutes. Fun!

"It was an exciting game," said Crew coach Sigi Schmid. "I don't think anyone can say they didn't get their money's worth. When we went up 3-1, I thought we had it, and then we gave up a very sloppy second goal, and then it got exciting. But we got three points at home and scored four goals. The rest will get better."

"Good game for the fans," said captain Frankie Hejduk. "We gave them a little scare, but we fought through it. It was a wide-open game, but we got the three points. Throughout the game, I thought we had the better chances. We were able to get Guillermo the ball in the spaces he wanted, Alejandro did an excellent job fighting for the ball and holding it, and Rogers came through big-time for us today."

Resiliency

One of the Crew's objectives this year is to finish off games. On one hand, it had to be dispiriting to see two leads slip away. On the other hand, the Crew bounced right back each time, which is surely much more difficult than holding a lead in the first place.

"I'm very proud of the way our team came back," said Schmid. "We gave up an incredible goal to Sasha Kljestan and then answered it, and then we got the winner right after giving up the goals to make it 3-3. That showed a lot of character."

In past years, blowing a two-goal lead at home would have been disaster, but Hejduk sees a difference in this year's team. "There wasn't a doubt in my mind that we were going to bounce back and win this game," he said. "We still had a positive attitude on the field. Taking two goals like that late in the game can be demoralizing, but we didn't let it get us down. Looking at my teammates' faces on the field, I don't think any of us thought for a moment that we were going to lose or tie that game."

Guille The Great

Guillermo Barros Schelotto gave his most mesmerizing performance yet in a Crew kit. Constantly on the ball, Schelotto delivered dangerous passes time and time again and truly was the engine driving the offense. He opened the scoring with a penalty kick in the 26th minute, then assisted on each of the Crew's next two goals. On the second goal, he collected a pass from Alejandro Moreno, drew a crowd of defenders in the box, then squared the ball into the path of Moreno for a one-touch finish. On the Crew's third goal, Schelotto angled a diagonal ball through three Chivas defenders to set up a streaking Robbie Rogers.

Guillermo Barros Schelotto works his magic against Chivas USA on April 12, 2008.

(Photo by Greg Bartram / Columbus Crew)

"Guillermo did what we wanted him to do, and the team gave him the opportunity to do what he can do," said Schmid. "We talked about getting guys behind him and defending, and I think Eddie Gaven did tremendous amount of work tonight both offensively and defensively. And Adam Moffat was up and down the field, along with Brian Carroll. That means Guillermo was given the freedom to do what he can do, and like I told the rest of the team, if he doesn't do it, then I get to scream at him."

Aside from providing defensive cover, the Crew were also encouraged to funnel the attack through Schelotto. "This week in training, we worked on transitioning in a way that would get Guillermo the ball more," said Hejduk. "He's supposed to be our big gun and we weren't getting him the ball enough. Today he saw the ball a lot more, and I think as a team, when we defended and got possession, we figured out where to get him the ball and we got it to him early so he could be more dangerous."

Schelotto tried to downplay his performance. "It doesn't matter what I did individually tonight," he said. "The important thing is that the team got three points. It was fun, but it is also our job. What made it fun is that we all did our job and everyone was involved."

But Alejandro Moreno said a lot of the fun was due to Guille. "It's great fun when he's up for a game because we depend a lot on what he does," said Moreno. "He can find the passes that many people in this league can't find, and we all know that."

Robbie Rogers: MOTM, Jr.

Young Robbie Rogers deserves some sort of Man of the Match designation for his play. He made great runs, unleashed ankle-breaking dribbling turns, and scored two goals, including the game-winner.

"On the first goal, the ball came to Guille and I made a run into the space and Guille got it to me," said Rogers. "When I took my first touch, I think Brad (Guzan, Chivas USA's goalie) thought I was going to the far post and so he cheated to the far post. Then I put it to the near post."

"I look for Robbie to make those runs," said Schelotto. "The important thing is that he stayed calm and put the ball in the back of the net."

Rogers scored the game-winner when he collected a long aerial pass from Danny O'Rourke, then unleashed a low knuckler that eluded Guzan. "The second goal was pretty lucky, I think," he said. "The defender misjudged the ball, I brought it down off of my chest, and thought 'why not?' with the way the game was going. Brad misjudged it and it went in."

Replays showed that what appeared to be a misjudgment on the part of Guzan was at least partially due to the movement on Rogers' shot.

Rogers' teammates were effusive in their praise. "Robbie has a very good future in front of him," said Schelotto. "What's important is that he brings that same performance as tonight every night. If he does that, (his opportunities will be limitless)."

"Robbie is going to be a star in this league," said Hejduk. "He has great pace, he can use both feet, he's good one-on-one.... when he gets his confidence up, it will be interesting to see what he does. I think tonight was a taste of what you're going to see in the future from him. Having said that, I don't want to get ahead of myself. He still has some things to work on, not just offensively, but defensively. But I think tonight was a great effort from him."

Robbie Rogers fights for the ball in the corner during his electrifying two-goal performance in the Crew's 4-3 victory over Chivas USA. (Photo by Greg Bartram / Columbus Crew)

Guille and Robbie

Schmid said he thinks that Schelotto sees a bit of himself in Rogers, and mentioned that Schelotto spends time mentoring the speedy youngster.

"Guillermo talks to me a lot in practice and in games and tells me what he wants me to do," said Rogers. "He's got a lot of experience and I'm pretty young and like to run a lot, so I try to get into spaces where he can get me the ball."

Schelotto downplayed the Rogers-as-young-Guille angle. "Every player has something that makes them special," he said, "and I think that people should focus on the player that Robbie is instead of trying to compare him to me."

Another Moffat Rocket

Rookie midfielder Adam Moffat elicited excited gasps from the crowd when he unleashed another long-distance howitzer on Saturday. This one nearly broke the sound barrier, then Brad Guzan's leg. The shot was hit so hard that Guzan couldn't have gotten out of the way if he had tried. (That's probably a good thing, since his job is to get in the way and all.) A left-footed, can't-get-my-foot-out-of-the-way "kick save" from Guzan thwarted another memorable Moffat Rocket.

"It would have been nice if that had gone in," said Moffat. "It was better than Robbie's. I told Robbie that I hit mine better, but he got the goal."

Yes, but because Guzan bore the brunt of Moffat's shot, maybe he got out of the way of Robbie's.

"That's what I'll tell Robbie," Moffat said. "But it just goes to show that if you keep it low and keep it on target, look what can happen."

Bad Brad

As a member of the U.S. national team, the MLS Best XI, and as the reigning MLS Goalkeeper of the Year, Brad Guzan is not prone to many off performances. On Saturday, he was badly caught cheating on Rogers' first goal, then saw Rogers' game-winner unexpectedly elude him.

When asked to assess Guzan's performance, Chivas USA coach Preki didn't mince words. "What do you think?" he asked rhetorically. "Brad has been very good for us, but everyone makes mistakes. Today was not his day. It is what it is."

On the game-winner, Guzan did get a smidge of sympathy from another member of the goalkeeping fraternity. The Crew's William Hesmer immediately had an idea as to how Rogers' shot eluded Guzan.

"To be honest, something I haven't seen talked about this year are these new balls," said Hesmer. "These balls are everywhere. They are moving a lot. I mean, Moffat's shot, Brad was leaning right and putting his hands up, and then it hit his left foot. These balls are made to score more goals and to be more explosive, so they're tough to deal with sometimes."

Lazy Random Quote "Intermission" So This Isn't An 8000-word Article
"They said they were OK with it the way it was, and we said we were OK with it, so we decided to keep playing. The one person we probably should have checked with was Will (Hesmer) to see if he was okay with it." – Sigi Schmid, on the decision to resume play during a partial lighting failure.

"Those things should be bright and shiny." – The ever-helpful Dwight Burgess, during the TV broadcast, as the cameras showed a bank of failed lights.

"We created a lot of chances. I think we're going to be a good attacking team, so four goals is pretty awesome, I think." – Robbie Rogers

"When they made the sub with Eric Ebert, we felt he was a guy that Robbie could go at and that proved correct as Robbie was able to get behind him a couple of times." -- Schmid

"Robbie and I were hanging out and I told him if I get the time, I'm hitting that ball to you. I love hitting that ball. He took it down brilliantly and finished it." – Danny O'Rourke, on his long-ball, game-winning assist that went over Ebert on its way to Rogers.

"Sometimes people dismiss a goal if it's a penalty, but I felt this penalty was an earned penalty. It was a good early ball by Schelotto, a good ball by Rogers, and a good run by Moreno, so those types of penalties can be deserving goals." – Schmid, on the Crew's first goal.

"We'll have to look at the tape on those two goals, but other than that 10-minute stretch, I thought we did a good job defensively. We lost the script for about 10 minutes, so we'll have to look at that." – Schmid, on the evaporation of the Crew's 3-1 lead.

"It was good that we built ourselves a lead, but we have to keep our concentration. Those 10 minutes almost cost us two points." – Adam Moffat, on the same subject.

"I still need to be better. That third goal, the tying goal…I need to save that." – William Hesmer.

"My landing was really dicey. All I could think was, 'God, when I said I was looking forward to spending time in Columbus, I didn't mean the rest of eternity.'" – Notebook Hall of Famer and Chivas USA color analyst Brian Dunseth, on his scary inbound flight.

Ding, Dong, The Streak Is Dead

When he arrived at the stadium, Danny "Two Penalties In Two Games" O'Rourke approached Dunseth and me with a very serious line of questioning. "Have you guys been on the field yet?" he inquired. "Have they marked off the penalty box with yellow tape that says DO NOT FOUL?"

Dunny and I said no, but that in its place, the Crew installed an invisible doggie fence around the box so that Danny would receive an electric shock upon entering the penalty area, which would alert him that he could no longer foul.

At that moment, the referees emerged from their locker room, stopped to say hi to Dunny and Danny, and then went out to check the field. As they walked into the distance, Danny jokingly commanded under his breath, "Don't call a penalty on me today!"

Then Dunny gave Danny a quick little pep talk about life as a central defender before everyone went their separate ways.

Fast forward four hours. As the victorious Crew walked off the field, O'Rourke came over with a high-five. "The streak is OVER!"

A little while later, in the locker room, we discussed it further. "Yes, the penalty streak is over," he said. "This is on par with when the Red Sox ended the Curse of the Bambino, or what it would be like if the Browns ever made it to a Super Bowl."

My smile vanished. Danny asked if I was a Browns fan. I said yes. He laughed at me.

(The worst part is that I don't have a leg to stand on. When I asked Danny who his team was, he said, "Whoever's on my fantasy team. I'm a Buckeye fan without an NFL team." So unless I get the inside scoop on Danny's fantasy league[43], I'm a sitting duck when it comes to football smack.)

---

[43] Little did I know that Danny's fantasy football obsession would become a regular Notebook topic later in the season.

Anyway, nobody ever accused Danny O'Rourke of being soft. Conceding penalties in the first two games at a brand new position could be devastating to one's psyche, but O'Rourke never shied away from the fact that it happened, and as mentioned, was even comfortable enough to crack jokes at his own expense before the game.

"There's no room to dwell on it," he explained. "If you think something bad is going to happen, it's going to happen. This game is 90% mental, so I had to keep a positive attitude and just learn from it understand that I couldn't take my midfield mentality out there. I gave up two penalties in the first two games, but Will saved both of them, so thankfully my learning didn't cost us any goals."

So what about those saves? Hesmer claims that O'Rourke owes him a steak dinner at Hyde Park.

"Hyde Park?" scoffed O'Rourke. "I don't owe him anything. It's his contract year, so I was just trying to get him paid."

Danny O'Rourke on April 12, 2008, the day the penalty streak died.
(Photo by Greg Bartram / Columbus Crew)

Padula's First Game

Gino Padula, the Crew's new left back, made his debut in Saturday's match. It was Padula's first competitive match since playing for the Crew on trial in England back on March 7. After a rough start, including an intercepted back pass in the 12th minute that required a bailout point-blank save from Hesmer, Padula finally settled into the game and displayed his talents.

Team captain Frankie Hejduk spoke at length about Padula's debut, shedding some light on the challenges that Padula faced as he was plugged into the starting lineup.

"It's tough because he just got in last week, traveling from Spain, going back and forth, staying in hotels…it's tough," said Hejduk. "And not only is it a new league, it's a different type of league. And I think he'll admit he's not 100% fit yet, but he's going to get there. But despite all that, I think we needed to implement him right away, because we brought him here for a reason. He's a guy with a left foot, and there were definitely flashes of brilliance out there tonight. He's a good one-on-one defender and he's not only good with the ball, but he's very calm on the ball, and we need that coming out of the back."

"I think after the first half hour, he finally got settled in," Hejduk continued. "He was much better in the second half, and I think he's going to get better with each game. I've been in his shoes before and it's tough. He's in a whole different country and that's not an easy thing because there is more than meets the eye. It's not just, 'Oh, you've got a new team, now go play.' I mean, not only does he have to learn a whole new team and a whole new league, but he's still got to bring his family over, get a car, find a place to live, and all that other stuff. So yeah, he had a few moments early in the game, but once he got settled in, you could tell that he is a good player and that he is really going to help our team this year. We're happy he's here."

Random Padula Numerology Note

Seeing a long-haired Argentine wearing No. 4 for the Crew made be think of Ricardo Iribarren. [44] And then I remembered Mario Gori also wore No. 4. Although others have worn that digit, No. 4 seems to be the unofficial Crew number for Argentine defenders.

---

[44] And how about that? Iribarren would join the Crew's coaching staff in 2009.

Moffat's Virtual Crew

Chris DeVille has been doing an outstanding job covering the Crew in Columbus Alive, one of the free weekly papers in town. Two weeks ago, DeVille wrote a feature on Adam Moffat in which Moffat revealed that when he played the soccer management simulation game Championship Manager as a kid, he often played with an American team called the Columbus Crew. Ten years later, he finds himself playing for that very club. "Now I know what it's all about," Moffat told DeVille.

That was great work by Chris, and I couldn't help but follow up on the groundwork laid by his piece. When I read that story, I immediately wanted to know if Moffat ever managed the Crew to an MLS Cup victory.

"I never did," he said with a shake of the head. "I got to a final, but never did win it. [45] I even cheated and got some more money and signed some new players."

So what type of talent infusion did the virtual fans of Columbus enjoy during the reign of GM Moffat?

"When I cheated?" he asked, seeking clarification. "When I cheated, I brought Ronaldo to Columbus. That was a good signing. You know, young Ronaldo from 10 years ago when he could really do it. But I think the game knew I cheated, so it still wouldn't let me win."

Will or William?

After turning in my first Notebook, I noticed that all references to "Will Hesmer" were replaced by "William Hesmer." Crew PR Director Dave Stephany then informed me that Hesmer is going by "William" this year.

Well, that's just insignificant enough to warrant a full-blown investigation. Let's start with the man himself, Whatshisface Hesmer.

"I grew up as William," explained Hesmer. "When I went to college, people started calling me Will, and my mom didn't like that so much because she said she named me William. People are still calling me Will, though. Danny O'Rourke's mom gives me a hard time because I introduced myself as William, and she said, 'I'm not calling you that. I'm calling you Will.'"

O'Rourke popped his head out from the around the corner. "What did he say about my mom? Yeah, that's right, I hear everything. I want you to write down everything he says about my mom so we can discuss it later."

So, William, what else do we need to know about Danny's mom?

---

[45] Seven months after this interview, Moffat would get his revenge by winning the real MLS Cup with the real Columbus Crew.

"Danny's mom is really cool," said Hesmer. "I have no idea how he came from her."

Rather than let the investigation get derailed by Danny's mom, it was time to focus on other aspects of the task at hand. Like, should we use a middle name or initial when referring to Hesmer? After all, nothing would bring me more joy than writing articles about The Honorable Mr. William Herbert Walker Hesmer IV, Esquire.

"No, you don't need to use my middle name," Hesmer said. "William or Will is fine. I am a junior though."

(Stephany was quick to point out that many juniors are given nicknames like "Skip" or "Chip," so his switch back to William from Will isn't terribly drastic within that context.)

The next witness called into this investigation was obviously O'Rourke, who addressed the Will vs. William conundrum. "Well, he grew up in the country club and flying around on his dad's private jet," said O'Rourke. "I think his dad runs half of North Carolina, so Will tries to be the senator of our apartment, but I don't let it happen. I will never call him William. To me, he is...Bill."

Although not present to testify, I know Duncan Oughton refers to Hesmer as "C.C. Willie." The initials stand for Country Club.

Moving on, there is a new problem to consider. If Will is now officially William, should the rest of the team follow his lead as a show of solidarity? Maybe Daniel O'Rourke? Edward Gaven? Robert Rogers?

"No," said O'Rourke. "No Daniel, no Edward, and no Robert. Besides, you got Robbie's name wrong. His name is Robbie Hampton."

Robbie Hampton?

"Yeah, because he acts like he's one of those kids in the Hamptons."

Okay. After weighing all of the testimony not related to Danny's mom or Robbie Hampton, I think Hesmer's official Notebook name will now be Mr. C.C. William "Chip" Hesmer, Junior.

Well, at least until I get tired of typing it or he beats me over the head with a polo mallet or something.

Mr. C.C. William "Chip" Hesmer, Junior, on the field just an hour or two before being subjected to the stupidest interview ever. (Photo by Greg Bartram / Columbus Crew)

Life Imitates Low Comedy

On Saturday, there was a small black rectangle of non-working panels on the scoreboard's video screen. I jokingly told Dispatch beat reporter Shawn Mitchell that the rectangle resembled one of the methods used by over-the-air TV programs when they have to censor nudity.

Wouldn't you know it, in the second half, the scoreboard showed a close-up of a Crewzer cheering and that black rectangle lined up perfectly across her torso. I almost spit my water all over Shawn's computer. The fact that the Crewzer could not have been mistaken in any way for being nude due to her puffy yellow coat made the image all the more amusing to me. That would have taken one heck of a wardrobe malfunction.

Speaking of Shawn…

Some readers may be happy to learn that Shawn's Crew blog is doing brisk business over at Dispatch.com. It is the third-most-popular blog on the site, trailing only the Blue Jackets and political blogs.

It would be folly to extrapolate too much meaning from those numbers. ("The Crew are more massive than Ohio State!") The numbers, however, do acknowledge that there was a segment of the reading public that needed a much bigger Crew fix than it was getting from the paper, and that Shawn's blog has been filling that need.

Plus my own personal game day experience has been greatly enhanced by the having the chance to hear Shawn say things like, "I'll be right back. I'm gonna go blog that." (And voila! Five minutes later, all of you get to read an update on The Ekpo Paperwork Crisis: Day 47.) [46]

The Nordecke

The Crew's supporters section in the Northeast corner once again got some love from players and coaches. After the game Frankie Hejduk tossed his jersey into the section, and in his press conference, Sigi tossed another verbal bouquet toward the groups that inhabit the corner.

"That corner is starting to become impressive," said Schmid. "I like that corner. Our team responds to it as well, which is why they go over there. That corner makes this a tougher place to play."

As a shirtless Hejduk walked off the field, he stopped for the fans at the tunnel entrance and screamed in jubilation while flexing his muscles Hans & Franz style. In typical Frankie fashion, he later joked, "I'm not gonna have this body forever, dude, so I gotta show it off."

Adam Moffat – Subliminal Marketer

I can't believe I missed this last time. After I turned in the Toronto article, I was looking over the quotes again, and I found a gem from Adam Moffat. I kicked myself that I didn't notice it and include it, so I am closing this week's Notebook with it.

---

[46] Shawn diligently reported on the Crew's quest to bring Emmanuel Ekpo over from Nigeria. Nearly every day Shawn would have a new update for his blog after talking to Crew technical director Brian Bliss, with Bliss serving up quotes to the effect of, 'We have reached a preliminary understanding of a sketch of an outline of a non-binding agreement that would tentatively advance the negotiation process to a hypothetical realm that could be construed as moving forward with our goal of signing Ekpo, pending any problems, difficulties, or other potential roadblocks that may or may not possibly occur, whether it be with us, the league office, the player, or his club, between now and the completion of this process, depending on whether it works out or not for the time being as the transfer deadline approaches. But we're cautiously optimistic that it will maybe get worked out somehow, but all we can do is wait until everything gets resolved, which it probably will at some undetermined point in the future, give or take 10 days or so. At least that's my impression based on the non-guaranteed verbal assurances I have been given by my anonymous sources within the Nigerian federation." And this went on for WEEKS. I am convinced that it would have been far less complicated and paperwork-intensive for the Crew to adopt a Nigerian baby than sign a Nigerian soccer player.

How could I miss it? Well, the first reason is that the line was delivered with such stone-faced subtlety that it was easy to overlook. And the second reason is that Moffat speaks with a thick Scottish accent, so he might as well be speaking Klingon for all it matters to those of us not born and raised in Scotland.

Anyway, a reporter asked him about being the "poster boy" for the Crew, since he's a hard working two-way player. In his reply, Moffat offered this gem:

"I like to work hard. And play harder." [47]

Questions? Comments? Got a light?[48] *Feel free to write at sirk65@yahoo.com.*

---

[47] The Crew's 2008 marketing slogan was "Work hard. Play harder."

[48] You know, because the stadium lights went out, remember?

Road Work: Crew 2, D.C. United 1

Match date: Thursday, April 17, 2008
Scoring:
32: CLB Moreno 3 (Hejduk 1, Schelotto 3)
42: DCU Namoff 1 (Emilio 1, Moreno 1)
43: CLB own goal (Peralta)
Attendance: 13,329
Crew's record afterward: 3-1-0

RETROACTIVE RECAP

Just when I thought the national espn2 telecast couldn't get any better than Adam Moffat's slow, careful, maybe-now-you-will-understand-me pronunciation of his name during the opening lineups, the Crew knocked off the defending Supporters' Shield winners on the road. Alejandro Moreno nudged home the first goal off a low, driven ball from Hejduk, and then looked to have nodded home a Moffat cross for the winner. Replays showed it was actually desperate United defender Gonzalo Peralta who got his head on the ball before Moreno could nod it into the empty net. It all counts the same, although Moreno and Moffat were denied the statistical recognition of their great goal-creating play.

QUOTES

Sigi Schmid: "This is a very difficult place to win. I thought D.C. was very good offensively. As much as I would have liked us to attack more, you could feel the rhythm of the game. We just had to defend and take care of business that way. Getting a win here was obviously very important."

"I think (Moreno's) much quicker than people realize he is. On the cross that he hit, he showed some good quickness. I've been very happy with Alejandro. He's got three goals and he could have had four if not for D.C.'s own goal. Three goals in four games for a center forward is pretty good."

Alejandro Moreno: "It's a great win because we can build on this. It gives us confidence to know that we can go into a tough environment against a tough team, a team people are touting to be the best in the MLS, and get a result. It speaks volumes to how organized we were and the things that we can do in the future."

Sirk's Notebook: Crew 1, Houston 0

Match date: Saturday, April 26, 2008
Scoring:
22: CLB Moreno 4 (unassisted)
Attendance: 15,271
Crew's record afterward: 4-1-0

In the last three weeks the Columbus Crew have done the following:

    * Scored four goals against the defending regular-season Western Conference champions to win a game in which they blew a two-goal lead late in the second half.

    * Went on the road to defeat the defending Supporters' Shield champions, winning at RFK Stadium for only the fifth time in club history.

    * Absorbed a desperate onslaught from the two-time defending MLS Cup champions, only to walk off the field with a shutout victory.

    Columbus 4, Chivas USA 3. Columbus 2, D.C. United 1. Columbus 1, Houston 0. Meet the new Crew, same as... the teams that used to beat up on the old Crew.

    Just one month into the season, the Crew have mathematically invalidated all those "America's Hardly Winning Team" jokes.[49] Four wins and 12 points have them sitting atop the entire league for the first time at any point since 2004.

    While there were flashes of style, Saturday's 1-0 victory over the Houston Dynamo was mostly about guts. After grabbing a first-half lead on Alejandro Moreno's fourth goal of the season, the Crew absorbed a second-half onslaught that would have buried previous editions of the club. Crew defenders ball-hawked as if they were Labrador retrievers and the Dynamo were playing with a tennis ball. And whenever something eventually broke down, another defender would fly in at the last minute to disrupt the play. The defensive third was full of yellow bodies looking for a grenade to hurl themselves upon.

    "That type of commitment... it's a goalkeeper's dream," said Crew keeper William Hesmer, whose acrobatic 89th minute save prevented a Wade Barrett shot from finding the upper corner of the net. "I love playing in front

---

[49] I have to admit, that was a pretty good twist on the Crew's "America's Hardest Working Team" motto.

of guys like that. It may not be the prettiest team, but they will do whatever it takes to win. We dodged some bullets, but at the end of the day, we made the plays we needed to make to win the game."

"We faced a team that was very hungry and desperate," said Crew coach Sigi Schmid. "From a soccer standpoint, you could say that they had the better of the game for sure, but I think our character, our resiliency, and our willingness to fight for one another... last year, we stood up here (at the post-game press conference) and said that we played better and had more chances but we lost. It's a lot better to be on the other side of the coin."

The Other Side of the Coin

Houston coach Dominic Kinnear was on the other side of the coin, left to talk about how his team played well and had nothing to show for it.

"You don't always get what you deserve in soccer," said Kinnear.

Kinnear was diplomatic when asked to assess the Crew's hot start. "Teams go on runs at different times of the season," he said. "Things are going well for them right now and they are taking advantage of the opportunities being presented to them. It doesn't surprise me when teams go on runs because you know every team has a run in them at some point in the season."

When asked if the Crew's run could continue, there were cracks in the political correctness. More than a little dammit-we-should-have-won-this-game leaked through. "If you were to watch that game and erase the goal, you'd probably say that Houston won that game," he said. "But it's not about playing well; it's about goals. Sometimes goals go well for you and sometimes they dry up. But of course their run can continue, because when you win, you have belief."

Belief

The Crew certainly have the belief.

"The guys are confident," said Schmid. "When they are in a game like this, and it's a war at the end, they have the feeling that they are going to win it. Last year, they were worried about when the bad thing was going to happen, whereas now they say 'OK, we're going to dodge a few bullets, make some saves, and sacrifice our bodies, but we're going to find a way to win the game.'"

"We are trying to win games instead of trying not to lose games," said Moreno. "When you have a mentality where you are going to be organized defensively and fight and win 50/50 balls, that adds up to a win. Those things count for something and tonight they counted for three points."

More Moreno Magic

How hot is Alejandro Moreno? Moreno is on such a hot streak that he has half as many goals as Landon Donovan.

(And how hot is Landon Donovan? His goal total has matched or surpassed 10 other MLS *teams*.)

Moreno did the whole score-against-the-team-that-traded-you thing in the 22nd minute. Chad Marshall made a brilliant diving header attempt off of a Guillermo Barros Schelotto corner kick. Marshall's low header hit defender Patrick Ianni inside the 6-yard box and fell in the vicinity of Moreno, who opportunistically blasted the ball home.

"It was a free header by Chad Marshall, so we were loose on the set piece," said Kinnear. "Then comes the scramble and it falls to them. It was one of their first forays into our half of the field, so you slap your thigh and throw out a couple of curse-your-luck words."

Schmid told the team that they would score on a set piece this week and, according to Marshall, it was a good thing they connected on that attempt. "After that one, they had two arms around me at all times," he explained. "To be able to get to one and to get the lead was crucial."

While certainly not a work of art, Moreno was happy to cash in on the opportunity that presented itself. "Goals are fickle, but right now they are going in for me," he said. "The most important thing is that I continue to work, and be dangerous, and create opportunities for myself and other people. If the opportunities are there, then it is up to me and the other guys to provide the finishing touch."

Alejandro Moreno hits the deck to knock home a rebound for the only goal of the game in a 1-0 victory over the defending MLS champs. (Photo by Greg Bartram / Crew)

The Beautiful Game

There are "inconsequential" moments in a soccer game that can take your breath away despite never appearing in the box score. One such moment occurred in the 30th minute when Robbie Rogers dispossessed Richard Mulrooney in the southwest corner of the stadium. Rogers took two controlling touches, then split two defenders with a burst of speed to advance the ball up the left sideline. Then he played the ball forward toward the center circle to Guillermo Barros Schelotto, who one-timed a give and go back to the in-cutting Rogers, who took one more touch and played a ball to Eddie Gaven on the right flank at the midfield stripe. Gaven then attacked with five dribbling touches before passing to an overlapping Frankie Hejduk down in the channel to the right of the penalty box. Alejandro Moreno made a run to the near post that lured three defenders with him, leaving Schelotto wide open for a run at the far post.

Sadly, Houston goalkeeper Pat Onstad intercepted Hejduk's cross to thwart the rally. Like Kinnear said, you don't always get what you deserve in soccer.

In the span of 20 seconds, the Crew advanced the ball the entire length and width of the field, from the southwest corner to the northeast corner, with 10 dribbling touches, 4 completed passes, a few great runs, and a good crossing attempt.

Beautiful. Simply beautiful.

Rugby Scrum

Another memorable (and much more peculiar) event occurred moments later in the 34th minute. Crew goalie William Hesmer muffed a low cross and the ball fell right to the feet of Dynamo forward Franco Caraccio inside the six yard box. Hesmer flailed at the ball with his legs which tied up Caraccio momentarily. Caraccio then took a shot that was blocked by Crew midfielder Brian Carroll. Each player's momentum caused them to collide, with the ball wedged between them.

Then it got even more interesting. As they fell to the ground, Crew defender Danny O'Rourke got between the players and the goal line, sticking his foot into the fray to further bolster the defensive fortification. However, O'Rourke was quickly swept into the pile, meaning three players were piled on top of the ball about three feet from the goal line.

And then Hesmer re-joined the fray, jumping over the pile as if he were Walter Payton on 4th and inches. From behind the pile, Hesmer sprawled out along the goal line while reaching his arms forward into the pile. Referee Terry Vaughn eventually blew the play dead when Hesmer secured the ball less than a foot from the Crew goal. (I half expected Vaughn to emphatically point in the Crew's direction to indicate that they had recovered the fumble at the bottom of the pile-up.)

Hesmer shook his head when reflecting upon the play. "The shot or cross came through and I probably should have held it or gotten it out of there, but then Caraccio came through and I'm trying to pin the ball to his leg and he's kicking at it and then everyone went down and Brian (Carroll) was in there and then Caraccio was basically trying to roll it in with his mid-section, so I just dived back in there and got my hands under the pile somehow."

Houston coach Dom Kinnear also struggled to make sense of it. "You can put that down to Columbus not giving up on the play, or us not having luck, or a combination of the two."

The Defense

The Crew undoubtedly had their finest defensive performance of the year. Chad Marshall owned the middle of the box, Danny O'Rourke played his best game at center back and, as has been mentioned, the team-wide sacrifice was evident.

"It's a good thing when you have 11 guys battling for each other defensively," said Hejduk. "Not just 9 or 10, but all 11. When you can withstand Houston throwing everything at you, it says a lot about your character. We're in it for the full 90 minutes. Or the full 95 minutes, like it was tonight."

"(The Dynamo) have good service from the flanks from Davis and Mullan, and they have some big bodies they can throw in the middle, so it was tough," said Marshall. "But we wanted to get that shutout for Will. We want to keep his goals against down and send him to the All-Star Game."

Hesmer's save on Wade Barrett's 89th minute shot a highlight reel moment. After going down injured twice, and after enduring a shaky moment or two earlier in the match, Hesmer was at his best with the game on the line. Not only did he make the diving save on a shot destined for the upper corner, but he caught it cleanly, leaving no rebound attempt.

"The difference between winning 1-0 and tying 1-1 is so small," said Hejduk. "Barrett took a great shot and Will made a great save. It could have easily been 1-1, but Will made the play. Things are going our way right now, but we are making our own luck."

Best of all, according to Hejduk, is that things should only get better in the back. "The good thing is that we're still learning each other in the back four. Gino Padula is new to the team and Danny is playing a new position. But we're learning how to play with each other while winning. If we're winning while learning, that's a good thing, because once we figure it out, we will be a tough team to beat."

Attitude

Danny O'Rourke likes to play with an attitude, so this game seemed to fit him perfectly. O'Rourke said the team's willingness to sacrifice and do whatever it takes stems from captain Frankie Hejduk.

"Frankie has said he wants us to play with a (mean guy) mentality, and in training and in games, he sets that tone," said O'Rourke. "I like to play that way anyway, so we just rev each other up. He gets in on a tackle and I try to rev him up, and when Chad Marshall gets in on a tackle, we try to rev him up. It feeds on itself, and if we can keep that mentality, especially at home, I think we'll be effective."

Hejduk's ribs

In stoppage time, Hejduk was given a yellow card for delay of game. He attempted to take a throw-in but was having a hard time lifting his arm, so he deferred. After the game, he spent a gazillion hours in the trainer's room, give or take.

"I took a shot in my side," he explained. "It's a bruised rib, and it takes a shot every game. Those types of injuries never heal during the season because you're always getting hit. It's just one of those things where I have to suck it up and deal with it, which is what our team is all about this year. Nobody wants to leave the field. We are out there fighting for each other and you have to drag guys off the field now."

100 Wins For Sigi

Crew coach Sigi Schmid earned his 100th career regular-season victory on Saturday night, becoming only the second MLS coach to reach the milestone. Former Ohio University (and current U.S. National Team) coach [50] Bob Bradley tops the list with 124 regular-season MLS wins with Chicago, New York, and Chivas USA.

"It means that I've been around for a while," said Schmid, of his milestone. "But what it really means is that I've had the privilege to coach

---

[50] As an Ohio Bobcat, I just love the idea of referring to Bob Bradley as "former Ohio University coach" and then mentioning his current job in parentheses. It's even more preposterous when I am putting the U.S. National Team job in parentheses, as if it is an afterthought compared to his former gig at the Harvard on the Hocking.

some good players. I'm proud of the fact that I have 100 victories, but I'm more proud of the fact that I've coached good players."

Schmid claimed he was caught off guard by the impending achievement, but don't confuse that for false modesty – Schmid willingly confessed that he does follow certain numbers pertaining to his career.

"Honestly, I didn't know (about 100 victories) until Dave (Stephany) mentioned it to me at the beginning of the week," he explained. "I'm a numbers guy, and I was more aware of my record at UCLA, and I knew when I was going to pass the guy ahead of me. The one MLS number I know is that I have 16 victories in the playoffs, and I want to add to that number. I know that's the most of any MLS coach, so I want to stretch that one out a bit. [51] That's the number I am aware of and the one that I want to expand on."

Sigi Schmid, during an unhappy moment in an otherwise happy occasion—April 26, 2008, the night of his 100th career MLS victory. (Photo by Greg Bartram / Columbus Crew)

Nerd Stuff, Part One: Is it still only April?

There is no need to adjust your calendars. Despite the fact that the Crew have earned 12 points, it is still indeed only April. For only the third

---

[51] That mission would certainly be accomplished in the fall.

time this decade, the Crew have met or exceeded the 12-point threshold before June. (And one of those sneaked in on May 31, 2003.)

Only the 1998 Crew earned 12 points at an earlier date on the calendar, but that is due to the vagaries of scheduling. The 2008 Crew have matched the 1998 squad by earning the 12 points in just five matches.

According to Schmid, the current players have been able to silence the back-in-OUR-day bragging of the assistant coaches. "The best part for the players tonight is that they don't have to listen to Robert (Warzycha) and (Mike) Lapper tell them about how they were members of the Crew team with the best start ever, because now we've matched them."

Here is a year-by-year look at when the Crew have reached or crossed the 12-point threshold:

1996: July 25 (20 games)	2003: May 31 (9 games)
1997: May 11 (8 games)	2004: June 6 (9 games)
1998: April 18 (5 games)	2005: June 11 (11 games)
1999: May 15 (8 games)	2006: June 3 (10 games)
2000: May 20 (11 games)	2007: June 20 (12 games)
2001: June 16 (11 games)	2008: April 26 (5 games)
2002: June 12 (11 games)	

Houston down, but not out

Despite Houston's 0-2-3 start, Kinnear said neither he nor his team is down about it, especially after what they felt was a hard-luck result Saturday.

"We've had some good luck in the past," he explained. "You don't win two MLS Cups without a little bit of luck. But you can see that these guys are hungry for success. They don't sit back and say, 'Look at us. We're the two-time defending champs.' There are expectations from the media and expectations from fans, but sometimes we need a reality check. Two championships in two years is pretty special. I think Columbus would take two championships in two years. I'm not saying that to be sarcastic, but the reality is that it has been going good for us. Our expectations in the locker room are the most important to me and our players, and that expectation is that we are going to try to win every game. And we are trying that."

And if Houston can maintain that hunger after two titles, don't look for the Crew to lose their own appetite after merely climbing to the top of the table.

"We haven't been there, so we should be hungry," said Schmid. "Once you climb to first place, it's harder to stay there than get there."

Duncan Responds To Danny O's Fashion Spread

Earlier in the week, Crew defender Danny O'Rourke was the focus of a Columbus Dispatch feature about personal expression. The paper picks a local personality and discusses their style with them. When asked what piece of advice he had for readers, O'Rourke told the paper, "Look at Duncan (Oughton), and do the opposite."

As many longtime readers know, I am nothing if not a crusader for truth and justice and for the right of an aggrieved party to give their side of the story, so long as it makes me laugh. So before Saturday's game, I tracked down Oughton to get his reaction to O'Rourke's potentially libelous advice, as it relates to fashion.

"They say that those who are jealous often lash out at others instead of looking in the mirror," said Oughton. "But I think Mr. O'Rourke needs to take a long look in the mirror because his fashion is absolutely shocking."

I mentioned that O'Rourke had been doing the opposite of Oughton, so I was curious as to what those opposite things might be. "That's the thing," said Oughton. "He's been doing the exact opposite of what I do. For example, I wash my hair, whereas he does not wash his hair ever. He's got a fauxhawk/mullet/I don't know what. He's trying to do so many things with his hair. When I had a mullet, I had a mullet. I was committed to it. Now I've tidied it up and it's more tidy than a mullet; it's your run-of-the-mill average haircut. He's trying to do six different things and, to be honest, not one of them is working at all."

After a brief pause for further contemplation, it was obvious that this was going to be a head-to-toe affair. "Working our way down," said Oughton, "I like to wear little kids' t-shirts. No wait, that's what he does because it's the opposite of the adult-sized t-shirts that I wear. I wear t-shirts that fit me in 2008, whereas Danny wears t-shirts that once fit him when he was just getting out of diapers, which was probably age 8 or 9 for him."

"As for pants," Oughton continued, "I'm happy with whatever he wears so long as he wears them. Then he wears these little slip-on shoes with squares of different colors painted on them. I think they wore them in the Karate Kid for that little dress-up party they had."

I did point out, in fairness, that in the article, O'Rourke said that his favorite TV show was Flight of the Conchords, starring fellow New Zealanders Bret McKenzie and Jemaine Clement.

"Really, I think Danny would like to do the things I do, but he's too immature so he can't quite yet," the Kiwi responded. "He'll get there someday. The fact that he said his favorite TV show is Flight of the Conchords just proves that he wishes he could learn to talk like me. He's told me, 'I wish I had an accent like yours', and now he's using those DVDs to teach himself. It's kind of weird. I've tried to tell him, 'You're cool in your own right, buddy, so there's no need to do every single thing I do.' He made a clumsy attempt at sharing that advice with the quote he gave the newspaper about doing the opposite of what I do."

So what advice would Duncs give to Danny O?

"My advice would be to get a new style. Danny thinks he has style, but it's obviously some sort of new underground style that nobody has heard of, like the Getting Dressed In The Dark Style. So if I could give one piece of fashion advice, from an older guy to a younger guy, it would be, 'When you wake up, open the curtains and turn on the lights before you get dressed, Danny. That way you can actually see what you are doing to yourself.'"

Duncan Oughton: Fashion Police

As we discussed O'Rourke's fashion, referee Terry Vaughn and his crew passed by and said hi to Oughton. The officials were identically dressed in their gray game shorts and socks, plus black Adidas shirts.

"What, do you fellas all shop at the same store?" asked Oughton.

After a brief exchange of jokes and pleasantries, the officials made their way toward the field. That's when Oughton noticed an unpardonable fashion faux pas. Three of the officials had the white adidas stripes running down the sleeves of their black shirts. The other official was wearing a solid black adidas shirt with no sleeve stripes.

"Hey! That man's not wearing stripes!" shouted Oughton as he pointed out the fashion offender. "Everyone else is wearing stripes, so why isn't he? Aren't you all on the same team? If so, dress like it, men! Be professional! Get that man some stripes for his shirt!"

Like O'Rourke, the officials found it hilarious to be on the receiving end of fashion advice from a Kiwi, so they all cracked up as they went on their way.

Crew Hometown In The News

San Diego native Frankie Hejduk was blown away by the news of the recent fatal shark attack near Solana Beach, Calif.

"I'm from Cardiff, and Solana Beach is the next city south," he said. "My friend texted me when the shark attack happened, and I couldn't believe it. I've surfed there a million times and I've never seen a shark. It's not like I ever went out there and worried 'is today the day it happens?' The only other shark attack I can remember near home was maybe 15-20 years ago when a woman was bitten, but she was already dead and had drifted way out into the ocean before the shark got her. But I know exactly where this guy was swimming. A great white just came straight up from underneath and chomped him once and he bled to death. It's crazy."

In all his years of surfing, Hejduk has only seen a shark once, but that was in Mexico.

Nerd Stuff, Part Two: MLS Cup Curse?

With Houston in town, it reminded me of a conversation that I had with my good buddy Flick about a month or so ago. We were discussing if Joseph Ngwenya had become the first ex-Crew player to win an MLS Cup. Ngwenya was traded to the Houston Dynamo on May 9, 2007, in exchange for current Crew scoring leader Alejandro Moreno. With Houston, Ngwenya went on to score the equalizing goal in the Dynamo's 2-1 MLS Cup victory over New England.

One thing that was apparent to us is that while the Crew haven't given away many championship pieces, they have been a massive importer of MLS Cup rings, hoping the luck would rub off.

Imported MLS Cup rings (21)

Tony Sanneh (D.C. '96, D.C. '97)
John Harkes (D.C. '96, D.C. '97)
Mario Gori (D.C. '96, D.C. '97)
Tom Presthus (D.C. '97, D.C. '99)
Ante Razov (CHI '98)
Manny Lagos (CHI '98, S.J. '01, S.J. '03)
Chris Henderson (K.C. '00)

Simon Elliott (L.A. '02)
Ezra Hendrickson (L.A. '02, D.C. '04)
Alejandro Moreno (L.A. '02, HOU '06)
Brian Carroll (D.C. '04)
Ned Grabavoy (L.A. '05)
Joseph Ngwenya (L.A. '05)

OK, so that's a total of 21 rings that have been earned prior to a stint in Columbus. But is Joseph Ngwenya seriously the first Crew export to go on to win a ring?

Well, let's see... hmmm... I immediately thought of two technicalities that probably shouldn't count. Frank Klopas was briefly Crew property during the 1997-98 offseason before being traded to Chicago for Jason Farrell. Klopas was a member of the Fire's 1998 MLS Cup championship squad. And Ramiro Corrales was also briefly Crew property. He was drafted by Columbus in 1996 but traded to San Jose for Mac Cozier before the season even started. Corrales won two MLS Cups ('01, '03) with the Earthquakes. Even though they never wore the Black & Gold, they have proven that legally belonging to the Crew in a name-on-a-spreadsheet sense is not in and of itself a barrier to championship success.

But it was time to do some digging. Surely there had to be at least one other ex-Crew who went on to collect a ring.

Sure enough, there were two more.

Exported MLS Cup rings (3)

  * **A.J. Wood** played a combined 19 regular season and playoff games for the Crew in 1997. In 1999, he tallied 8 goals and 6 assists in 24 regular season games for D.C. United. He also logged 75 minutes in four playoff games that year. He did not see the field in United's 2-0 MLS Cup triumph over Los Angeles.

  * **Bo Oshoniyi** played 13 games in goal for the Crew during their inaugural season, including a shutout in the Crew's first-ever game. In 2000, he had the best seat in the house for Tony Meola's career year with the Kansas City Wizards. With Meola starting 31 regular season games, Oshoniyi pitched a shutout in his lone appearance of the season—his first MLS action in four years. Meola gave a legendary MVP performance in Kansas City's 1-0 MLS Cup shocker over Chicago while Oshoniyi watched from the bench.

  * **Joseph Ngwenya** tallied 5 goals and 4 assists in 25 games with the Crew in 2006 and 2007. After being traded to Houston on May 9, 2007, he notched 7 goals and 3 assists in 25 regular season matches, plus two assists in the first three playoff matches. Then he started MLS Cup 2007, played 80 minutes, and scored the equalizing goal in the 61st minute of Houston's 2-1 win over New England.

So now we know that Ngwenya became the *third* former Crew player to ever go on and win an MLS Cup. However, he earned the distinction of being the first former Crew player to actually see the field (much less score a goal) in a winning MLS Cup performance.

When's the Crew's birthday?

After the game, Crew fan Janet Handler was trying to make sense of the Crew's 4-1-0 start. She wanted me to get to the bottom of this unnatural occurrence and suggested maybe it had something to do with the team's Zodiac sign. This, of course, begged the question: When is the Crew's birthday?

It was suggested that it should be the date the team was granted. I nixed that because that was basically announcing, "Hey everyone! We're pregnant!"

Someone else suggested it should be when they officially became the Columbus Crew. I nixed that because that was basically looking at the ultrasound and saying, "It's going to be boy, so we will name him (insert-name-here.)"

I am going to have to stand by the notion that the team was born when it played its first ever game. Of course, that means that every club in the league is an Aries, which means that club-based astrology plays no role in the fortune of the league's teams. Hard to believe, I know. If only there were a more viable hypothesis to explain the Crew's hot start…

"Hopefully the fans saw that this team will give you everything they have for every minute of the game." – Sigi Schmid.

I suppose that explanation will suffice until more supernatural/paranormal research can be conducted.

Questions? Comments? Get three points from the Crew as a wedding gift on Saturday and feel that it is a good omen for your marriage? [52] Feel free to write at sirk65@yahoo.com

The Nordecke buries Houston's Brad Davis in a shower of black and gold streamers as he attempts a corner kick during the Crew's 1-0 win over the Dynamo on April 26, 2008. This was during the brief window of time when MLS encouraged streamer tossing as a fun and festive activity brought to us by the great fans of Toronto. (Photo by Sam Fahmi)

---

[52] That was for Jason and Carrie, who got married that day.

Sirk's Notebook: Crew 2, Kansas City 1

Match date: Saturday, May 3, 2008
Scoring:
4: CLB Moffat 2 (Marshall 1, Schelotto 4)
34: CLB Rogers 3 (Moreno 2, Hejduk 2)
79: KC Lopez 2 (penalty kick)
Attendance: 10,447
Crew's record afterward: 5-1-0

In this bizarro Crew season, what could be more bizarre than taking a large, open, yellow, steel and aluminum structure and making it resemble a woodshed?

After Saturday's 2-1 win over the Kansas City Wizards, the Columbus Crew, who had won just 16 of 45 homes in the last three seasons – and just 9 of 30 in the last two seasons – are suddenly 4-0-0 at Crew Stadium this year.

"We only won five games at home last year, and we are within one with 11 home games left, so I think we will top that mark," said Crew coach Sigi Schmid. "I am pretty confident in that prediction. This is something we talked about all pre-season. We wanted to take care of business at home. The fans have been great, and it helps spur us on, so we have become a difficult team to beat at home."

The Wizards learned that the hard way on Saturday when the Crew jumped out to a 4th minute lead, and played such attractive and dominating soccer that the 2-0 halftime score felt unjustly low. To their credit, the Wizards rebounded in the second half and made a game of it despite being down a man. The final 10 minutes were heart-pounding stuff, but as has been their custom this year, the Crew dug in and held on for the three points.

As always, here is a collection of notes, quotes, observations, nerdy research, and general stupidity from Saturday's match...

Mr. Moffat Strikes Again

The Crew took a 1-0 lead in the 4th minute on Adam Moffat's second goal of the year. Guillermo Barros Schelotto swerved a 30-yard free kick to the far post, and Chad Marshall (who else?) headed the ball back across the goalmouth. As Alejandro Moreno and two Kansas City defenders waited for Marshall's looping header to come down, Moffat barreled into the mix, bowling everybody over as he nodded the ball home from maybe six feet away. From the man who has brought us The Moffat Rocket, it was much, much, much too close to the net to be a true Adam Moffat goal.

"Yeah, yeah, it was a bit close, but I decided to get my head on it and knock it in," said the stubbled Scotsman. "It was good ball back across by Chad. When he goes for a ball, you know he's going to win it, so you just run to the back post. I was in the right spot at the right time. If it's me, you know I am going to go for it. There were a few of us challenging for the ball, but I guess I am bit taller than all of them."

Actually, Moffat is listed at 6'0" while his most prominent challenger on the play, Jimmy Conrad, is listed at 6'2". But we probably shouldn't let facts get in the way of a perfectly good self-deprecating Adam Moffat quote.

Adam Moffat scored a goal in his final appearance of the season. The midfielder left the game in the 54th minute after he tore the ACL in his left knee. Emmanuel Ekpo subbed in for Moffat, so Ekpo's season began as Moffat's ended. (Photo by Greg Bartram / Columbus Crew)

Racing Robbie Rogers

The Crew took a 2-0 lead in the 34th minute on Robbie Rogers' third goal of the season. It was a strange play. First of all, how many goals are set up by a bicycle kick at midfield?

Alejandro Moreno biked a pass from Frankie Hejduk, sending it into Kansas City territory. Wiz defender Chance Myers chased down the ball while his goalie, Kevin Hartman, came off his line. Sensing that the ball was going into no-man's land near the edge of the box, Rogers never gave up on the play. He raced into the fray, and a split second before either Myers or Hartman could clear the ball, Rogers stuck his right foot between the two KC players and sent a slow roller that trickled into the gaping goalmouth.

"I have some speed[53], so I like to run those down," said Rogers. "If the defender is running toward his own goal and the goalkeeper is coming out, there's always the possibility of some miscommunication, and this time I got lucky."

It was the third such dicey no-man's land misadventure for Hartman and his defenders, and they finally got burned after escaping the first two incidents with a Moreno crossbar and a smothered attempt by Schelotto.

"We played a very high line today," explained Wizards coach Curt Onalfo. "The Crew dropped off so we were pushing way up the field. There were a couple times where our defenders were stepping when they should have been dropping. We have some very young players back there who are going to make some mistakes, but we can live with it because we feel we are building a team for the future that is also a good team right now."

Espinoza's Scarlet Card

Former Ohio State standout Roger Espinoza was ejected in his professional homecoming in the 36th minute after throwing a forearm toward Frankie Hejduk's face. As the two players battled for the ball in front of the benches, arms started flying around. Espinoza turned toward Hejduk and threw a forearm that more resulted in shoving Hejduk off by the face. Espinoza was shown a straight red for the forearm, while Hejduk was given a yellow for his role in the sideline tussle.

"From what I understand, he's a very nice guy, and he's going to live and learn from it," said Hejduk. "He was complaining that I had fouled him, then he turned and looked at me as he was throwing his elbow or whatever you want to call it. That's something he'll learn not to do. You don't look at a

---

[53] Understatement.

guy as you're throwing a blow on him. If your elbow comes up while you're still looking at the ball, then it's just a foul, but if you turn and look at the guy…"

10 v 11

The Crew battled two soccer clichés in the second half. The first is that a two-goal lead is the most dangerous lead in soccer. The second is that a 10-man team can be more dangerous than an 11-man team. Sure enough, the Wizards made a game of it in the second half, pulling to within a goal on a 79th minute penalty kick goal by Claudio Lopez, then creating several tense moments the rest of the way.

"I thought we made the second half more difficult than we needed to," said Schmid. "K.C. did a good job of moving the ball despite being down a man, but I think what happens psychologically, no matter what you tell your team, is that guys start thinking, 'Hey, we're up a man,' so guys start dropping off and thinking they can sit in a space without stepping up, so we started giving up a lot of possession. Part of that was Kansas City raising their game. When a team is playing down a man, guys all know they have to give 10% more to make up for it. Then the guys on the team that is up think they can do 10% less, and suddenly things equal out again[54]."

The Crew seemed intent on building a 10-0 lead by halftime, but in the second half, Schmid felt that they may have been wiser to try to hold their 2-1 in the final 10 minutes lead instead of trying to bump it back up to 3-1.

"I think we could have done a better job of taking the ball to the corners and killing time," he said. "Going for the third goal is great if you get it. But if you swing it in there and they clear it out and come the other way, it's a long way to run back."

Why I Didn't Ask O'Rourke About His "Penalty"

When Danny O'Rourke was whistled for a dubious looking penalty, I immediately returned to the press box to see if the call was legitimate. Replays showed that while O'Rourke did have a fistful of Scott Sealy's jersey, he did not push, pull, hold, tug or otherwise alter Sealy's position. Sealy simply flopped to the ground. As if that were not bad enough, Sealy had his back to the goal a good 16 yards from the net. There was no imminent danger or

---

[54] Fun with math: A 10% reduction of 11 men is the equivalent of 9.9 men. A 10% increase in 10 men is the equivalent of 11 men. So suddenly the team playing down a man is actually up by 1.1 men. That's not equal. To make Sigi's equation work, where the teams would equal out, the respective teams would have to increase and decrease their play by 4.76% instead of 10%.

scoring threat. So the Wizards were awarded a penalty on a non-foul that took place on a non-scoring threat.

(At least it wasn't as bad as last year's game at Arrowhead when the Wizards were gifted a stoppage time penalty when Kerry Zavagnin reached out and kicked a stationary Stefani Miglioranzi in the shin, then fell down to garner a penalty call.)

Flops and bad calls happen. And if you play central defender long enough, they are going to happen to you. But the last person any Crew fan wanted to see victimized by a bad penalty call at this stage of the season was Danny O'Rourke.

Once I saw that the call was soft (to use the charitable term used by the television announcers), all I could think was, "Imagine being Danny O'Rourke." You've spent your first few years in the league being a pit bull defensive midfielder assigned to maul anyone and everyone that poses a threat. Aggression was encouraged, and the consequences of physical play were nothing more than the occasional booking or suspension.

In 2008, you have switched to a brand new position. This position requires infinitely more subtlety than the bloodthirsty aggression that has been your forte. You're an intelligent guy, so you work hard at un-learning your prior habits while picking up the nuances of your new position.

And then in the first two games, nature triumphs over nurture and you commit two brainfarts that lead to penalty kicks. Your buddy between the posts bails you out both times, but the trend is established. The imaginary tabloids in your mind start spinning hot-off-the-presses extra-extra-read-all-about-it headlines like: "Thug d-mid good for a penalty per game as thug center back!"

But you don't let it get you down. It motivates you to work harder. You bust your butt every day in practice, focusing on field awareness, when to challenge, when to hold your ground, and when to shepherd an attacker toward your help. You keep a sense of humor about your foibles and you refuse to play scared.

You finally break the streak, and then play two more penalty-free games. Your improvements and adaptations with regard to your new position are evident. Your confidence is growing.

And then, out of the blue, you are whistled for a phantom penalty. It has to seem like a cruel joke. All the work, all the learning, and all of the practical application goes up in smoke when that whistle is blown. You have worked so hard and focused on keeping it clean in and around the penalty box… and this is your reward? You surely feel like the luckless contestant on

Fox Soccer Channel's newest reality game show, "How Many Penalties Will They Call On Danny O'Rourke This Year?"

To make matters worse, your buddy can't maintain his miraculous penalty save streak. And the goal from your penalty has now changed the complexion of the game so that victory, once assured, is now in some feverish degree of doubt. In some way, you feel you have a let your team down, even if you didn't do a thing to deserve the distinction.

As backward as it seems, the fact that it was a bad call makes it harder to deal with. It's not a defect in your play, but a defect in your reputation in a referee's mind. If it's your mistake, you can fall on your sword and then work your butt off to get better. There's a solution to that. It's in your hands. But if you're getting a bad call just because you're the guy that gave up two PKs already… how do you fix that? Especially now that it's three?

It would be impossible not to take the whole thing to heart. Simply impossible.

When I took one look at O'Rourke in the tunnel after the game, it confirmed my suspicions. I knew I wasn't going to interview him about the play. What would be the point? What would be his options? Rip the refereeing? How counterproductive. Accept culpability for a crime he didn't commit? Unlikely. Do the smart thing and say "no comment"? How print-worthy.

So I let Danny be. It didn't take Dr. Phil to figure out what was likely going through his head. His body language said he was upset about it. His teammates clearly didn't blame him and were behind him 100 percent. Sigi made a point to stop by his locker and offer a few words.

And really, that was the story. No quotes needed. Had it been a legit penalty, we would have needed to talk about it, and I am positive Danny would have done his part. But in this case, two open eyes and healthy dose of empathy were all that were needed to figure this one out. Why pick at the scab on the open wound?

I have few fears about how this will affect Danny going forward. When we talked about his penalty streak previously, he stressed that he doesn't dwell on the past and doesn't worry about bad things happening. If anything, this call will just make him work harder. If he feels he has to hold his breath in the box so as not to get a bogus penalty call for breathing on somebody, he'll probably work on that until he is blue in the face.

Hesmer's Take

Although I didn't ask Danny about it, someone asked Crew goalkeeper William Hesmer what he thought of the penalty call. "I played with Sealy and I know how strong he is," said Hesmer. "There wasn't enough there to bring him down. I don't blame Danny for that penalty at all."

Hesmer Plays

Hesmer was a game-time decision due to what is being called a "left shoulder AC joint sprain." Regardless of the medical terminology, Hesmer's shoulder was pronounced fit enough to play.

"I made it through the whole week without training, then did a little training (Friday) to make sure that I could handle some hard shots," Hesmer said. "Then I came in today, doc gave me a shot, I went and warmed up and felt OK, and then it was time to play."

The Debut of Emmanuel Ekpo

After 17 million Shawn Mitchell blog updates about vague paperwork complications that made it seem as though Crew Technical Director Brian Bliss was trying to purchase Emmanuel Ekpo from the Nigerian equivalent of the Ohio Bureau of Motor Vehicles, the midfielder was seen in the flesh on Saturday night, subbing for a hobbled Moffat in the 54th minute.

"We felt that this was a good time to get Ekpo into the game," said Schmid. "Just like when Gino Padula played his first game, until you get out there and feel the rhythm of the game, the game in MLS is… people work, people run, people move. At times he got caught with the ball and wasn't making decisions soon enough, but he also gave a few glimpses of what he is capable of. Now he has a better feel for the game and how it's going to be, so he'll know he has to play quicker."

Emmanuel Ekpo in the flesh! (Photo by Greg Bartram / Columbus Crew)

From the Recycling Last Week's Material Department

Last week, I looked at the dates when the Crew have historically met or exceeded the 12-point threshold. With another three points in their pocket from game number six, we can see that the 2008 Crew have met or exceeded the 15-point threshold earlier than any other team in club history in terms of the number of games played, and it is the second-earliest date ever on the calendar. The 1998 team took 7 games to do it, but their season started earlier, so they reached 15 points on April 30 of that year.

Here is a year-by-year look at when the Crew have met or crossed the 15-point threshold:

> 1996: Aug. 4 (23 games)
> 1997: June 21. (15 games)
> 1998: April 30 (7 games)
> 1999: May 29 (10 games)
> 2000: May 27 (12 games)
> 2001: June 23 (12 games)
> 2002: June 15 (12 games)
> 2003: June 7 (10 games)
> 2004: June 12 (10 games)
> 2005: July 16 (17 games)
> 2006: June 21 (13 games)
> 2007: June 23 (13 games)
> 2008: May 3 (6 games)

No Overconfidence Here

Despite their hot start, the Crew aren't getting ahead of themselves.

"Of course we're aware that this is a good start, but you can't let up in this league," said Hesmer. "There are no easy weeks. Kansas City got off to a start like this last year and they barely made it into the playoffs."

"We're all excited and there's a buzz," said Hejduk. "There's a buzz around the entire stadium. Then fans are buzzed, and we're a little buzzin', but do we think about it? We think about it for a few hours tonight and pat ourselves on the back, but then it's on to next week. I think we've done a good job of that. We keep our focus from game to game. Winning five games isn't going to get us into the playoffs, so we still have a lot to do."

Schmid isn't worried about complacency setting in. "Every week is a new challenge," he said. "Every week is a new adventure."

Somewhere in all those streamers, Kansas City's Claudio Lopez contemplates taking a corner kick. It's all part of the growing "buzz" in Crew Stadium.
(Photo by Greg Bartram / Columbus Crew)

Danny Responds To Duncan

In last week's notebook, Duncan Oughton spoke at length about Danny O'Rourke's fashion sense, claiming, among other things, that Danny utilizes the Getting Dressed In The Dark Style of personal fashion. Again, in the interest of being fair and impartial, it was my journalistic duty to give Danny O a chance to respond to Duncan's latest assertions.

"I want to first start off by saying that Duncan is someone I've looked up to for awhile," said O'Rourke, sounding not at all like a man with retaliation on his mind. "I look up to Duncan not only because he's pushing 40, but because of his amazing heart and work ethic."

Danny did take umbrage with Duncan's classification of his personal style, mostly because of the source. "If my style is 'getting dressed in the dark', then his (stuff) is from the dark ages."

I thought that might be a good Kiwi Lord of the Rings joke, but Danny meant the dark ages of American culture. "Some of Duncan's outfits were seen on mannequins even outdating the disco era. But that's a typical Kiwi. I'm sure that style is all the rage back there."

Just when it seemed like Danny was going to get on a roll, he eased up on his elder teammate. "I am going to stop there because I like and respect

97

Duncan so much," he explained. "But if you talk to him, could you please get my kitchen bowl back? He borrowed it to use when he cut his hair and I haven't seen it since."

I assured Danny that I would attempt to get his kitchen bowl back, assuming that Duncan isn't now using it to eat his Cocoa Puffs, which are part of a nutritionally balanced Kiwi breakfast, along with wombat sausage, freshly squeezed sheep's milk, Vegemite pop-tarts, and a Hobbit-shaped chewable vitamin.

From the Lineup Consistency Department

The injury to left back Gino Padula snapped the Crew's streak of using the same starting lineup at three consecutive games. It may not seem like much, but as Crew PR guru Dave Stephany has pointed out, the Crew have only equaled the streak on two other occasions since their last playoff appearance.

Here are the players involved in the three-game lineup streaks:

JULY 20 & 23 and AUG. 6, 2005

Jonny Walker	David Testo
Robin Fraser	Eric Vasquez
Chad Marshall	Knox Cameron
Chris Wingert	Cornell Glen
Simon Elliott	Kyle Martino
Chris Henderson	

JULY 22 and AUG. 4 & 11, 2007

William Hesmer	Danny Szetela
Frankie Hejduk	Ned Grabavoy
Chad Marshall	Eddie Gaven
Marcos Gonzalez	Guillermo Barros Schelotto
Stefani Miglioranzi	Alejandro Moreno
Danny O'Rourke	

APRIL 12, 17 & 26, 2008

William Hesmer	Adam Moffat
Frankie Hejduk	Eddie Gaven
Chad Marshall	Robbie Rogers
Danny O'Rourke	Guillermo Barros Schelotto
Gino Padula	Alejandro Moreno
Brian Carroll	

Chad Marshall is the only starter from the 2005 streak that was still a part of the 2008 streak. (And for good measure, he participated in the 2007 streak as well.)

Also, the Crew's modest 2008 streak is somewhat misleading. Sigi is a big believer in consistency, and in the first six matches, he has actually used the exact same lineup at 10 positions. The only changes have occurred at left back. Stefani Miglioranzi started the first two matches, Padula started the next three, and then Ezra Hendrickson started there on Saturday.

Ambiguity—The Devil's Volleyball [55]

I overheard a fun post-game conversation starter between Dante Washington and Sigi Schmid…

Dante: "101…"

Sigi: "Huh?"

Dante: "Victory number 101."

Sigi: "Ohhhh. I see."

Dante: "Did you already forget your 100th was last week?"

Sigi: "No, you just said '101' and my mind couldn't figure out what you meant. When I hear '101', I think 'That's a highway in California.' Or 'That's the Columbus alternative rock station.' I didn't know where you were going with that."

Weird Wizards / Kansas City Weekend

At this time of year, I have three pro sports teams that are currently in action. It was a strange weekend in that the Cleveland Indians played Kansas City, the Cleveland Cavaliers played the Wizards, and the Crew played the Kansas City Wizards.

---

[55] That was an old Emo Philips line.

Questions? Comments? Have your lightbulb-lighting "Man, I forgot Brian Carroll was on the field… Oh my God, what would the Crew do without Brian Carroll?!?!?" epiphany yet? Feel free to write at sirk65@yahoo.com

A Crew fan proudly raises his scarf on May 3, 2008.
(Photo by Sam Fahmi)

Road Work: Crew 3, San Jose 2

Match date: Saturday, May 10, 2008

Scoring:

42: SJ Corrales 1 (O'Brien 1)

73: CLB Rogers 4 (Ekpo 1)

81: CLB Rogers 5 (Moreno 3)

83: CLB Evans 1 (Schelotto 5)

89: SJ Johnson 1 (Grabavoy 2)

Attendance: 9,318

Crew's record afterward: 6-1-0

RETROACTIVE RECAP

The Crew and Guillermo Barros Schelotto set a club record by taking 18 corner kicks, but the story of the game was the Crew's 10-minute burst of breakaway soccer that turned a 1-0 deficit into a 3-1 lead. First, newcomer Emmanual Ekpo rolled a beautiful, diagonal, 30-yard through ball to spring Robbie Rogers for the first goal. Then Alejandro Moreno beat four players with an exquisite lead pass to again spring Rogers, who dribbled the keeper and potted his second goal of the night. Then Guillermo Barros Schelotto flipped a ball into space for Brad Evans, whose semi-breakaway was capped with a blast into the roof of the net. Those ten minutes in one word? I'll go with, "WOW!"

QUOTES

San Jose coach Frank Yallop: "I think Columbus is a good team and we can't take that away from them. We weren't at our best closing them down in our half in the first half, and we did not do it really well in the second half in critical parts of the game. It was two good runs and goals from Rogers, but I wish we could have caught up to him. It is just disappointing."

Alejandro Moreno: "I think at times (the Earthquakes) were pretty good, but we found ways to get through their defenders. We exploited Robbie Rogers' speed; we created chances in the first half and were able to take advantage of the chances on the second half. It is a well-deserved victory for us."

Road Work: Crew 0, Toronto 0

Match date: Saturday, May 17, 2008
Scoring: None.
Attendance: 20,538
Crew's record afterward: 6-1-1

RETROACTIVE RECAP

The game was a dud, but the post game war of words was a real treat. The 0-0 draw ran the Crew's unbeaten streak to six games, and set a mark for the best 8-game start in club history. William Hesmer collected his third shutout of the season. The most notable on-field aspect of the game was that Guillermo Barros Schelotto was a one-man frustration machine. He endured plenty of hacks, and made a meal of every foul. His display frustrated the Hosers and their coach, John Carver, as the Crew bled out a 0-0 draw and a trip back home, none the worse for wear. Carver blew up afterward, giving Guille the opportunity to get in one of his funniest quotes of the year.

QUOTES

Toronto coach John Carver: "They've come to spoil the game. They've come to take their time. They've come to fall over and dive all over the park, and I think that's what they did. Any team to go six wins out of seven and have a game plan like that surprises me a little bit. Today, we saw a professional diving all over the park. Is there anything going to be done about it? The whole game, continuously, it was as if the wind was too strong for him. I'm not here to be a part of that. That's not honest and professional. I've never seen anything like it."

Guillermo Barros Schelotto, in response: "His team play very bad. He must feel frustration for his team." [56]

---

[56] Quote from Shawn Mitchell's May 18, 2008, story in the Columbus Dispatch.

Sirk's Notebook: New England 1, Crew 0

Match date: Saturday, May 24, 2008
Scoring:
89: NE Dube 2 (unassisted)
Attendance: 15,621
Crew's record afterward: 6-2-1

All good things must come to an end. Seinfeld... back rubs... the Crew's 376-game, not-losing-on-an-89th-minute-penalty-kick-rebound streak.

Saturday's 1-0 loss to the New England Revolution was a heartbreaker. It was the Crew's first home loss of the season, and the dramatic climax betrayed the game that had preceded it. Chad Marshall was once again dominant, combining with Danny O'Rourke to lock down the middle of the Crew's defense. New England had a wicked shot from distance by Jay Heaps, but that was about it for them.

The Crew, meanwhile, conducted a near-miss clinic at the offensive end. They put only two shots on goal, but both required heroic saves from New England goalkeeper Matt Reis. The first robbed Alejandro Moreno in the 26th minute, and the second inconceivably denied an all-but-certain Eddie Gaven header in the 75th minute. Moreno also hit a post. Gaven also whistled another shot wide by inches. Frankie Hejduk dipped a shot just over the crossbar. Brad Evans snapped a header just high. And then there were some promising set-ups in the box that were broken up at the last minute by solid defending from the Revs.

Three points to Columbus would have been fair, but disappointing from a New England perspective. A point for each team would have been fair, but disappointing from a Columbus perspective. But to come away with nothing at the last minute? Ouch.

"All it comes down to is that we played well, but the result didn't go our way," said captain Frankie Hejduk. "That's soccer sometimes. That's what makes it such a wonderful game. You have to stay concentrated for the full 90 minutes. You can come out and play great, but if you lose concentration for one minute, it's that one minute that can cost you the game."

The Penalty

The fateful penalty occurred in the 88th minute after a lovely two-man game between Steve Ralston and Shalrie Joseph on the defensive left side of the Crew's penalty area. As Ralston received another pass from

Joseph, he made his move to the middle, carrying the ball just inside the top of the box. The box was crammed with players, giving Ralston nothing to shoot at, but then Crew defender Ezra Hendrickson stepped on Ralston's right foot, bringing him down for a penalty.

Neither coach felt there was any doubt about the call, nor did the man who committed the foul. "I think (Ralston) played it well. I didn't really go into a tackle. I put my leg up to block a shot and then we got tangled up. It was a PK. It wasn't like I went into a tackle, but it was basically one of those soft PKs. We defended so well for 88 minutes, and then to have that happen was unfortunate. But it was a PK. Our feet did get tangled."

To clarify, when Ezra said it was a soft PK, I got the impression that he didn't mean the call itself, but rather the circumstances of the foul. He just meant that Ralston didn't have much going on, and it wasn't a hard foul, and it was at the edge of the box…not exactly a vicious foul that robbed a goal-scoring chance. Even Ralston conceded that if he even got a shot off, it was probably just going to hit somebody.

Hejduk, however, did his captain's duty and stuck up for his teammate for those very reasons. "I thought it was a soft call," he said. "In the 88th minute of a tie game, I think you have to be 100% sure it was a nasty foul or takes a good chance away. I don't think that was a nasty enough foul to award a last-minute penalty kick for, but that's just my personal opinion. I think it's a shame because that's the second soft penalty against us this year. That one and the one against Kansas City were very soft, especially playing at home. Maybe on the road you are going to get those calls against you, but at home? I've seen plenty of refs wave those off, but that's how it goes. That's what we signed up for when we decided to play a refereed sport."

Danny O'Rourke also stuck up for his penalty-stricken teammate, but in his own self-deprecating O'Rourkian fashion. "I told Ezra not to lose any sleep over the penalty because he's nowhere close to catching up to me."

The Save and the Goal

Shalrie Joseph stepped to the spot for New England, and for the third time in four tries, Crew goalie William Hesmer made a penalty kick save. Hesmer dove to his left and parried the ball away, but the elation lasted mere seconds before Kheli Dube nutmegged a recovering Hesmer on the rebound shot.

The penalty kick rebound is the cruelest and most deflating of goals.

"It's disappointing to do the hard part, and then not make the second save," said Hesmer. "After you make the (penalty) save, you're hoping that's the end of it."

Dube blew past Hendrickson to get to the rebound, but Schmid had his doubts. "Dube is either very, very fast, or he got in early for the rebound. We'll just assume he was very fast. It's one of those things that happens."

Replays showed that Dube took two steps[57] into the box before Joseph struck the ball. Technically, the goal should have been disallowed, but Hesmer had no intentions of dwelling on it.

"That's not what I'm focusing on," he shrugged. "That's the referee's job. It's unfortunate if he missed it, but he's got a lot on his plate."

Attitude

Whenever a great run ends, especially for a team that's new to this whole winning thing, there is always concern about the team's attitude when a result finally goes the other way.

"We played a team like New England, who is perennially one of the top teams in the league, and if you look at the game, we played very well," said Schmid in his press conference. "We're disappointed that we didn't get the result. You're going to hit some speed bumps along the way. We just need to make sure it's a speed bump, not a detour, and we need to keep our confidence up."

Fifteen minutes later, the players didn't seem to be lacking confidence in the locker room.

"It's good to be in the locker room this year and feel the disappointment," said Hesmer. "We feel that we played well enough to get three points. We had a great week of practice, came out and played a good game, and then we get nothing to show for it. But we know that when we wake up tomorrow, we're still going to be a good team. We haven't lost our confidence."

"We were trying to get three points and win the game," said Alejandro Moreno. "We had our chances to put the game away. We would be more concerned if we weren't getting chances or if we were getting outplayed. New England is a good team and an experienced team and we still created chances. That said, we have won games where we didn't play our best, and that's just the balance of the game and how the season goes."

---

[57] Actually, after looking at the replays a few more times after turning this in, it wasn't as egregious as it first appeared. Dube's first step didn't really go anywhere, so he really only advanced one step. It looked worse than it was. I am sure plenty of people take one step on most penalty kicks. He was still early, but it wasn't as bad as I originally wrote. It gets downgraded from "egregious refereeing error" to "tough break."

"We're not down about it," said Hendrickson. "We fought hard and we played well. At worst, we deserved a point tonight. But that's how it goes."

"I think we can hold our heads high," concluded Hejduk.

Sigi's Sub

Despite the 0-0 scoreline for almost the entirety of the match, Schmid made only one substitution. Midfielder Emmanuel Ekpo entered the match in the 80th minute to replace Eddie Gaven.

"(I only made one substitution) because I thought we weren't playing badly," said Schmid. "Sometimes people want you to use subs just for the (heck) of making subs. I thought we were playing well. We thought Ekpo could give us a lift like he did in the second half at San Jose, and thought he could provide that again, even though I thought Eddie was playing much better in the second half. The team was playing well, so I'm not going to make changes just for the sake of making changes."

On Streamers…and Bananas?

I'll be the first to admit that I have totally changed my mind on the streamer issue. Twice. I enjoyed seeing Toronto's Todd Dunivant being buried in streamers moments after the Hoser fans tried to do the same to Guillermo Barros Schelotto in the season opener. Then I thought it was kind of played out. But now I have come to embrace it. In fact, I confess to eagerly anticipating the first corner kick taken in front of the Nordecke, just to see a shower of black & gold cascade upon the enemy kick-taker. And I must say that it looks beautiful on television.

Is it juvenile? Sure. But prank calling is a lost art these days thanks to cell phones and caller ID, and Steve Ralston lives too far away to toilet paper his house, so toilet papering Steve Ralston himself will have to do.

Aside from appealing to the juvenile in me, the other thing that has swayed my opinion is seeing the reaction of random patrons throughout the stadium. The streamer thing has become an event. It gets the rest of the stadium into it. And the Crew players love it too.

There have been plenty of "slippery slope" arguments against streamers, saying that the tossing of streamers would lead to the lobbing of more dangerous items. After Saturday, there will be plenty of told-you-so's. That's because near the end of the game, a handful of numbskulls pelted Ralston with beer bottles as if he had joined Jake and Elwood on stage at Bob's Country Bunker.[58] Ralston would go on to tell the Boston Globe that

---

[58] If you don't understand this, rent "The Blues Brothers" at once.

he was also hit with all manner of objects including, almost laughably, a banana. That's right. He said a banana. If Ralston's version of events is accurate, some fruit-smuggling drunkard apparently mistook Ralston's corner kick for a Fozzie Bear routine. [59]

Although some of the exact projectiles can be debated, there is no mistaking that a line had been crossed. I asked a couple of Crew players about it, and their responses were great. I'm not talking about the words they used, which were just fine. Rather, I am talking about the way in which their words were delivered. There were no freaked-out overreactions. Rather, just acknowledgments that it went too far this time, and the hope that next time will be better.

"We'd rather not have beer bottles be thrown," said Ezra Hendrickson. "Someone could get hurt. It's the first time they've done something like that. We love those guys. We feed off their energy. We don't want them throwing beer bottles though. That can make even one of our guys get injured. At the end of the day, we want them to get keep supporting us like they have, and as long as they stop throwing dangerous things like beer bottles, we will have no problems."

"Obviously, we want to keep it clean," said Danny O'Rourke. "Bury guys in streamers and make it intimidating. That's fine. It even gives us a little breather and a chance to get set. All we ask is that everyone keeps it clean."

And if you can't trust Danny O'Rourke when he tells you to keep it clean with the opposition, who can you trust?

Anyway, the players recognize that a good thing is going in the Nordecke. There was no panic or overreaction to the bottle episode, assuming it was a one-time event as part of the section's growing pains. Even Ralston himself commented on the improved atmosphere and said he didn't mind the streamer shower until it got out of hand later.

So I say follow their lead. It's not a time for the organization or the league to overreact and ban streamers based upon one bad night. Going forward, it would be unfair and unfeasible to expect the supporters to police themselves without help from security. People are there to enjoy the game, not play policeman. And the last thing anyone needs is vigilante justice in the stands. Also, it would be unfair and unfeasible to expect security to be able to

---

[59] I got some stick for joking about this, but nobody ever produced the alleged banana. I received verification from stadium workers that beer, water bottles, ice, coins, lighters, and half-eaten bratwurst were among the thoroughly unacceptable items that were thrown, but nobody saw a banana. (Nor a machete, which was Matt Reis' hyperbolic object of choice.) I wasn't making light of throwing objects at players, but the banana thing struck me as funny, as it reminded me of Fozzie Bear.

discern who is throwing what once the corner kick melee starts. And nobody wants heavy-handed security meddling with the Nordecke. But perhaps having a few extra bodies hanging around, specifically for Projectile Patrol, wouldn't be a bad thing.

Hopefully a compromise can be reached whereby supporters can discretely point out the small minority of knuckleheads in their midst, and then the club provides adequate security to handle the issue from there. Both the supporters and the club owe it to the team to work together to keep a great thing going. [60]

Dunc & Danny

In the last two notebooks, we have had a little bit of playful fashion sniping between the DO Duo: Duncan Oughton and Danny O'Rourke. Before Saturday's game, Oughton told me that O'Rourke delivered a "weak response" in the last notebook. I told him that Danny said it was out of respect. Oughton scoffed. "Respect? I'd call it lack of wit."

When I spoke with Danny after the game, he declined to discuss the Oughton matter. "We lost the game tonight, so I'm not going to start on Duncan," he said. "People might think that I'm a sore loser and that I take it out on senior citizens."

London Calling

After the game, Frankie Hejduk received word that he was called into the U.S. National Team to replace the injured Jonathan Spector. Hejduk flew out the next day to join the team in London for Wednesday's match against England. He will rejoin the Crew on Thursday in Los Angeles.

As you can imagine, a last minute oh-by-the-way-you-have-to-fly-to-London-tomorrow phone call set off a flurry of activity once he finished his post-game treatment in the trainer's room. First came the congratulatory conversations with teammates, along with the take-care-of-Salt-Lake-and-I'll-see-you-dudes-Thursday-in-LA reciprocation. Then came the phone calls. Then logistical conversations with the equipment staff. Then logistical conversations with the training staff. Then Michael Arace from the Dispatch ran back in to get some quotes. Then more phone calls. Then conversations about phone calls that needed to be made. Then phone calls were made to set up other phone calls that needed to be made in the morning. Then…oh yes, a

---

[60] I immediately caught some crap for this section because in the time between when I turned this in and when it was published, the racist YouTube video surfaced. More on that after this Notebook.

shower. After a half-hour of scrambling around in a towel to get things in order, there was time for a post-game shower after all.

Meanwhile, I just sat in front of Guille's locker and watched the Colorado-Chivas match on television.

After the shower came another phone call. Then another logistical conversation with team staff. And then, at long last, once he was dressed and had a moment, I finally butted in. Frankie seemed amazed.

"Dude, you waited through all that just to talk to me?"

I explained I wasn't on deadline, and it was obvious he had a lot of stuff to take care of, so I just watched the game on TV instead.

"Naw, man. You just should have interrupted. All this other stuff will get taken care of anyway, dude."

And then on that gracious note, Frankie took a break from the madness to speak for several minutes about Saturday's Crew game and his international call-up. The Crew quotes have been scattered throughout this article, but here are his thoughts on his call-up and his SoCal rendezvous with the Crew.

"It's going to be an awesome game," he said of Wednesday's friendly against England. "Any time you get called into your national team, it's an honor. It's good that someone is getting noticed from the Crew, and that comes from our team playing well. My teammates have helped me play well, and if we keep playing the way we are playing, more guys will be seen and might get some looks."

"It's going to be a great atmosphere," he continued. "The England fans are obviously not happy about their team not qualifying for Euro 2008. From the squad I've seen, it looks like they've called in all their big guns, so it's going to be a big challenge for us."

Hejduk noted that the England match is just the tip of the iceberg. "We have three great games coming up," he said. "They're considered friendlies, but they aren't going to be that friendly. As I said, England wants to win that game to prove to their fans that they are still a soccer power. Then we have Spain, who is in Euro 2008, so they will be tuning up and all gung-ho. And then we play Argentina, and 10 days after we play them, they start World Cup qualification, and one of their first games is against Brazil. That'll be three great tests for us, so if there is any way I can contribute, I want to. I'm probably going over to London as a back-up, but I want to help out any way I can."

Hejduk has his fingers crossed that two of his Crew teammates will get similar call-ups during this run of high-profile friendlies. "Eddie (Gaven) and Robbie (Rogers) are both in the player pool for these games, so hopefully they will get their looks," he said. "That would be big for them, especially since they are getting ready for the Olympics. The more guys we can get noticed on that level just shows the year that we're having in Columbus. In years past, it wasn't like that. Now guys from the Crew will get some looks."

Meanwhile, it will make for an eventful week for Hejduk, who will play for the Crew Saturday after his transatlantic voyage. "It's a lot of frequent flier miles," he joked. "Those plane rides can take a lot out of you, so you have to do everything you can to keep yourself ready to play that next game. U.S. Soccer does it right and flies us business class, which is great of them to do. They do it the right way, and that allows us to recover correctly."

And not only is he making a transatlantic voyage, but in a double whammy, as he also has to make a transcontinental trek to meet the Crew in California. "Yeah, it's going to be an eight-hour difference, so it's going to be a weird one," he laughed. "Sleep is going to be a little bit off. It's something that I'm used to and that I've done before. It's part of being a professional. Sometimes you have to suck it up and do whatever you need to do to be ready for the game."

Frankie Hejduk dribbles the ball against the Revs, just hours before his last-minute trip to England with the U.S. National Team.
(Photo by Greg Bartram / Columbus Crew)

Dwight's Spiffy Jacket

Now that Dwight Burgess anchors the CSN Rotating Cast of Bald Television Broadcasters Booth, I do not cross paths with The Voice of the Crew as often as I used to back when he plied his trade on the radio. But before Saturday's game, I ran into Burgess as he walked along the concourse in his bumble-bee striped Crew warm-up jacket from the late 90s.

"Like my jacket?" he asked with an excited smile. "I'm trying to relive the Rob Jachym era!"

(Jachym was the Crew's first-round pick in 1997, and he appeared in just three games during his one-year Crew career.)

Bugging Elias Sports Bureau: William Hesmer Edition

Now that William Hesmer has saved three penalty kicks this season, he is knocking on the record book. After bugging the ever-helpful Peter Hirdt at Elias Sports Bureau, we have learned that Hesmer is the first MLS goalkeeper to make three penalty kick saves in one season since Dallas' D.J. Countess in 2003. That year, Countess saved four PKs to tie Joe Cannon's league record, which he set in 1999 with San Jose.

Armed with that helpful info from Elias Sports Bureau, I dug deeper into the record book, and here is a look at those two historic seasons.

Joe Cannon (San Jose, 1999)
4 saves, 2 goals
Progression: Save, Save, goal, Save, goal, Save.

D.J. Countess (Dallas, 2003)
4 saves, 6 goals
Progression: goal, goal, goal, goal, goal, goal, Save, Save, Save, Save

How about Countess? Practice makes perfect, huh? He allowed six consecutive penalty kick goals, and then finished up with four consecutive saves. He capped that streak with two penalty-kick saves against the MetroStars on October 11, 2003. The penalty saves bookended the match. In the 2nd minute, he stoned Amado Guevara, and then in the 86th minute, he denied Clint Mathis. To top it off, the two saves preserved a 0-0 draw.

As for Cannon, it seems that Hesmer is following his exact progression, albeit much ahead of schedule. Cannon did not make his third penalty save of 1999 until August 7.

Dumb Conversations With Dwight, Part One

Should you ever have the occasion to speak to Burgess, be aware that the man has a comeback for everything. [61] Take this instance, whereby Dwight put on some tiny old man glasses to read something in the radio booth, and then I made the mistake of opening my mouth, allowing Burgess to use the irrefutable facts of history to defend himself.

ME: "Wow. If you took that ring of functioning follicles around the bottom of your skull and let them grow the hair out until it was part way down your back, you'd look just like Benjamin Franklin."

DWIGHT: "Ben Franklin could have had any woman he wanted. The guy was a legend with the ladies. The similarities are obvious. Thanks for noticing."

(For any readers who happen to be married to Dwight Burgess, let the record show that Dwight purposely keeps his entire head bald so as not to unintentionally entice the modern day equivalent of Ben's Bimbos. You should only become concerned if he ever grows one of those shaggy semi-circles of hair, which is a telltale sign of philandering with a Franklin Floozy.)

Bugging Elias Sports Bureau: Lineup Consistency Edition

In the last notebook, I shared a fun fact passed along by Crew PR Director Dave Stephany, which was that earlier this year, the Crew fielded the same starting lineup three games in a row for only the third time in the last four years.

This raised the question, when was the last time the Crew fielded the same starting lineup FOUR games in a row?

Once again, Peter Hirdt at Elias Sports Bureau came to the rescue with a most astonishing answer: _Never._

Thirteen seasons in, and not once have the Crew fielded the same starting lineup for four consecutive matches.[62]

---

[61] That is the most indisputable statement in this book.

[62] This would change come playoff time. From the season finale through MLS Cup, the Crew fielded the same lineup for five consecutive matches: Hesmer, Hejduk, O'Rourke, Marshall, Padula, Gaven, Carroll, Evans, Rogers, Schelotto, and Moreno.

Dumb Conversations With Dwight, Part Two

Like part one, this conversation also has nothing to do with soccer, but Dwight hasn't been in the Notebook for a while, and I can't help but marvel at how sharply convoluted Dwight can make any conversation. Moments after rubbing it in that his Cincinnati Reds swept my Cleveland Indians last weekend, the following exchange took place...

DWIGHT: "You know what? I had two tickets to last Friday's Reds-Indians game that I couldn't use. I should have called you. I didn't even think of it."

ME: "I couldn't have gone either, but hey, thanks for not thinking of me."

DWIGHT: "Any time. In fact, it's more like *all* the time, so it was really no trouble for me at all."

Frankie, the Fans, and the Beautiful Game

The Crew talked about holding their heads high and not letting the loss get them down, and I saw no more concrete evidence of this concept in action than when Frankie Hejduk left the field. Despite a last minute loss, Frankie was all smiles as he ran toward the tunnel, stopping to give a few high fives and sign a few autographs along the way.

For a notorious competitor like Hejduk, it was noteworthy to see him in such high spirits after a loss. Part of it was because he felt the Crew played well despite the loss. But just a part. Mostly, it was because of the fans.

"They were still cheering, even after we lost," he said with a smile. "In years past, you didn't see that. We probably would have gotten booed a little bit here and there. I think they appreciate how we have been playing and the effort that we have been giving, and in turn, we appreciate the extra boost that they have given us. They gave us that extra boost tonight, so it's a shame that we couldn't come through for them. But they still showed appreciation for us after the game, and it felt really good. I've seen that plenty of times in Europe, and I think we're finally starting to get that European feel in America, which I think is a good thing. People try to dismiss soccer by saying it's a 'European sport', but you know what? Where I'm from, it's one world and one game. If people are passionate all over the world, why shouldn't we be just as passionate in the United States? It's not European or South American or anything else. We're all in this together, and it's just a beautiful game."

Questions? Comments? Unaware that Crew radio announcer Neil Sika is a dead ringer for Cleveland Indians pitcher Jake Westbrook, finely trimmed beard and all? Feel free to write at sirk65@yahoo.com

A cross-field view of the Nordecke, which was a source of both good and bad on May 24, 2008, during the Crew's 1-0 loss to New England.
(Photo by Greg Bartram / Columbus Crew)

The Incidents, Part I:
The YouTube Video

In the days that followed the Crew's 1-0 loss to the Revs, all heck broke loose when a YouTube video clearly chronicled a camera-toting idiot shouting a racial epithet toward New England's Kheli Dube after he scored the winning goal. The video understandably and deservedly rocked the MLS community.

It also completely changed the context of the previous Saturday's events. On game night, nobody was aware that any such racist event had occurred. Instead, the talk was about the bottles and debris that had come from the Nordecke. When I went to the Crew's locker room, my goal was to get a few Crew players on record advising the fans to quit throwing dangerous objects onto the field. It was the first major problem of this sort with the Nordecke, and my hope was that by having Crew players appeal to them with how it affects the home team too, it would help nip it in the bud without any sort of draconian security crackdown. Danny O'Rourke and Ezra Hendrickson came through, asking the fans to keep it clean and pointing out that objects on the field are equally likely to hurt home players as visiting players.

As far as I was concerned, it was mission accomplished. And I laughed when word spread to the Crew's locker room that Steve Ralston mentioned bananas and Matt Reis mentioned machetes when speaking about the thrown objects. Both cases seemed like humorous hyperbole, especially since nobody associated with Operations or Stadium Grounds could recall any evidence of a single banana or machete. (But plenty of beer and water bottles, ice, coins, lighters, half-eaten bratwursts, and other such inappropriate and dangerous objects. It was a shameful mess, no doubt.)

When I wrote my story, I remembered Ralston's banana comment and it made me laugh because it reminded me of a bad Fozzie Bear routine. As a kid, I always used to wonder who brought tomatoes to a comedy show with the intent to hurl them at unfunny comedians, and the same thought struck me about Ralston's unsubstantiated banana. So I made a Fozzie Bear joke in my article. No biggie, right?

Well, once the YouTube video hit, I was suddenly accused by a few of encouraging the throwing of objects and laughing off racism toward black players. Uh…what? Those few personal accusations were easily rebuffed, but the larger attacks on the Nordecke, the Crew, and the city of Columbus went on. I understood a lot of the fury, as the act itself was reprehensible, but much of the anger directed at anyone beside the perpetrator was fueled by misinformation.

The grapevine produced stories of multiple racial incidents, organized taunts, and even conflated Ralston's banana comment with the racism incident so as to make it sound that Crew fans were tossing bananas at black players, as had been done in Europe in the past. None of these items were true, but if that's the story I had heard through the grapevine, I'd be furious as well.

Another popular misconception was that fans stood around and did nothing while the racist idiot mouthed off in front of everyone. This claim ignored both the physics of sound and human physiology. At the time the goal was scored, some 2,000 people in the Nordecke began screaming random words. Some were shouting at the referee, others were shouting at the Revs, and others were simply booing or releasing general frustration. That's one mighty wall of noise. The video revealed that the person shouting the epithet was standing in the very front row, facing the field. So with 2,000 people screaming 2,000 different things, this person was in the very front, saying his reprehensible word while facing away from the mass of humanity behind him. In addition to the physics of sound waves, throw in the fact that it's virtually impossible to listen while you yourself are screaming, and so the odds of this person being heard by anyone, with the possible exception of the person on either side of him, were slim and none. Unlike the 2,000 other human beings in the Nordecke, the camera's microphone was in position to capture the imbecile's words. Also, video cameras are not distracted by their own screaming.

With that wall of indistinguishable noise, the word never even made it to the players. That night, at the stadium, nobody had a clue that a racial incident had occurred. But the word at 22 seconds into the video clip was clear as day. It had in fact transpired.

I got a call from Dante Washington that Tuesday morning. He had been out of town and just caught word that something had happened in Columbus. I had to explain to Dante that some idiot at Crew Stadium had hurled an n-bomb at Kheli Dube. And I had to explain that Columbus was getting raked over the coals. I had to explain that other fans were referring to the Crew as the "KKKrew" and were redoing the Crew's shield so that it featured three hooded Klansmen. I had to explain that disreputable websites were manufacturing "evidence" of the Nordecke's neo-Nazi affiliations. I had to explain that due to the actions of one ignorant person, many other ignorant people were suddenly equating Columbus with the Jim Crow South.

Dante and I talked for about an hour that morning. We were disappointed that Columbus was getting dragged through the mud on racial issues. I have had many conversations over the years with friends from both Cleveland and Cincinnati about how, when we return to our respective hometowns, it's almost like going to another world. Living in Columbus, we have forgotten the racial divides of our hometowns, where both whites and blacks seem to lug around a perpetual chip on their respective shoulders. We've often tried to figure out why everyone gets along so well in Columbus, and the best we could come up with as that the Big C's at either end of the state are old manufacturing cities where the tension and resentment became entrenched over many decades, whereas Columbus is a newer city dominated by the intellectual center of a large university, which is an environment where diversity is celebrated. Or something like that. I don't think we've ever truly figured it out, but the truth remains that Columbus is a very low-stress city when it comes to melding different races, religions, sexual orientations, or anything else. In both 2004 and 2007, Black Enterprise magazine rated Columbus as a Top-10 City for African-Americans in its tri-annual rankings. That's not to say Columbus is without problems or is some sort of utopia, but it's definitely got a more communal vibe than most major cities. It was sad and disheartening for Dante and I to see our club and our adopted hometown lumped in with some foul-mouthed miscreant.

I'm a pretty laid back person, but I came to loathe this individual, who I derisively referred to as Drunky the Racist D-Bag. I loathed that he used the word in the first place. I loathed that he was such a coward that he anonymously hid behind the roar of a crowd, then posted the video like he was some tough guy who had the balls to shout it to someone's face, when all he did was shout it into a microphone far from Dube's ears. I came to loathe the fact that the very usage of that word disrespects so many people that Drunky the Racist D-Bag had ostensibly cheered for over the years. Would he shout that word at Andy Iro? Ezra Hendrickson? Emmanuel Ekpo? Dante Washington? Jeff Cunningham? Edson Buddle? Brian West? Ansil Elcock? Stern John? Robin Fraser? Nelson Akwari? It doesn't matter how many guys I list—could he look any of those men in the eye, man to man, and shout that word?

I loathed that he unfairly piled upon the Nordecke, which deservedly had problems enough with the object throwing from that game. I loathed that he besmirched a Crew organization whose foundation was built by men of high character and class— Lamar Hunt, Jamey Rootes, Tom Fitzgerald, and Brian McBride. I loathed that he gave ammunition to every grossly inaccurate "podunk backwoods" stereotype that most outsiders have of Columbus.

And when this awful pall he had cast seemed to be the first domino in a series of Crew-related misfortune that would spread into early June, I loathed him even more. It was if his bad karma was single-handedly destroying all of the positive momentum from the Crew's great start.

But that's not what happened. The Nordecke forged a tighter bond and became stronger. The team eventually regained its footing. And once the sensationalism died down, most anyone outside of the most rivalry-fueled corners of the internet came to realize that Drunky the Racist D-Bag was not a fair representation of anyone but his own stupid self.

The funny thing about hate speech is that hating the hate speech still produces hate. Isn't that why the Klan has rallies in the first place? To provoke outrage? Hate and anger are unproductive emotions. I thought of all the hours I spent being enraged at Drunky the Racist D-Bag for his cowardly actions toward Dube, and all the time I spent being enraged by the people who used his actions to poke at Columbus. That was a lot of time and energy wasted on something that had nothing to do with the reality of who Kheli Dube is as a human being, nor the reality of what Columbus is like as a community or the Crew are like as an organization. So I let the anger go.

In the end, when some drunken idiot uses a racist epithet in an attempt to get a rise out of an opposing player, or some message board moron or tawdry web site exploits racism to get a rise out of a fan base, it's a far greater condemnation of the perpetrator than the target.

Well, then. Sorry for that grim detour. However, when looking back at the 2008 season, it would be folly to pretend that such a thing never happened. It was a major news story in Columbus and around the league, and it's the sort of thing that needs to be talked about. Letting go of one's anger about the incident is not the same as failing to condemn the incident or pretending it never happened. It happened and it deserves to be talked about.

The racist YouTube video was the first of three newsworthy off-the-field incidents that could have derailed the Crew's magical season. I will get to the others when the time comes in our story. In the meantime, let's get back to the games.[63]

---

[63] Although at this stage in the season, you'd probably prefer that we didn't. You can skip ahead to June 14 if you want. The games are pretty much all smiles from then on.

U.S. Open Cup: Crew 2, Salt Lake 0

Match date: Tuesday, May 27, 2008
Venue: Columbus Crew Stadium
Scoring:
26: CLB Lenhart (unassisted)
53: CLB Rogers (unassisted)
Attendance: 4,816

RETROACTIVE RECAP

The Crew ran out a largely reserve-laden lineup and knocked off Real Salt Lake, 2-0. Emmanuel Ekpo, Steven Lenhart, Ryan Junge, and Jed Zayner made their maiden first-team starts with the Crew. Also, George Josten made his first appearance in an official Crew match, while Andy Gruenebaum saw his first first-team action of the year. Lenhart scored his first professional goal after corralling a deflected ball in the box and sticking it home. Go figure. And Robbie Rogers doubled the lead in the second half with one of his vintage cut-ins from the left flank, allowing him to laser a right-footed shot inside the far post.

Robbie Rogers works the end line during the Crew's USOC victory.
(Photo by Sam Fahmi)

Road Work: Chivas USA 2, Crew 0

Match date: Saturday, May 31, 2008
Scoring:
20: CHV Flores 3 (unassisted)
21: CHV Marsch 4 (Braun 2)
Attendance: 12,338
Crew's record afterward: 6-3-1

RETROACTIVE RECAP

Earlier that evening, the nefarious numbers runner known as Z-man and I were celebrating our friend Rob's 30th birthday (observed.) We recorded the game at Z's place. When we got back there, his wife greeted us by saying, "I was asleep on the couch, but I woke up for a part that you guys are going to hate." So much for going in fresh. As the opening quarter hour played out, we thought that maybe she had hallucinated the whole thing. But then Jorge Flores scored in the 20th minute. And then Jesse Marsch (him again?) scored in the 21st minute. And then Danny O'Rourke got ejected for a tackle from behind in the 22nd minute. The game was essentially decided within 120 seconds of pure suck.

QUOTES

Frankie Hejduk: "We didn't come out ready to play in the first 20 minutes. They came out like the home team and pressured us, and we didn't really respond. They got two early goals and by then we're chasing the game for the rest of the game. Of course the red card doesn't help out either. They did well. I thought we battled for the most part. After that first 20 minutes, I thought we played decently. It's going to be tough to come back from 2-0 with a man down so the whole game we're chasing but that's just the way it goes sometimes."

Steven Lenhart, on making his MLS debut in front of friends and family in LA: "It's a good support crew. I definitely appreciate that and it's good to get out there in front of family and a bunch of friends. Obviously it's a bummer that we lost. Good to get in there at the end and run around a little bit, but the outcome wasn't what we wanted. Not much to say about that one."

120

Sirk's Notebook: San Jose 2, Crew 0

Match date: June 7, 2008

Scoring:

10: SJ Johnson 2 (O'Brien 2)

60: SJ Corrales 2 (O'Brien 3)

Attendance: 11,704

Crew's record afterward: 6-4-1

In baseball, they call it a June Swoon. If it's true that when it rains it pours, the Crew are suffering a June Swoon Monsoon. The Crew entered the month on a three-game winless steak and a 277-minute scoring drought in league play. Then in the first week of the month, they lost budding folk hero Adam Moffat to another knee injury. Then the Crew's captain, Frankie Hejduk, continued to be pulled in all directions on two continents, racking up more flight miles than John Glenn in 1962. Then the team's exclusive local TV partner, CSN, announced that it was ceasing production operations.

Clearly something evil was at work. It was obvious that some malevolent entity had brought forth a plague of misfortune to Crewville. But who? Who saw to it that our blue skies turned gray, that our sevens became snake eyes, and that what had previously been coming up roses was coming up, uh, giant man-eating Venus fly traps that smelled like stinky cheese?

Before Saturday's home game against the expansion San Jose Earthquakes, Crew PR Director Dave Stephany told me that there was a surprise guest waiting for me in the press box. Aha! Surely this was the culprit! Thinking back to Ghostbusters, I cleared my mind, hoping not to provide a tangible form to this shapeless evil.

Alas, Dave spilled a name. I got a mental picture. I was doomed. I trudged up the press box to greet evil incarnate in the form of Craig Merz. The Crew beat writer for the Columbus Dispatch from 1996-2005, Merz was subbing in for the Associated Press. While sitting in the front row of the press box, Merz's eyes glowed red as he used his evil telekinetic powers to direct San Jose's only two shots on goal of the game into the Crew's net. He also lifted a scaly, clawed hand and pinched Chad Marshall's neck from afar, Darth Vader style, forcing him out of the game in the 27th minute. I don't even want to think about what he did to Ezra Hendrickson's groin in the 44th minute. He cackled a nefarious cackle when the game ended 2-0 in San Jose's favor, extending the Crew's league winless streak to four games and league scoreless streak to 367 minutes. Then Merz dematerialized to go back to the evil spirit world where he can orchestrate his Crew ruinations from afar in a parallel dimension.

Or something like that.

Of course, Merz isn't really evil. I'm sure all of this was just a coincidence. But I told him if the Crew capped off this miserable week with a home loss to an expansion team, I was going to murder him in print and blame the whole thing on his return. Come to think of it, since he told me to bring it on, it's probably at least partially true then anyway, right?[64]

Roughing Robbie Rogers

In what has become a troublesome and annoying pattern, at least judging by the reactions of coaches, players, fans, and media, the Earthquakes mugged the Crew to the tune of 21 fouls. That's 21 that were called.

Understandably, San Jose coach Frank Yallop offered no apologies. In fact, when a reporter commented that the Quakes were physical early on, Yallop was quick to correct him. "Not early on. The entire game. That's one of the things that's been missing for us. It may not be pretty, but I'll tell you what-- we fought for every ball. We might have mistimed some tackles. We might have got in some challenges that were fouls. That's football. The other team has to handle it and move on. We've been overpowered in away games, but I thought today was an example of a fantastic away performance. We made it miserable for the other team to play us, we took our chances when they came, and we didn't roll over. That was excellent."

Excellence is in the eye of the beholder. Crew coach Sigi Schmid was uncharacteristically terse in his assessment of the physical play. "You'll have to talk to the referees. I have no comment. We have been beaten up in the last four games."

Nobody has been beaten up more than Crew speedster Robbie Rogers. MLS teams might want to share the secrets of their success with Wile E. Coyote.

"The first eight games, people couldn't figure out how to defend Robbie," said Crew goalkeeper William Hesmer. "Once one team started kicking him, now everybody is kicking him. That's the way to defend him now. If the refs could come in here and see Robbie's legs, they might call things differently too."

---

[64] I suppose it would be fair to note that, after this game, Merz never personally witnessed another loss for the rest of the season.

Rogers' legs were on full "Exhibit A" display as he sat in front of his locker answering questions from the press. Each shin had at least one bleeding wound and a couple of bruises to match. At his age, one might expect Rogers to whine about the roughhouse treatment, but he did not. His tone was annoyed, yet defiant.

"Everybody asks me about it, and I am getting tired of talking about it," he said, which clearly suggested that the annoyance in his tone was more from the repetitive line of questioning than the hacking itself. "I just have to be quick enough that they can't touch me. I have to figure something out. Maybe I need to play more physical too. I don't care what happens, but I am not going to let this ruin the game. It would be nice if the refs helped me out a little bit, but the reality is that I'm only 21 years old. I can't expect that. It's up to me to figure something out."

While an undaunted and determined Rogers works on upping his maximum sprinting speed from Warp 5 to Warp 6, his teammates had their own suggestions on how to end the weekly hackfest:

- Guillermo Barros Schelotto thinks the Crew just need to play to their abilities: "We need to play the same (as we did before.) I knew before the game that San Jose would play with many fouls, but we did not play (like we are capable of)."
- Frankie Hejduk thinks the Crew need to let the ball do the work: "To be honest, we need to get rid of the ball sooner. We need to play a two-touch game. When you take 3, 4, 5, 6, 7 touches, you're inviting tackles. We need to play the ball quicker instead of dribbling around the field, which is what we're doing, and that's inviting tackles and fouls. So yeah, teams are hacking us, but that's because we're not playing two-touch soccer."
- And Hesmer thinks the Crew need to make the other teams rue their trip and tug transgressions: "The way to stop it is to make them pay on set pieces, and we're not doing that right now. If teams know that fouling us in the final third could lead to a goal a game, they would have to ease up."

The suggestion box is full of good ideas. Now it's time for the team to implement a few. [65]

---

[65] They pretty much spent the rest of the year doing all three of those things.

Goalless

The Crew's offense, which was the league's most potent in the opening month of the season, has now sputtered to four consecutive league shutouts for the first time in club history. However, the 367-minute scoreless drought in league play is not a club record. The 2004 Crew put together a 420-minute drought in April and May that spanned only three shutouts and the large part of each game on either side of those shutouts. But maybe it's a perverse good omen, since the 2004 Crew rattled off an 18-game unbeaten streak and went on to win the Supporters' Shield for the only time in club history. [66]

Anyway, the goalless drought was another hot (and surely annoying) line of questioning in the locker room.

"It's not that we're not getting the ball into the offensive end or we're not getting chances," said Schmid. "We're not catching the breaks right now."

"It's frustrating, but we're creating chances, so there's not much more we can do," said Rogers. "I don't know what to say. We're going to score goals. And to be fair, in the middle of this, we scored two goals in the U.S. Open Cup game against Salt Lake. Tonight we got off to a bad start and fell behind. We can't start out flat like we did tonight. Starting out flat is more of a concern to me, because I know that we are going to score goals."

(UPDATE: To follow up on Robbie's point, the Crew scored two more goals in Tuesday's U.S. Open Cup match against Chicago, meaning the Crew have scored four goals against MLS clubs while in the midst of their league scoreless drought. Now back to Saturday's comments...)

"Bounces were going our way earlier in the season, and now they are not," observed Hejduk. "Scoring goals can be a hot and cold thing. We need to get our forwards some goals to get their confidence back up. When we had confidence, we were leading the league in goals. Now, for whatever reason, it has stopped. And that doesn't mean it's just the forwards. Goal scoring is a team thing. We need to look at video, see what we're doing wrong, and then get back to the drawing board."

Big Brown

The Crew did put the ball in the back of the net once on a diving attempt by Alejandro Moreno, but it was correctly called back because Moreno hit the ball into the goal with his arm.

---

[66] It was indeed a perverse good omen. It's official: Long scoreless streak = Supporters' Shield.

The play did inspire Sigi to briefly break his no-comment pledge about the refereeing, as he delivered this Triple Crown inspired gem about the defensive effort of San Jose's Jason Hernandez on that play: "I'm not doubting that the play with Alejandro was handball, but the guy was riding him like Big Brown.[67] It has to be either a goal or a penalty."

Moffat-less Rocket

Adam Moffat may be out of the lineup for the foreseeable future, but strange as it may seem, the fans were still treated to a Moffat Rocket on Saturday. The stand-in rocketeer was Jed Zayner, who roasted a 35-yarder off the crossbar in the 35th minute of his first career league start.

"The ball came down, I heard 'man on', and I thought, 'Why not have a go?'" said Zayner. "I didn't think I hit it that well, but then I looked and thought '(gasp) Oh my God!' Then it cracked the crossbar from 35 out. It's one of those things that you might pull off one in a hundred, but you take your chances and hope it goes in. That time it didn't, but at least I hit it well."

Katie's Curls

Knowing that the Crew were in a funk, television sideline reporter Katie Witham took matters into her own hands. And by "matters" I mean "a curling iron." She curled her hair. It seems that the Crew were undefeated when Katie's hair is curled. "They're at least 4-0," she said before the game. "It better not rain tonight. It's bad for the curls, and we need a win."

With her main employer, CSN, shutting down production operations the day before, it had to be a rough couple of days for Katie. It was the elephant in the stadium, but we joked around for a few minutes anyway. When a wayward soccer ball rolled our way from the little kid scrimmages out on the field, Katie hit a 20-yard ball right to a kid's instep. I told her she hadn't lost a thing from her playing days at Capital. "I hit that ball in heels too," she proudly noted. When another ball drifted our way and a kid raced after it, I urged her to go after the 50/50 ball Danny O'Rourke style. Given her footwear, she jokingly threatened to go in "stud up."

Anyway, let's fast forward a few hours. Thanks to the June Swoon Monsoon, we all know which of the available streaks got snapped on Saturday. When I saw Katie after the game, she forced a wan smile and said, "So much for the curls, huh?"

---

[67] Earlier that day, a Kentucky Derby and Preakness-winning horse named Big Brown raced for the Triple Crown, but finished dead last in the Belmont Stakes.

Snakeless?!?

One of the great things about soccer is that it is such an international sport, one can't help but learn about the world when conversing within the diverse community of players, coaches and fans. I have known Duncan Oughton for eight years now, and while Dante, Dunny and I have cracked just about every New Zealand joke imaginable, there is still so much to learn about the Kiwi's homeland.

This weekend, Duncan informed me that New Zealand does not have any snakes. Zip. Zero. Nada. I couldn't believe it, so I did some research. Sure enough, the New Zealand government advises visitors, "New Zealand doesn't have any snakes, scorpions, bears, wild cats (of the ferocious variety) or alligators/crocodiles. We do have spiders but only one of them is capable of causing a nasty bite - and it's never fatal." Further reading also revealed that New Zealand is free from rabies, so should you be bitten by a bat, a hedgehog, or a naughty, naughty sheep, there is no need for big needles in your bellybutton.

"It's a very peaceful land where I come from," said Oughton.

This is all the more astonishing when one considers New Zealand's proximity to Australia, where Steve Irwin made a (shortened) career out of wrangling an endless assortment of deadly animals commonly found in people's back yards. The New Zealand government goes through great pains to keep unwanted plant, animal, insect and disease pests out of the country. They have a Biosecurity Ministry that maintains strict preventative measures to deny entry to unwanted pests and, failing that, the government is quick to quarantine and eradicate. The country's snake policy is so unyielding that snakes may not even be brought onto the islands for display in a zoo or for research purposes. New Zealand's miniscule swat team of biosecurity snake handlers receives its training in Brisbaine, Australia.

In late April of this year, a yellow sea snake made its way to shore at Baylys Beach on the north island. A few dead sea snakes wash ashore every year, but the frigid Pacific waters typically serve as a protective barrier from living specimens. Once the live snake was discovered by a man walking his dog, the beach was shut down as if it were a Jaws movie. The snake was captured and deported.

More alarming is the prospect of deadly eastern brown snakes, common to Australia, which are sometimes intercepted at port or at shipping facilities. Should the eastern brown snake take hold, it would have disastrous consequences for New Zealand, whose ecology would have no defenses. When your national symbol is a flightless bird, one has to shudder at the thought of six-foot snakes quickly making the kiwi as relevant as the dodo.

Eastern browns would also change everyday life in New Zealand, where residents currently experience nearly risk-free enjoyment of the natural beauty their homeland has to offer. Hikes through fields or forests would suddenly shift from carefree to cautious, from delightful to dangerous.

The Biosecurity Ministry works tirelessly so as not to duplicate the problems created by other foreign species that have taken hold in New Zealand in the past. These include wild goats, deer, weasels and possums, all of which have caused great harm to the environment by eating and destroying plant life while competing with native species for food. The possum in particular is cited for the decrease in kiwi numbers, as the omnivorous marsupials have been known to eat kiwi eggs and chicks.

Here in Ohio, it must seem funny that possums were introduced to New Zealand in the mid-1800s in the hopes of establishing a fur trade, or that the possum, which we consider harmless in our environment, has become Rogue Wildlife Enemy No. 1.

However, it seems that New Zealanders at least share our sense of humor about the possum's typical fate. From NewZealand.com, concerning wildlife pests and invasive species: "Possums are the worst - their population is estimated to be about 70 million despite intensive eradication programmes and the presence of their formidable foe - the car."

Story Time With Todd Yeagley

For those of you who actually thumb through FreeKick, the game program, you may have noticed I have been doing a "Where Are They Now?" with former Crew players. I have a bunch of leftover material that I will have to slip into notebooks at some point, but here's one I can't wait to share. While chatting with Todd Yeagley last week for the next batch of programs, I asked him about a story that former Crew coach Tom Fitzgerald told me about a year before his passing.

I advised Yeags that Fitz had told me a story about a game in L.A., and Yeags was quick to cut me off. "The $100 bill under my chair?" he asked. Bingo. The Crew had just fired coach Timo Liekoski after a 6-16 start. They were buried in last place with virtually no hope of making the playoffs. And then Brad Friedel arrived and Tom Fitzgerald took over as coach, and the Crew won nine of their last 10 games to make the playoffs. Now that the scene is set, I'll let Yeags tell the story from the first game in that run...

"It was Fitz's first game as coach," said Yeagley. "We were in L.A., and the Galaxy had a really good team that year. We were in last place. Nobody expected us to do well. I had only started a couple games to that point, and one of Fitz's changes was to insert me into the lineup. Before the game, without me knowing, he taped a $100 bill to the bottom of my chair. We won the game and I played well, although certainly no better than the other guys. It's not like I won the game or anything, but I played well. Afterward, Fitz was giving his post-game speech. He said he was proud of the team for playing so well, but he wanted to recognize one person in particular for stepping up when given the chance. He said, 'Todd, great job.' Then he reached under my chair, pulled out the $100 bill, and said, 'I was bettin' on ya!'"

This exactly matches the story Fitz told me, minus Todd's modesty. After telling me the story, Fitz joked that for the rest of the season, players were always looking under their seats to see if there was any money taped to the bottom. But as Yeags went on with his recollection, Fitz's postscript took on added hilarity.

"After he said he was betting on me, he put the $100 bill in his pocket!" Yeags continued. "I never got that $100 bill! I think he had good intentions, but just forgot in the excitement of the moment. Of course, I couldn't just ask him to give it to me. That's OK, though, he more than made up for it with all the times he had us over to his house for cookouts. That game really meant a lot to me. It's one thing for a coach to put you in the lineup, but for him to believe in you so much that he puts $100 under your chair before the game as proof of his belief in you, and then to come through for him, that was a special moment that I will never forget."

Hopefully this silly anecdote will give you a reason to smile the next time you pass Fitz's memorial rock on the west side of the stadium grounds.

New Zealand Wildlife Tidbit #2

Sorry if I am boring anybody with the Kiwi wildlife stories, but Duncan's offhand comment fascinated me and inspired a lot of reading, so I just felt like sharing in case anyone else was interested. I mean, do you really want me to write more about the two-goal home loss to an expansion team? Didn't think so.

Anyway, here's the other interesting tidbit I found: New Zealand has no native land-roaming mammals. Strange, huh?

The only mammalian wildlife species that existed naturally within its shores were bats and seals. All other mammals were artificially introduced. Most of these were brought over intentionally, such as cattle, sheep, horses, rabbits, and the aforementioned Blight of the Possums.[68] As would be

---

[68] You know, like "Flight of the Conchords." Such a subtle NZ reference!

expected, some undesirable species such as mice and rats gained entry as stowaways on ships that came to port. Even to this day, there are just 46 total species of wild and feral mammals in New Zealand, including oft-domesticated farm animals like horses, cattle, pigs, and sheep.

To contrast that locally, there are 58 species of wild mammals in Ohio, excluding all mammalian pets and farm animals. This means your neighbor's golden retriever and the bovines at Don Scott Field don't count. Alas, it also excludes the native mammals that have been extirpated from the state over the last 150 years, such as bison, grey wolves, cougars, elk, lynx, and those dastardly wolverines, among others.

See, isn't learning more fun than wallowing? [69]

There was a lot of anguish in the stands on June 7, 2008. Heartbroken that her Crew lost to an expansion team, Chelsey was better off learning about New Zealand's reptiles and mammals than reliving that 2-0 nightmare. (Photo by Sam Fahmi.)

Frankie the Indefatigable Frequent Flyer

In the span of 16 days, Frankie Hejduk played in six games while making four transatlantic flights and two transcontinental flights covering the breadth of eight time zones. From May 24 to June 8, he went from Columbus to London to Los Angeles to Santander to Columbus to New York, all while

---

[69] I sure hoped so. It seemed a lot more fun to me than writing about the game.

playing 270 minutes for the Crew and 91+ minutes for the U.S. National Team.

Frankie and I were born a day apart, but the gulf is so much wider. I got more exhausted typing that itinerary than he did living it. It blows my mind. After Saturday's Crew game, he was ready to depart again to play against Argentina the next day in New York. It didn't appear to phase him.

"It's all part of it," he said with a big grin. "It's a grueling process, and it's great, and it's an honor to be a part of it."

Meanwhile, I need a nap just thinking about it.

U.S. Open Cup Shocker!!!

Well, the Crew lost to the Fire, 3-2, in overtime. That's not much of a shocker. The Crew have faced the Fire in the U.S. Open Cup three times since 1998, losing all three games in overtime. It's annoying, not shocking.

The U.S. Open Cup shocker Tuesday night came in the form of Hollywood United FC, an amateur side run by "Without A Trace" TV star Anthony Lapaglia. HUFC stunned the Portland Timbers of USL1 with a 3-2 upset in the Rose City. Of particular interest to me, of course, is that Notebook Hall of Famer Brian Dunseth plays midfield for HUFC when his broadcasting schedule permits. ("I usually play in the Sunday games," he said.)

HUFC is made up of amateur players with a few former pros sprinkled in. Dunny was by far the most decorated player to take the field for HUFC Tuesday night, although Matt Taylor (6 goals in 64 games from 2004-07) and substitute Jason Boyce (3 assists in 19 games from 1998-99) had MLS experience. A few other players had second or third-division experience, and the rest were flat out amateurs. To get themselves ready for their Open Cup showdown with Portland, HUFC upped their after-work practice schedule to Mondays, Wednesdays, and Fridays. Although HUFC has different teams at various age and skill levels, the current "open" team has been playing together since September of 2007.

"This team is mostly made up of hard-working California guys who never got their opportunity for whatever reason," said Dunseth. "They all have jobs, but they keep playing for the love of the game. It's a cliché, but it's true. Thanks to Anthony Lapaglia, these guys finally got their shot."

Making the upset all the more stunning is that Hollywood United overcame two deficits to win the game. Matt Taylor converted two equalizing penalty kicks, and then Earl Alexander found the upper-90 in stoppage to cap the, er, Hollywood ending.

The biggest play of the game was a penalty kick save by HUFC goalkeeper Javier Barragan in the 53rd minute. A goal would have given

Portland a 3-1 lead. In another Hollywood twist, Barragan is HUFC's back-up goalkeeper. The starter, Mike Littman, was forced to serve a red-card suspension that he earned back in 2003. That's right, HUFC was down its starting keeper because of a five-year-old Open Cup red card Littman had picked up with the third-division Utah Blitzz. The team is long gone, but the suspension remained.

You want another crazy story? How about starting center back Nas Koubouras? Affectionately known as "Spartan" because he's the team's Greek warrior, Koubouras was forced to leave the game in the 70th minute with what is believed to be a torn ACL.[70] After celebrating his team's improbable upset Tuesday night, Koubouras caught a stand-by red-eye flight back to LA, hopped in his truck, and was on time Wednesday morning for his job as a construction welder. [71]

"I'm not even going to rank this game," said Dunny, "because it's not about me. I was so proud of these guys. I am so happy for them. This game was their World Cup. They finally got a chance to prove themselves, and they made the most of it."

"Look, we know realistically that Portland didn't start their first team," he continued. "Fair enough. Neither do a lot of MLS teams when they play USL sides. But when an amateur team beats a USL team, everyone says they were so lucky, but if a USL team beats an MLS team, they turn around and say it shows that the USL is just as good as MLS.[72] That's just how it goes, but we played better than most will give us credit for, especially as our confidence grew in the second half. This result just goes to show that anything can happen on any given day in a cup competition."

So what of Dunny the midfielder? "I should've played midfield my whole life," he said. "I don't have to chase really fast guys all night long. But the truth is that by the 65th minute, I was ready to die, especially playing on wet turf. My back hurt, the hip flexor was acting up, and I didn't even want to think about overtime."

But thanks to Earl Alexander's stoppage-time heroics, Hollywood United did not need overtime to set up their June 24 showdown with the

---

[70] Later confirmed.

[71] My dad, a factory worker, called Koubouras his hero after I told him the story.

[72] Dunny points out one of my favorite myths, as it accentuates the upsets in favor of the broader reality. From 1996-2008, MLS and USL1 teams have met 102 times in the U.S. Open Cup. The MLS teams, despite rolling out reserve lineups in most cases, hold a decisive 70-32 edge in advancement.

Seattle Sounders. "We've got two weeks to recover and get ready," said Dunny. "We know it's going to be even harder against Seattle, but anything is possible. We are a team without a fan base, so hopefully we'll pick up some underground support along the way. Every little bit helps."

Now that the Crew are out, count me in.

Questions? Comments? Think that only Moffat can hit Moffat Rockets, and therefore I should have called Jed's shot a Zayner Zoomer or something? Feel free to write at sirk65@yahoo.com

Nas Koubouras (center) battles with Portland's Chris Brown during Hollywood United's stunning Open Cup upset of the Portland Timbers. Nas would blow out his knee later in the game, catch a red-eye flight back to LA, then report to his construction welding job first thing in the morning. Such is the glory of the Open Cup. (Photo by Allison Andrews / SoccerCityUSA.com)

U.S. Open Cup: Chicago 3, Crew 2 (OT)

Match date: Wednesday, June 11, 2008

Venue: Shea Stadium at Bradley University (Peoria, Illinois)

Scoring:

10: CHI King (unassisted)

63: CLB Ekpo (Gaven)

65: CHI Herron (Mapp, Plotkin)

67: CLB Garey (Zayner, Rogers)

116: CHI Herron (penalty kick)

Attendance: 3,829

RETROACTIVE RECAP

The Crew faced Chicago in the U.S. Open Cup for the third time ever, and for the third time, they lost in overtime. This latest overtime loss came when William Hesmer was called for bringing ex-Crew elbow specialist Andy Herron down in the box. Herron then converted the winner.

There was next to nothing written about this game, and I think I followed it via a thread on Big Soccer or by refreshing the scoreboard on USOpenCup.com or some other non-sensory means.

That being the case, I don't have much to add except for some tidbits that the Crew's PR staff passed along at the time. For example, the goal was Ekpo's first goal in a Crew kit. And Jason Garey's goal was his first with the first team in 2008, and it came one minute after he entered the game as a sub. And, hey, that crowd of 3,829 was the biggest crowd to ever pack Shea Stadium. (The one in Peoria, not the one in Queens.)

SOOPER DOOPER INTERESTING FACTOID OF MY OWN

Brian Plotkin, who would be signed by the Crew in August, assisted on Chicago's second goal. Plotkin would be a member of the Crew all the way through their MLS Cup run, but he would never enter a competitive match. That means that Brian Plotkin is, and always will be, a Massive Champion, yet his lone game day on-field contribution to the Crew's 2008 season was to help eliminate Columbus from the U.S. Open Cup. How effed up is that?

Yet maybe the clearing of the Crew's schedule was a vital component of their Shield and Cup runs. So maybe by hurting the Crew, he helped the Crew, and therefore eventually helped himself to a championship. I smell a conspiracy—a delightful conspiracy, but a conspiracy nonetheless. Let's call it Plotkin's Plot.

Road Work: Crew 3, Kansas City 0

Match date: Saturday, June 14, 2008
Scoring:
3: CLB Marshall 1 (Schelotto 6)
21: CLB Moreno 5 (O'Rourke 2)
67: CLB Moreno 6 (unassisted)
Attendance: 10,385
Crew's record afterward: 7-4-1

RETROACTIVE RECAP

Picking up from the mid-week Open Cup revival of the offense, the Crew torched Kansas City for three goals. Chad Marshall headed home a Schelotto corner kick in the 3rd minute for his first goal of the year, and Alejandro Moreno continued his torrid scoring pace by notching his fifth and sixth tallies. The first was a looping shot over an out of position Kevin Hartman, while the second was a hammered half-volley that beat Hartman to the near post.

The game featured many notable lineup events. Duncan Oughton made his first league start of 2008, while Jason Garey saw his first league action as a second half sub. Even more notably, rookie Andy Iro and second-year man Ryan Junge earned their first career MLS starts, while rookie midfielder Cory Elenio made his MLS debut when he replaced Emmanuel Ekpo in the 81st minute.

QUOTES

Alejandro Moreno: "I think we believe in what we're doing a little bit more. I think we're a little more consistent in the way we are playing. We're more organized in the back. The team believes we are capable of getting results whether it is at home or on the road. It's good to start out the season the way we did. It gave us confidence. We hit a patch there that last month or so, but we're back on it with a good result tonight. I'm looking forward to next week."

Road Work: Crew 3, Los Angeles 3

Match date: Saturday, June 21, 2008
Scoring:
4: LA Donovan 10 (unassisted)
47: LA Buddle 9 (Randolph 3)
67: CLB Evans 2 (unassisted)
71: CLB Schelotto 2 (penalty kick)
83: LA Donovan 11 (penalty kick)
88: CLB Lenhart 1 (unassisted)
Attendance: 27,000
Crew's record afterward: 7-4-2

RETROACTIVE RECAP

In retrospect, this game mentally forged a lot of what this Crew team was to be the rest of the way. After giving up goals in the opening minutes of each half, the Crew rallied to tie the game. When the referee made the unconscionable decision to call Danny O'Rourke for a phantom penalty on a preposterous David Beckham flop,[73] the Crew fell behind 3-2 in the 83rd minute.

Steven Lenhart, however, was about to start making a name for himself, and that name would be "The Equalizer." When LA goalkeeper Joe Cronin fumbled a Frankie Hejduk shot in the 88th minute, Lenhart dropped to the ground and knocked in the rebound, giving the Crew an improbable point.

In a perfect capper to the night, the Soccer Gods exacted revenge on Beckham for his earlier flop. In the closing moments, he had a clear shot at the winner from close range. It looked to be a certain goal, but Beckham sent his shot into orbit. Afterward, he concluded that the only explanation was that the grass must have given way a little bit. "To hit it so far off from that distance, something must have happened." Yeah, and that something is called karma.

QUOTES

Sigi Schmid: "I was proud of our team that we came back being two-nothing down, especially the way we gave up the goals. Psychologically, those are tough blows, but we were able to come back. Overall, I was very proud with our effort and our ability to come back."

---

[73] This prompted Merz to joke to me, "Beckham flopped worse than his wife's acting career."

Sirk's Notebook: Crew 2, Colorado 1

Match date: Saturday, June 28, 2008
Scoring:
53: CLB Schelotto 3 (penalty kick)
60: COL LaBrocca 2 (Casey 1)
70: CLB Ekpo 1 (unassisted)
Attendance: 12,254
Crew's record afterward: 8-4-2

What's the opposite of the June Swoon Monsoon? The June Boon Typhoon? Whatever it is, the Crew have used it to erase any premature doubt and apprehension about this enjoyable season. We have now seen this team walk across the hot coals of a cold streak, only to safely arrive at the other end of the mixed metaphor.

On Saturday night, in front 12,253 mortals and one Brad Friedel, the Crew capped a stellar month with a 2-1 victory over the Colorado Rapids. What an amazing turnaround. Just three weeks earlier, the Crew were mired in a scoreless drought and had dropped a home decision to an expansion team. It seemed like a distant memory on Saturday. Once the final whistle blew, Frankie Hejduk flexed in front of the Nordecke and celebrated with supporters there. Fans crowded around the tunnel to give the team one last round of applause as the guys exited the field. The lines at Autograph Alley extended beyond the length of the tent. Everywhere I looked, everybody was smiling.

More than an hour after the game had ended, I was talking with Dr. Johnson, one of the Crew's team physicians. Over his shoulder, I could see Friedel honoring every last autograph and photo request from his fellow Crew fans. Over my shoulder, Dr. J could see current Crew players laughing and conversing with supporters.

"If you write about nothing else," said Dr. J, "make sure you mention how much FUN it was tonight."

Confidence

I don't know how this season will end up, of course, but in the past few weeks, I have been thinking about the confidence and mental toughness this team possesses. Whether it's Danny O'Rourke shrugging off his penalty troubles, or Frankie Hejduk sucking it up and flying around the world to play six games in 16 days, or Alejandro Moreno's dogged and determined play,

136

there seems to be a common thread running through this team. These guys believe in themselves, they believe in each other, and they refuse to back down.

As I watched the Crew go on the road to demolish Kansas City and then overcome separate two-goal and one-goal deficits to earn a draw in L.A., I kept going back to my conversation with Robbie Rogers after the loss to San Jose. The Crew were in a four-game winless streak, a four-game scoring drought, and Robbie had been hacked to pieces during that stretch. As I sat next to Robbie and his visibly battered shins, he was irritated, but resolute. He told me that the team is getting chances and will score goals, so the scoreless drought was just something for the media to make a big deal about even though he wasn't worried. He assured me that the winless streak was just a cold stretch that all teams go through, but a good team like the Crew will snap out of it quickly before it spirals out of control. And as for the hacking, he promised he was going to figure something out and was going to run even faster so people couldn't kick him anymore.

I didn't know if it was the brash exuberance of youth, or if the wisdom of older players like Hejduk and Moreno had rubbed off on him. Or both. But what struck me was how much he meant the words coming out of his mouth. He wasn't just parroting platitudes, Nuke LaLoosh-style.[74]

I didn't get a chance to talk to Robbie after he finished carving up the Colorado defense on Saturday, although he certainly deserved a shot at an I-told-you-so. But I did briefly relay the story of that June 7 conversation to Hejduk, the team's captain.

Frankie cracked a smile. "We've scored eight goals in the three games since then."

Hejduk reaffirmed that there was never any crisis of confidence in the Crew locker room. Not only did they take care of business on the road, but they knew they would get back on track at home as well. "We knew before we took the field tonight that we were going to win this game," he explained. "I know that's how I personally felt, and I think a lot of guys in the locker room felt the same way. We felt this was the game to get our home streak going again."

And whether it's falling behind in Los Angeles, or coughing up an equalizer at home to Colorado, Hejduk says the team is quick to shake off setbacks while getting back to the task at hand. "Last year, we would give up a

---

[74] One of the many great scenes in Bull Durham is when Crash Davis gives Nuke LaLoosh a tutorial on bland sports clichés.

goal and hang our heads and think 'here we go again.' This year, it's almost a wake-up call. It's more like, 'Come on, what are we doing? Let's go get this back.' When the whole team has that belief, not just one or two guys, but when everyone has that look in their eyes, it usually happens. It's a testament to how we have played all year. None of this would have happened last year."

The more I think about this team, and the more I contemplate the men who comprise it, the more I am convinced that Crew fans are in good hands. Win or lose, this is a good bunch that will work to do you proud. [75]

Go Go Ekpo!

As for "getting it back," Emmanuel Ekpo gave the entire stadium a jolt in the 70th minute when he scored a breathtaking game-winning goal. After flipping a header over the defender on his back while on his own side of midfield, Ekpo spun around and raced 50 yards with the ball at his feet, all while surrounded by five Colorado defenders. The defense seemed content to let him dribble, so dribble he did. Once he got within 20 yards of the goal, Ekpo uncorked a worm-burner to the far side netting. It was a stunning strike to cap a stunning run – the ol' Run & Stun.

"That goal was outstanding," said Schmid. "That has to be a goal of the week candidate."

Even Ekpo couldn't hide his enthusiasm. "Yeah, it was a nice goal," he conceded with a smile. "I thought that maybe I should try something this time. I tried to pass in those situations before, but this time I had a couple of touches and they gave me room to shoot, so I thought why not? And now it will give me the confidence next time."

Schmid feels that with that confidence, the best is yet to come for the young Nigerian. "You have to remember that he's only played about 300 MLS minutes," said Schmid, who came within 18 minutes of pegging Ekpo's actual total of 318. "As he plays more and more, he'll get a better and better at playing on the outside. It's a new position for him, but he's getting comfortable out there, even though he's still learning when to tuck in defensively and things like that. But tonight he showed that there's a specialness about him – that he has a special quality – and that's why we want to get him on the field."

---

[75] Really, this group was so special that even an idiot like me, as far back as June, could pick up on the idea that they were something else.

Emmanuel Ekpo on the ball against the Colorado Rapids on June 28, 2008.
(Photo by Greg Bartram / Columbus Crew)

Save of the Game

Crew goalkeeper William Hesmer saved his best for last. A series of deflections near the edge of the Crew box put the ball at the feet of Colorado's Colin Clark, whose ensuing shot was also deflected. Hesmer went low to his right, and was able to tip the ball just enough so that it caught the outside of the post and rolled out of play, preserving the Crew's three points.

"That was one of those where the ball was bouncing around and I didn't know which way it would ultimately go," said Hesmer. "When I dove for it, I honestly thought it was destined for the side netting, but luckily I was able to get a fingernail on it."

The Twin Towers

Sigi unveiled a new defensive alignment for the Rapids game. He paired rookie Andy Iro with Chad Marshall in the middle of the defense, while moving Danny O'Rourke to left back. As a result, the Crew had 12 feet, 9 inches of unfriendly persuasion patrolling the box, while O'Rourke and Hejduk hassled Rapids on the flanks.

"We knew…well, we didn't know for sure because you never know for sure until the game gets played…but we figured Terry Cooke was probably going to start, and that would mean a lot of crosses since that his is forte," said Schmid. "And then Colin Clark on the other side hits a lot of crosses. When you look at their attack, it was crosses, free kicks into the box, and long throw-ins. So having those two guys in the middle helped us win a lot of headers. Then late, we went with five in the back and put Danny in between those two guys to clean up anything that came in over the top."

O'Rourke didn't mind the transition to left back at all. "Sigi wanted Andy and Chad in the middle for the crosses, and he wanted me to go outside to try to shut down Cooke," said O'Rourke. "I thought it was an excellent game plan and it panned out. I'll play anywhere if it helps the team. I played left back a couple of games last year. It's different, but I think Robbie (Rogers) and I have good chemistry out there."

And while it's not exactly a Wayne Gretzky-Dave Semenko [76] situation, I kind of liked the idea of having O'Rourke playing behind the speedy kid with the bull's-eyes on the front of his socks. His presence alone ought to give pause to Robbie's would-be shin-kickers.

No All-Star Coaching for Sigi

Despite the Crew's victory, it wasn't enough to give Schmid the reigns to the MLS All-Star team. New England defeated Toronto on Saturday, giving the honor to Revs coach Steve Nicol.

"Like I have said a couple of times, sort of tongue-in-cheek, the last time I coached the All-Star Game, I got fired," said Schmid. "Hopefully (not coaching the All-Stars) will keep me here through the end of August. I have no problem with it. Stevie Nicol's wife can spend the bonus money, and hopefully she'll buy Stevie something with it. He could use a new coat and tie. Or maybe a new cell phone with a different ring."

That Was....Weird

I have been to hundreds of press conferences in my life. Several of them featured the mad ramblings of Ray Hudson. But I'm not sure I've encountered anything as perplexing as Rapids coach Fernando Clavijo's response to a question about the repeated cramping of his team's goalkeeper, Bouna Coundoul.

"He was cramping up," said Clavijo. "Bouna was called up [to Senegal's national team] and was away for a month in Africa. He didn't play,

---

[76] Semenko was the baddest of all of Gretzky's enforcers. To paraphrase an old Monty Python skit, I've seen grown men pull off their own heads rather than fight Dave Semenko.

and really, we don't even know if he trained or not. We have no idea. It's one of those things we have to endure and suffer. We don't know what players do when they go away. So yeah, he was cramping. There's not much else to say there."

Obviously. After suggesting that Coundoul's cramping was the result of some sort of classified couch-napping vacation to Senegal, what else is there to say?

Well, except for, "Bouna, I see you didn't play when you were called up, but tell me about the training that you did while you were away." I'm no expert, but such an unconventional approach might eliminate some of the mystery that the Rapids have had to suffer and endure.

The Return of Craig Merz

In case anyone has missed it,[77] former Columbus Dispatch soccer beat writer Craig Merz has been hired by MLSnet.com to be the Crew's beat writer. Anyone who regularly visits TheCrew.com has surely noticed that Craig has been pumping out about four stories per week over the last few weeks. ("I will run out of ideas by August 7," he assured me, so read him while he's hot!)

Craig's return is another great development on the media front over the last year. After Chris DeVille was granted space for a weekly Crew column in Columbus Alive midway through last season, Shawn Mitchell was given a Dispatch blog to supplement his newspaper coverage, and now Merz is banging out stories left and right for MLSnet. That's not even mentioning the various fan sites and blogs that have sprouted from the resurgent supporters section. All in all, it's been a banner year for those who wish to read about the Columbus Crew.

Stats of the Night

* Emmanuel Ekpo's game-winning goal means six different players have scored game-winning goals for the Crew this year. (Stat courtesy of the Columbus Crew.)

* Ever since I blamed Craig Merz for the home loss to San Jose, the Crew are 2-0-1 despite Craig's almost daily presence. (Stat courtesy of Craig Merz.)

---

[77] I remember broadcaster Dwight Burgess being one of those who missed it. His explanation? "I already know everything, so why would I bother going online to see what either of you two have to say?"

Sooper Dooper Exclusive Adam Moffat Interview About Cornhole

Speaking of Chris DeVille, I just had to follow up on another nugget that he unearthed. In this week's story about Steven Lenhart, DeVille casually mentioned that Lenhart and Adam Moffat are the Crew's undefeated cornhole champions. (For those reading from areas outside of Ohio, cornhole is a popular tailgating game whereby the participants attempt to toss beanbags through a hole cut out of a board that sits on the ground. Any bag through the hole is worth three points, and any bag that lands on the board without going in the hole is worth one point.)

So DeVille threw this interesting tidbit out there, but I wanted to know more. To that end, I conducted the following world exclusive interview with champion beanbag tosser Adam Moffat.

SS: I understand that you and Lenhart are the Crew's cornhole champions.

AM: Cornhole is a great game. Super game. One day I plan on becoming a professional cornhole player.

SS: There's a professional cornhole league?

AM: They don't have a professional league yet, but I am going to start it. I'll found it.

SS: How's the ACL holding up while you play?

AM: It's good rehab for my knee. I recommend it. I get to bend my knee. The bag's a light weight. It's perfect.

SS: They don't have cornhole in Scotland, do they?

AM: No. I never heard of cornhole until I came here.

SS: But it makes sense that you are good, since Scotland invented another game where you have put an object through a hole in the ground.

AM: That's true. You're right. It's built in.

SS: In this room, who could challenge the Lenhart-Moffat team for your crown?

AM: Robbie Rogers and Brad Evans are close, but they're not there yet.

SS: And who's the worst? Who do you guys dominate?

AM: The worst players are George Josten and Ryan Miller. We demolish them. Comfortably.

Annoyed by the Lack of Annoyance

In the days leading up to Saturday's game, I struggled to identify any personal emotion toward the Colorado Rapids other than utter apathy. They are a Charter Member of Major League Soccer, yet to me, they are the blandest, most nondescript franchise in league history. They haven't won anything of importance. They've never had much in the way of heroes or villains. Heck, they don't even have easily identifiable colors. In the span of 12 years, they have gone from green & gold to green & black to black & blue to burgundy & sky blue.

Living in Columbus, it's even worse, since they only play the Crew two uneventful times per year. Apparently the Rapids have gone 14-7-7 all-time against the Crew, and I never even noticed.

When I think of the Colorado Rapids, these are about the only things that immediately come to mind:

    * Marcelo Balboa's incredible bicycle kick at Crew Stadium.

    * That bomb of a goal that Mike Lapper scored at Mile High Stadium on July 4, 1999.

    * The Crew once beat them in a season opener when Mike Clark, of all people, scored the winning goal in the farcical shootout.

I ran my list by Merz in the press box, and he was pretty sure that there was one time where the Rapids won in overtime to keep the Crew from having a shot at the playoffs. As he remembered it, a Rapids tie or loss would have given the Crew a chance to take the last playoff spot the next day. Instead, Paul Bravo scored in overtime to eliminate the Crew on the season's penultimate day. Then we cracked open the Rapids media guide and verified that Craig was spot on. It was back in 2000. The Crew lost to Chicago the next day anyway. But technically, the Rapids broke the Crew's hearts once upon a time, but they are so bland that I didn't even remember.

After a little more thinking, I also remembered that the 1997 Rapids were the second-worst MLS Cup finalist ever, that the Crew won the Supporters' Shield in Denver in 2004, and that Colorado choked in Crew Stadium during the 1999 U.S. Open Cup final, providing me with the career highlight of listening to Doug Miller claim that the '99 Rochester Rhinos were "The Team of the Century." [78]

The Rapids haven't even had many notable or identifiable players—players that you hear their name and immediately think "Colorado Rapids." The club's all-time appearance and minutes leader is Chris Henderson, who was a very good player and an exceptionally nice guy, but when I think of Henderson, I immediately think of his great season with the 2000 MLS Cup champion Kansas City Wizards. The two most identifiable Rapids are Pablo Mastroeni and Marcelo Balboa, a defensive midfielder and a center back, respectively. They are/were U.S. National Team stalwarts, but they aren't exactly headline-grabbers.

I quizzed Merz to see if he could name the Rapids' all-time leading goal scorer. After hemming and hawing, Merz finally spit out a name. "Paul Bravo?" he asked, probably since Bravo's name was in his head from our conversation moments earlier.

We grabbed the media guide. Yup. Paul Bravo. With 39 goals. In 135 games. Dazzling stuff.

Stern John scored 44 goals in just 55 games in a Crew kit. In addition to John, Edson Buddle had 42 goals, while Brian McBride and Jeff Cunningham obliterated Bravo's mark with 62 goals apiece.

In fact, Bravo's club-leading 39 goals are dead last amongst MLS clubs founded in 1990s. The only other club whose career leading scorer has a total fewer than 60 goals is New York, who are led by Giovanni Savarese's 41 tallies. (But New York is not a team I struggle to hate, so who cares.)

On the other end of the field, the Rapids' all-time leader in most goalkeeping statistics is Joe Cannon, who most everyone associates with the San Jose Earthquakes.

It just blows my mind that in the 13th season of MLS, I still cannot find anything to make me care about the Rapids one way or the other except for the 180 minutes per season that they are the Crew's anonymous opponent. The only other team that is even in the same ballpark, apathy-wise,

---

[78] I still remember telling Burgess that the next day, and he replied, "What color is the sky in Doug's world?"

is Real Salt Lake, but they are only three years old. And I at least hate their ridiculous name.

All this got me to wondering if *anybody* feels emotion about the Rapids. Five minutes of research reminded me that the Rapids have won all our playoff match-ups against FC Dallas, even though the Hoops were the favored team each time.

I e-mailed Buzz Carrick, proprietor of the excellent independent FC Dallas site 3rdDegree.net, and told him of my Rapids-related apathy and wanted to know his thoughts.

"I'd love to help," he wrote back, "but I don't care about them either."

In fairness, Buzz did go on to say that many Dallas fans do indeed hate Colorado, and suggested that I search the BigSoccer archives to read the message board posts following the 2005 and 2006 playoff fiascos.

Here is an excerpt from a sample post from the 2006 elimination, which featured some severe crowd taunting from Colorado that ended with Dallas goalkeeper Dario Sala decking Colorado's Hunter Freeman.... "I'm just so beyond upset and so beyond angry that I'm ready to just lock myself in my room for days on end. (Bleep) Clarke, (bleep) this team, (bleep) Abbey, (bleep) Clarke, (bleep) MLS, and (bleep) Clarke, but especially (bleep) Colorado. You stupid pieces of cheating, diving, ugly (jerks). It wasn't enough that somehow you got our number, you have to come taunt us after the game and flick us off and everything else. My heart goes to Sala, he layed one of you (jerks) out on your (butt). You don't (make wee-wee) on someone when they're down."

On second thought, after looking at the alternative, maybe Rapids-apathy isn't such a bad thing after all.

U.S. Open Cup Update

The second round was not kind to my adopted team, Hollywood United FC. Two weeks after stunning the Portland Timbers in the Rose City, HUFC's underdog roster traveled to Seattle, where they were summarily thumped 6-0 by the Sounders.

Notebook Hall of Famer Brian Dunseth, the ex-MLSer in the middle of an amateur lineup, offered his summary of the match. "We got beat by a Seattle Sounders team that was well prepared and outclassed us pure and simple," he said. "It's unfortunate, as this group of players is better than what they showed, but all credit to Seattle as they thoroughly deserved the win. We just couldn't overcome the loss of our center back, Nas Koubouras, and our starting forward, Matt Taylor, who had taken off for Australia for a trial with Sydney FC."

If you'll recall from the last notebook, Koubouras injured his knee in the upset of Portland, caught a red-eye flight home after the game, and then reported to work at 8 a.m. for his job as a construction welder. As a follow-up note to that item, making the story all the more incredible, Koubouras received confirmation a few days later that he had suffered both a torn ACL and MCL. (Maybe he will play cornhole as part of his rehab.)

So with Hollywood United joining the Crew on the Open Cup sidelines, I need a new team to root for. There are two logical bandwagons for Crew fans to hop aboard, and I am hopping aboard both.

The first obvious candidate is my hometown team, the Cleveland City Stars. Who better to ask about the City Stars than their most famous alum, Adam Moffat? During a break from figuring out how to pay himself for playing in his own professional cornhole league, Moffat offered his reasons why Crew fans should get behind the City Stars.

"The Cleveland City Stars are the team to watch out for," he said. "They are from Ohio, so that's good. They've got a good fan base. The Green Army is the supporters group, and they're a bit crazy. And Cleveland is playing the Chicago Fire, who knocked us out, so there's a bit of revenge there."

Sounds good to me. What soccer fan in Columbus can't identify with revenge on the Chicago Fire?

The other obvious bandwagon candidate is the Charleston Battery, who also wear black & gold, also opened a soccer-specific stadium in 1999 and currently employ one of the nicest players to ever wear a Crew kit, Nelson Akwari. How can anyone not cheer for Nelly?

I sent Nelson an e-mail asking for him to make the case for Crew fans hopping aboard the Battery bandwagon, and he replied with this list of bullet points:

* "I get to wear the black and gold, and when people see pictures of our stadium or me playing, they ask if I'm playing for the Crew again or if I am at Crew Stadium."

* "My wife and I met while I was playing for the Crew....this should get the 'girl support,' or at least that's what my wife says because girls like romantic stories."

* "My wife's family and my cousins live there, so I still come to visit Columbus all the time and I miss it!"

* "The fans here LOVE and support the Battery, just like the Crew fans, even during HORRIBLE weather."

* "Have you seen our pub?? It's an amazing gallery of pictures, jerseys, and sports memorabilia."

* "One of our players, Stephen Armstrong, briefly played for the Crew, and has been down here for a few years now."

* "Our assistant coach, Mark Watson, is also a former Crew player."

* "When the Crew supporters watch us play, they'll see a bunch of black guys with bald heads…it'll feel just like they're supporting Ezra Hendrickson." [79]

* "I'm the captain of the team, and I want your support!!"

From the fact that the team has two ex-Crew players, is assistant coached by a Crew original and the scorer of the first own-goal in Crew history, and is also carrying on the long Columbus Crew tradition of playing bald black guys, Nelly has made many compelling arguments.

I look forward to both Charleston and Cleveland advancing until they eventually meet in the semifinal or final, at which time I will make Nelly and Moffat engage in a public debate in an effort to sway our affection toward one team or the other.

Nesta

Nesta Hejduk, Frankie's 10-year-old son, was hanging out in the locker room as Merz and I talked to his dad. As Frankie spoke about how the Crew knew they were going to win this game, Merz jokingly turned to Nesta and asked if he felt the same way.

"Definitely," said Nesta. "Every time. Every time I come here."

Frankie busted up laughing. "Dudes, this is on the record!"

"Like, last year," Nesta continued, "they lost every game, but when I came, they won every game."

"That's true," Frankie added. "We got hot last summer."

Emboldened, Nesta went on. "They have never lost a game when I am here."

Frankie couldn't let that one slide. "His nose is growing bigger! Pinocchio!"

At that point, Danny O'Rourke, who had been listening from a few lockers over, deftly slipped into his role as the ever-agitating big brother. He

---

[79] This still cracks me up. It's even funnier since Nelly was called "Dante Jr." when he and fellow bald black guy Dante Washington were on the Crew together.

grabbed Nesta by the arm and said, "Does that mean if we lose, you will go home?"

Nesta, being a Hejduk, refused to back down. He responded with a furious assault on O'Rourke that could only be halted by the threat of Danny's secret big brother weapon – the dreaded Indian burn.

Questions? Comments? Stick around to watch The Goonies? Feel free to write at sirk65@yahoo.com

A pumped-up Frankie Hejduk flexes with the Nordecke after the Crew's 2-1 victory over the Colorado Rapids on June 28, 2008. (Photo by Sam Fahmi)

Sirk's Notebook: Crew 2, Chicago 2

Match date: Saturday, July 5, 2008

Scoring:

8: CHI Rolfe 3 (unassisted)

25: CHI Carr 2 (Segares 1, Rolfe 3)

36: CLB Ekpo 2 (Schelotto 7)

87: CLB Lenhart 2 (Schelotto 8)

Attendance: 17,172

Crew's record afterward: 8-4-2

How do the Crew do the voodoo that the Crew do so well? No clue, dude. But Crew voodoo turned deep doo-doo into a 2-2 "woo hoo!" against the loathsome Chicago Fire on Saturday night at Crew Stadium. [80]

Twenty-five minutes into the game, with the Crew trailing 2-0, I was already trying to imagine cheesy holiday-themed newspaper headlines (e.g. "Fire Works Crew At Stadium"). Ninety minutes into the game, I was standing above the stage, all my thoughts drowned out by the jet-engine roar of the Nordecke, as everyone on the railing twitched with anticipation of a seemingly imminent Columbus game-winner. What a night.

On the whole, the Crew's performance may not have been a work of art, but it was definitely a work of heart. At this point, it would be foolish to expect anything else.

"You wish to have a team like this that will fight until the end," said Crew assistant-turned-head-coach-for-a-day Robert Warzycha. (Head coach Sigi Schmid was in Los Angeles for his daughter's wedding.) "If you give up after the first 15 minutes, then why even be here? We've tried to get a group of guys who fight until the end and I think today was a very exciting game."

Bad Start

The Crew fell behind early when Chris Rolfe converted a rebound in the 8th minute, snapping Chicago's 341-minute scoring drought in league play. The Fire doubled their advantage in the 25th minute when Calen Carr

---

[80] Crew communications coordinator Jason Smith would later point out that this was, like, my third rhyming Notebook opening in a row, following the June Swoon Monsoon on the June Boon Typhoon. This one was way more preposterous, and it every much felt like a goofy Jim Ingraham tribute. I cannot emphasize enough how much his Indians coverage imprinted itself on my young mind.

capped a nice Chicago counterattack with a sliding finish from the middle of the Crew's box.

"To be honest with you, I wasn't worried," said the unflappable Warzycha. "Chicago came out flying and the two goals they scored were pretty good. They caught us on the counterattack. With Rolfe and Carr, who are so fast, they did good. But I wasn't worried, to be honest with you.[81] I knew we were going to score goals."

When asked if the early deficit was the result of poor Crew defending or excellent Chicago attacking, Warzycha split the difference. "In soccer, it is always a combination of things," he said, "but those were good counterattacks by Chicago. As I said, they came out flying."

The Comeback Begins

The Crew started their comeback in the 36th minute. After Bakary Soumare dispossessed Alejandro Moreno at the edge of the box, Moreno battled long enough to give Guillermo Barros Schelotto time to enter the fray. Schelotto picked Soumare's pocket, then quickly played a low cross into the box that was redirected into the net by a streaking Emmanuel Ekpo.

Fire coach Denis Hamlett thought that play was the turning point. "We had a very good start to the game," he said, "but I think giving up that first goal off our mistake gave them life when we had control of the game."

Steven "The Equalizer" Lenhart

With the Crew trailing late, Warzycha made some moves to bolster the offense. The most notable was the 77th minute pulling of defender Andy Iro in favor of forward Steven Lenhart.

"I knew the guys in the back were going to do their job and not allow any more goals. To be honest, it wasn't much of a gamble," Warzycha explained. "(Lenhart's) the type of player who can change a game for you. As a coach, when you're 2-1 down, you have to decide on Steven Lenhart or Jason Garey. I decided on Lenhart, and sometimes you're right."

Lenhart, who tallied the 88th-minute equalizer at Los Angeles two weeks ago, made a genius out of Warzycha by netting the 87th-minute equalizer against the Fire, bouncing home a cross from Schelotto. The ball literally bounced off of Lenhart and went into the net.

---

[81] To be honest with you, Robert is always very honest with you.

Lenhart was equal parts giddy and goofy when asked about his late-game heroics.[82] "I just ran into the ball," he said. "I have no idea what happened. My eyes were closed. I ran to the far post and Guillermo put it there. I got lucky. The ball was as good as it could have been."

He shrugged off his knack for scoring big goals in the waning moments of matches. "I feel great, but that's soccer," he said. "I'm happy any time I can help the team, but someone else scored the first goal, you know?"

Since Lenhart was reluctant to toot his own horn, we'll let his captain do it for him. "Steve did well to battle in the box again," said Frankie Hejduk. "He's a beast in there, and he makes it tough for defenders. He's in the right spot at the right time, and that's what a forward does. He's hot right now, so he gets in the right area and the ball is coming to him."

A freshly-shorn Steven Lenhart (center) celebrates his 87th minute equalizer with Robbie Rogers, Emmanuel Ekpo, and members of the Nordecke. (Photo by Sam Fahmi.)

Frankie on the Two-Goal Comeback

Hejduk shared his thoughts on the Crew's two-goal rally. "The first 20 minutes killed us, and then we had to chase the game," he said. "Having said that, we chased it pretty well. We created a lot of chances. It was a strange game in that it felt like there was no midfield for either team. It was

---

[82] Actually, Steven is almost always equal parts giddy and goofy. The guy radiates a joy for life.

back and forth, back and forth. I thought we played well enough in the end to win the game, but Chicago did well with what they had to do too. They are a thorn in our side. They made it difficult for us, but we did well by battling back and not giving up. We easily could have lost this game 2-1 if we didn't believe in each other."

Hamlett on the Loss. I Mean Tie.

"It's disappointing," said first-year Fire coach Denis Hamlett. "It feels like a loss, but there were some positives. We haven't been scoring goals, and we got two goals tonight. We got a point, but we're pissed off because we thought we had three points in the bag and we let it slip away tonight."

Loud Crowd

The combination of the Crew's good play, the hated Fire, Mexican star Cuauhtemoc Blanco and a beautiful night contributed to the largest crowd of the season at 17,172. Not only was it a large crowd, but it was passionate. The Fire fans did their thing in the south end of the stadium, but unlike years past, when the Chicagoans dominated the proceedings, the Nordecke drowned them out from the northeast corner. It was an exciting game for both sets of fans, giving everyone a reason to go at it in full voice.

The action in the stands did not go unnoticed by the participants. "It's always fun playing Columbus because our fans come down and it makes for a good atmosphere," said Hamlett. "It was a good game and a good crowd."

"You can't ask for anything more," said Hejduk. "We're in Columbus, it's against the Fire, and it's the day after the Fourth. It was awesome. Both teams' fans were into it and were singing the whole time. It would have been more of a storybook ending if we could have sent all those people home with a win, but the fans never gave up on us, and it keeps us motivated because we don't want to let them down."

Rolfe Rules Crew Stadium

Fire forward Chris Rolfe played his college ball for the Dayton Flyers after growing up in the Dayton suburb of Kettering. Although it's an hour east from his true hometown, Columbus Crew Stadium has been Rolfe's personal playground as a professional. Rolfe's goal in the 8th minute was his fifth goal in just six career matches at Crew Stadium. He's been consistent, too, scoring in four of those six games.

"Whenever you come home, I think there's some extra incentive," said Fire coach Denis Hamlett. "He's from this area and I think he wants to play well in front of his friends and family."

Rolfe confirmed his coach's comments. "It always feels good to get a goal, especially in front of my friends and family here at home."

For those who like to extrapolate statistics just to make your teeth hurt, Rolfe's career pace at Crew Stadium is the equivalent of a 25-goal season. That's Stern John territory.[83]

At one point a year or so ago, my good buddy Flick, in an effort to simultaneously boost his Flyer pride and Crew loathing, conducted research that revealed that at that time, no active Crew player had scored more career goals at Crew Stadium than Chris Rolfe had for the Fire. If I recall, Eddie Gaven was tied with Rolfe at four Crew Stadium goals, with at least one of Gaven's tallies coming when he was with the MetroStars.

Thankfully that's one stat that's in the past. Without doing too much research and/or compiling a thorough list, since all I want is a single exception to knock Rolfe off the top spot and to make everyone (especially Flick) feel better, I can verify that Alejandro Moreno has six goals at Crew Stadium as a member of the Crew, not even digging into his pre-Columbus past. And best of all, Moreno's got time to pad his lead since Rolfe isn't scheduled to score again at Crew Stadium until next year. [84]

Robbie's Chance to Say "I Told You So"

Since I didn't catch up with Robbie Rogers for last week's Notebook, I made a point to visit with him Saturday. I rehashed our conversation from after the San Jose game, when he very convincingly stated his case that the Crew would score goals and turn their slide around. Credit where credit is due, he was right. The Crew have gone 2-0-2 in league play since that conversation, scoring 10 goals in those four matches.

I gave Robbie his shot for an I-told-you-so, but he kindly declined, instead opting to reiterate his belief in the Crew.

"Well, I have a lot of confidence in this team, and we all have confidence in each other," he said. "I knew the media – no offense [85] – was

---

[83] As many of you know, Stern John holds the Crew's single-season goal scoring record with 26 tallies in 1998, which was one goal short of Roy Lassiter's league record.

[84] Although it wasn't scheduled, Rolfe would come back to Crew Stadium later in the year for the Eastern Conference final. He would not score.

[85] None taken.

going to make a big deal out of that scoreless stretch, but we had scored goals in Open Cup games and I knew we have guys that can put the ball in the back of the net. We knew we were going to turn it around. We didn't stop believing in each other."

Robbie said that belief came in handy in Saturday's comeback against Chicago. "After we got that first goal, it was like we knew we could do this and we didn't panic," he said. "We eventually tied it up and had even more chances at the end. We wanted that third goal, but that's the way it goes."

The Importance of the Regular Season

At 8-4-3, the Crew have reached the midpoint of their schedule while locked into second place in both the Eastern Conference and the overall league table. They trail first-place New England by six points, but control their own destiny in terms of making up that ground since they have two games in hand.

It has been a popular theory amongst soccer traditionalists that the regular season does not matter in Major League Soccer because of the existence of playoffs. The argument is that as long as you sneak into the playoffs, you can get hot for four weeks and walk away with the trophy, rendering the games in June and July meaningless.

It would be a fantastic theory if 12 years of MLS history didn't say otherwise. For example, 22 of the 24 MLS Cup finalists have finished first or second in their conference. The two exceptions were both fourth-place finishers—the 1997 Colorado Rapids and the 2005 Los Angeles Galaxy. That's it. Two squeaker-inners[86] out of 24 finalists.

Of the 12 MLS Cup champions, 11 of them finished first or second in their conference. The lone exception was the 2005 Los Angeles Galaxy.

Looking at it from a league table perspective, 17 of 24 MLS Cup finalists have finished in the top three in the league, and that number becomes 19 of 24 when you look at the top four. There have been three #5 finishers in the final—the 2001 San Jose Earthquakes, the 2002 New England Revolution, and the 2006 Houston Dynamo. The aforementioned '97 Rapids finished 7th overall, while the '05 Galaxy finished 8th.

When it comes to winning MLS Cup, eight of the 12 champs were top-three clubs, and nine of 12 were top-four. The two fifth-place teams that won the title (the '01 Quakes and '06 Dynamo) were each two points away

---

[86] Sure, "squeaker-inners" is a word. To me. Besides, I couldn't think of any other concise way to describe those teams. Well, besides "pieces of crap", which wouldn't have been very website-friendly.

from leapfrogging from fifth to third in their respective seasons, so they were certainly in the mix.

That basically leaves the awful 2005 Galaxy as the exception that people can latch onto when saying that the regular season does not matter. The Galaxy finished 13-13-6 that season, with a (-1) goal differential. While that may seem more mediocre than awful, consider that they feasted on expansion Chivas USA and Real Salt Lake that year. Against established clubs, the Galaxy were 7-12-5 with a (-10) goal differential, yet this was the team that nobody could beat with everything on line. One could argue that MLS had no deserving champion that year, and the Galaxy were proof of that.

Anyway, one of the most encouraging signs about the Crew's season thus far is that they are in the thick of the race for the conference and the league. The last dozen years have shown that to be a serious MLS Cup contender, conference and league contention are more or less a prerequisite. Whether it's because teams who don't value the season as highly learn harsh lessons about trying to restart their motor come playoff time, or whether it's something as simple as the notion that the better teams win more often no matter the time of year, I don't know. But the idea that just squeaking into the playoffs is sufficient for a shot at winning the title doesn't hold up. Sure, we all know a low seed may upset a higher seed in the first round, since many in Columbus still carry the razorblade scars from the Crew's ill-fated 2004 playoff campaign. But only twice in 12 years has such an upset been an underdog's stepping stone toward suiting up in the MLS Cup final.

Intrigued by these numbers, I decided to run them past Frankie Hejduk for his thoughts.

"Those stats speak for themselves," said Hejduk. "There's always some chance for a dark horse team to have a good run, so obviously making the playoffs beats missing the playoffs, but I think that the people who believe that the season doesn't matter as long as you get in are the teams that are squeaking in to begin with. It's been a few years since I've been in the playoffs, so I know squeaking in beats staying home, but the ultimate goal is to win a championship."

Hejduk wasn't too surprised to learn that 22 of the 24 MLS Cup finalists finished first or second in their conference, or that the odds of appearing in the final are heavily slanted toward teams that finished in the top three or four of the league. He believes that championship-caliber teams have the desire to win every time they set foot on the field, and as a result, that is also his approach to the game.

"Personally, I take it one game at a time, week by week," he explained. "I want to win every week, and I think that's important. I don't think things like, 'We can coast because as long we get in the playoffs, it doesn't matter.' I can tell you that the guys in this room are focused on playing hard every week. And like I said, if anyone thinks playing hard every week doesn't matter so long as you make the playoffs, I think those numbers will shut them up."

While finishing near the top of the conference and league does not guarantee playoff success, failing to do so is a strong indicator that a team will be watching MLS Cup from their couch, just like you and I. It's something to keep an eye on as the Crew begin the second half of their season. [87]

Who Was That Masked Moron?

Late in the game, the proceedings were interrupted by a chubby chump in a luchador mask who ran onto the field from behind the north goal. He didn't get as far as the 18-yard box before his jiggling, shirtless carcass was slammed into the turf by Director of Stadium Grounds, Brett Tanner.

After the game, I had a mega-brief chat with Tanner about his closing speed and textbook tackling technique. "My first 20 yards is exceptional," he said. "I hope Jim Tressel was watching because I still have four years of college eligibility left. If he needs an outside linebacker, I am ready."

Despite a Horseshoe-worthy tackle that earned the cheers of over 17,000 people at Crew Stadium, our dunce-dumping hero did have one tiny regret. In the heat of the moment, he forgot the conclusion of every Scooby Doo episode he had ever watched.

"I really wish I would have thought to take his mask off," Tanner lamented. "I had him in a headlock, so it would have been pretty easy to unmask him, but I didn't think of it at the time." [88]

---

[87] Wow. 2008 would go a long way toward vindicating this whole section. New York became the third-ever lame team to upset their way to the MLS Cup final. New York finished #5 in their conference and #8 overall. But quality won out in the end, like it almost always does. Columbus finished #1 in the east and #1 overall, then beat New York 3-1 in MLS Cup.

[88] Here's an awesome story that may or may not be true. A team source told me that one of the players was told by some Hispanic fans that the masked pitch invasion was part of a bet. The runner could win the bet by making it across the field without being captured...OR...if the runner was captured and deported, he could still win the bet by making it back to Crew Stadium by a certain home game later in the season. According to these fans, the guy had allegedly been deported. As far as I know, no one ever heard if he made it back by the specified date. Again, I heard this story third hand, and maybe the fans were pulling the player's leg with this story, but it's such a great story that I had to share anyway. Like they say, when the legend becomes fact, print the legend.

The masked luchador is escorted off the field by stadium security, including the Nordecke's favorite security man, Mike Havely[89], who is the bald guy on the left side of the photo. (Photo by Greg Bartram/ Columbus Crew)

U.S. Open Cupdate

Oh my. Such a clever word-merging that was. Anyway, last week, I spoke with Adam Moffat and Nelson Akwari, who urged Crew fans to throw their U.S. Open Cup support behind the Cleveland City Stars and Charleston Battery, respectively.

Last Tuesday, the City Stars were dumped 4-1 by the Fire, while the Battery advanced past the Houston Dynamo on penalty kicks after a 1-1 draw, which the Battery finished while playing 9 v. 11.

I spoke with our two experts to find out what happened with their teams last week.

"Cleveland had a terrible start," said Moffat. "It just wasn't to be. I talked to their coach and he told me it was just a terrible start. They went behind 3-0 in the first 25 minutes. They got a goal back, but it wasn't enough. It was kind of like tonight's game, except we only fell behind by two and we were able to come back."

---

[89] Sadly, Havely passed away on January 9, 2009. The Nordecke has hung a banner in his memory.

Meanwhile, it was a happier story from South Carolina. "I was a pretty crazy game," said Akwari. "Our fans were there in full force and going crazy, so I think that's what got us through those last 15 minutes in the second overtime while we were down two guys.

"Houston really didn't field their full team and the game was pretty even throughout the first half," he went on. "Once the second half began and we got the red card, Houston started to press, and we pretty much began to defend our 1-0 lead. Houston deserved the goal they scored because they played well throughout the second half and created a lot of chances. The second red card, which came in overtime, was a kick below the belt because the referee could have easily kept the card in his pocket. Despite going down another man, we actually played well and still created some scoring chances. I felt like we deserved to go to PKs because we limited a lot of Houston's scoring chances. We both know that it's anyone's game when it comes to PKs. Our shooters did well to score their goals and our goalie, Dusty Hudock, came up big on one of their shots. I was actually supposed to be the fifth shooter for our team, but I didn't need to take my shot. I'll be ready if I'm called on in the future!"

Tuesday night, the Battery travel to Pizza Hut Park for a quarterfinal matchup with FC Dallas. "We'll see what happens," Akwari said. "It will be cool to be back in the MLS atmosphere."

With the City Stars eliminated, Moffat has joined me on the Battery Open Cup Bandwagon. "I think Charleston is the way to go," he said. "Let's all cheer for Nelson."

Nelly welcomes the well-wishes from Ohio. "Thanks for giving the Battery a chance to get some extra fans," he said. "I know how die-hard C-bus fans can be, so we appreciate the support."

Questions of the Night

- "What is this, a doily?" – Fox Soccer Channel announcer / fashion critic Brian Dunseth, while fondling Duncan Oughton's white paisley necktie before the game.

- "It was good to see me, wasn't it?" – Standard Dwight Burgess farewell comment after our pregame chat.

- "What's the right order of swear word symbols for (bleep)?" – Columbus Dispatch beat reporter Shawn Mitchell, trying to accurately convey Crew President/GM Mark McCullers' pre-game speech to the denizens of the Nordecke. (For the record, Shawn[90] settled on "@&*%#!")

- "Can we get a translator, please?" – MLSnet's Craig Merz, ribbing acting head coach Robert Warzycha before the Polish Rifle even said a word at his postgame press conference.

Apples Not Far From the Tree

The Crew's postgame locker room saw Alejandro Moreno Jr., playing with Maximo and Nicolas Barros Schelotto. The three youngsters giddily chased each other around the room, with each taking turns getting thrown to the carpet by his exuberant pursuers. Considering that the elder Moreno and Schelotto are tied for the league lead in fouls suffered, it was as if the kids took turns preparing themselves for a career in MLS as imagined from watching their padres play.

Questions? Comments? Think Shawn should have gone with "&#@^%$" or "@!*$^#&" instead? Feel free to write at sirk65@yahoo.com*

---

[90] This has nothing to do with anything other than to remind me years from now...but after finishing our duties following the awesome Crew-Fire game, Shawn and I were able to weasel our way into the second half of the Jason Isbell & The 400 Unit show at the Basement. It was a tremendous half-concert. All in all, it was a fantastic night.

Road Work: Salt Lake 2, Crew 0

Match date: Saturday, July 12, 2008
Scoring:
4: RSL Morales 3(unassisted)
78: RSL Findley 4 (Deuchar 1)
Attendance: 12,378
Crew's record afterward: 8-5-3

RETROACTIVE RECAP

An awful game on an awful field. The Crew fell behind early (again) on a Javier Morales free kick, then Salt Lake iced the game on a Robbie Findley breakaway in the 78th minute.

The game itself was largely unwatchable due to the fast green concrete that served as a field at Rice-Eccles Stadium. Real Salt Lake's new park, Rio Tinto Stadium, would not open until October, which was much too late to save the Crew, who looked like they would have rather been anywhere else than Rice-Eccles that night.

QUOTES

Sigi Schmid: "I thought Real Salt Lake was better than us tonight, and I thought Salt Lake came out aggressive. They played a lot of long balls and tried to stretch us early, which they did well. It's something I wanted our team to do, but we didn't execute that part of it. I just thought they were a hungrier team tonight. They won more of the 50/50 balls, they won more of the challenges, and got more of the loose balls."

Frankie Hejduk: "(Real Salt Lake) were just the better team tonight, that was it. They were better; they fought a little bit harder. We came out a little slow and whenever you take a goal early away from home, it's tough to fight back."

Robbie Rogers: "Obviously we just weren't clicking. We're not used to playing on a turf field like this. It's really fast. I don't really think it allows you to play as much soccer as you would like. We just didn't make the right adjustments for it and we kind of learned our lesson from it."

Sirk's Notebook: Crew 3, Kansas City 3

Match Date: Thursday, July 17, 2008

Scoring:

22: KC own goal (Hejduk)

24: KC Espinoza 1 (Jewsbury 3, Morsink 2)

26: CLB Schelotto 4 (unassisted)

33: CLB Moreno 7 (Schelotto 9, Rogers 1)

38: CLB Marshall 2 (Schelotto 10)

75: KC Wolff 1 (Jewsbury 4, Morsink 3)

Attendance: 16,117

Crew's record afterward: 8-5-4

The Crew and Kansas City Wizards hooked up in a 3-3 Rorschach test on Thursday night. Was it a point won for the Crew after going two goals down? Or two points lost after going a goal up? Or two points lost for the Wizards after leading by two goals? Or a point won while trailing by a goal in the second half? Or all of the above?

To friends and co-workers who hate the very notion of ties in any sport, I have tried to explain that ties in soccer come with a full spectrum of emotions. Some ties bring elation, while others result in fury or despair, while the rest fall somewhere in between. But then there was this—a tie so convoluted that everyone had a hard time figuring out how to appropriately weigh the positives and negatives. It was furious elation. Or was it elated despair? Each team's gutsy comeback was the other team's unfortunate collapse. And each team's crucial lead was the result of the other team's misfortune or mistakes. The 3-3 draw was a yin & yangy, tart & tangy clusterfudge of conflicting emotions. Finally, in order to keep things simple, each team eventually agreed to be angry because they should have won.

"I think both teams are disappointed," observed K.C.'s Josh Wolff.

"It feels like a loss," said Crew midfielder Robbie Rogers.

"We'd rather have a 1-0 (crap) win than a 3-3 tie," grumbled Crew defender Danny O'Rourke.

"We'll take a point, while knowing that we pissed away a two-goal lead," grumped Wizards coach Curt Onalfo.

And the source of all this bipartisan despair can be traced back to one simple sentence uttered by Crew coach Sigi Schmid: "Any time you score three goals, you should win the game."

Bad Habit

The Crew played well for the first 22 minutes, then found themselves down by two goals by the 24th minute. The Wizards opened the scoring by not scoring themselves, but rather benefitting from a Frankie Hejduk own goal. There was a nice service into the box, and Hejduk was one of three players challenging for the ball. Unfortunately, the ball bounced off of his head and into the upper corner of the net. Two minutes later, the Wizards took a 2-0 lead when former Ohio State Buckeye Roger Espinoza buried the first goal of his MLS career.

"We were playing well, but we went down 2-0," said Crew midfielder Robbie Rogers. "That can't happen at home. We can't go down 2-0. This isn't the first time it's happened, and it's becoming a bad habit for us."

We'll have more on that bad habit a little later in this rambling article.

The Guile of Guille

The Crew got on the board just two minutes after Espinoza's goal. Hovering over a free kick, Guillermo Barros Schelotto took advantage of the Wizards as they attempted to set up their wall. While the defense was in a state of confusion, Guille ripped a shot over the wall and inside the near post, beating goalkeeper Kevin Hartman, who had hopped in the other direction to check on the wall just as Schelotto surprised everyone by taking his shot.

"Their first goal was a quick freekick, and we need somebody standing on the ball," said Onalfo. "We had nobody standing on the ball, and that just can't happen. Credit to Schelotto for being savvy and capitalizing on our slowness to react."

Schelotto had a simple explanation for his quick kick. "I ask the ref, 'Can I play?' He tells me yes, so I play."

Guille's guile would also lead to the Crew's second goal in the 33rd minute. As the teams debated a throw in, Guille picked up the ball and threw it in quickly to Robbie Rogers. After receiving a deft return pass from Rogers, Guille fed Alejandro Moreno in the box, and Moreno's shot trickled across the goal line before Hartman could belatedly swat it back to the feet of Moreno, who kicked it back in the net for good measure.

"Their second goal was the result of some indecision," said Onalfo. "Our players thought it was our throw, but again, credit to Columbus for playing it in quickly. They did that throughout the game and they caught us a few times."

Guillermo Barros Schelotto, doing his best to look like Jerry West in the NBA logo, cuts through the Kansas City defense. Schelotto scored a goal and added two assists in the Crew's 3-3 draw with the Wizards. (Photo by Greg Bartram / Columbus Crew)

Air Marshall On Duty

Guille capped his amazing half by serving a perfect corner kick in the 38th minute. Crew defender Chad Marshall rose up from the depths and attacked the ball like an orca does a seal, lasering a header into the upper right corner of the goal. They don't have radar guns at Crew Stadium, but Marshall's header traveled at an estimated speed of at least 6.1 SPKs. (Sanneh Penalty Kicks.)[91]

Concluding his rundown of the Crew's goals, Onalfo said, "The third goal was a corner kick. We went over that all week, so that, for me, was troublesome."

---

[91] That's like the second or third time in 2008 that I busted on Tony Sanneh and his playoff penalty kick that traveled at the speed of Mr. Burns' bowling ball in that early Simpsons episode. Anyway, suffice it to say, I was still bitter about the 2004 playoff collapse. Thankfully, thanks to the Massive Bananas, my bitterness has now subsided. Starting in 2009, whenever I rip on Tony Sanneh, it will simply be out of Crew fan obligation.

The Wizards may have gone over it, but it seems that Marshall displayed some guile of his own. "I scored against them at their place, so they were kinda grabbing and watching me," Marshall explained. "So on that one, I made a late run. I made it look like I wasn't going to go, and then Guillermo hit a great ball. I have no idea where it went. I just heard the crowd roar, so I knew it went in."

Let's Pause to Go Down Memory Lane

By halftime, I was already extrapolating crazy scores, and it brought to mind one of the highest scoring games in league history, when Kansas City beat the Crew 6-4 on May 2, 1996.

Earlier this year, when I interviewed Mike Clark for the "Where Are They Now?" piece in the Freekick game program, I asked him which game was most memorable for him. I didn't have room for it in the article, but his reply seems fitting to share on this occasion.

"Aside from the obvious ones, a game that really stands out is the game we lost 6-4 in Kansas City in 1996," said Clark. "I scored my first ever goal in that game, and in the process, the goalie punched my cheek and fractured my orbital bone. I was in a daze for the rest of the game. We were up 4-2 and gave up four goals in the last 20 minutes to lose 6-4. The thing was, blowing that lead sounds horrible, like it was some sort of wacky 1996 MLS game, but all four of those K.C. goals were great goals. It was an amazing game."

Sadly, Thursday's game only brought us one goal in the second half, which brings me to…

The Danny O'Rourke / Car Fire Story

I completely missed Kansas City's tying goal in the 75th minute because I was busy checking out the car fire. Yes, the car fire. Upon seeing and smelling the clouds of acrid smoke that wafted into the stadium, it didn't take much investigation to discover the flaming car in the parking lot.

According to witnesses, some tailgaters had dumped the coals out of their grill into an adjacent parking spot. Later, a car parked in that spot, but didn't pull in all the way so as not to park over top of the coals. However, the car was still close enough that the heat radiating from the coals was sufficient to eventually ignite the tires and then rest of the vehicle. (This type of thing is evidently more common than I thought. My good buddy Flick told me that he once read an interview with a Goodyear blimp pilot who said that he usually sees at least one car fire at every football game he hovers over. The pilot said that the cause is almost always hot coals from tailgate grilling. So as a pubic service announcement, be sure to douse your coals when you are done grilling.)

Anyway, I had completely missed K.C.'s equalizer. I had no idea what had happened. Then Sigi testily made the following comment in his press conference: "It's a nice long ball, but if Danny O'Rourke is going to step up there, he needs to win the ball. He can't get beat there."

Okay. So while I still didn't know what happened, I gathered Danny screwed up, and it may have been really, really bad.

When we were allowed into the locker room, Danny wasn't in the trainer's room. He wasn't in the shower. He wasn't on his way out the door. He wasn't on his cell phone. He wasn't staring into his locker with his back to everyone. Instead, he was already dressed, and he sat facing the center of the room. He had eliminated every possible interview barrier and was openly waiting to face the music.

I was in the first group of reporters, and given that I hadn't the slightest clue about the play, I waited for someone else to ask him about the goal. Nobody did. Awesome. And if they weren't going to ask after seeing the play, I wasn't going to do the hard part without even knowing what I was talking about. My plan was to circle back to Danny later, where I could explain my predicament, and then ask him about the goal.

After getting off easy with the first group, Danny still waited around as Shawn Mitchell had not had his turn, and a quote about the goal would surely be needed for the newspaper. So Danny waited for Shawn too.

Once I saw Shawn and Danny talking, I never circled back around. Danny had already done his duty, and sure enough, he explained his thought process in the next morning's paper. (Hint: The quote that appeared in the Dispatch ended with the words, "Oh (bleep)!")

I didn't see a replay of the goal until Saturday night. My goodness. His attempt to cut out that ball was miscalculated "Wendy I can fly" defending at its worst. It was a ghastly play, especially given the game situation. But having seen the play, it made me further appreciate Danny's availability and willingness to face up to it. (Well, had any of the first five people asked about it.)

As I've written before, this team seems to exude good character, so I don't mean to imply that Danny is an exception in comparison to the rest of the team. But undoubtedly one of the suckiest parts about being a player is having to answer questions from the dummies in the press after a bad game or boneheaded play. And one of the suckiest parts about being in the press is having to prod someone about their bad game or boneheaded play. Given the situation, I can't help but respect how Danny made sure he was ready and available after Thursday's game.

While it won't bring that awful goal back, it's just another example of how this team goes about its business.

Too Much Space

Apart from the goal itself, Sigi was also dismayed with the defensive positioning in the second half.

"When you're ahead, you're going to absorb some pressure, but our thing was that we didn't step out," he explained. "We stayed in, and when the ball is 30 yards down the field, we need to step out. That made for a big field in the second half. We need to do a better job of possessing the ball in the second half when a team is pressuring us, and we need to make the field more compact."

Mr. Numbers Nerd: Opponent-Torching Edition

[Redacted for statistical inaccuracy. Embarrasing.][92]

Robbie Goes To China

Robbie Rogers, the Crew's all-star midfielder, was named to the USA's Olympic roster this week. He will play for Peter Nowak's team in this summer's Beijing Olympics.

"I'm excited, but I don't think it's really hit me yet," said Rogers. "Maybe when I am training in China I will realize it. I am really looking forward to it. We have a great team, and I am looking forward to getting back together with those guys."

While there are myriad international competitions for soccer, and the Olympics is not the be-all, end-all that it is for some sports, it is nevertheless a thrill for the players who take part. "I always watch the Olympics," Rogers said. "Believe it or not, I've never watched the soccer part of it, but I've watched the Olympics since I was kid. I never knew I'd get to compete in them, so it's exciting."

The road to the Olympics was not a smooth one for Rogers, who was left off of the Olympic qualifying roster. But based on his all-star play with the Crew, he seemed to be a no-brainer when it came time to name the final roster.

---

[92] This will be explained in the Crew-Dallas Notebook.

"I went from disappointment at not making the qualifying roster, to hoping that the team would qualify, and once they qualified, I told myself that I have to make this team," Rogers explained. "It took a little bit of luck and hard work, but I made it."

There are two notable Crew links to the Olympic tournament. The first is that Rogers is going to get to play with Brian McBride, who was named the roster as one of the over-age players. "McBride is a Crew legend, and I just got here," said Rogers. "You always hear about him in the locker room and stuff. I've never met him, so I am really looking forward to playing with him."

And the other link is that Rogers will be facing off against the man with the locker right next door to his, Emmanuel Ekpo of Nigeria. "We've been talking a little bit," Rogers said with a smile. "I am trying to get the scoop on the players they have. I'm trying to do some scouting."

Frankie the Alternate

Crew captain Frankie Hejduk could possibly join Rogers in China, as he was named an alternate. This means that if one of the overage players on the U.S. roster should suffer an injury, Hejduk could be called in as a replacement. Given that Hejduk suffered a torn ACL after being named to the 2006 U.S. World Cup squad, he knows what it's like to be on the other side of the equation.

"Hopefully nobody gets hurt, but if they do, I will be ready to go over," he said. "It's always an honor when your country calls. That Olympic tournament is going to be a great tournament, and the U.S. has a great team, so hopefully they'll do well. I wish them the best, and I hope I don't get called in because that would mean somebody got injured, and I don't wish that on anyone."

In the meantime, Hejduk is looking forward to watching his young teammate in Beijing. "Robbie's an up and coming player and he's had a great year," he said. "This could be a breakout tournament for him. The big stage is the time to shine, so I wish him the best."

Random Moments

* After concluding his press conference, Wizards coach Curt Onalfo stopped on his way out the door and asked if anyone had the minutes of the first-half goals. Columbus Dispatch columnist Michael Arace had his notebook open and rattled them off, "22, 24, 26, 33, 38." Onalfo stood there for a moment, let the numbers sink in, shook his head, and then walked out of the room without saying another word.

* As the press gathered around Robbie Rogers, Adam Moffat decided to join in the interview session by holding an unpeeled banana amidst all of the media's recording devices.

* Upon concluding his one-minute, 12-second chat with reporters, Chad Marshall turned toward his locker and sardonically stated, "I'm such an AWESOME interview."

(Chad has never sought out a microphone in his life, and typically doesn't have much to say on the occasions he's asked. Often said to be one of the funniest people on the team once you get to know him, I've always accepted/respected that talking to the press isn't really Chad's thing. But credit where credit is due—despite his post-interview proclamation, he did give a pretty good description of his goal earlier in this article.)

Mr. Numbers Nerd: 0-2 Edition

What are the odds that the team with the second-best record in all of MLS would be a team that has fallen behind 2-0 in 41% of its games? Pretty long, right?

Well, the 2008 Columbus Crew have fallen behind 2-0 in 7 of their 17 league matches, including the last two home games, and three consecutive games overall. The Crew, astonishingly, are 0-4-3 in those seven games, having earned a point on June 21 at Los Angeles, on July 5 vs. Chicago, and now on July 17 vs. Kansas City. This got me to wondering how rare this point-gathering feat has been in club history.

In a word: in-frickin'-credibly.

A two-goal lead may be "the most dangerous lead in soccer", but a 2-0 lead against the Columbus Crew has been three points in the bank, historically. After digging through media guides, MLSnet.com, and enlisting the help of Shawn Mitchell to research the Dispatch archives for the two games for which I had no box scores, I can tell you that with Thursday's draw against Kansas City, the Crew's all-time record after conceding the first two goals of a match has improved to 3-64-3. (Miraculously, none of the relevant games from 1996-99 went to a shootout, so that's a pure 3-64-3.)

That's right. You read that correctly. In the span of just 26 days, the Crew equaled the amount of non-losses that they had "piled up" in the previous 12-plus seasons. Of course, the other three historical instances were victories. We'll get to those in a minute, but for now, you might want to pause and see if you can recall the Crew's only three league victories after trailing 2-0. As a (hopefully) easy bonus question, see if you can also name the club's one other victory after going 0-2 down, which was not a league game.

<Whistling the "Jeopardy" theme>

Okay, moving on. We'll get to the victories in a second. But first, some more 0-2 numbers from the 2008 season.

With seven matches in which they've been behind 0-2, the Crew are nearing the franchise record despite having almost half of a season to play. The record is nine games with an 0-2 hole, set in 2005. The 1996 and 2000 Crew teams fell behind 0-2 on eight occasions. The 2008 Crew already rank 4th all-time in club history.

It is obvious to anyone that the 2008 Crew are better than their predecessors from 2006 and 2007. However, in barely half a season, the current Crew have already fallen behind 0-2 an equal number of times as the 2006 and 2007 clubs *combined*.

The Crew's three-game streak of conceding the first two goals is tied for the second longest in club history, equaling the three-game run from September 1-9, 2000, when the Crew fell behind 0-2 in losses at San Jose (0-3), at Chicago (1-3), and vs. Chicago (2-3).

The all-time Crew record is four consecutive games of conceding the first two goals, which occurred during the ghastly 2005 season. From April 23 to May 14 of that year, the Crew fell behind 0-2 in consecutive losses at Colorado (0-2), vs. Chicago (0-2), at DC (1-3), and vs. KC (0-4).

In allowing the first two goals in their last two home games, the Crew have equaled their club record, which has been done four times, most recently in 2005 with the Chicago and Kansas City home matches during the four-game overall streak. (What is it with those two teams?) The club also fell behind 0-2 in consecutive home matches on two separate occasions in 1996.

Another facet to this year's crazy performance is that the June 21 draw at Los Angeles snapped the Crew's 41-game road losing streak when conceding the first two goals. It was the very first road point in club history under such circumstances. After losing 2-0 in their subsequent road game at Salt Lake, the Crew's all-time road record after conceding the first two goals currently stands at 0-42-1.

Not only did they pick up the first road point in club history and equal the previous total of non-losses, but the 2008 club's points per game when falling behind 0-2 is staggering. In seven games this year, the Crew are averaging 0.43 points per game when trailing 0-2. Talk about a "never say die" team. In the previous 12 seasons, the Crew averaged barely a third of that, at 0.15 points per game.

In fact, from 1997-2007, the Crew picked up three points in 55 games when trailing 0-2. The 2008 Crew have equaled 11-years' worth of points in the span of 26 days.

When Chad Marshall headed home Schelotto's corner kick on the Thursday, it was only the fourth time in regular season history that the Crew had ever taken a lead after falling behind 0-2. Unfortunately, it was the first time the Crew had not hung on to win after staging such a comeback. Here are the other three regular season instances, all of which ended in Crew victories:

May 11, 1996: After digging a 2-0 hole against the New England Revolution, Brian McBride got the Crew back in the game with a 48th minute penalty kick, but the real drama came in the closing minutes, when Pete Marino's 87th minute goal tied the score, and then McBride won the game with an 89th minute shot that angled just inside the right post. The improbable last-minute victory caused many in the crowd of 24,750 to rush the field after the game, which in turn prompted Doctor Khumalo to hurdle the sign boards on a dash to the locker room while apparently fearing for his life.[93]

August 10, 1996: D.C. United held a 2-0 second half lead before Ricardo Irabarren's bicycle kick goal electrified not only the Ohio Stadium crowd, but his teammates. McBride and Adrian Paz scored within four minutes to give the Crew a 3-2 lead that they would carry until the final whistle. This was one of the many thrilling victories in the Crew's magical, nearly-impossible late-season run to the playoffs that year.

October 26, 2003: In one of the more comical games in Crew history, the Crew went into the locker room trailing the Chicago Fire 2-0. The Fire emptied their bench to the extent that they could, even subbing in rookie goalkeeper Curtis Spiteri. In the only 45 minutes of his MLS career, Spiteri was beaten SIX times as the Crew sent their fans into a playoff-less winter with a bit of a giggle after a 6-2 thumping of the hated Fire. For those who love ridiculous rate stats based on small sample sizes, the Crew's Jake Traeger racked up 2 assists in the only 12 minutes of his career that day, meaning he retired with an assists-per-90-minutes ratio of 15.0. Meanwhile, Carlos Valderrama, considered the finest passer in MLS history, retired with an assists-per-90 of 0.66. It would take almost 23 Valderramas to equal the career assist rate of one Jake Traeger. THAT's the kind of game it was.

And as for the bonus non-league comeback…

---

[93] The best part is that a fan tried to do likewise and impaled his crotch on the top of the sign board. I simultaneously laughed and cringed.

September 10, 2002: Hosting a U.S. Open Cup semifinal, the clock hit 75:00 with the Crew down 2-0. Edson Buddle scored in the 76th minute to breathe some life into his slumbering team, and then John Wilmar Perez forever etched his name into Crew lore by not only scoring the equalizer in the second minute of stoppage time, but also scoring the golden goal in the 109th minute. Only 2,103 were on hand to witness the miracle. Six weeks after Pelusa's heroics, the Crew beat Los Angeles in the U.S. Open Cup final to win the franchise's first piece of hardware.

Crew Records, By Year, When Conceding the First Two Goals of a Match

For those who want year-by-year-numbers, here you go:

2008: 0-4-3 [94]
2007: 0-2-0
2006: 0-5-0
2005: 0-9-0
2004: 0-3-0
2003: 1-3-0
2002: 0-6-0
2001: 0-2-0
2000: 0-8-0
1999: 0-5-0
1998: 0-6-0
1997: 0-5-0
1996: 2-6-0
TOTAL: 3-64-3
(Home: 3-22-2 Away: 0-42-1)

Morons in the Media

Everybody loves a good "morons in the media" story. The dumbest thing I ever personally witnessed happened in the press conference following MLS Cup 2000. A reporter noted that before the game, he observed Chicago head coach Bob Bradley wishing Kansas City head coach Bob Gansler "good luck" before the game. The reporter wanted to know if that showed that the Fire were overconfident heading into the game.

---

[94] The Crew would finish 2008 at 0-6-3, falling behind two-zip in a 2-0 loss at Houston and a 3-1 loss at New York. At the end of 2008, the updated franchise totals would then be 3-66-3 overall, and 0-44-1 on the road.

I just about peed myself.

Anyway, here's a gem from Thursday. As Robbie Rogers talked about leaving for the Olympics, one intrepid reporter asked Robbie, "Obviously some of the veterans like Frankie have gone through this many times, but will it seem strange to be leaving your team like this in the middle of the season for the first time?"

Robbie processed the question and then delicately informed the numbskull, "Well, uh, I was away last year with the U-20s, so it's pretty much the same thing."

Then all the other reporters laughed at the dunce who asked the question.

That dunce, of course, was me. I apologized for asking such a stupid question, then doffed my cap and took a bow for the rest of the reporters.

Extemporaneous thinking is not my strong point at the end of a long day. I didn't even factor in last year since he was mostly a reserve player until the end of the season. So in my mind, this was his first time leaving a team in mid-season when he's a starter and integral part of the team's success. That's what I was going for. But that's not what I asked. And I wish I could say it was just clumsy phrasing, but the truth is that at that precise moment, I had forgotten all about the U-20s last year, which is why I phrased the question as I did. So I basically made a fool of myself, although Robbie was nice enough to laugh it off without making me feel too terribly stupid.

There's still a lot of season left, so I am throwing down the gauntlet. I challenge Mitchell, Merz, and everyone else. I dare anyone to ask a stupider question before the season is over. If you want to take my Dunce of the Year cap away from me, you'll have to earn it!

Who the Heck's in the Nordecke?

If some of you thought you saw a familiar face in the front row of the Nordecke during the first half, your eyes were not deceiving you. Crew television analyst and former former former Crew player Dante Washington wanted to experience the Nordecke for himself.

"I met with the Hudson Street Hooligans at Ruby Tuesday," he explained. "We made the walk down Summit Avenue to get from Ruby Tuesday to the stadium, and they had people leading the chants and stuff, and people were coming out of their houses wondering what the heck was going on. Other people in Crew jerseys were driving by and honking their horns. It was like there were two groups of people: people who get it, and people who haven't gotten it yet. I think the people who haven't gotten it are starting to get it. Like Grant from the Hudson Street Hooligans told me, it was the first time these people had seen all of this on a Thursday, so when they saw all these OSU students who are die-hard Crew fans, they were probably like 'What the (heck) is gong on'?"

Dante wasn't just HSH for the night. "I met with La Turbina and some Crew Union people once I got inside," he said. "There are so many different experiences. This is all a big experiment. Hanging with Hudson Street Hooligans is one experience, but then I go to La Turbina and I'm dancing with the drums and enjoying the Latino feel. It's such a different feel depending on where you're at, but it's all for the game."

Dante Washington watches the Crew-Wzards match with the Hudson Street Hooligans. Much to Brian Dunseth's dismay, Dante's bar scarf is obscuring that Bumpy Pitch t-shirt. (Photo by Greg Bartram / Columbus Crew)

For someone used to quietly watching the game from an aerial view, watching the game from the front row of the Nordecke had to be a bit of a shock. "It was difficult," Dante said. "I am used to watching the game from higher and analyzing it from a broadcast perspective, and part of me is trying to do that, while part of me is trying to watch it as a fan, so I had these two parts of my head fighting. You can't really analyze the game from that low in the corner, but man, it was unbelievable. Watching from the Nordecke is just an unbelievable experience. I just told Alejandro Moreno that as much as the players can show them love, they should, because those guys are absolutely nuts."

When asked to describe his personal experience in the front row, Dante said, "The Hudson Street Hooligans kept bumping into each other. I felt bad, because I was bumping into people and saying 'excuse me' all the time, but I don't think they cared if people bumped into them. Also, there were 21-year-olds looking at me like 'who the hell is this guy walking right up to the front?' There's a whole new generation of Crew fans. We're getting old, Sirk."

Ugh. Let's change the subject. Did Dante bow to Guille on the corner kicks? "No, I don't bow. Guille is a good player, but I don't bow. Instead, I pat him on the back." (He then patted a laughing Guille on the back.)

The bottom line is that Dante had a great time, and he recommends that other fans give it a try. "I definitely think everyone should get in touch with their inner supporter for even just one half. Stop by the Nordecke, visit any of the three groups, and just soak up the experience."

When told that Dante was in the front row of the Nordecke, Frankie Hejduk busted up laughing. "Man, I wish I would have seen him!" he said. "That's good that Dante was over there, because once I'm retired, I'm going to be over there too!" [95]

Questions? Comments? Slow to recognize de-mustachioed faces?[96] Feel free to write at sirk65@yahoo.com

Amidst the Hudson Street Hooligans, Dante appears to be praying for good fortune during a tense moment in the Crew's 3-3 draw with against the Wizards. (Photo by Greg Bartram / Columbus Crew)

---

[95] Forget retirement. Little did we know that two and a half months later, Frankie would be tailgating with the Crew Union while serving a suspension against the Galaxy on October 4.

[96] Former Crew GM Jim Smith was at the game, but no longer had his famous mustache. He said that fans would look at him like they sort of recognized him, but couldn't place where.

The Incidents, Part II:
West Ham United and the Importance of Diction

On July 20, 2008, a story went out on a prominent news wire. It was quickly picked up by newspapers and websites around the globe. That's because the article opened with this juicy sentence:

A brawl among more than 100 fans at halftime marred an exhibition match Sunday between West Ham United of the English Premier League and the Columbus Crew of Major League Soccer.

When one receives copy about a 100-person brawl, at a soccer game, featuring West Ham's notoriously combative fans, it's news in every corner of the world. British hooliganism had arrived on American shores! And for the second time, those rowdy Columbus fans were in the middle of a controversy! Let's not forget that racist YouTube guy!

And so it was. Columbus found itself in the middle of another media poopstorm and internet message board frenzy.

"A brawl among more than 100 fans" conjures up any manner of fantastically violent images of two columns of furious fans rushing together in a Braveheart-style battle to the death. But there were neither pools of blood nor piles of broken bones on the Crew Stadium concourse. In fact, there were hardly any punches thrown.

The skirmish began when several West Ham United fans waltzed into the Nordecke and began to tussle with Crew fans. Several punches were thrown as Crew fans and security removed the West Ham fans from the section. A few more punches were thrown once the scene moved to the concourse, but police and security used pepper spray to quickly diffuse the situation, with security lining up between the two groups of fans. From that point, the only other notable event occurred when a West Ham fan threw one more punch and was quickly tackled to the pavement by police in a persuasive show of force.

Having spent much of my formative years attending Cleveland Browns games, the actual violence was negligible by comparison. I have seen more punches thrown at just about every Browns game I have ever attended, especially those games back at old Cleveland Municipal Stadium.

One thing that made this incident a little more alarming, however, was that I had never experienced two walls of opposing supporters facing off against one another. Although security was between them, the numbers of Crew fans and Hammer fans on either side of the security divide were growing by the second. Most were curious onlookers coming to rubberneck at the commotion, but it was still unsettling as the numbers grew. At Browns games, most of the fighting involves a handful of drunken pugilists, much like the incident that started this commotion. However, these two swelling masses of opposing fans were a new experience for me. For a moment, I was genuinely fearful that one wrong move could set off a legitimate brawl.

But that's not what happened. Crew fans chanted "USA! USA! and "Relegation!" at the West Ham fans while Hammer fans responded with insults of their own, and that was pretty much it. The crowds dispersed by the start of the second half. In the end, it was lots of bark after very little bite.

The strangest sight for me came after the crowds had dispersed. A member of Hudson Street Hooligans tracked down the shirtless, tattooed West Ham fan that started the original confrontation in the stands. I thought I was about to witness another fight, but the two men shook hands, assured each other that all was well, then engaged in a series of forceful-yet-friendly head butts.

And so it was that the making of peace landed harsher blows to the skull than did the original skirmish.

I came away from the West Ham incident awed by the importance of diction. I learned that when writing the news, there is a lot of power in every single word. There was certainly a newsworthy incident at Crew Stadium on July 20, 2008, but it was amazing to see how one unfortunate word choice changed the entire framework.

A few fans of each team threw punches. Then 100+ people congregated. At no point was there a "brawl" much less "among 100 fans."

Had the article said that there was a "confrontation" or a "standoff" between Crew and Hammer fans, it would have told the story. But through use of the word "brawl", the brief, somewhat scary, and largely nonviolent confrontation/standoff literally became worldwide news as the latest incidence of large-scale soccer violence.

One word. The choice of one little word. What a powerful lesson.

Road Work: Crew 2, Colorado 0

Match date: Sunday, July 27, 2008
Scoring:
21: CLB Lenhart 3(Miglioranzi 1)
75: CLB Garey 1 (Evans 1)
Attendance: 10,647
Crew's record afterward: 9-5-4

RETROACTIVE RECAP

The Denver area had been historically inhospitable to the Crew, who had previously managed just one win in 13 matches at mile high altitude. However, on this night, the Crew bucked historical trends. Steven Lenhart, in the first start of his MLS career, registered a 21st minute goal and a 42nd minute red card for accidentally, yet recklessly, elbowing Facundo Erpen in the face.

Crew goalkeeper William Hesmer stood on his head as the Rapids threw everything at him, and then Jason Garey iced the game with a spectacular, sliding, off-footed, rooftop finish of a bouncing ball in the Colorado box. Hesmer made 7 saves to preserve the shutout.

During stoppage time, The Voice of the Crew, Dwight Burgess, told the ONN viewing audience, "The Crew…well…they are a *massive* club, and this would be a *massive* win."

QUOTES

Sigi Schmid: "Soccer is a funny game. Today we got dominated and came out with a win. That's just the way it goes."

Jason Garey: "Finally got a chance to get on the field and I was able to finish one. I almost had another one. I wish I would have finished that one too because that would have given us a little more breathing room. I can't say enough about the guys in the back. What I did was really very small compared to what those guys did tonight. Especially Will. I have been to a lot of soccer games, but that was the best goalkeeping that I have ever seen in person. He had an unbelievable game."

Rapids coach Fernando Clavijo, regarding Hesmer: "Their goalie played some inspired soccer tonight; he played a lot bigger than his size. He looked like he covered half the goal, and came out well on corner kicks. And you have to credit them for playing an absolute flawless defensive game."

Road Work: Houston 2, Crew 0

Match date: Saturday, August 2, 2008
Scoring:
13: HOU Davis 2 (Mullan 2)
43: HOU Ching 8 (Jaqua 1)
Attendance: 15,371
Crew's record afterward: 9-6-4

RETROACTIVE RECAP

The Crew were massively shorthanded for this road game against the two-time defending MLS Cup champs. Robbie Rogers and Emmanuel Ekpo were away at the summer Olympics. Steven Lenhart (red card) and Frankie Hejduk (yellow accumulation) were suspended. Gino Padula and Stefani Miglorianzi were unavailable due to injury. As if that weren't enough, Chad Marshall and Brad Evans left the game the 28th and 53rd minutes, respectively, with injuries.

A left-footed volley by Brad Davis gave the Dynamo the lead early, and then Brian Ching's low liner doubled the lead just before halftime. Despite outshooting the Dynamo 12-6, the Crew couldn't find the back of the net.

QUOTES

Sigi Schmid: "I thought they finished their chances well in the first half. They took them well. I thought we had enough chances to win the game. In all the times I've coached Columbus, in the three times we've played here, this is the most chances we've created here, and if we finished, I think we're in the game.

"What hurt us the most, though, was losing Chad Marshall and Brad Evans to injuries. That dictates what you can do. Tactically, that limits the decisions you can make."

Guillermo Barros Schelotto: "They took advantage at the beginning of the game, then they started concentrating on possession and controlling the ball for the rest of the game. We had a couple of opportunities to score a goal, but then they scored their second goal. We kept on trying, but their goalkeeper was playing very well. That's why we lost -- we couldn't finish our plays.

"We were missing some players who went to the Olympics, like Robbie Rogers, and Frankie (Hejduk) for having five yellows, but we played well. They scored on us when we made mistakes, and we couldn't finish."

Sirk's Notebook:
Oughton's Intro-Dunc-tions (2008)

Greetings, Crew fans. It's that special time of year when everyone's favorite Kiwi, Duncan Oughton, takes time out of his busy splinter-picking schedule in order to enlighten Notebook readers. Each season, as a public service, Duncan gets to know all of the team's newcomers, then reports his findings in the hope that the fans will be able to bond even more strongly with the new players once they know more about them.

This tradition started in 2006. I had to miss the first half of the season due to a family emergency in Cleveland. When I got back to Columbus, I realized that Sigi Schmid had completely gutted the Crew's roster to the point that it was unrecognizable from that of the 2005 team. Wanting to know who was who, I turned to the most reliable, believable and trusted man to ever set foot in a Crew locker room—Duncan Oughton.

I knew I could count on Duncs to give us the straight scoop on the new players. He did not disappoint. For example, in 2006, we learned that goalkeeper Andy Gruenebaum had parlayed his extensive personal DVD collection into a thriving underground business called "Rabbi Rentals."

2007 saw another drastic roster turnover, and Duncan again came to the rescue. Among other things, we learned that:

* Goalkeeper William Hesmer is "C.C. Willie" (short for Country Club Willie), "a man who enjoys the finer things in life, like rocking his Polo polos and khaki shorts, imported brew in hand" while chatting with the upper-crust at the country club bar.

* Midfielder Brad Evans "is an Arizona boy who was repeatedly bitten by poisonous snakes and scorpions in his early years and has obviously never fully recovered."

* Defender Danny ("Meathead") O'Rourke "is well known in the community, because if people don't know who he is, he tells them forcefully."

* Guillermo Barros Schelotto had become so enamored with burritos that he had taken to "eating all of his meals in burrito form." Not only would he turn McDonald's or filet mignon into a burrito before eating it, but on road trips, Duncan claimed that Guille would pour milk and cereal onto a tortilla and then roll it up. ("It's a soggy mess, but it's the only way to make sure that Guillermo eats the most important meal of the day.")

To the uninitiated, Oughton's Intro-Dunc-tions may appear to be a roast; a rite of passage that every player must endure on the path to becoming True Crew. However, it's worth noting that Duncan provides these descriptions with a straight face, so he's obviously telling the unvarnished truth.

I gathered this year's "intro-Dunc-tions" after training on July 11, 2008. Newly acquired Pat Noonan is obviously not included, but I may catch up with Duncan later in the season once he gets to know Noonan a little. Likewise, Adam Moffat joined the Crew late last year after we had already done our intro-Dunc-tions, so now he appears in this year's edition.

Before we proceed, we must remind everyone of that these intro-Dunc-tions describe the new players as seen through the eyes of Duncan Oughton and only Duncan Oughton. His views may not be indicative of the views of the Columbus Crew, Major League Soccer, or objective reality.

I believe him though.

OK, enough of my yapping. Without further ado, here is the 2008 edition of Oughton's Intro-Dunc-tions!

#4 GINO PADULA

"Gino Padula? I'm not sure. He must train in the evenings. But seriously, Gino came in with a bit of a roar and then has hit some speed bumps with injuries. He's got lovely hair. His English is decent, which is good, so he can understand all of the rude Spanish I am saying to him. He's a really good guy, although I am a little disturbed about his mafia connections. I think Guillermo brought him in so they could start a little Argentine mafia in the locker room. I think Nico Hernandez was involved too, but then he disappeared.[97] We're all concerned that Nico may have wronged Gino or Guillermo in some way and then the mafia got him. You have to be careful around those guys. I've probably said too much."

#6 ANDY IRO

"Big Andy. Where do you start? He's an Englishman who is desperate – and I mean desperate – to be a California boy. Apart from the fact that he sticks out like a sore thumb because he's seven-foot and has an English accent, everything else about him is completely Californian. It's hard to explain what's going on in his head sometimes. It's so high up there that I'll never have a chance to get a good look inside anyway. 'G.I.' is what we call him—Generation Iro. He's in his own world and I think he's on some sort of International Wealth Plan. He's sewing his own cleats because he doesn't

---

[97] The Crew waived Hernandez on June 28, 2008.

want the shoe companies telling him what to do. He does what ever G.I. wants to do, like sometimes talking in the third person."

#16 BRIAN CARROLL

"BC…that little rat. Obviously BC has been around the league a while. He's a very sneaky little man. You think he's a shy and quiet 12-year-old-boy lookalike, but underneath that lovely image is a little raging rat that's ready to break out. OK, he really is a great guy. And all joking aside, when his playing days are done, I really do think he has an excellent future as a decoy on that Dateline NBC show."

#17 EMMANUEL EKPO

"Manu loves the geese. He is fascinated. I had to have a conversation with him about the geese, because he is fascinated by all of the geese around Columbus and he didn't understand that there was no owner to all these geese. I've seen Manu try to herd some of them at Obetz, so if all of the geese disappear from the streets and ponds of Columbus and are being farmed somewhere, I think we'll know exactly who the farmer is. Manu is a lovely man and we're glad he's on our team."

#18 KENNY SCHOENI

"Kenny came in and thought he was a field player. He did the beep test and scored a 412, which is unheard of. As a goalie, he's a madman around the goal box. Sometimes we play a crossing and finishing game at the end of practice for a little bit of fun and Kenny's out there trying to punch people's heads off their shoulders. He's not the type of guy you'd ever want to wrong. That's because he has to get you back 400 times worse or he'll never be satisfied. I've played the odd trick on him and he's always come back with anger. I think he has a lot of pent-up anger. He's ready to explode at any time. As a warning to fans out there, don't ever play a trick on Kenny Schoeni. If you do that 'what's that spot on your shirt' trick to him, he's likely to rip out your jugular with his bare hands."

#21 RYAN MILLER[98]

"Ryan is a Notre Dame boy, so he is a smart and sophisticated young man. He's a quiet guy who keeps to himself or hangs out with the other young guys. I think there might be some deviousness going on there with

---

[98] The Crew waived Miller on September 12, 2008.

those boys because they gather together in a dark corner of the locker room and talk amongst themselves. I don't know if maybe they've been recruited by the Argentine mafia as low-level peddlers who do business in the dark corners of the locker room, or what. But that group of Miller, George Josten, and Kevin Burns...I think Kevin is the mule who does all of the dirty work, hauling questionable weightlifting supplements to Danny O'Rourke. I think that's how that group makes most of their money. So Miller is part of the young group that moves protein powder from the Argentine mafia to Danny O'Rourke."

#22 ADAM MOFFAT

"Adam Moffat? Oh, goodness. The Scotsman? He seems like a great guy, but I honestly haven't had a single conversation with him where I've understood even one word that he's said. I mean, he could be a really bad guy. He could be saying the worst things ever, but I wouldn't know. He seems like a nice guy, though, because he's always smiling. He never stops smiling. When he's out there playing? Smiling. Scores a goal? Smiling. Doesn't score a goal? Smiling. Tears his knee ligaments? Smiling.

"I think he's gone ahead and decided that he's not going to shave until he's back playing again, so he looks like a caveman at this point. He's got a longer, thicker beard. He grows it quickly, and right now he looks like the episode of Family Guy when Peter Griffin had birds living in his beard. That's Adam Moffat right now and it's only been a month. I hate to think of what it's going to look like in four months. Goodness. By then, maybe one of Manu's geese will be living in his beard. That would be lovely."

#25 GEORGE JOSTEN

"He's one of those devious boys in the dark corner of the locker room. George is a quiet lad as well, but he's got that Miller-Burns connection going on. He seems like a nice kid, but there's a devious side due to his connections to the Argentine mafia. I think it's a shame that the mafia got to those kids first, instead of the nice folks, like myself for instance. But George tells a decent joke now and then, and he's quick-witted. I've been working on getting some dirt on him and Ryan Miller, so maybe I need to go undercover and hide in the corner of the locker room."

#26 CORY ELENIO

"Big Red, as he's fondly known around here. He's doing the red-headed nation proud, isn't he? He can be found streaming down the right wing while obviously in danger of terrible sunburn. But there he is, streaming down the right wing, despite not being allowed to wear a hat. I think MLS should sanction the wearing of hats for his benefit, to protect him from the sun.

"Cory knows a New Zealand guy that I know and I think it rubbed off on him during college. He has a bit of New Zealand wit. If you get to know him, there's a real sharp wit ticking in his head, so I think there could be good times ahead with Cory."

(Since New Zealand has rubbed off on him, does he eat Vegemite?)

"No, he doesn't eat Vegemite. He hasn't gone that far New Zealand. I hear he's a big fan of ginger though."

#29 RICARDO PIERRE-LOUIS

"He came late this year. If I see him in the morning, he'll say, 'Good morning, Duncan,' and that's about all I've gotten out of him. I haven't figured out if that's the extent of his English or if he just doesn't want to talk to me. But he's another guy that's always smiling. What's up with all of these younger players smiling all the time? Are they making more money than me or something? These guys are always smiling. Goodness. But Ricardo definitely seems like a pleasant lad who is enjoying his time here. He hasn't been around as long as the other guys, so we will have to do a follow up once I get to know him better. "

#31 KEVIN BURNS

"As we discussed, Kevin is a mule for the Argentine mafia. I think that's why he has faked an injury. It allows him to earn good money running supplements from the Argentine mafia to Danny O'Rourke. The only time Kevin shows up at training is on food days. Every time I see him in line, he's got handfuls of food that he is stuffing into his mouth. I can't tell if it's because he's really hungry from working crazy hours for the Argentine mafia and making all those night runs for them, or if it's because Miller and Josten ate all the food back at their house. It has to be something, though, because he's always double-fisting chicken and whatever else he can get his hands on. It's really weird."

#32 STEVEN LENHART

"He's the super-sub, as some people have called him. He's a Cali boy who grew up right near where I played college ball. He probably watched me play in my younger Fullerton days. I bet he was in the stadium cheering me on. He's a good religious boy and he's another one of these young guys who's always smiling.

"He has long, loping arms, so sometimes if you're anywhere near the same room as him, you can take an inadvertent elbow to the face or a hand to the back of the head without warning because his arms are flailing all over the place. I'd hate to be the opposition going against him in a game. I've done it in training and I get black eyes...my nose becomes swollen even more so than normal...it's a nightmare."

(NOTE: This interview took place two weeks before Lenhart was red-carded for elbowing Colorado's Facundo Erpen in the face. Good call, Nostraduncus!)

"Steve can be seen driving his big truck around town, like he's still back in Cali. He's got it raised up a bit, bouncing around as he sings along to N'Sync and stuff like that. I've had the pleasure of riding in his truck a few times and it's an experience, let me tell you. You can't miss it if you see him on the road. He's the one with the windows down shouting lyrics to Backstreet Boys.

"It's a shame he cut his hair. He had quite the afro going. It was a less cultured Will Hesmer, with no country club style, that Steve had going on there. It was a sad day when he came in with that buzz cut. I think he got made fun of a bit when he first got here, though. People were calling him Cabbage Patch Kid because he really did look like that one Cabbage Patch Kid with the curly blond hair.

(Yeah, that Ben Winkler one.)

"Well, I don't know what they're called. Guys called him Cabbage Patch Kid and I just went with it. I never had one, unlike you, Sirk, so I don't know all the dolls' names. You're a weird guy. I'm done with this interview. Get away from me."

Questions? Comments? Think Duncan's nose would grow more if it could? Feel free to write at sirk65@yahoo.com

Oughton's Re-intro-Dunc-tions
Mining the 2006 and 2007 introdunctions

In the interest of completeness, here are the Oughton's Intro-Dunc-tions for the other members of the 2008 squad, as provided in 2006 or 2007. So let's hop in the time machine and see what Duncan had to say about...

#9 JASON GAREY (2006)

"Jason Garey is also known as Jason Scary. He will probably feature on HGTV, the home-fixing network, as he is quite the handyman. This offseason, he may start a dry-walling business.

"He also has a Chia Pet. It doesn't like me. It growls at me. But Jason is a good team man, except for his Louisiana instincts that cause him to eat Jambalaya."

#12 EDDIE GAVEN (2006)

"Eddie Gaven is a youngster who has already been in the league forever. When Eddie Gaven yells, it is like you or I whispering, so it is hard for him to get a point across in a conversation. [Inaudible whispering.] That's how he talks.

"He's a great young guy. You can't get him to swear. He's a good Catholic boy. I am trying to corrupt him, but it's not working, so that is going to be my goal. I am going to try to get Eddie Gaven to swear."

(I interject: "It's funny you say that. My roommate at Ohio University was the same way. Jay would never swear. He would never say something was s***. He would say, 'That's a bunch of stool' and stuff like that. We were always trying to get him to swear to no avail. Then one night we were playing NHL hockey on the Sega Genesis and Jay lost to someone who wasn't very good. He slammed down the controller and said, 'I suck at this f***ing game!' I couldn't believe it. I ran through all three floors of our dorm, banging on everyone's doors while screaming 'JAY SAID F***! JAY SAID F***! JAY SAID F***!' I was the town crier. This was after midnight.")

"What a sensational, magical moment! I hope to experience that with Eddie Gaven some day. I've heard him swear on the field, but that doesn't count. My goal is to some day get him to consciously swear off the field. Also, if I could get him to drink a Coca-Cola or something, that would be good too. But Eddie is a very nice kid. You couldn't meet a nicer kid."

#23 EZRA HENDRICKSON (2006)

"Ezra. Eazy-E. I've known Ezra for a long time since he played in LA with Simon. He has the longest legs in the league. Lucky legs, actually. He's lucky that they don't snap off and go up his own bottom. He's very funny and a great team guy. He's never afraid to have a laugh."

(I interject: "When I see him out there, he reminds me a lot of Ansil Elcock. Based on what you said, is there some Ansil inside of him?")

"Yeah, I think all Caribbean boys have a little bit of Ansil Elcock inside of them."

(Me: --dying of laughter--)

"Whoa. That was not intended. That came out completely wrong.

"Moving on, Ezra and Knox Cameron speak this special tongue. It's all Caribbean, so I understand maybe every five words. If I put the words I understand together, it can sound pretty bad, but I really have no idea what they are saying. I'm trying learn Spanish, and now I am also trying to master the Caribbean language so that I can talk to everyone on the squad."

#24 JED ZAYNER (2006)

"Jed is another IU boy. He doesn't quite share the same traits as the Crew's previous IU people. I don't think he ever saw the party side of IU like the previous IU guys, who are now family men I might add.

"Jed refers to himself as The Rev. I think his self-proclaimed nickname speaks for itself. He is obviously a religious man. I've caught him on many occasions staring at his own reflection in the locker room mirror. I'm not sure if he's looking into the mirror in order to gaze into the depths of his inner peace and tranquility, or if he's just doing his hair. I'm a bit worried that he could be the next Brian Dunseth."

#28 ANDY GRUENEBAUM (2006)

"Andy is the half-Jewish boy. He claims his Jewishness…is Jewishness a word? No matter, I'm going with it. He claims his Jewishness is a half, so he is half wealthy and half poor. But I can truly tell you that he also has the most amazing video collection. I often stop by Rabbi Rentals for DVDs. I am a subscriber to Rabbi Rentals. I think some of the other guys are learning about this amazing collection, and now he is earning a bit of money on the side. And that's great. He's got a bit a free time and he's got a selection that is second to none. It's incredible.

"Andy is always good for a laugh, and he's not afraid to laugh at himself. When you have a Family Guy chin, where your chin looks like two testicles, you HAVE to be able to laugh at yourself.

"He's from Kansas and then went to school in Kentucky, so it doesn't get worse than that. But despite all that, he's a good young goalkeeper and he's got a thriving secret video rental business on the side, so he's done well to get as far as he has."

#1 WILLIAM HESMER (2007)

"Ricky Bobby, as he is often referred to, is not the unsophisticated slouch that this nickname might suggest. More tellingly, he is also known as C.C. Willie. That is short for Country Club Willie, a man who enjoys the finer things in life, like rocking his Polo polos and khaki shorts, imported brew in hand, while circulating with the regulars and making small talk at many a country club bar. A top man who can also play goalkeeper...who would have thought such a combination existed?"

#3 BRAD EVANS (2007)

"Many fans might not have seen Brad yet as his rather flimsy body has needed numerous touch-ups, thus confining him to his nurse's quarters for extended periods of time. Brad is an Arizona boy who was repeatedly bitten by poisonous snakes and scorpions in his early years, and has obviously never fully recovered. It has affected his dress sense, showering ability, and has led to some of his previously mentioned flimsiness. Brad is a genuinely nice lad with loads of ability, so we hope to see him on the pitch soon."

#5 DANNY O'ROURKE (2007)

"Where do I start with Danny 'Meathead' O'Tool? Danny is a local Columbus lad who finally, after playing for numerous teams all the way from the west coast to New York, found his way home. His smile has not left since arriving here, as now he can study the habits of 'Mr. Muscle', Jacob Thomas, and try to move from his Baby Meathead title up to compete with the big boys in the Heavyweight Meathead division.

"Around the soccer field or training facility, his motto seems to be 'If it moves...kick, hit, or inflict some pain on it', so most people give him lots of space and let him hurt himself, which he enjoys nonetheless.

"Being a local lad, Danny is well known in the community, because if people don't know who he is, he tells them forcefully.

"He is also a great guy in the locker room. His jokes are improving, along with his wig, and he is slowly breaking his Starbucks addiction. Mr. Columbus? He may just be the well-rounded figure to take the title!"

(I ask: "Anything else about Danny O?")

"Why? Has he been making rude comments and talking s*** about me? Has he?!?"

(I reply: "No, but he just seems like a character that you could talk about for an hour or two.")

"I probably could, but, I mean, I don't want to kill the guy. I mean, take a look. He wears his sister's t-shirts. He's doing it to himself, really. It's not my place to pile on."

#7 GUILLERMO BARROS SCHELOTTO (2007)

"Again, like last year, when we had a translation issue with the Chilean, we had one this year with the Argentinian. But Guillermo…I have heard many different pronunciations of his last name… SkuhLOATo… ShehLOTToh…. Ess SchkuhLOAToh…and another one that sounds a bit like 'escargot'…I'm not sure which is correct.

"Guillermo is a great guy who came here not knowing a lick of English, but he is picking it up quickly. Even more importantly, he isn't afraid to pick up the bad words along the way. He has used these words to create some very unique phrases that keep the guys laughing at training.

"Guillermo is a family man, and his wife is nearly due to give birth again, meaning he has been spending a bit of time picking up the family dinner from various local restaurants. I think he has been enjoying the burrito aspect of this task. Burritos are more Mexican than Argentinian, so it is possible that he had not been introduced to a burrito before. His addiction started with actual burritos, but before long, he was converting all of his food into burrito form. He would stop at McDonalds for a burger and fries, and then he would wrap them into a burrito. Pizza? He would roll it up into a burrito. He would go to a nice restaurant and ask for a filet mignon burrito.

"We have really noticed this on the road trips, where he'll pour milk and cereal onto a tortilla to make a burrito for breakfast. It's a soggy mess, but it's the only way to get him to eat the most important meal of the day. Eating all foods only in burrito form is a unique concept that Guillermo has brought into the team, along with his amazing soccer talents."

#10 ALEJANDRO MORENO (2007)

"Alejandro is our DT, or Designated Translator. He is the official mediator for the group of players that has been nicknamed The Espanols. He translates for the Espanols, so on top of his salary, he is also earning translator money.

"We acquired Ale specifically because we needed a translator for the Espanols who could also play soccer. That way, it was only one roster spot."

(I asked: "Joseph Ngwenya was not much help as a translator?")

"Joe is a terrific person and a talented player, but he cannot speak English, or even his native tongue of Zimbabwean, in any sort of understandable form. He is a leally leally bad translator.

"Alejandro is a tank of a forward, plus he can translate, so the squad is very excited that only one roster spot was needed to fill these two urgent necessities. His versatility has saved someone's job, so we are all thankful to have Ale on our team."

#13 ANDREW PETERSON (2007)

"Andrew is very quiet. He came from that Cleveland team...the Cleveland Steamers? No, wait, it's the Cleveland City Stars. My fault. Andrew is a very nice young lad, and I have learned that he has taken a liking to the golf facilities in the region, and that he has been playing a little golf."

(I follow-up: "With Andy 'The Hebrew Hammer' Gruenebaum?")

"Yes, with the Hebrew Hammer. They have become golf buddies, and you can only imagine how important free golf is to the Hebrew Hammer. Lucky for Andrew, he has been able to tag along with the Hammer, so he too has been enjoying his free golfing."

#15 STEFANI MIGLIORANZI (2007)

"Big Stef is well traveled. He's a nice guy who was born in Brazil, went to school in the United States, married a girl with a European background...his kids are pretty much going to be the ultimate melting pot. I think the only thing they won't have is a bit of Kiwi, which is a shame, because it would put a touch of class into the mix.

"Stef is a good man who likes to have the odd laugh. My wife and I have really taken to Stef and his wife. They are good people to hang out with, as any of you out there who have talked to him already know."

(I said: "I'm surprised you didn't mention the fact that he always wears a suit on game days.")

"To tell you the truth, at first I didn't know if he was coming straight to the game from a wedding or a funeral. I didn't know whether to offer my congratulations or sympathies. Then I thought he was going to post-game parties with a higher class of people than the rest of us. But now I know he just likes to dress…for nines? What's that saying?"

(I correct: "Dressed to the nines.")

"That's it! There you go! I pulled it out of the hat! I can speak a bit of American now and then."

#19 ROBBIE ROGERS (2007)

"Robbie is a little guy from California who spent last year with Heerenveen in the Dutch league. He got homesick, so he signed with MLS, and then got sent to Columbus, which is probably just as far from his home as Heerenveen was in the first place.

"In Columbus, Robbie is living at the Daddy Day Care Center with Timmy Ward and Danny Szetela. It's frightful to think that he has two bad influences bringing him up nowadays. I feel bad for the guy, because I think there is a genuinely good guy buried deep down beneath the Ward and Szetela influences.

"Robbie is also a ladies man. Or at least all the ladies want him to be their man. I have heard many catcalls at various games. All kinds of catcalls. It's really bad."

[At this point, our interview is interrupted by Andy Gruenebaum, who needs Duncan's keys so he can get his cell phone out of Duncan's car. Duncan originally declines the request, saying, "If I give you my keys, you will siphon gas out of my tank and steal the spare change from my ashtray."]

#27 RYAN JUNGE (2007)

[I struggle pronouncing Junge's last name.]

"No, I think it's Yoong…or Joong…Jungah…Jingles…Jungle… Juggler…I haven't yet got that sorted out, and I think it frustrates him. Every now and then I will say it correctly, and he will get really, really, really excited, but then I'll forget what I said and get it wrong five seconds later. Now I've just settled on calling him Jungle Jim because he is a big guy and a meathead. He spends his time wrestling with Danny O'Rourke, who is a self-professed meathead.

"Ryan is from Creighton, which I think is in Nebraska. There isn't much to do in Nebraska, which allowed him time to develop some unique talents. He can finish off a full apple juice in less than three seconds. If you give him an apple juice, it's gone in three seconds."

(I ask: "Are we talking a Hejduk apple juice, here?")

"No, we're talking real apple juice...the apple juice that comes from apples instead of grains. It's unbelievable what that man can do to a bottle of apple juice."

NOTE: Chad Marshall and Frankie Hejduk predate the inception of Oughton's Intro-Dunc-tions. Also, I figured I would get the official intro-dunc-tions for Pat Noonan and Stanley Nyazamba for the 2009 edition, but Noonan was traded and Nyazamba was waived before that could happen. As a result, they both escaped scot-free.

Sirk's Notebook: Crew 2, Dallas 1

Match date: Saturday, August 16, 2008
Scoring:
35: DAL Cunningham 4 (Serioux 2)
62: CLB Carroll 1 (Schelotto 11, Moreno 4)
65: CLB Evans 3 (Schelotto 12)
Attendance: 17,647
Crew's record afterward: 10-6-4

Man, the 2008 edition of the Columbus Crew has these milestone games down to a science.

* The 2008 Crew's record when Moffat Mania came to town and Adam Moffat made his historic regular-season home debut, which was broadcast live in two countries[99] around the world? 1-0-0.

* The 2008 Crew's record when amassing a club-record 18 corner kicks? 1-0-0.

*The 2008 Crew's record when finally getting their historic chance to play a league match at a minor league baseball stadium? 1-0-0.

* The 2008 Crew's record when conceding a club-record 17 corner kicks? 1-0-0.

* The 2008 Crew's record when an opponent records his 100th career goal? Fittingly enough, 1-0-0. Get it?[100] It's almost like they did it on purpose.

It was yet another fun night at The House That Lamar Paid More Qualified People To Build, as the Crew overcame Jeff Cunningham's 100th career goal to defeat FC Dallas, 2-1. Although not as sexy of a milestone, the third career goals by both Brian Carroll and Brad Evans lifted the Crew to a come-from-behind victory and put Columbus atop the league table.

Rough First Half

Playing in front of their largest crowd of the season, the Crew took the field and laid more eggs than a bunny rabbit at Easter time. Dallas created several dangerous scoring chances and took a 1-0 lead into the break.

---

[99] The U.S. and Canada. Even though they are right next to each other, one could still take the long way and travel around the world to get from one to the other.

[100] In case you didn't, 1-0-0 = 100.

"The first half was not good," said Crew coach Sigi Schmid. "Will Hesmer made some big saves to keep us in the game, especially that 1v1 with Cunningham. We were lethargic."

Dallas head coach Schellas Hyndman, naturally, was pleased with the opening 45 minutes. "We had a great first half. It almost felt like we were the home team. We were unfortunate not to get more than one goal."

Hyndman felt that lateral movement was the key to Dallas' early success. "What we tried to exploit was that we have two good strikers, and we had Victor Sikora playing his first game for us on the left side," he said. "We tried to move the ball laterally. We did not want the ball in the center of the field. We wanted to get it in the middle and then move it out wide, and we were finding a lot of success that way. Early in the game, Columbus had trouble shifting from one side to the other after overloading the side with the ball."

Schmid, meanwhile, could not pinpoint just one source of his team's first-half malaise. "We didn't play well," he said. "It wasn't any one specific thing. We didn't get out of the back, we were too stretched on the field, we didn't put pressure on their back four, we weren't stepping up to their midfielders in time, we were too slow, we didn't try to play the ball behind them at all…those were all things we talked about at halftime."

Fortunately, as anyone who has watched the Crew this year knows, a one-goal deficit is a mere trifle. This team has the ability and attitude necessary to shrug off bad stretches, and they proved it again on Saturday.

"We've said this all year, and we believe it – one goal is nothing," said goalkeeper William Hesmer. "Obviously, we don't want to give up that one goal, but if that's what it takes to get guys fired up to come back and fight to the end, I'll take it. A win's a win."

"I told Robert (Warzycha) that as long as we get in at 1-0 and don't get annihilated in the first half after playing so poorly, we have the character to come back in the second half," said Schmid. "The character of this team is great. They listened to what we had to say at halftime. They came out with more energy and were much more direct in their play. We were able to stretch their defense and get in behind them. As a result of that, we created some chances and then the goals came."

And Then The Goals Came…From Whatshisface and That Other Guy

With so many high-profile offensive players, Columbus got goals from surprising sources. The Crew tied the match in the 62nd minute when Brian Carroll buried a half-volley off of a knock-down header from Guillermo Barros Schelotto. It was Carroll's first goal in 25 months.

"It's awesome for BC," said Brad Evans. "We're all happy for him."

In the 65th minute, Evans beat Kenny Cooper to a Schelotto free kick and flicked a glancing header into the net for his third career goal, which gave the Crew a 2-1 lead.

"You know Guillermo's service is going to be great most of the time," said Evans. "Cooper wasn't playing loose on me, but he wasn't as tight. I took advantage of that and got around him, and the ball was perfectly placed. It was a good finish and a good ball from Guille."

Evans almost put the game away for good in the 78th minute, but his rocket clanged off the right post. "I didn't even see where the ball went," he said. "I hit it and then I hit (Adrian) Serioux and my hamstring cramped up. I didn't see it hit the post, but I thought I had it. I want that one back so I can move it a few inches to the left."

The Carroll-Evans scoring combo left Hyndman flummoxed. "I don't know how many goals he scores, but Carroll scores a goal," he said. "And then Evans scores a goal, and I don't know how many goals he scores. The guys we thought might score their goals didn't score goals."

Evans knows that's a good thing. "If we can get more goals out of the midfield, we're going to be so successful," he said.

Jeff Joins the Century Club

Congratulations to Jeff Cunningham for scoring the 100th goal of his career on Saturday. Cunningham joins Jaime Moreno, Ante Razov, and Jason Kreis in the MLS Century Club, and it's a milestone that was 62 percent achieved while wearing black and gold. After a torturous stint in Toronto[101], Jeff was all smiles as he prepared to make his Hoops debut. "I'm happy," he said before the game. "I'm excited. I'm ready."

Cunningham knew he was on the cusp of history, and he wanted it to happen in Columbus. "Hey," he said, while gesturing toward the Crew locker room. "Go in there and tell those guys I want an easy one. Tell them to leave me unmarked so I can get a tap-in or something."

Once the game started, it seemed that Cunningham was cursed. Numerous chances were thwarted at the last moment. There was a goal-line clearance from Chad Marshall. Hesmer made a diving save on a header, and also bravely charged out to snuff a breakaway attempt. Danny O'Rourke deftly defended an open-field one-on-one opportunity.

---

[101] Cunningham was a favorite whipping boy of Toronto coach John Carver, who even went so far as to force Cunningham to change in the reserve locker room rather than with the first team.

But the fifth time was the charm. It wasn't exactly the easy tap-in that he attempted to order before the game, but it was close enough. Cunningham capped a perfectly timed near-post run with a three-yard poke-in that resulted in a high-speed, three-body pileup.

Jeff did not look happy coming off the field after the final whistle, and the Hoops were already gone by the time I got out of the Crew locker room, so I never got to talk to Jeff after the game. I did speak with Duncan Oughton, who had gone over to offer his congratulations after the game, and had also walked off the field with Cunningham. As one might expect, Duncan said that Jeff was down on the whole thing because of the loss.

That said, it was only fitting that goal No. 100 came at Crew Stadium. With the exception of his first playoff goal, which was scored on the road in Tampa, all of Jeff's milestone goals have been scored in Columbus:

* First career goal – May 17, 1998, at Ohio Stadium
* First goal in Crew Stadium history – May 15, 1999
* 50th career goal – May 10, 2003, at Crew Stadium
* First All-Star goal – July 30, 2005, at Crew Stadium
* 100th career goal – August 16, 2008, at Crew Stadium

According to the pool quotes provided by MLS after the game, it appears that Cunningham realized all this. "Sometimes people say the stars are aligned and things are meant to be, and I just felt like this was destiny for me to get it here (in Columbus)," he said. "This is where it all started. I have special place in my heart for Columbus and the fans appreciate me, so this is where it was supposed to happen. Maybe all the things I went through in Toronto was because it wasn't meant to happen there."

More on Cunningham

Given that the opportunity was there to score goal No. 100 in Columbus, Dallas coach Schellas Hyndman had no qualms about starting Cunningham, who arrived in Dallas on Tuesday. "This was his comfort zone," Hyndman said. "I think it was the first goal he had ever scored against this club, so it was something personal for him. I thought he had an outstanding first half, getting behind the defense and creating opportunities. He's going to be a good player for us."

Meanwhile, Hesmer shrugged off the idea of being the answer to a trivia question that will never be asked on Jeopardy. "Going in, we knew Jeff wanted to score his 100th goal in Columbus," Hesmer said. "It sucks it was against me, but good for him."

Jeff Cunningham possibly asks Danny O'Rourke for an easy tap-in goal as Cunningham sought his 100th career tally on August 16, 2008. While Danny wouldn't give him a tap-in, Cunningham achieved the milestone anyway. (Photo by Sam Fahmi.)

Helloooooooo Noonan[102]

In his first game since transferring from Norway, Pat Noonan started and played 58 minutes in a fairly uneventful Crew debut.

"Noonan is going to play better than he did tonight, but he was able to get his feet wet," said Schmid. "He suffered along with our team because the team was not playing well (in the first half.) As the new guy, it's tough for him to change our play when the team is playing that way."

Noonan acknowledged some fitness issues and rust, and he also delivered the quip of the night. "It was nice to be a part of a victory," he said. "All they had to do was sub me out in order to start scoring some goals."

Guille The Great

It's obvious that Guillermo Barros Schelotto has been an offensive dynamo since joining the Crew early in the 2007 season. After Saturday's two-assist performance, Schelotto now has 9 goals and 23 assists in his Crew career. That means he has been on the feeding or finishing end of 32 goals, which I will simplify by referring to as "goals produced." In just 42 games, not even a season-and-a-half, Schelotto ranks 10th all-time in Crew history for goals produced.

---

[102] I'm sure that variation of the Seinfeld joke never gets old to him.

CREW ALL-TIME GOALS PRODUCED LEADERS

1. Brian McBride - **107** (62 G, 45 A)
2. Jeff Cunningham - **105** (62 G, 43 A)
3. Robert Warzycha - **80** (19 G, 61 A)
4. Edson Buddle - **57** (42 G, 15 A)
5. Stern John - **51** (44 G, 7 A)
6. Brian Maisonneuve - **50** (23 G, 27 A)
7. Brian West - **47** (18 G, 29 A)
8. Dante Washington - **42** (28 G, 14 A)
9. John Wilmar Perez - **34** (12 G, 22 A)
10. Guillermo Barros Schelotto - **32** (9 G, 23 A) [103]

Naturally, Guille hasn't been around long enough to catch many of the big names on that list. So let's flip it around and compare those 10 players on goals produced per 90 minutes.

CREW ALL-TIME GOALS PRODUCED PER 90 MINUTES LEADERS
(Minimum of 30 goals produced)

1. Stern John - 1.143
2. Guillermo Barros Schelotto - 0.882[104]
3. Jeff Cunningham - 0.830
4. Dante Washington - 0.764
5. Edson Buddle - 0.749
6. Brian McBride - 0.689
7. Robert Warzycha - 0.593
8. John Wilmar Perez - 0.513
9. Brian West - 0.473
10. Brian Maisonneuve - 0.323

So if you've been watching Guille and have had the feeling that you've been seeing something special...you have. In the entire history of the Columbus Crew, only Stern John has produced goals at a pace that exceeds

---

[103] Guille would finish the 2008 regular season tied for 8th with Dante Washington at 42, based on 12 goals and 30 assists.

[104] Guille would finish the 2008 regular season at 0.989 goals produced per 90 minutes.

Guille's rate of production. The Nordecke has every reason to genuflect in the Argentine's presence.[105]

On to the Races

If you were an assistant referee on Saturday night, you would have spent your evening running up and down the sideline. You would have directed some throw-ins. You would have pointed to the corner flag every now and then. You might have cleared a wayward streamer or two. You might have even wiggled your flag to alert the center referee to a foul. But what you would not have done is raised your flag and held it high, proudly nailing some scurrying scofflaw or lollygagging loiterer for getting a head start behind the defense.

Yup, the Crew and Hoops combined for zero offside infractions. How rare is that? The last time the Crew were involved in an offside-free contest was May 6, 2006, in a 1-0 win at Salt Lake. That's a span of 77 matches.

Cynics might scoff that the odds against an offside-free game involving Jeff Cunningham are astronomical. Then again, during that 2006 offside-free match, Cunningham played 90 minutes for Salt Lake, and one of the Crew's starting forwards was the unfailingly flag-tastic Kei Kamara. Go figure.

Correction Time! (a.k.a. "I Am An Idiot!")

After praising Danny O'Rourke for facing the music after that Kansas City game last month, I would be a hypocrite if I didn't do the same.

While researching the previous offside item on Sunday morning, I realized much to my horror that the Crew's first victory over Kansas City this year was by a 2-1 score, not 3-2 like my brain was convinced it was. This means all the stuff that I wrote in the Kansas City notebook about scoring nine goals against the Wizards and averaging three goals per game against them this year, and how that compared historically, was complete and utter bull(poop).

Meticulous historical research means nothing when you start out with a premise based on flawed 2008 data that you "know" to be a fact when it isn't. While no readers or colleagues called me on it after publication, it's embarrassing, and I apologize for screwing that one up.

---

[105] One of my favoriteNordecke traditions is when the group chants "Guillermo! Guillermo! Guillermo!" and gives the we're-not-worthy bow to Schelotto as he lines up over a corner kick.

I learned my lesson while researching the next tidbit...

Cunny's Kill List

After Saturday's game, I saw it reported that with Cunningham's first-ever goal against the Crew, he had scored against every MLS club. So I thought it might be fun to compile "Cunny's Kill List," whereby he is the goal-scoring assassin, and then listing the dates on which he first "killed" each club with a goal. Obviously, the list would finish up with "Columbus – August 16, 2008." So I started working on the list...

Los Angeles - May 17, 1998
New England - May 22, 1998
San Jose - May 30, 1998
Miami - July 29, 1998
New York - August 12, 1998
Kansas City - August 16, 1998
D.C. United - June 13, 1999
Dallas - July 24, 1999

Chicago - September 23, 1999
Tampa Bay - June 16, 2001
Colorado - May 10, 2003
Chivas USA - May 14, 2005
Salt Lake - October 1, 2005
Houston - April 22, 2006
Toronto - ....

Uh-oh. I got all the way down to Toronto before I noticed that...well...contrary to published reports that Cunningham has scored against every MLS team, I can find no record of Jeff Cunningham scoring a goal against Toronto. Not only that, but since 2007 was Toronto's first season, and since Salt Lake did not play Toronto for the first time in 2007 until after they had already traded Cunningham to the Hosers, that means that Jeff Cunningham has NEVER PLAYED A GAME against Toronto FC, much less scored a goal against them.

In light of that, I'm betting Jeff has October 11 circled on his calendar, as that is when John "It makes you wonder how he ever scored 99 goals in this league" Carver[106] and the TFC Hosers make their trip to Pizza Hut Park.

The 16 Kill Club

In light of the original reports that Cunningham had scored against every team in MLS history, I became fascinated with the concept of The 16 Kill Club. To be in this club, a player would have to be enough of a veteran to

---

[106] The "he" in that quote was Cunningham, after Carver was dismayed that Cunningham failed to score on a glorious chance late in a game in the Canadian Championship. Seriously, was there a more mismatched manager for Jeff Cunningham than John Carver?

have scored against Miami and Tampa Bay before they were contracted after the 2001 season, would have to be recent enough to have scored against Toronto, would have had to play for at least two different teams, and would have needed to score a boatload of goals in order to gun down everybody.

Those criteria make it easy to weed out people. Roy Lassiter? Too old school. Jason Kreis? Never scored once Toronto joined the league. Taylor Twellman? Could never have scored against the Revs. Carlos Ruiz? Joined MLS the year after contraction. Landon Donovan? That search ended once I saw he never scored against Miami as a rookie.

It's no surprise that the three leading candidates to serve as the founding member of The 16 Kill Club are already members of the Century Club.

* As mentioned, Cunningham has 15 kills. All he needs is Toronto.
* Ante Razov has 14 kills, but his situation is a bit tricky. While he'll have a chance to cross Chicago off his list next year, he won't be able to score against Chivas USA unless he gets traded elsewhere. (Except to Chicago, which would gum up the works from the other direction.)
* Jaime Moreno, the league's all-time goal scoring leader, is tied with Cunningham at 15 kills. Moreno has scored against every franchise in MLS history except for the Houston Dynamo.

Since it's unlikely that Razov will have a chance to bag kills 15 & 16 anytime soon, it's a two-horse race between Cunningham and Moreno.

And here's where it gets good – each player has one more shot at their white whale this season.

And here's where it gets even better – Cunningham faces Toronto on October 11. Moreno faces Houston on October 12.

Such serendipitous scheduling! The 16 Kill Club could grow from zero members to two members in the span of 24 hours![107]

Hoosier Daddy

Pat Noonan's debut vaulted Indiana University back into a first-place tie with UCLA as a source for Crew players, with nine all-time players apiece.

Hoosiers: Mike Clark, Brian Maisonneuve, Brandon Ward, Todd Yeagley, Juergen Sommer, Ned Grabavoy, Danny O'Rourke, Jed Zayner and Pat Noonan.

---

[107] Neither player would accomplish the feat in October. Oh well.

Bruins: Paul Caligiuri, Billy Thompson, Brad Friedel, Mike Lapper, Jorge Salcedo, Nelson Akwari, Chris Henderson, Ante Razov and Frankie Hejduk.

(Man, if only Tony Sanneh had gone to UCLA like "fan favorites" Caligiuri and Razov. The Bruins could have had a monopoly on the Abominable Crewmen. UCLA's loss is Wisconsin-Milwaukee's gain. Or something. I guess. Thank goodness the Bruins are redeemed by those other seven guys, plus Sigi.)

Anyway, despite the tie, Columbus has the reputation of having an Indiana pipeline, and that is largely true since Hoosiers have made 648 appearances for the Crew, compared to 446 appearances by Bruins. That Hoosier advantage is bound to grow with three Hoosiers on the current roster and only one Bruin.

Noonan said he is happy to join up with O'Rourke and Zayner and to be a part of the Crew's IU legacy. "Obviously there have been some IU guys who have gone through here," he said. "It's nice to see some familiar faces coming out of the program and into the league and doing well. It's good to be a part of that."

Turn Back the Clock Night: October 4

One of the things I like about MLSnet beat writer Craig Merz is that he is A Man of Great Ideas. You don't believe me? Fine. Then how about this one?

Before the game, in the usual press box BS session, we got to talking about Bruce Arena's impending hire with the Los Angeles Galaxy. This caused us to reminisce about some of our favorite Bruce Arena moments, which included Bruce's constant harping about games at Ohio Stadium in his D.C. United days, from the narrow field, to announcements during the game, and other such crimes against the game.

(After pretty much nailing the paraphrase in the press box, Craig went through his records and dug up Arena's exact quote, in all its condescending glory, from October 16, 1997: "You wouldn't play a college soccer game there, not to mention a professional game. They play music during the game. It's a circus. But it's probably very good entertainment for Middle America.")

After we had our little chuckle-filled trip down memory lane, Craig hit upon a great idea…

If Bruce Arena is named head coach of the Galaxy (which he now has been), the Crew should make the LA game on October 4 "Turn Back the Clock Night."

"First, for one game only, the Crew would make the field 62 yards wide," Merz explained. "Since there's a high school football game the night before, they could just leave the lines on the grass and use the football field. Instead of the MLS anthem, they can play circus music as the teams walk onto the field. During the game, it will be non-stop Jock Jams and public address announcements. The scoreboard clock can count down. And if they still have the thing, the Crew could even put that old shootout clock behind the north goal."

As great as all that sounds, Merz had not yet revealed his piece de resistance. "As a show of our Midwestern values," Merz said, "the Crew could put a large butter sculpture[108] of Bruce Arena out on the plaza. A Butter Bruce would be very good entertainment for Middle America."

Merz is a genius. For any readers who happen to be named Mark McCullers, please note that you have a month and a half to make this happen.

Mascot Soccer

When the annual mascot soccer game was rained out a few years ago, I thought I reached a new low when my good buddy Flick and I engaged in a mascot soccer fantasy draft, complete with detailed rationales for each pick, and then had readers vote on which team would win. (Answer: Mine.)

As they say, all lows are made to be eclipsed, and another friend of mine did some major eclipsing on Saturday night. The nefarious numbers runner known as the Zman decided to augment his traditional Crew goal pool with a mascot soccer goal pool. That's right – Z accepted money from people as they wagered on which mascot would score the first goal during the annual mascot game. He found six other suckers, including me, so there was $7.00 in the pool. (I took Stinger, the Columbus Blue Jackets' mascot, which was clearly the wrong choice given the goal-scoring prowess the Jackets have displayed since their inception.)

I suppose I should start by giving the officially unofficial scoring summary, as Team East and Team West tied 1-1. (Team East defended the east goal, and Team West defended the west goal.)

Scoring summary:
EAST: Gravy the Bob Evans Dog (Stinger) 4'

---

[108] For those reading this who are not from Ohio, the "butter cow" is always a big hit at the Ohio State Fair. It's a life-sized cow carved from butter. It is usually augmented by other butter sculptures. If I recall, there was a butter Crew logo the year the stadium opened, so Craig's idea is not without precedent.

WEST: Shawnee Bear (unassisted) 7'

Sure, Shawnee Bear came up with a late equalizer, but money changed hands on Gravy's goal. And who was it that was literally riding the Gravy train? Why none other than the nefarious numbers runner known as Zman. Naturally, the other contestants were suspicious.

Zman explained his selection via e-mail on Sunday. "Without seeing Gravy's footwear, I made my selection based on the slenderness of the costume," Z said. "Mobility is a major factor in these games. Regular footwear is a big advantage over the floppy oversized costume shoes that many of the mascots are burdened with, but second to that is the size of the costume itself, and Gravy was a very slender dog. Gravy ran on to a nice through ball, held off the challenge from behind and buried his shot. It was a nice finish and a big chunk of change in my pocket."

Any suspicions of foul play were brushed aside by the Zman. "There were cries of 'rigged!' from the other wager-makers, but how is one to rig a mascot soccer match?" Z asked. "There are no officials to pay off, and there are no team officials as each player represents their own organization. It would dig considerably into my profits if I were to bribe even three of them. It was a completely fair win based on the usual things – scouting, odds, and a bit of luck."

Attempts to at least get my dollar back because Stinger played the through ball that led to Gravy's goal were ignored.

U.S. Open Cupdate

The Charleston Battery, who are the Official Notebook U.S. Open Cup Bandwagon Team Of Destiny, defeated the Seattle Sounders in their U.S. Open Cup semifinal match and will face evil D.C. United in the final on September 3 at RFK Stadium.

The semifinal against the Sounders ended in a 1-1 draw, with Charleston advancing 4-3 on penalties. Former Crew defender Nelson Akwari converted what proved to be the decisive penalty in the 5th round, as his score was followed by the game-winning save by Dusty Hudock.

"It's always a 50/50 chance of winning when you go into a penalty shootout, but we had the home field advantage, and I had a good feeling," said Akwari. "Our keeper came up big with some great saves, and our shooters did a great job of staying composed and scoring goals."

Not only did the Battery avenge Hollywood United's 6-0 loss to the Sounders from back when Hollywood United was the Official Notebook U.S. Open Cup Bandwagon Team Of Destiny, but now Charleston has the chance, in their own way, to avenge everything that D.C. United has ever done to the Crew over the years.

"(Playing D.C.), there's no better time for the Crew fans to jump on the bandwagon and cheer for the Battery," Akwari said. "To the Crew fans that have been cheering for us from the beginning, I've got to say thanks. The whole team, the organization, and the fans are excited about the opportunity that's in front of us. We'll see what happens in D.C. We'll be sure to give them a good game!"

Godspeed, Nelly. May D.C. United smash their own coffee pots in frustration after another Charleston victory.[109]

Yet Another Bandwagon

I would be remiss if I failed to mention that the Cleveland City Stars defeated the Richmond Kickers 1-0 on Saturday to advance to the USL-2 final. The City Stars, of course, are the team that gave us budding Crew folk hero Adam Moffat. Their back line is anchored by former Crew defender Mark Schulte.

In their quest to win the first-ever outdoor soccer title in Cleveland history, the City Stars will be hosting the Charlotte Eagles on Saturday. I'd recommend heading up to Krenzler Field to show your support, but the Crew are at home against Real Salt Lake, so forget that. The good news, however, is that the game will be televised by Fox Soccer Channel, so you can set your DVR and watch it when you get home from the Crew game.

Here's hoping that the Cleveland City Stars bring home another trophy to Titletown USA.[110]

Interesting Cleveland Soccer Factoid

While doing a quick search to see if the NASL's Cleveland Stokers, the ASL's Cleveland Cobras, or the USISL's Cleveland Caps ever won an outdoor soccer title, I came across the following factoid:

---

[109] Charleston upset D.C. United in the 1999 Open Cup by the score of 4-3. Afterward, United's players were so upset that they trashed the visiting locker room at then-brand new Blackbaud Stadium in Charleston. Among the damaged items from the D.C tantrum were the locker room's coffee pots and shower heads. Starting in 2004, the fans of the two teams created the official Coffee Pot Cup that serves as a 'title belt' between the two teams. The loser must fill the Coffee Pot Cup with as much beer as it will hold and present it to the winner. Sadly, United has held the trophy ever since its inception.

[110] Sure, it was in 1948 that the Browns, Indians, and Barons all won titles in the same year, but if I always have to hear about a river fire from 1969, I can cling to a championship year from 1948 since they both happened before I was born.

Randy Lerner, who owns the NFL's Cleveland Browns and Aston Villa of the English Premier League, got his start in sports by working as an equipment manager for the Cleveland Cobras.

Crew team administrator Tucker Walther also got his start in sports by working as an equipment manager for a soccer team. I hope Tucker will still be my friend in the event that he inherits a multi-gazillion dollar company from his dad.

Katie Updatie

And you thought "U.S. Open Cupdate" was bad. Anyway, for you Katie Witham Fan Club members out there, I am happy to pass along some good news. Katie will be picking up freelance work with the Big Ten Network, where she will help cover Ohio State athletics. (As if Buckeye fans didn't already have enough of a reason to write to their local cable company...)[111]

But Crew fans whose cable provider possesses unflinching negotiating willpower should fear not. Katie confirmed that she will also be working the four remaining ONN home broadcasts, so she will be back on the sidelines at Crew Stadium starting next week.

Katie was so happy that I could have sworn that she was going to do back flips. Like, on the grass outside the post-game tent or something. Or did that really actually happen?[112] It was a long night.

Sight of the Night

At 10:55 p.m., Crew players Chad Marshall, Steven Lenhart, Brian Carroll, and Ezra Hendrickson joined the Crew fans gathered around the TV to see if Michael Phelps could set an Olympic record with his eighth gold medal of the Beijing games. He did. And there was much rejoicing.

Before people accuse Ezra of being a front-running, bandwagon swimming fan, in stark contrast to the majority of the USA (which actually stands for United Swimming Aficionados), let the record show that St. Vincent & the Grenadines did not have a contestant in the race, so it's all good.

---

[111] Ah yes, the golden days of the great "Big Ten Network vs. Time Warner Cable" battle that gripped Columbus for a solid year before the two entities could finally reach an agreement that would allow Central Ohioans to receive a 24/7/365 network that they will watch for a grand total of 9 hours per year when OSU football plays the likes of Otterbein, Denison, and Indiana.

[112] Yes, that really actually happened.

The Danny O Goal Watch

Now that Brian Carroll has scored, the attention has turned to the Danny O Goal Watch. So, when can we expect Danny O'Rourke to finally score a goal?

"2012," said Brad Evans.

"I was going for 2011," said O'Rourke. "2012 would be okay, but I was planning that in 2011, I would make a run forward. The other idea is that maybe if we're up 6-0 in a game, I would ask Will to let me score in our own goal, just so I could celebrate."

One would think that a guy like Danny O would have no idea how to celebrate a goal, but that's not true. According to O'Rourke, "I score all the time in practice, so during the games, I let guys like Brian Carroll and Brad Evans see what it feels like."

Questions? Comments? Think mascot soccer would become more popular if they opened the checkbook and signed a Designated Player like Ronald McDonald or Mickey Mouse?[113] Feel free to write at sirk65@yahoo.com

Alejandro Moreno receives a congratulatory head rub from the Nordecke after the Crew's 2-1 victory over FC Dallas on August 16, 2008. (Photo by Sam Fahmi.)

---

[113] First it's mascot soccer fantasy drafts. Then it's mascot soccer goal pools. Now I am proposing a Beckham Rule to take mascot soccer to the next level? I need help.

Sirk's Notebook: Crew 3, Salt Lake 0

Match date: Saturday, August 23, 2008
Scoring:
15: CLB Marshall 3 (Schelotto 13)
25: CLB Schelotto 5 (penalty kick)
55: CLB Evans 4 (Gaven 2, Schelotto 14)
Attendance: 12,448
Crew's record afterward: 11-6-4

The pen is said to be mightier than the sword, but the mightiest implement of them all may be the keyboard on Shawn Mitchell's laptop computer.

After last week's comeback against Dallas, the Columbus Dispatch reporter asked Crew coach Sigi Schmid and defender Danny O'Rourke if the Crew would be better served by blowing out an opponent instead of staging comeback victories. Then in Saturday's paper, in the "How It Might Play Out" section of his game preview, he eschewed the normal "if X happens, then Y might happen, and the result could possibly be Z" format in favor of a flat out declaration that the Crew would score multiple goals and collect the full three points.

Before the game, when I commented in the press box that he had thrown down the gauntlet, Shawn said, "This team is due to blow somebody out, and I think it's going to be tonight."

From Shawn's lips to the Crew's ears. Fueled by the confidence infused in them by the bloodthirsty newspaper writer, the Crew went on a regicidal rampage and slaughtered Real Salt Lake by a score of 3-0. Guillermo Barros Schelotto had a goal and two assists, Eddie Gaven regained his form in a big way and goalkeeper William Hesmer recorded his sixth shutout of the season. All because of the local scribe.

"There, Shawn, are you happy?" Schmid cracked as he took the podium for his postgame press conference. "You wanted a more lopsided score, so we got a more lopsided score."

Modesty and/or corporate policy forced Mitchell to name an actual athlete, in this case Schelotto, as Man of the Match in Sunday's paper. Nevertheless, it's clear to me that the true Man of the Match was none other than Shawn Mitchell.

Furious First Half

From the opening whistle, the Crew ran laps around Real Salt Lake. The right side of the Royals' defense, Robbie Russell and Jamison Olave, suffered ritual abuse at the feet of Schelotto, Robbie Rogers, and Alejandro Moreno, then Eddie Gaven took care of the abuse on the other side of the field, and all of that was possible because the Salt Lake midfield never got off the plane. Amelia Earhart's plane.[114]

The Crew scored both goals off of desperate defensive challenges. Russell brought down Schelotto outside the left corner of the penalty box in the 15th minute. It was the third deep foul conceded by RSL in the opening stretch, and those are some long odds with the accurate Argie standing over the ball. Schelotto's free kick found Chad Marshall's noggin for an easy nod-in to give the Crew a 1-0 lead. Then in the 25th minute, a scorched Nat Borchers had no choice but to body-block Gaven in the box for a penalty. Schelotto calmly converted the spot kick to make it 2-0.

And so it went for 45 minutes. The Crew imposed their will and the Royals had no answer.

"It's a game where, defensively, I don't think we were quite there," said RSL coach Jason Kreis. "I don't think we had the energy or commitment level in the first half. It looked like we had already played 45 minutes before the first whistle blew. A team like Columbus is going to punish you for that."

(That's polite coach-speak for "Our beat writer for the Salt Lake Tribune didn't want this game as badly as that guy from the Dispatch did.")

Goal of the Week Redux?

The Crew's exclamation point came in the 55th minute with a beautiful bit of team play. Schelotto collected a cross-field pass at the midfield stripe, and then fed Eddie Gaven who made a great run into the right channel. Gaven then curled a cross that was met in stride by Brad Evans, whose close-range header hit nothing but net. Beautiful stuff.

"That's the way you'd draw it up," said Schmid.

Evans downplayed his role in the goal. "It's all in the service," he said. "I don't want to say it's easy, but service like that makes it a lot easier."

With Brian Carroll winning Goal of the Week last week, Evans' team-play tally could have a shot it making it two in a row for the Crew.

"If I could get all of the votes that BC's family made for him, I might have a chance," he laughed.

---

[114] Not sure where I was going there. Sure, RSL looked lost, but they were physically present. Amelia Earhart was a completely different kind of lost.

Brad Evans moves the ball against Real Salt Lake on August 23, 2008.
(Photo by Greg Bartram / Columbus Crew)

Goal City

Last week, I mentioned that Craig Merz is a Man of Ideas. This week, Merz noticed that Chad Marshall has scored all three of his goals this year against teams playing in a "City" city. He has two goals against Kansas City and one goal against the team from Salt Lake City.

"I don't what it is," said Marshall. "There aren't any more 'Cities' in the league, are there?"

There will be now. As a result of Craig's research, I am working on a plan whereby the team will constantly refer to their match against "Dallas City" this weekend, not to mention next weekend's big showdown with "New England City."

Go get 'em, Chad![115]

Playoff Push

The Eastern Conference race could be one for the ages. The top five teams are separated by just six points. From Thursday to Sunday, when each

---

[115] In the playoffs Chad would score Massive and legendary goals against "Windy City" and "New York City."

of those teams played their 21st game, the top five went 4-0-1, scoring 11 goals and conceding just one. Let the one-upmanship begin!

The Crew have a potent offense and an uncanny resiliency. The New England Revolution have the cohesion and experience. The Chicago Fire have the best defense in the league. The New York Red Bulls have...well...they are in the race.[116] And as Dante Washington and I discussed Saturday night, D.C. United is probably the scariest team of them all. When they are good, they are VERY good. It's just that they're not good all the time.[117]

It's staggering to think about the possibilities as these teams enter the stretch run. I am frantic and frazzled with pennant-race fever, and so is Danny O'Rourke! Tell 'em Danny!

"I can talk to you about (next weeend's) Dallas game if you want," he said. "That's the only thing we can think about and the only thing we have any control over right now."

Oh. I guess it's just me, then. Apparently the players are going to focus on doing their jobs or something.

Sigi Schmid and Danny O'Rourke NOT discussing playoff races during a break in the action against Real Salt Lake. (Photo by Greg Bartram / Crew)

Updates on Last Week's Notebook

* With a goal and two assists against the Royals, Schelotto has vaulted past John Wilmar Perez and is now 9th all-time in Crew history with 35 goals produced (10 goals, 25 assists). Perez had 34. The next target on

---

[116] Needless to say, if you would have told me in August that New York would make the MLS Cup final...

[117] And it turns out they weren't good down the stretch either, so they missed the playoffs entirely. Thanks to the Crew of course. Hahahaha.

Guille's list is Dante Washington, who is 8th with 42 goals produced. At the rate Guille's going, Dante could be eating his dust in a few weeks.[118]

* Now that Pat Noonan has leveled the all-time Indiana-UCLA pipeline at nine Crew players apiece, recent developmental signing Brian Plotkin has a chance to put the Hoosiers on top once again. Right now, Plotkin is in Leonard Griffin purgatory. Griffin is a Bruin who was on the Crew's roster, but never made an official appearance, and therefore is not on the list. If Plotkin can find the field, he would be the 10th Hoosier to appear in a Crew uniform, restoring IU's traditional crown. (No pressure, Brian. All you have to do is impress that ex-UCLA coach.)[119]

Lots and Lots of Bests

The Crew have the best record in MLS when...

* ...scoring the first goal (9-0-0)
* ...allowing the first goal (2-6-3)
* ...trailing at the half (2-5-2)
* ...playing in a game decided by one goal (7-1-0)

Not too shabby, huh?

Bagpipes

Earlier this week, Shawn Mitchell published an interesting tidbit in his "Covering the Crew" blog over at Dispatch.com. He noted that after training last Wednesday, Adam Moffat tore out of the Obetz parking lot with bagpipe music blaring from his car stereo. What a brilliant piece of observational reporting from Shawn and, naturally, I wanted to know more.

"Shawn heard me listening to a Scottish folk band called RUNRIG, who play traditional and contemporary bagpipes," Moffat explained. "I recommend the band to anyone out there who just feels sometimes like they need to rock out to some bagpipes.[120] My friends and I back home used to

---

[118] Guillermo would finish the season with 12 career goals and 30 career assists, tying him with Dante at 42 goals produced in the regular season. He wouldn't blow past Dante until the start of the 2009 season.

[119] Plotkin would never see the field with the first team, therefore cementing his place in Leonard Griffin purgatory.

[120] Don't we all?

love playing it max volume out the car as we drove, so I still keep it up over here."

As anyone who has been stuck at a long red light knows, rap aficionados typically gut their cars of unnecessary parts, such as the radiator, in order to create more room for enormous speakers that produce bass sounds capable of crumbling the skeletal structure of anyone over the age of 40. It made me wonder if Moffat had installed massive speakers with extra treble, allowing even the highest squeals from the bagpipes to be blasted from his car at full force.

"I haven't yet, but if it would produce a clearer and louder sound for my bagpipes, then it may be a good investment," Moffat said. "I will look into it, so watch out Columbus. If you hear the noise of bagpipes getting closer as you're walking about, don't worry. It's just me driving in your neighborhood with RUNRIG blasting out of my new speakers."

Moffat concedes that his taste in music is different from that of his teammates, but he thinks his taste compares favorably to that of some other guys. "Duncan likes to listen and sing along to some band from New Zealand[121]," he said. "It's decent, but it just doesn't match up to the bagpipes. And Steve Lenhart is well educated in speaking Spanish and loves the Gypsy Kings, but again, it's decent music, but just not in the same league as the bagpipes."

While a voracious consumer of bagpipe music, do not expect Moffat to become another one of those athletes who tries to cash in on his athletic fame by releasing a bagpipe album.[122]

"One of the most common questions I get asked when people find out I'm Scottish is 'can you play the bagpipes?'" he said. "I would love to say yes, but the truth is that I have never even tried. My uncle Will is the only one in my family who can play. Whenever he would stay at my house, he would play his bagpipes at like 7 in the morning. Let me tell you that you cannot sleep through someone playing the bagpipes in the same house. It is one loud instrument."

And to think that Uncle Will wasn't even hooked up to the enormous extra-treble car speakers...

---

[121] It has to be either Crowded House or Flight of the Conchords, right?

[122] Andy Murray, Rowdy Roddy Piper, Shaq, etc.

The Spirit of St. Louis

I have only met Crew television analyst Bill McDermott a few times over the years, but to call the man gregarious would be an understatement. He is never without a joke or a story. Believe it or not, I think he actually calms down on TV.

As I walked into the press box, Bill was in the middle of a tale about some travel woes. From what I gathered, there was a time when he had broadcast a game at the Meadowlands, but his direct flight home from Newark to St. Louis had been canceled. McDermott was at the reservation desk, trying to find a new flight home.

"The lady types a few things into the computer," he explained, "and then she says, 'Mr. McDermott, we can put you on a flight from Newark to Chicago to St. Louis…' and I'm thinking that's not too bad, considering there are no direct flights."

But the woman kept typing, trying to find better alternatives. "Then she says, 'Or we can put you on a flight from Newark to LAX to St. Louis.'"

Needless to say, Bill was stunned by this second option, especially in comparison to the route that was already on the table. "I asked her, 'Who do you think I am? Vasco da Gama?'"

Apparently the woman did not pick up on his explorer joke. Either that, or she would have preferred he used Magellan, since Magellan circumnavigated the globe.

Anyway, one cannot expect to tell such a story to Dwight Burgess and Craig Merz without the inevitable avalanche of comments.

Burgess: "So did you take the LA flight? Think of all the magazine reading you could have done, plus all the in-flight movies you could have watched."

Merz: "Maybe if you got on the LA flight they would have given you a parachute."

Burgess: "And a breathing apparatus, since you'd be at 38,000 feet."

Merz (as an airline employee): "Mr. McDermott, when you see the big arch, jump."

Burgess (as an airline employee): "Don't worry. We'll be more than happy to give you a little push out of the plane."

It was also noted that if one were to land just the right way on the Gateway Arch, one could ride it safely to the ground like a slide.

Story Time With Tucker

With former Crew trainer Craig Devine in town, team administrator Tucker Walther was in full-blown storyteller mode after the game. Here's one of Tucker's many great stories from the Crew's pre-season trip to England. Also present at the telling of the story, and in the story itself, was Dr. Johnson (aka "Dr. J"), one the Crew's team physicians.

"We had just watched West Ham play Liverpool at Anfield," Tucker said. "We were walking down this road to the team bus. The group was me, Dr. J, and (team trainer) Jason Mathews. As we were walking down the street, this hammered Liverpool fan comes rushing up to us. 'ColumbusCrewMLSDavidBeckham!' That's all I could make out of it. Almost everybody over there would say Beckham's name when saying something about MLS. Kinda like here, really.

"So this guy is all excited that we're with an MLS team. He is so drunk he can hardly stand or walk, and for some unknown reason, he has worn a Brazil national team jersey to a Liverpool match at Anfield. Not only that, but he wants us to autograph his Brazil jersey.

"First of all, we're not players. Second of all, we're not from Brazil. But this guy is so smashed he doesn't care. He's determined to have the Chicago Fire sign his Brazil jersey. Oh, that was the other thing. One time he would call us the Columbus Crew, and the next time he would call us the Chicago Fire. He kept switching between the two. I don't think it mattered since it was all 'MLSDavidBeckham' to him.

"So this guy wants to have the Columbus Crew, or maybe the Chicago Fire, sign his Brazil jersey, but he has nothing to write with. So what does he do? He takes off his jersey, hands it to me, and then takes off running. Keep in mind it was friggin' cold out there. We all had winter jackets on, and this drunk guy is stumbling and staggering around with no shirt on while trying to find something to write with. It was actually a good move on his part. We would have just walked away and got on the bus, but since we had this guy's Brazil jersey, we felt like we had to stay there so we could give it back to him.

"The guy eventually comes back, but does he have a Sharpie? No. He has a ballpoint pen. Seriously. A ballpoint pen. We tell him a pen won't work, that he needs to get a marker. So he takes off again. Then he eventually comes back with ANOTHER ballpoint pen. We tell him again that a pen won't work and that he needs to get a Sharpie."

(By this point Dr. J is nearly convulsing at the table.)

"So what does the guy do? He goes to the cop that's right near us. The cop is on a horse. He asks the cop if the cop has a Sharpie."

("This cop is waaaay up there on a HUGE horse!" confirmed Dr. J through his tears.)

(Later, Mathews, who is 6'4", confirmed that the horse was "massive" and "the largest horse I have ever seen that wasn't pulling a Budweiser wagon. That thing could have pulled a Budweiser TRUCK.")

Anyway, back to the story.

"The cop says he doesn't have a marker," Tucker continued, "so the guy takes off again. He finally stumbles back with yet another pen, but it was a little better than the first two. We have to get going, so we decide to sign the guy's shirt so he'll leave us alone. We asked the guy one more time, and told him we were not players, but he insisted that he wanted us to sign his Brazil jersey because it's yellow just like our colors.

"OK, then. We signed his shirt. I think I signed it Brian McBride, Doc signed it Dr. J, and Jason signed it Carlos Bocanegra, since the guy kept calling us the Fire and Jason used to work for the Fire when Carlos was there. The thing is, you couldn't read any of what we wrote anyway because it was a pen. Basically, all we did was ruin the guy's Brazil jersey with pen marks, but he couldn't have been happier. He was so excited. It was so strange."

Speaking of Autographs...

After the game, one of the fun things to witness in the tent is when autograph seekers request autographs from people who don't play on the team. If you're dressed up and look athletic, someone may unwittingly ask you to sign something.

With Brian Dunseth in town to broadcast the game for RSL, he was the subject of several such requests. Each time, he would take care to point out he no longer plays for the Crew and that he's a TV announcer now. His little truth-in-autographing disclaimer was meant to make sure that people aren't blindly having him mess up their quest to have the entire 2008 Crew autograph their jersey or something. Of course, some folks remembered him and wanted his autograph anyway.

Which leads me to this adult woman who approached Dunny and asked for his autograph. As he started to explain he doesn't play for the Crew, she cut him off.

"I don't care. You're hot. Sign it."

Dunny looked over at me, gave a shrug, signed the shirt, and then she went merrily on her way.

After all these years, I still can't comprehend what it's like to be Brian Dunseth.

Sights of the Night

* Dante Washington holding up his Hudson Street Hooligans jersey in the Crew locker room. (As Matt Bernhardt told me during the game, "You know it's a blowout when the supporters are ignoring the game and chanting the name of an ex-player.")

* The normally reticent Chad Marshall celebrating another successful media session by pumping his fists into the air and saying, "Yes! That year and a half at Stanford paid off!"

* Dunseth being floored at the sight of Devine's teenaged son, who had grown a ton since Dunny had last seen him. "When I was your age, I was this tall," Dunny said while holding his hand on his arm, a few inches below the shoulder. "I was little, and my voice sounded…exactly like it does now, actually. It never changed."

* Kristine Fidler, a Canadian even Bill Archer would love[123], hugging people goodbye on her final night of work after a decade in the Crew's front office.

Cleveland Wins the USL-2 Title

In last week's Notebook, I said that people should not go to Cleveland to watch the City Stars compete for the USL-2 title, but should instead record the game and watch it after returning from the Crew-RSL match at Crew Stadium. At least one person ignored my advice.

Adam Moffat, who is out for the year with a torn ACL anyway, received permission to go to Cleveland to watch his friends and ex-teammates play for the USL-2 crown.

"That was great of (Sigi)," said Moffat. "He knows I still have a good relationship with the people up there and that it was the biggest game in their short existence. I have some real good friendships with the players, coaching staff, and fans up there, so it was great to see them win the championship in only their second year. I was also disappointed that I didn't get to see us have a great victory over Salt Lake, but I was getting score updates on the phone and enjoyed seeing the goals add up."

By defeating the Charlotte Eagles, the City Stars became the first professional outdoor soccer team in Cleveland history to win a league championship. (The Cleveland Crunch won indoor soccer titles in 1994, 1996,

---

[123] Toronto FC fans are convinced that Big Soccer blogger Bill Archer is an anti-Canadian hate criminal who should be prosecuted at The Hague.

and 1999.) Let's turn it back over to Moffat for his thoughts on the evening…

"Cleveland won 2-1, but could have made it much more convincing with the chances they created," he said. "But they got the victory they deserved. Charlotte had a great season, but couldn't produce it in the final. They showed great respect to Cleveland when the City Stars picked up the winner's trophy, and that was great to see. It was an enjoyable match and I'm very happy for the Cleveland manager, Martin Rennie, who is a fellow Scot[124]."

And thus is the story of yet another championship for the city of Cleveland.

Normalized Point Scores

One of the frustrating conundrums about soccer is that it's hard to put a team's performance in an overall perspective. In baseball, football, basketball, and pre-shootout hockey, we Americans could easily reference winning percentage, with ".500" being the most obvious dividing line. Anything above ".500" is a winning season, anything below ".500" is a losing season, and anything at ".500" is the very mathematical definition of mediocrity.

The traditional use of winning percentage does not work in soccer since there are three points for a win and one point for a draw. All ".500" records are not made equal. A 4-4-2 record is a better ".500" record than 3-3-4. So that's the first way winning percentage is misused in soccer. I've also seen winning percentage used as literally the percentage of games won, and also the percentage of points won versus points possible. The problem here is that as a percentage, these things do not in any way correlate to winning percentages as most Americans, me included, know them. There's no easy frame of reference, like the traditional ".500" mark.

Some people prefer looking at points per game. It's a fine way to look at how a team compares to perfection, but it also lacks an easily definable frame of reference or any normalization.

Part of the problem with all of this is that with there being three points for a win and only one for a draw, there is a variable disbursement of points. Some games produce three points. Others only produce two total points. Over the years, some seasons find points tough to come by, whereas others see more points put into the standings.

---

[124] I wonder if he plays the bagpipes?

And then when looking at MLS, there is also the matter of fluctuating schedule lengths and competition structures. Seasons have varied from 26 games to 32 games, and there was that whole shootout era where games produced either three points or just one total point.

Wanting a way to compare teams across all seasons, and in relation to a fixed mid-point a la the ".500" mark, I took a cue from baseball stats such as OPS+ or ERA+, which compare those stats to the league norm, and give you an idea of how a player compared to that norm in any given season. An average season has a score of 100. Anything above 100 is better than average, and anything less is below average.

Just like ERA+ shows how a pitcher's 3.50 ERA means one thing when the league's ERA is 3.00, and another thing when the league's ERA is 4.50, I wanted to create something that reflected the strength of a team's point total in any given season compared to the average point total in any given season. I wanted to compare how teams did in relation to their actual league environment that season.

So what I settled on was something called a Normative Point Score (NPS). It's pretty simple, really. All it consists of is the number of points a team earned, divided by the league average of points per team. Then that number is multiplied by 100 to remove the decimals. Just like OPS+ or ERA+, 100 is average, or ".500" in the traditional sense. The higher the number, the better.

And even better is that you can subtract 100 from a team's NPS to find out how a team compared to average, percentage wise. A 120 team was 20% better than the average ".500" team that year. A 75 team was 25% worse.

(Note: For 2001, I had to break the league average down to a per-game level to calculate the NPS for teams who played 26 or 27 games, respectively. In the Crew example below, the average is based on the 26 games the Crew played.)

Just like winning percentage, NPS isn't the be-all end-all. In 2006, the St. Louis Cardinals finished five games over .500, but won their division and the World Series. In most other seasons, finishing five games over .500 would have put them 10+ games out of first place. But like winning percentage, I hope it gives a clearer view of winning and losing seasons, and how teams fared when compared to the norm. You know, just like everyone knows that the 2006 Cardinals were a joke based on their winning percentage.

For starters, let's take a look at the Crew's history, with the year, the Crew's points, the league average in parentheses, and then the Crew's NPS.

As you can see, the Crew's three 45-point seasons and four 38-point seasons are all different when viewed within the context of the league norms for those seasons.

1996: 37 (41.2) **90**   **2002:** 38 (39.8) **95**
1997: 39 (41.4) **94**   **2003:** 38 (40.9) **93**
1998: 45 (42.5) **106**   **2004:** 49 (40.4) **121**
1999: 45 (38.5) **117**   **2005:** 38 (44.3) **86**
2000: 38 (45.2) **84**   **2006:** 33 (43.3) **76**
2001: 45 (37.1) **121**   **2007:** 37 (41.2) **90**

Yup, in 12 seasons, the Crew have been "above .500" (or 100) just four times. It's also fun to note that, in relation to the norm, the 2001 team fared just as well as the 2004 team, but the latter won the Supporters' Shield while the former finished 8 points behind Chicago.

For those who think this Crew season has been special, you'd be correct. The Crew's current NPS is 129, which would be the best in club history.[125]

[BOOK NOTE: I have updated the following lists and final factoids with the final 2008 numbers.] A few other quick lists...

BEST NPS IN MLS HISORY
1. 1998 Los Angeles – 160
2. 1999 D.C. United – 148
3. 2005 San Jose – 144
4. 2001 Miami – 143
5. 1996 Tampa Bay – 141

WORST NPS IN MLS HISTORY
1. 2001 Tampa Bay – 36
2. 1999 MetroStars – 39
3. 2005 Chivas USA – 41
4. 2005 Real Salt Lake – 45
5. 1999 Kansas City – 52

---

[125] The 2008 Crew finished with 57 points against a league average of 40.9, for an NPS of 139. It's the best mark in team history, 8th-best all-time in MLS history, and the second-highest NPS of the 13 MLS Cup champions.

MLS CUP WINNERS RANKED BY NPS

1. 1999 D.C. United – 148
2. 2008 Columbus – 139
3. 1997 D.C. United – 133
4. 1998 Chicago – 132
5. 2002 Los Angeles – 128
6. 2000 Kansas City – 126
*. 2007 Houston – 126
8. 2003 San Jose – 125
9. 2001 San Jose – 121
10. 1996 D.C. United – 112
11. 2006 Houston – 106
12. 2004 D.C. United – 104
13. 2005 Los Angeles – 102

TOP FIVE MLS CUPS RANKED BY COMBINED NPS

1. 1999 (DC-LA) – 288
2. 1998 (CHI-DC) – 268
3. 2003 (SJ-CHI) – 255
4. 2000 (KC-CHI) – 252
5. 2001 (SJ-LA) – 248

WORST THREE MLS CUPS RANKED BY COMBINED NPS

1. 2006 (HOU-NE) – 217
2. 2002 (LA-NE) – 223
3. 2004 (DC-KC) – 225

TOP THREE CLUBS IN ALL-TIME AVG NPS (through 2008)

1. Houston – 119.0
2. Chicago – 114.0
3. Los Angeles – 110.8

BOTTOM THREE CLUBS IN ALL-TIME AVG NPS (through 2008)

1. Toronto – 73.5
2. Real Salt Lake – 74.8
3. Chivas USA – 93.5

Other random factoids...

* Supporters Shield winners have averaged an NPS of 136.3. The 1998 Galaxy had the highest at 160, while the 2004 Crew had the lowest at 121. There have been four scores in the 120s, four in the 130s, four in the 140s, and then the Galaxy's ridiculous 1998 campaign.

* MLS Cup winners have averaged 123.2. Only three below-average teams have made it to the MLS Cup final. Shockingly, the 2005 Galaxy is not one of them. The 1997 Rapids (92), 2002 Revolution (95), and 2008 Red Bulls (95) hold that distinction.

* Come to think of it, the 2005 Galaxy and the 2006 World Series champion St. Louis Cardinals would have had identical NPS scores of 102, converting the Cards' 83 wins into the NPS format. Wow. What a pair of sucky champions.

* If one throws out the expansion teams from 2005 and beyond, New York has the lowest all-time NPS among existing teams at 94.5.

* The Crew's all-time average NPS after 2008 is 100.9, placing the Crew 5th all-time behind Houston, Chicago, Los Angeles, and D.C. United.

So that's this week's interesting/boring research portion of the Notebook. I rather like this NPS idea and find it intriguing, but maybe I am a moron. I am sure it can be improved upon, so if any of you math/stat freaks out there have ideas for refining it into some sort of NPS+ stat that accounts for schedule strength or something, please feel free to send me an email at the address listed below.

Since I can't let readers leave on a nerdy research session, I will leave you with one last tidbit about...

Olympic Sports

The Olympics are over. The Beijing games were the last time America's Pastime, baseball, will be an Olympic sport. I guess some other country's pastime will have to fill the void. Then I thought back to something Moffat said during our discussion...

"For anyone who watched the Olympic opening ceremony, they would have heard the bagpipes being played numerous times," Moffat proudly noted. "That's an event us Scots would have taken gold in – bagpipes."

Uh-oh. By 2012, Adam could be demoted to the second most famous athlete in his family if Uncle Will brings the bagpiping gold home to Glasgow.

Questions? Comments? Have any idea who is the Jimi Hendrix of bagpipers? Feel free to write at sirk65@yahoo.com

William Hesmer watches the action waaaaaaay down at the other end of the field as the Crew destroy Real Salt Lake, 3-0, thanks to Shawn Mitchell's request for a blowout. (Photo by Sam Fahmi)

Road Work: Crew 2, Dallas 1

Match date: Saturday, August 30, 2008
Scoring:
35: DAL Cunningham 5 (Guarda 1)
37: CLB Moreno 8 (Marshall 2, Schelotto 15)
40: CLB Gaven 1 (Schelotto 16)
Attendance: 10,590
Crew's record afterward: 12-6-4

RETROACTIVE RECAP

For the second time in two weeks, the Crew allowed Jeff Cunningham to open the scoring before overtaking FC Dallas by a 2-1 score. This time, the speed of the comeback was stunning. Just two minutes after the Dallas goal, the Crew equalized on a double header off a Schelotto corner kick. Chad Marshall hung back and nodded the ball forward toward the goalmouth traffic. Alejandro Moreno then nodded the ball into the net. Just three minutes after that, Schelotto undressed Dallas defender Drew Moor in the left channel before serving a left-footed cross that was headed home by Eddie Gaven.

The victory vaulted the Crew into sole possession of first place in the Eastern Conference. For good.

QUOTES

Sigi Schmid: "Obviously I'm very happy with our team character; our ability to go down a goal and continue to play and get two goals back. We've done it a few times this season. I think we've done it as well as anybody has this year. It's something that I'm proud of— it's the fight, it's the character that our team has that allows us to do it. The team believes in themselves, they have great confidence in each other, and they work hard for each other. So to be right now in first place and have the most points, it's something that they can be very proud of, and it's a reflection of the team we've built, and they're all part of that."

On the play of Guillermo Barros Schelotto: "He's definitely a special player. He had the assist on the first goal as he swings the ball in. But the move he made prior to the second goal was unbelievable: the quick cut back and then swinging it in with his off foot. He has the ability to make special plays. He has the ability to make plays that decide games. And he's done it for us all season, and the guys know what he can do."

Sirk's Notebook: Crew 4, New England 0

Match date: Saturday, September 6, 2008

Scoring:

40: CLB Schelotto 6 (unassisted)

45: CLB Iro 1 (Schelotto 17)

67: CLB Garey 2 (Schelotto 18)

90: CLB Garey 3 (Noonan 1)

Attendance: 16,918

Crew's record afterward: 13-6-4

Upon opening Saturday's Dispatch and seeing that the Buckeyes were hosting the Ohio Bobcats and that the Crew were hosting the New England Revolution, any local sports fan could have guessed that the city of Columbus would be playing host to a nailbiter and a blowout on that gorgeous day. But only a wall-bouncing wacko could have correctly predicted which game would be which.

Just hours after the Buckeyes rallied in the 4th quarter to squeak past the mighty Bobcats[126], the Crew nuked New England, 4-0, in a game that was nowhere near as close as the score would indicate. The Crew outshot the Revs 27-4. Shots on goal were 14-1 in favor of Columbus. It was a game that felt like it could have been 5-0 or 6-0…before the Crew actually made it 1-0 in the 40th minute.

Both Crew coach Sigi Schmid and Revs coach Steve Nicol were quick to qualify the result by referencing the oppressive schedule that has seen the Revs play 11 matches in 39 days and 18 matches in 71 days. It is undeniable that the Revs were playing with leaden legs and burned-out brains.

However, as the Buckeyes showed earlier in the day, the advantage of physical superiority is meaningless if you don't take care of business. On Saturday night, the Crew showed up for work, punched the clock, and then punched the Revs in their gaping jaws. Over and over. For 90 minutes. It's what good teams do.

In the past, this is the type of game that the Crew teams of yesteryear would have found a way to squander. They'd play down to a wounded rival or buckle under the pressure of expectation. But once again, this Crew team has proven to be a different breed.

---

[126] Thanks in large part to a preposterously blown call on a blatant block in the back that turned a 19-14 game into a 26-14 game in the final minutes.

"I told the guys I wanted them to be nervous," said Schmid. "I wanted them to feel the weight of the big game. I wanted to see how they responded. They passed with flying colors."

Cue the Violins

I know most Crew fans are going to have little sympathy for the three-time defending Eastern Conference champions as they bemoan the ravages of the heavy MLS, U.S. Open, SuperLiga, and CONCACAF Champions League schedule that is the price of their success. And if I were dating Charlize Theron, I'm sure nobody would want to hear me complain about how little sleep I've been getting after the bedroom lights go out. But since Sigi went out of his way to comment on it, let's give Revs coach Steve Nicol his say.

"One thing we have to do is understand where we are," said Nicol. "When you can't run, you can't compete, and at the present time, we can't run. We can't close the ball, and when we do get it, we can't go past people. When you go to make challenges, you're a half-yard short. It's an impossible task. They played well – they closed us down real quick, made some chances – but as I said, if you can't run, you can't compete, and we can't compete at the present time."

Nicol said there was no way to compare this game to the Revs' first visit, which resulted in a 1-0 New England victory. "We can't run," he reiterated. "Last time we were here, we could get around the field. Today, we couldn't get around the field. When you travel 20,000 miles and play a game every three or four days for almost three months, it's an impossibility."

While the major clubs in Europe play a heavy schedule, Nicol said the wear and tear they face is negligible compared to what the Revs have endured. "It's a huge difference," he said. "They don't travel like that. They travel an hour and a half. They leave at 6:00 and get there at 7:30. We leave at 6:00 and get there at 3:00 in the afternoon. We have to deal with time zones, time differences, different countries...we were in three different countries in seven days last week. It's a unique situation that we find ourselves in."

Schmid was sympathetic, but also knew that business is business. "Let's understand that New England is a team, as Stevie mentioned, that has played a lot of games and has guys injured," he said. "They're a quality team. Our goal going into the game, our mantra for the last two days, was to make it a 90-minute game. Don't let New England off the hook. Don't let a tired team have a 45-minute game. We stuck to the gas pedal right from the start of the game.

"We were fortunate a bit that we got to play a tired team, but there's also a thing that when you go into a game like that that you're supposed to win, it can be difficult to accomplish. I was very proud of them because they came out and did the job."

Oh, and before we put the violins away, let's not forget that the Crew were playing without their leading goal scorer, Alejandro Moreno, and their energizing captain, Frankie Hejduk, both of whom were away on national team duty.

Guille Great Again

It seems that every week, Guillermo Barros Schelotto is setting some new statistical benchmark or another. It's becoming a broken record of broken records. With a goal and two assists, Schelotto wormed his way into the record book two more times just a week after setting the Crew's single-season assist record. (We'll address his new records in the Mr. Numbers Nerd segments below.)

After hitting the crossbar and serving up several dangerous free kicks during the Crew's first half onslaught, Schelotto finally put the Crew on the board in the 40th minute when he scored his sixth goal of the season. After Robbie Rogers scorched down the left wing, he sent a low ball into the box. Steven Lenhart challenged Michael Parkhurst for the ball, which deflected off of Parkhurst and into the path of Schelotto. Guille buried his first run-of-play goal of the season when he one-timed the ball from, well, about a foot from the penalty spot.[127]

In the 45th minute, Schelotto picked out the head of Andy Iro on a free kick, resulting in the Crew's second goal. In the 67th minute, his no-look, Magic Johnson, Showtime Lakers pass to Jason Garey created a 3-0 advantage for the Crew.

Schmid said three things have led to Schelotto's torrid play. "The first thing is just that Guillermo is playing very well," he said. "Every time our team gets a free kick, we think we can score. If you watch him before the game, he as a routine where he takes free kicks from different parts of the field. The second thing is that as a team, I think we do a better job of getting Guillermo the ball in better positions so that he doesn't have to come as deep or as wide to get the ball. And then the third thing is that you don't win that many championships without the ability to raise your game. So many times

---

[127] Which is where he scored 5 of his 7 goals in 2008.

this season he has raised his game at crucial moments. Tonight was another example of that. He was in the moment."

Big Game For Big Andy

With Frankie Hejduk away with the U.S. National Team, Schmid had a decision to make with the Crew's backline. He ultimately decided to stick rookie Andy Iro in the middle, while sliding the Crew's Swiss Army knife, Danny O'Rourke, to right back.

"Andy played inside last week while Danny was suspended, and to be honest, our original thought was to put Danny back in the middle and play someone else at outside back," said Schmid. "But because of the way Andy played last week and trained this week, we rewarded him. Competition brings out the best in everyone. He wants to stay on the field, and his focus and his concentration has been good in the past few weeks."

Iro's biggest challenge, of course, was trying to contain the Revs' lethal striker, Taylor Twellman. "I'd never played against him before," said Iro. "I had seen him play before, but within the first 10 minutes, I could instantly tell how sharp he was. His movement is so quick, so it required some extra concentration. But honestly, it was easier for me to defend him because there was no service coming in. We put so much pressure on their service. This was the best team defensive game I have seen us play."

But the big fella's contributions were not limited to the defensive end of the field. The man affectionately known as "Generation Iro" generated some offense of his own, heading home a Schelotto free kick moments before the halftime whistle.

"I saw the ball coming in…and it's been a bit of a team joke about my heading…but I was able to judge it early enough and accurately enough to know it was going to go over Chad's head," G.I. explained. "I backed up, and luckily I didn't back up to the point that I was jumping backwards, but I back up to where I could move forward. Good ball, good finish."

The finish had to make up for some the disappointment of being robbed moments earlier, when Iro's 43rd minute shot was cleared off the goal line. That shot was a product of Iro's soon to be patented knee-ball.

"It was pure instinct and reaction," he laughed. "I used to be a forward, but people don't believe me. It was too high to kick and too low for a header, so I just said 'whatever' and lifted my knee."

Scary Garey

Boy, Jason Garey is nothing if not efficient. In just 85 minutes all season, Garey has taken seven shots. Five of those seven have been on goal, and three of them have gone in.

Upon entering Saturday's game in the 66th minute, Garey's first act was to make an offside run. He doubled back to get onside again, and then made another run that was rewarded with a pass. His first touch was to chest down the pass from Schelotto. His second touch was to hammer a left-footed shot past Matt Reis to put the game away at 3-0.

"When I came onto the field, Guillermo waved me over," said Garey. "He said, 'You come here. When I get ball, you go.' So he got the ball and I went. The very first ball was a goal, so I was like, 'All right, I'll keep doing it!'"

As a forward, Garey appreciates how special it is to play with a visionary like Schelotto. "You think he doesn't know you're there, but he knows," Garey explained. "He's not even looking in my direction, but I know that if I make the run, he'll get the ball there. I'm making blind runs all the time. He will find you. That's the key – just make the runs and he will find you. And with Pat Noonan it's the same thing. Nobody thought he was going to play that ball through, but I knew if I made a run, those guys are so good at playing the ball through that it worked, so it was good."

Yes, in the 90th minute, Garey ran on to a beautiful through ball from Pat Noonan and finished the breakaway to make it 4-0. Not a bad night's work.

The Unsung Heroes

Players and coaches went out of their way to praise the midfield tandem of Brian Carroll and Brad Evans, whose contributions toward shutting down New England's superb midfielder, Shalrie Joseph, will not show up on the scoresheet. Well, except for the New England goose egg.

"Carroll and Evans did a great job on Shalrie," said Schmid. "It is tough to restrict Shalrie's touches, but they restricted the ability of Shalrie to play balls forward. They forced him to play sideways and back more than he wanted to play sideways and back."

"BC and Evans were great," added Garey. "They didn't give New England a chance to play their game. They were all over them."

"That zero is the most important thing," said Danny O'Rourke of the shutout. "Chad and Andy held down the middle, and I think Gino and I did well on the outside. And then Will is our leader back there. But I can't say enough about Brian and Brad controlling the midfield in front of us."

In one of my favorite photos of the year, Jason Garey celebrates as the ball rolls toward the gaping New England net. Garey put the final two nails in the Revs' coffin in a 4-0 Crew romp that saw them take control of the Eastern Conference and never look back. (Photo by Sam Fahmi.)

Run Robbie Run

Another guy whose name will not show up on the scoresheet is Robbie Rogers. It would be criminal to overlook the havoc caused by his relentless runs. The exhausted Revs had no answer as Rogers took on double and triple teams, serving dangerous balls and winning several deep restarts for Schelotto.

"I thought Robbie was the best he's been since he came back from the Olympics," said Schmid. "I thought he was aggressive in getting behind people. Albright is not a slow defender, and I think Robbie did a good job getting behind him."

In the opening moments of the second half, Rogers' head was on the receiving end of a high kick from Shalrie Joseph. After the game, Rogers was seen walking around the locker room with an ice bag held to his head. When he removed the ice bag, one could clearly see a big horn growing out of his right temple, as if he were the offspring born of two unicorn cousins.

(Thankfully, when the Crew contemplated bringing me back to the organization this year, the ability to craft unicorn incest similes was NOT part of the interview process.)

Lenhart's Bike

Steven Lenhart brought the crowd out of their seats in the 7th minute when smacked a bicycle kick that forced a last-second tip save from New England goalkeeper Matt Reis.

"The ball went up over my head, and I'm not a bicycle kick specialist, but I just went for it," he said. "I didn't think I could do that, to be honest with you. It almost worked."

Sigi seemed as baffled as anyone by the sight of Lenhart striking the ball while fro-side down. The coach made a special trip to the rookie's locker to ask if Lenhart left the kickstand down while attempting that bike.

"I think so," said Lenhart. "I had no idea what I was doing. I just did it."

Lenhart's Surpise Visitors

After receiving word that he would be starting against New England, Lenhart called to tell his family. Little did he know what that would mean.

"My mom and sister flew out last minute to surprise me," said Lenhart. "They left this morning to come here. It's awesome."

Across the room, Generation Iro's eyes lit up. "They bought plane tickets this morning? I wish my family was as rich as yours! Do you know how much it would cost to fly across the country at the last minute like that?"

"No idea," said Lenhart. "They probably took the family jet."

Lenhart was quick to add that he was only joking about the private plane. Besides, I think it's an unofficial team rule that all jokes about mythical family jets are supposed to be directed at "Country Club Willie" Hesmer.

Atmosphere

The size and exuberance of the crowd had Dante Washington reminiscing about the The Good Ol' Days on the radio, and it made an exciting game even more exciting for everyone involved.

"The crowd was amazing," said Crew goalkeeper William Hesmer. "It was electric. They are in tune with the game, and they were loud. Like we've said all year, this crowd has definitely played a huge role in our success this season. They've really taken on that corner and made it their own and made a good statement to other teams in the league that Columbus is going to be a tough place to come in and play, and we're proud of that."

"When we walked out and saw all those people in the upper deck, it was tremendous," said Schmid. "Our section in the corner was superb. We could feel that all night. You want to feel those nervous butterflies, but you aren't actually nervous. When there's a big game, it brings a smile to my face. I get excited. This is why I coach. And as a player, this has to be why you play."

Both the Nordecke and the upper deck brought their A-games to support the Crew in their crucial 4-0 victory over New England on September 6, 2008. (Photo by Sam Fahmi.)

Mr. Numbers Nerd: Guille Edition (Part one)

Schelotto has now strung together four consecutive multi-assist games. That ties the MLS record, originally set by Marco Etcheverry in the league's inaugural 1996 campaign.

Here's a look at the two streaks…

MARCO ETCHEVERRY
8/7/96: 2 assists in a 3-1 win at Tampa Bay.
8/10/96: 2 assists in a 3-2 loss at Columbus.
8/18/96: 2 assists in a 2-1 win vs. Los Angeles.
8/25/96: 2 assists in a 3-0 win vs. Tampa Bay.

GUILLERMO BARROS SCHELOTTO
8/16/08: 2 assists in a 2-1 win vs. Dallas.
8/23/08: 1 goal and 2 assists in a 3-0 vs. Salt Lake.
8/30/08: 2 assists in a 2-1 win at Dallas.
9/6/08: 1 goal and 2 assists in a 4-0 win vs. New England.

The totals are 0 goals, 8 assists, and a 3-1-0 record for El Diablo, compared to 2 goals, 8 assists, and a 4-0-0 record for Guille. I think it's safe to say that Guille wins the tiebreaker on the strength of those two additional goals and an additional victory. Of course, he could negate all debate with a fifth consecutive multi-assist game this weekend in Toronto against the Hosers.

Mr. Numbers Nerd: Guille Edition (Part two)

After Schelotto was subbed out of the game, Pat Noonan and Jason Garey rudely combined on a goal without Guille's participation. It snapped a streak whereby Schelotto had participated in 10 consecutive Crew tallies either by scoring or assisting each goal. That has to be some sort of record, right?

Indeed it is. By participating in 10 consecutive tallies over the last four games, Schelotto broke Jeff Cunningham's Crew record of participating in nine consecutive Crew goals. Cunningham accomplished the feat by scoring 6 goals and dishing 3 assists in an eight-game stretch from May 9 to June 26 of the 1999 campaign.

(Cunningham's streak was snuffed out when Ansil Elcock scored an unassisted goal in the 37th minute against San Jose on June 30, 1999. That game is most notable for Stern John's amazing blast past Joe Cannon with three seconds to play, forcing a shootout that was won by the Crew.)

Guille's streak, while impressive, fell short of the league record. The single-season record for consecutive goal participation is 12, set by San Jose's Ronald Cerritos in 1998. From Aug. 9 to Sept. 20 of that year, Cerritos strung together 5 goals and 7 assists in nine games. His streak was snapped at Spartan Stadium on Sept. 27, when Braden Cloutier scored on assists from Francisco Uribe and Victor Mella in the Clash's 2-0 win over the Wizards.

While Cerritos holds the single-season record, Landon Donovan holds the overall record by participating in 13 consecutive Galaxy goals from Oct. 7, 2007, carrying over through April 26, 2008. In nine games, Donovan racked up 8 goals and 5 assists. He had a string of 1 goal and 4 assists in the final four games of 2007, then a string of 7 goals and 1 assist in the first five games of 2008. His steak was snapped in the middle of the Galaxy's 5-2 pasting of Chivas USA, when Alan Gordon scored an unassisted goal for Los Angeles.

For good measure, Donovan scored another goal a minute later, added another assist that night, and then assisted on the first goal in the Galaxy's next game, putting him on a 16-out-of-17 run. (You know, in case Guille needs something else to aim for in the next couple of games.)

Mr. Numbers Nerd: Weird Happenings Edition

Crew radio man Neil Sika noticed something peculiar about the Crew's performance this season—the Crew have garnered at least one point in every league match in which they have so much as tallied a goal. For the 2008 Crew, the equation has been simple:

At least one goal = At least one point[128]

The Crew are 13-0-3 when erasing the goose egg from their side of the scoreboard. Neil thought that was a bit peculiar...and boy was he right.

Not only do the Crew have a shot to become the only team in MLS history to garner at least a point in every game in which they have scored a goal, they have room for error in terms of setting this peculiar league mark. The 2005 New England Revolution lost only two matches in which they erased their goose egg, and that is the current record. The Revs scored and lost on August 6, 2005, in a 2-1 loss vs. Kansas City, and then improbably scored four goals and lost, 5-4, at New York on September 17, 2005.

---

[128] This streak would be snapped on October 18 in a 3-1 loss at New York. They would finish 17-1-5 when scoring a goal. (20-1-6 including the playoffs.)

The 2008 Crew have already established a new calendar record in terms of converting goals to points. The previous record belonged to the 2002 Dallas Burn, who lost for the first time when scoring a goal on August 21 of that year, dropping a 3-1 decision at San Jose.

(In case you're wondering about the shootout era, no team topped either of these marks even if one counts shootout losses as draws.)

Revolting

The Revs are a good team, but when they lose, they LOSE. Saturday's match was the third time this year in league play that the Revs have dropped a 4-0 decision on the road. They also lost 4-0 at Chicago on April 3 and at San Jose on Aug. 16. They've also suffered a 3-0 home loss to the Fire in league play on May 3, and an embarrassing 4-0 home shellacking from Joe Public (Trinidad & Tobago) during CONCACAF Champions League play last Tuesday.

Massive Ideas

* In the spirit of the in-stadium displays that are common when a slugger is approaching a home-run milestone, Dante Washington thinks that the Crew Stadium stage should host a pair of big numbers counting up Schelotto's assists, with a ceremonial in-game update every time he adds another one to his tally.

"And they better make sure they have a '2' all ready to go for that first digit," he noted.[129]

* On the drive home, it occurred to me that Crew goalkeeper William Hesmer probably felt like the kid who got stuck playing right field in tee-ball. I wondered if Hesmer passed the time Saturday night with a rousing rendition of "99 Bottles of Imported Brew on the Wall." When I talked to them, I should have asked Danny O or Generation Iro if they overheard any such thing during the rare instances in which they had to venture near their own penalty area.

* Crew fans seem to be in a tizzy that Dispatch columnist Michael Arace insists on calling the Crew the Canaries. He started with the Fighting Canaries, but after getting wise to the fact that the Crew are a massive club, he recently made the switch to the Massive Canaries.

---

[129] Guillermo sat out some games down the stretch, so he finished with "only" 19 assists.

While an improvement, this has still evidently caused some consternation amongst supporters. I think this is because Crew fans long ago adopted the banana as the yellow comparison object of choice. After all, the Crew's immediately identifiable uniforms have been famously referred to as "the banana kit" ever since they belatedly debuted in 2000.

Arace is a gifted writer, and he has produced some outstanding pieces about the Crew, so it's a shame that this canary issue seems to be overshadowing his excellent work. Since Crew fans are still resisting the canary comparisons, and since Arace clearly likes using a nickname for the Crew, there is only one practical solution:

The Massive Bananas.[130]

That, my friends, is a nickname you can boast about. So let's give it a try. It will now be the Notebook's Official Crew Nickname. Sure, I might have to nix or rewrite a few sentences, such as one I originally wrote about the Crew sticking it to the Revolution's exhausted players for 90 solid minutes, but it's no bother.

U.S. Open Cupdate

The Charleston Battery, who were the Official Notebook U.S. Open Cup Bandwagon Team of Destiny, saw their championship dreams end with a 2-1 loss to D.C. United in the final. It was a shame too, as the Battery controlled large portions of the match and were a bit unlucky. Not only did the ball work some fortuitous magic on both D.C. goals, but the Battery were denied by a post and had a spectacular volley by Lazo Alavanja whistle just wide in the final minutes. And then they had a stoppage time equalizer wiped out by a questionable offside call.

"I think we are all still a bit disappointed," said former Crew man Nelson Akwari, who has been kind enough to offer his thoughts throughout the tournament in order to help us bandwagon Battery fans. "To get that far and to fall short is tough. D.C. United did well to finish off the chances they created, but I can't help but think that we could have done a better job defensively to not give up those opportunities. I still haven't seen the full game, but I've seen some highlights. I did hear about the offside call, and I

---

[130] Almost the name of this book, bit I thought it was too obscure of a book title.

guess a lot of friends and family are saying what a lot of people have said…it was a close call.

"I was proud to see our team respond positively after going down a goal, and it was awesome to see our fans in black and gold cheering us on throughout the game," he continued. "Our organization is first class and it truly was an honor to represent them in the U.S. Open Cup Final. Thank you to the Crew fans that cheered us on throughout our run. I know you would have loved to see D.C. go down in the final. Congrats to you all on being in first place in the league, and I wish the Crew the best of luck the rest of the way."

Nice guy, that Nelson Akwari. Here's hoping the Battery follow the Cleveland City Stars' blueprint, whereby they lose in the Open Cup to a Crew rival, then go on to win their league. I'll keep the Notebook Bandwagon on standby for the USL-1 playoffs.

Help Name Duncan's Pub!

A few weeks ago, Shawn Mitchell's "Covering the Crew" blog on Dispatch.com unearthed another interesting nugget. It seems that when his playing days are over, whenever that might be, Duncan Oughton hopes to open his own pub in Columbus. This pub may not exist for years, but the prospect has nevertheless excited the beer-drinking subsection of the Crew's fan base.

As we know, Duncan is currently living the life of a jet-setting international footballer. Between his worldwide commitments to club and country, one can't expect Oughton to devote time to the minor tasks associated with planning a future business.

Being the helpful sort, that's where I come in. Or more specifically, my newly-formed company, Sirk Marketing Research, Inc. My goal is to develop a surefire name for Duncan's future pub.

Alas, I will not be naming the pub. That would not be fair to Duncan. Rather, Sirk Marketing Research, Inc., will oversee a rigorous test marketing and focus group campaign to ensure that the very best name is chosen for Duncan's pub.

The first phase was to solicit ideas. For this purpose, I consulted with the Dante-Dunny Think Tank Foundation, a group dedicated to brainstorming brilliant New Zealand-themed ideas. However, in the interest of getting the best names possible, I did not put all my eggs in one basket. I also consulted with "green light thinkers" from within the Crew locker room. As a result of these various consultations, I am compiling an alphabetical list of potential names for Duncan's pub.

Phase two will be a two-pronged approach. Based on the list of potential names, I will then poll future potential customers—you, the fans. (Instructions are below.) That's the first prong. The second prong will be a media vote because, let's face it, media people know a lot more than everyone else, and if it's simply left up to the fans, you end up with a situation whereby Guillermo Barros Schelotto is not an MLS All-Star. But if you let the media's unbiased, rational, and superior judgment into process, Guillermo Barros Schelotto is still not an MLS All-Star. So, um, I guess the name of this pub will not be "Guillermo Barros Schelotto."

(NOTE: Crew PR guru Dave Stephany, who has an incurable fact fetish, made a point to let me know that Guille finished fourth in both the fan and media voting, which would have made him an All-Star. It was his appallingly sparse vote totals amongst players and coaches/GMs that prevented him from being voted into the All-Star First XI. Now that this information has come to light, I will not be retracting my joke, but instead will proudly point out that at least I'm not letting coaches/GMs vote on Duncan's pub name.)

Once I have combined the fan and media votes, I will submit the five finalists to Tucker Walther, head of the Walther Polling Institute. The WPI will canvas those within the clubhouse to determine the final name. (I still feel good about this, despite Dave's facts. Since players are not allowed to vote for their teammates, the Crew's players were not the problem with the All-Star voting. It was all the clowns on those other stupid teams.) Once the voting has concluded, all results will be verified by the accounting firm of Paco, Mathews, & Associates, and then forwarded to me.

Once this exhaustive, multi-faceted process is completed, we can all be sure that Duncan's future pub will have a name that is guaranteed to stand the test of time. The winning name will be published in the next Notebook.

Let's all do our part to make life easier for our favorite Kiwi entrepreneur!

Fan Voting Process

The list of potential names will be published on the Crew's official blog, The Black & Gold Standard, either Tuesday night or Wednesday morning. To vote, simply register and leave your vote as a comment in the comments section. Your vote must be time-stamped by 5 p.m. on Sunday, Sept. 14, 2008.

Reactions to Duncan's Pub Idea

The news that Duncan hopes to open a pub someday in the future elicited a full spectrum of emotions. On one end, you had people like Dante Washington, who gleefully noted, "It's good to know that I will always have a place where I can eat and drink for free."

Other folks, however, were turned off by Duncan's comment to Mitchell that he envisions his pub being "something with a little more of an English feel, a proper pub."

It seems that this comment did not go ever well with the locker room's Scottish demographic, which probably fears that the jukebox will be lacking in bagpipe selections.

"Yeah, well maybe he should just call it 'Duncan's English-Feel Proper Pub'," said Adam Moffat. "I hope Duncan will sell crumpets and tea in his English pub."

Metric Conversion

During the radio broadcast, Dante Washington kept making a mess of Andy Iro's height. At first, Dante kept calling him 6'4", which is the height of Iro's shrimpier partner in the central defense, Chad Marshall.

Dante happened to walk into the locker room as we were talking to Iro, and here's how it went down between me, Iro, and Craig Merz.

SS: Do you care to tell Dante how tall you really are? He kept getting it wrong on the radio.

AI: How tall did he say I was?

SS: He started at six-four, but I heard as high as seven-ten.

AI: I'm six-five. Six-five. (Turns to Dante.) I'm six-five, dawg!

CM: What's that in metric?

AI: Uh, in metric? I think it's like one meter and...97 centimeters.

So close! Rounded up to the nearest centimeter, 6'5" is 1.96 meters. Then again, there could be rounding on the inches, so maybe Andy is really 1.97 meters if we measured directly in metric.

Either way, be sure to tune in next week when Craig asks Andy to convert his weight into stones!

All 1.97 meters of Andy Iro dribbles the ball against the Revs on September 6, 2008. Iro would do the most damage with his head, scoring to put the Crew ahead 2-0 just before the half, en route to a 4-0 pasting of the Revs. (Photo by Greg Bartram / Columbus Crew)

Beardo-Weirdos

You may have noticed a few strange pieces of facial hair amongst the team's staff. A week ago, I suspected that there may be some sort of beard contest going on, and it turns out I was right. From what I understand, there are only a handful of participants. Danny O'Rourke has obviously grown a beard, but he's sticking with a normal person's beard, so he may have just grown that on his own.

The contest was the brainchild of assistant trainer Skylar "Paco" Richards, according to Moffat, who had all sorts of crazy angles carved into his facial hair. "Paco came up with four categories: thickest, sickest, best design, and most air time," Moffat explained. "Kenny Schoeni has led the way in the thickest. I think he may have glued some head hair on there, though. I'm hoping for victory in the sickest and best design categories, but there is some competition as you saw from Jason and Skylar on Saturday."

Paco had some massive dagger muttonchop sideburns, and head trainer Jason Mathews was showing off a crazy mess that he referred to as "The John Quincy Adams."

Moffat knows that there is one category he has no shot to win. "Most air time looks to be going to Jason after Robbie took that kick to the head. There was a brief television appearance which heavily boosted his beard's air time. I was hoping to do a Phelps and take gold in all categories, but my lack of playing time means no TV or interview time, so the 'most air time' category is one I have no chance in. But when I'm not rehabbing my knee, I'm thinking of sick designs for my facial hair. It's fun."

The saddest part of this very small competition is that strength and conditioning coach Steve Tashjian had the "sickest" and "best design" categories all wrapped up. Paco showed me a cell phone video in which Tashjian had a Mr. T mohawk that split and looped around to form a pair of chin straps that ran along his jawline before jumping up over his mouth to form a mustache. Alas, Tashjian was disqualified because he shaved it all off after it was documented.

Although the disqualification gave Moffat a new lease on life in the competition, even he was blown away. "How awesome was Steve Tashjian's?" he asked. "I couldn't believe it!" [131]

Yellow Card Danger

Crew fan Andrew Goodrich has noticed something amusing about the official game previews for each Crew game. Despite being out for the year with torn-up knee, Moffat is continually listed on the yellow card danger list. It seems that with two more cautions this season, Moffat will be suspended for a game.

The Scot says that people needn't worry, as he is all about fair play these days. "I have been on my best behavior up in the stands when I watch the games," he said. "I have tried not to trip anyone when in the line for food at halftime, so if I keep it clean, I'm sure I will avoid the suspension. I really don't want to get the five yellows because if I were forced to sit out a game, I would be distraught."

Trust me, Moffat. Watching your teammates play is anything but distressing.

(Although after Saturday's Massive Banana attack, the Revs might beg to differ.)

---

[131] Tashjian's concoction would become known as The Legend, and it would make a return appearance after the Crew won MLS Cup. Photos appear later in the book.

Questions? Comments? Like Dwight's new Elvis Costello glasses? Feel free to write at sirk65@yahoo.com

Danny O'Rourke sports a normal person's beard during the Crew's 4-0 thrashing of New England on September 6, 2008. (Photo by Greg Bartram / Columbus Crew)

Road Work: Crew 1, Toronto 1

Match date: Saturday, September 13, 2008
Scoring:
6: TOR Robinson 1 (Guevara 4)
40: CLB Noonan 1 (unassisted)
Attendance: 19,657
Crew's record afterward: 13-6-5

RETROACTIVE RECAP

The Crew clinched the inaugural Trillium Cup with a 1-1 draw on the shores of Lake Ontario. Guillermo Barros Schelotto and Brad Evans missed the game due to injury, but it was Schelotto's replacement, Pat Noonan, who hit the equalizing left-footed strike from 21 yards after slaloming his way through the middle of the Hosers' defense.

The Crew fell behind early, when Carl Robinson took a set-piece feed from Amado Guevara and stuck a looping shot toward the upper corner of the Crew's goal. William Hesmer got a hand on the ball, but the shot ricocheted into the net after hitting the bottom of the crossbar. The Crew had a chance to equalize six minutes later, but Alejandro Moreno's penalty kick was easily saved by Hoser goalkeeper Greg Sutton. No worries, though, as Noonan saved the day and the Crew collected their first piece of hardware, winning the Trillium Cup by virtue of their 1-0-2 season record against the Hosers.

QUOTES

Sigi Schmid: "Being able to come back from being down a goal, I thought that was a positive. Being able to deal with the psychological blow with missing a penalty kick was also something we needed to come back from., and that was what our team did. I was very proud of that.

"Our squad's depth is good. Obviously, today you know Stefani Miglioranzi stepped in, and one of the reasons we brought in Pat Noonan is we knew he could play [Schelotto's] position. He scored a great goal today. Emmanuel Ekpo, you know he's only been back over a week after being gone for a month with the Olympics, and we're trying to round him into shape, but I think everybody saw his quality in the last 15 minutes of the game. I've never been disappointed about our depth."

Pat Noonan: "It was a very good result, especially the way the game started. They got on the board early, and it's a tough place to play with the crowd and how well they play at home. Obviously you want to win the game, but we're happy with the point."

The Incidents, Part III:
A Scare in the Air

NOTE: This incident only got a passing mention in the upcoming Notebook, and at the time, I didn't fully grasp the enormity of what had transpired. In the months that followed, I learned a lot more about what happened, and this book would have seemed incomplete had I stuck to my nearly non-existent scribbling from the time when all this went down. (I had an offhand "barf bag" quote from Sigi and a basic recap, and that was about it.) So on Labor Day 2009, I circled back around to talk to some of the participants so that they could retell the story in more detail now that the passage of time and many more flights have put at least some distance between them and the trauma/drama of September 14, 2008.

September 13 was a good day. Playing without Guillermo Barros Schelotto and Brad Evans, the Crew earned a draw to clinch the Trillium Cup thanks to Pat Noonan's strike. With the Trillium Cup decided in the Crew's favor, Toronto Mayor David Miller had to pay up on his bet with Columbus Mayor Michael Coleman. As agreed, Miller posed with Crew captain Frankie Hejduk and the Trillium Cup…while wearing a Columbus Crew jersey.

"It was a fun bet, and you can always laugh a bit harder when your team wins," Hejduk said. "We didn't want our mayor to have to wear their jersey, so I am sure (Coleman) enjoyed seeing their mayor in a Crew shirt. Their mayor was a good sport about it and we joked around a bit."

A few hours after the mayoral shaming and photo op, traveling Crew supporters were in for a special treat. Since it was a Saturday afternoon game and the team wasn't scheduled to fly out until Sunday afternoon, that left plenty of time for revelry. Crew players and fans celebrated the Trillium Cup together and further cemented the bond between the team and their supporters.

"Later that night, we shared the Trillium Cup with the fans at the hotel," said Hejduk. "It was a chance to have fun, have a few beers, and laugh about it. We know that our fans and the Toronto fans have a bit of a rivalry, so our fans loved it. Not only is it a trophy that we can play for every year as players, but it always feels good when you can go out on the field and make your fans happy and give them some bragging rights."

First place in the Eastern Conference, the Trillium Cup in hand, a fun-filled night of celebrating with supporters…what a great weekend.

All that was left was to fly home on Sunday to prepare for Thursday's nationally televised match against the New York Red Bulls.

Toronto Mayor David Miller (left) poses with the Trillium Cup and Crew captain Frankie Hejduk on September 13, 2008. Per the terms of his bet with Columbus Mayor Michael Coleman, Miller had to have his photo taken while wearing a Columbus Crew jersey. Frankie and the Crew were all smiles on Saturday. That would change within 24 hours. (Photo courtesy of the Columbus Crew)

Hurricane Ike had just finished a week-long rampage across the Atlantic Ocean and Gulf of Mexico, killing nearly 200 people and causing well over $30 billion in combined damage in the Turks and Caicos Islands, Haiti, the Dominican Republic, Cuba, and the United States. On Friday, September 12, the storm made landfall in Galveston, Texas, knocked the windows out of skyscrapers in Houston, and caused yet more flooding in hurricane-ravaged Louisiana. All told, it was the third-costliest Atlantic hurricane in American history.

Although Ike was no longer a hurricane by the time he reached Columbus on Sunday afternoon, he still packed a wicked wallop. His 75 mile-per-hour winds[132] uprooted trees, damaged roofs, and left hundreds of thousands of Central Ohioans without power for days.

And he was absolute hell on small aircraft.

The Crew's flight home started out like any other. As the team boarded their Dash 8 Turboprop, the jokes started right on cue. Even the more experienced fliers felt a little skittish on a 35-seat prop plane.

"It was totally old school," said Hejduk. "We were calling it a bus with wings, and we were joking together before takeoff, saying things like, 'Since this is our last flight, it was nice knowing you' and stuff like that."

As one of the people who hates flying on smaller prop planes, Hejduk made a point of having a couple of beers beforehand to calm his nerves and to keep him loose. It would turn out that the phrase "liquid courage" needn't always have a negative connotation.

The seemingly uneventful flight became exponentially bumpier as the plane approached Columbus. When the serious turbulence first started, guys still tossed jokes around the cabin. Players laughed off their nervousness by commenting about their pending doom to the deeply religious Eddie Gaven… "Hey Eddie, put in a good word for me!" or "Hey Eddie, when we get to the Pearly Gates, can I be your plus-one?"

Hejduk, fortified by those pre-flight beers, tried to treat the turbulent tumult as if it were an amusement park ride. "We were getting thrown all over the place," he recalled. "Guys were sweating and their faces were turning green or white, but I was trying to keep a cool head by joking around. We would suddenly drop 50 feet straight down and I'd scream 'Oh yeah!' like we were on a roller coaster. One time I thought we were actually going to flip over, but I yelled 'That was (bleeping) gnarly!'"

At another particularly tense moment, Crew PR Director Dave Stephany remembers someone shouting "Guillermo is the smartest man on the face of the earth!"

(Guillermo Barros Schelotto, often lauded for his wisdom and ability to see game events unfold before they actually happen, was at home resting

---

[132] The National Weather Service had no record of stronger winds in the city's history.

his hamstring from the rigors of Toronto's plastic field. As a result, he was not on the flight.)

While some tried to keep the mood light, the turbulence increased its ferocity with each passing mile. Soon, the flight crossed the threshold from "terribly bumpy" to "sickening and scary."

"You try to start off lighthearted," said William Hesmer, "but after a while, it was serious."

As the plane jerked and jolted up and down and side to side, people literally lost their stomach for it. "I think the smell of one person getting sick....not only was it hot in there," said Hesmer, "and not only were we getting bounced around, but I think the smell of people getting sick made other people get sick and pretty much everyone on the plane got sick."

"I am not exaggerating," said Jed Zayner, "when I say there were points where we were looking at each other and saying, 'Should we be praying? We may be about to die.' We just kept going up and down and side to side, and we were getting slammed hard.

"I was grabbing onto the seat in front of me with both hands and both of my arms went numb because I was squeezing so tight," Zayner continued. "I had a barf bag on my lap and I kept thinking, 'Don't barf. Don't barf. You're gonna die. You're gonna die. Don't barf.'"

As if nauseating motion and noxious odors weren't enough, the guys were confronted with more bad news. "Steam was coming in through the air conditioning vents," Zayner said. "It was freaky, some of the stuff that was going on. It was like smoke, but it was a white mist. And it was so hot in there. Some guys were taking off their shirts because it was so hot. And then you look outside and the wings are tipping all over the place. It is something I never want to go through again."

"It was getting way too intense," said Hejduk. "Some guys were getting sick, others were reading Bibles, and others were gripping on for dear life."

But amidst the chaos was a voice of reason. Landing would be her vindication.

On the plane with the team was an off-duty flight attendant. Sitting next to Hejduk, she had been going out of her way to matter-of-factly assure the sickened and terrified passengers that everything would be okay.

"When we got near Columbus and the landing gear came down, she said that we were all going to be fine," Hejduk recalled. "She told us she's been through things like this before, and once the landing gear comes down, that means we're in good shape."

Except it seemed obvious to everyone on board that landing gear or not, the plane was not in good shape.

"I thought we were in trouble when we were still crabbing in and we were about 500 feet off the ground," said Hesmer.

Seeing as I was not familiar with the aviation term "crabbing", Hesmer gave me a quick demonstration using my extended arm as a runway and his hand as an airplane. When there is a severe crosswind, a plane cannot approach the runway head on or it will be blown off course by the crosswind. Instead, the plane's trajectory is tilted into the crosswind, thereby allowing the crosswind to push the plane back onto its actual course. The more severe the crosswind, the more severe the crabbing angle. The term gets its name because the plane is essentially traveling sideways in the air, much like a crab scurrying across the sand. When crabbing a landing, the plane will straighten itself out at the last moment so that it hits the runway straight.

It's this last detail that had Hesmer worried. "I knew we weren't going to be able to get it straightened out in time for the landing," he said.

Others noticed similarly ominous and alarming details upon their approach to Port Columbus. The view from the windows offered little comfort. "There were trees getting blown across the highways and roads," said Duncan Oughton. "We could see that it was windy. There were people's barbeques being blown into the sides of their houses."

"We're maybe a few hundred feet off the ground," said Hejduk, "our tail is going sideways like we're going to do a 180, we're still getting tossed around, and it's like nobody has any control of the plane."

Unable to align with the runway vertically or horizontally, the plane was mere seconds away from disaster. The landing had to be aborted.

"The landing gear came up and we tried to get back up into the sky," Hejduk said. "Then the flight attendant next to me reached for her barf bag and even she started puking. That wasn't good."

A year later, Zayner could only shake his head when recalling that moment. "That stewardess that sat next to Frankie threw up five times!"

While the voice of reason had been muzzled by a rapidly filling air sickness bag, Hesmer—ever the analytical one—focused on the landing.

"You could hear them kick the landing gear up, so you knew it was bad," he said. "It was like, 'Okay, they missed the first one. Maybe it was just a gust of wind and we'll land the second time.' But then they tried to climb out of it, and they were struggling to even climb out of it so that we could turn around. They couldn't really turn around without us almost losing control. The second time around, it was even worse. On the second try, we were coming in perpendicular to the runway."

After the second nearly calamitous landing attempt, the plane was diverted to Cleveland[133]. The unrelenting turbulence barely diminished on the way to Lake Erie. Some of the guys estimated that the Cleveland portion of the trip was still rocking in at 80 percent of the horror of the Columbus portion. Nevertheless, the plane safely landed at Cleveland Hopkins International Airport.

It was a good first step.

A safe landing was a welcome development, but it only offered some relief. Since the plane was not scheduled to land in Cleveland, there was no gate reserved for the plane and therefore no place to put it. The guys were still stuck in the broiling, barfy, claustrophobic confines of the Dash 8 for the foreseeable future. That is, until they took matters into their own hands.

"They wanted us to stay on the plane because we were on the runway," said Zayner. "We were like, 'Heck no! You better open this door!'"

"There was basically a mutiny," Hesmer concurred. "We got off the plane and were standing around on the runway. Then they told us we needed to get back on the plane, but not a single person listened. We were enjoying being on land."

"Guys were kissing the ground and giving each other high fives," said Hejduk. "Even the pilots seemed a little shocked by the whole thing, saying things like, 'Wow, that was a crazy one.' I think everyone was happy to be on the ground and to not be dead."

The basic plan was that once the wind passed through, everyone was to board the plane so they could make another go at landing at Port Columbus. The Crew nixed that plan in a heartbeat. Team administrator Tucker Walther placed a call to the bus company that the team uses locally. As luck would have it, the company had an empty bus in Cleveland that was

---

[133] Port Columbus shut down immediately after the Crew's second aborted landing. For those wondering why the Crew's flight left in the first place, Ike was not predicted to come so far north or to do so as quickly as he did. Airline officials remarked that had they known it was going to be so treacherous in Columbus, the flight never would have left Toronto.

on its way back to Columbus. Within 45 minutes, the team was on a well-stocked bus heading home to Central Ohio.

The trip down I-71 was anything but smooth, not that anyone minded. "Even the bus was getting blown around," said Zayner, "but by then, we were drinking beers and watching movies, and we were just so happy to be on the ground that we didn't care. The worst thing that could happen if the bus tipped over is that we would all fall down. We were already on the ground."

A year later, the Toronto flight is still a topic of conversation amongst those who went through it. Discussing it is liable to produce wide eyes, an increase in speaking volume, or a fresh sigh of relief.

"The best way I can describe it is that it was like a movie," said Walther. "Think of every plane crash you have ever seen in a movie, like in 'Almost Famous', and that's what this was like, except we didn't crash."

"Yeah," said Hejduk, "except in a movie it's like that for two minutes and then the plane crashes. We went through that for a solid hour."

Duncan Oughton seemed to be the only one who downplayed the event, based on his experiences when flying home to New Zealand. "The airport at my home town of Wellington is between two mountains and the harbor, so if it's a smooth landing, it's a miracle," he explained. "It's always rocky and crazy. To get a non-windy day in my home town is pretty rare, so I didn't mind it too bad. I mean, it was obviously a hairy one, but it wasn't my time yet. I love roller coasters, so it was like an expensive roller coaster ride."

Hejduk and Hesmer shared none of the Kiwi's bravado. The former is the son of a flight attendant, while the latter is the son of a pilot. From their formative years, they have been familiar and comfortable with aviation. As experienced and as knowledgeable as these two men are, each deemed the turbulent misadventure aboard the Dash 8 to be his most terrifying moment in the air.

"I have been flying all over since I was six years old," said Hejduk. "In all that time, plus all my time as a professional athlete with club teams and the U.S. National Team, that flight was by far the scariest and most intense flight I have ever been on."

"It's by far the scariest flight I have ever been on," said Hesmer. "I have flown in Cessnas and single-engine and twin-engine planes. I got caught in a thunderstorm in a Cessna flying back from the Bahamas with my dad and my little sister hit her head in the turbulence, but that was nothing compared to this."

It's an experience that nobody on board will ever forget. The Crew were already a close team, but this incident took team unity to a deeper, subconscious level.

"I don't think it was ever talked about or ever put in that perspective, but I think that's true," said Hesmer. "It's funny that you go on preseason trips and try to manipulate the team bonding process, but then to go through something like that for real, it's a bonding moment for sure."

Hejduk was even more emphatic. "Whenever you experience a life-threatening moment like that, it bonds you together forever."

We will never really know how close the Crew came to joining Manchester United and the Marshall University football team among famously tragic sports-related air disasters. One shudders at the thought. When split second decisions had to me made just hundreds of feet off the ground, the pilots and air traffic controllers made enough of the right choices to ensure that everyone on board could eventually transition from freakish terror to terra firma. Instead of an abrupt and unspeakably tragic ending, there were many joyous chapters yet to be written about the 2008 Columbus Crew. Thank God, thank the pilots, and/or thank dumb luck.

Or maybe…just maybe…thank Breanne Rice. According to Walther, the Crew's Assistant to GM may have been the unwitting hero.

"We didn't have the Trillium Cup on the plane," Walther explained. "Breanne drove it back to Columbus, which was good because that thing is the heaviest (bleeping) trophy ever made. It's ridiculous. Maybe that extra 40 pounds would have been enough to take us down when we were trying to land. Who knows?"

Sirk's Notebook: Crew 3, New York 1

Match date: Thursday, September 18, 2008

Scoring:

21: NY Angel 10 (unassisted)

41: CLB Hejduk 1 (unassisted)

46: CLB Rogers 6 (unassisted)

85: CLB Gaven 2 (Hejduk 3, Noonan 2)

Attendance: 10,881

Crew's record afterward: 14-6-5

Neither Ike's gusty winds[134] nor Schelotto's gimpy hamstring could knock the power out of the Columbus Crew's high-voltage offense on Thursday night. With MVP candidate Guillermo Barros Schelotto in a suit, and many central Ohioans in the dark, the charged-up Crew generated 3.0 goalawatts of scoreboard-lighting electricity to jolt the New York Red Bulls, 3-1.

Despite carrying the better of the play in the first half, the Massive Bananas found themselves in their usual uphill battle. Playing with 10 men for 10 solid minutes as players received medical treatment, Columbus fell behind in the 21st minute when Juan Pablo Angel scored a 30-yard bomb of a free kick. It was the 14th time in 25 games that the Crew had given up the first goal and, as usual, it wasn't that big of a deal.

"I felt like we played a man down for the first 20 minutes because we always had somebody out cut and injured," said Crew coach Sigi Schmid. "It was a questionable foul that led to the goal. It was a well-struck free kick for sure, but after that I thought we took over the game and I was very proud, again, of our ability to come back."

Red Bulls forward Mike Magee was a one-man demolition derby in the opening stages of the game. In the 15th minute, his midfield collision with Stefani Miglioranzi knocked the Crew midfielder out of the match. Television replays showed blood seeping through Miglioranzi's shin guard as trainer Jason Mathews helped him off the field.

"Stefani took 20 stitches – 10 inside and 10 outside," said Schmid. "It was down to the bone. No foul, by the way."

In the 17th minute, Crew forward Alejandro Moreno went up for a header and knocked noggins with Red Bulls defender Andrew Boyens, who

---

[134] The remnants of Hurricane Ike slammed Columbus on Sunday, September 14, leaving hundreds of thousands of people without power for several days.

temporarily left the field with a bleeding gash on his forehead, making it 10-on-10.

Three minutes later, Magee ultimately sent another Crew player to the bench, although it was the result of a seemingly innocuous play. He and Danny O'Rourke were standing at midfield, making a play on a bouncing ball, when Danny busted his eye open on Magee's skull.

"I went up for the ball with Magee," O'Rourke explained. "He's a buddy, and we were battling and whatever. He's smaller than me, so I tried to get up over him and my eye hit the back of his head. It was a fluke play. He didn't do anything."

A minute later, the bleeding forced O'Rourke to the bench as Emmanuel Ekpo came on in place of Miglioranzi, and as a head-wrapped Boyens returned for New York. At the next whistle, New York scoring ace Juan Pablo Angel bent in his Beckham-esque 30-yard free kick to give the Red Bulls a 1-0 lead.

Meanwhile, O'Rourke received treatment for the same eye wound he had suffered against New England. After originally being closed with three stitches two weeks ago, the Crew's medical staff opted for four stitches when reclosing it on the sideline.

"Whatever it takes to keep it from opening again," O'Rourke said.

The Crew finally returned to 11 men at the end of the 25th minute. It would take another quarter hour of solid play before they'd change the game in their favor.

Frankie's Floater

The Crew equalized in the 41st minute on a stunning goal by Frankie Hejduk. After duping Jorge Rojas into making the always-solid defensive move of leaping high into the air on a hip fake, Hejduk walked around the airborne Rojas, noticed that Red Bulls goalie Jon Conway was cheating off his line, and then chipped the stranded keeper from the top right corner of the box. Frankie's shot floated down under the crossbar and beyond Conway's desperate, backpedaling "oh fudge" swat.

"It certainly lifted our spirits," said Schmid. "We thought we were playing well and were taking the game to them. We were probably frustrated, too, since not only did we feel like we were playing with 10 men for much of the first half, but we also felt that they were playing with 12. That goal from Frankie lifted everyone's spirits. Then we could just settle down and do what we knew how to do instead of worrying about good calls and bad calls."

Given that it was an unorthodox goal, and given that Frankie's crosses can sometimes get away from him, many wondered if the strike was a cross, a shot, a crot, or a shoss. Hejduk was glad to clear it all up afterward.

"It was definitely a shot," he said. "After the guy jumped in the air, I was going to hit it hard on the ground, but then I looked up and saw the keeper was off his line. It was either going to be a goal for me or a tap-in for somebody running in. I was definitely trying to chip it over him. Right when it left my foot, I knew it was a goal."

"I wasn't really surprised that it went in," said Crew midfielder Robbie Rogers. "If you take a look at the replay, you can see Frankie looking to see where the keeper is. The keeper thought he was going to cross it for sure, and Frankie just chipped him. That's just experience. Frankie has been playing forever. He probably won't like me saying that, but then again, he still runs around way more than I do."

Robbie Rips a Rocket

Rogers turned the game on its ear before half the players on the field were fully stretched out for the second half. Just 19 seconds in, No. 19 put the Crew on top, 2-1, with a net-seeking missile from 30 yards out. After receiving a scoop pass from Gino Padula on the left flank, the Olympian slalomed through the defense from left to right before unleashing a swerving rocket that beat Conway to the far post.

"I haven't seen it yet," Rogers said from his locker. "I kept my head down trying to keep the ball down. I heard it was pretty good, so I am excited to see a replay of it later tonight.

"(Coming out after halftime) is a dangerous time for us attackers," he continued. "We like it when defenders are trying to get back into a game. I think Parke may have been flat-footed, and their keeper as well. We just have to punish teams if they come out like that."

Putting pressure on the defense is what the Crew wanted to do from the half's opening whistle. Having the kick, the Crew dropped the ball to Brian Carroll, who played a long ball into the New York end for a Red Bulls throw-in. New York restarted play, Padula intercepted a pass, and the rest was Goal of the Week material.

"That's something we always want to do," said Schmid, of playing the kickoff deep into the opponent's territory. "We just want to put the ball in their end and put them on the defensive. If we get on the end of it, great, but even if we put it out deep in their end, we'll make them play down there. If you start by playing it back and then turn it over in the middle of the field or in your third, suddenly they have some momentum coming out right after halftime."

Instead, all of the momentum belonged to the Crew. Rogers' goal was a stunning punch to the gut for New York.

"It destroyed everything we talked about at halftime," said Red Bulls' coach Juan Carlos Osorio.

A Trip Down Memory Lane With Sigi

Rogers' goal brought back memories for Sigi, who was on the receiving end of such a devastating half-opening goal in the past.

"One time when I was in L.A., we took a goal like that," he said. "I think it was one of those afternoon games in Dallas when it was 118 degrees. I don't even think I had made it to the bench yet. I was still walking behind the goal. It's certainly something that demoralizes you. Especially the kind of goal it was. You've had your halftime talk, you've went over your game plan, and you plan to get back into the game and settle into the game, and then before you even have the chance to make your first run, the ball is in the back of your net. It's a shock to a team. Obviously, it was great for us and great for Robbie."

Gaven's Goal

The Crew put the game away in the 85th minute when Eddie Gaven scored his second goal of the season. Gaven's goal was the culmination of 12 passes and 38 seconds of possession. And that wasn't even the Crew's most breathtaking stretch of sexy soccer of the night. (More on that later.)

At the end of the play, Pat Noonan played an incisive through ball to Hejduk, who raced into the box and laid the ball off to an unmarked Gaven, who had a rather simple finish.

It capped a night where the offense once again came from different sources.

"It's like we always said, we've got different people that can score goals," said Schmid. "Tonight, it was Eddie Gaven that scored a goal. Robbie Rogers finally got off the mark and had a great goal. And Frankie was chipping the ball over the goalkeeper, he wasn't crossing it. He scored a great goal, as well. Obviously, those two goals, I think, are Goal of the Week candidates. We find goals from different places."

The Depth of This Team Is Deep

Ha! That subject heading is a quote I got from Chris Armas after a World Cup Qualifier earlier this decade. It still cracks me up.

Anyway, it's kind of weird to contemplate a Crew team that is so amazingly deep in talent. Missing an MVP candidate? No sweat. Replace him with an MLS All-Star and U.S. National Team player. The replacement starting d-mid has to leave with a gash in his shin? Oh well. Time to mix it up and put in an every-game player for the Olympic silver medalists. Heck, on the bench, the Crew have a soul-of-the-team guy in Duncan Oughton, and not even dressing is a young talent like Ricardo Pierre-Louis, both of who seem to get more first-team action with their respective national teams than they do with their massive club. It's mind-boggling.

"This is the deepest team I have ever been on," said Gaven. "From guy one to the last guy on the bench, everyone can step in and do their job. We've seen it all season and it is going to help us as we head toward the playoffs. Guys are going to get cards or injuries, so it's good to know that guys can come in and play at that same high level."

"I think one of the great things about this team is how many good players we have, the depth of our team," added Rogers. "That's why I think it would've been great if our team was in the CONCACAF Champions League or one of the other tournaments because I think our depth is one of the greatest in the league. Guillermo is a great player, and he adds so much, but then we also have some other players that can attack and create and do some things."

"I think we're a tough team to play against because you can't focus on one guy," Schmid said. "If you focus on one guy, somebody else is going to come through and be the one to put it in the back of the net."

True enough. Hejduk's goal means the Crew have gotten goals from 14 different players, which is tied with Colorado and Toronto for the most in MLS. The difference, obviously, is that the Crew gave gotten plenty more goals out of those 14 players, whereas the other teams have taken the "blind squirrel finds a nut" approach to goal diversification. Columbus has scored 44 goals, Colorado 33, and Toronto 25.

An In-Depth Look At Depth

I did not do the research in this sub-section. Rather, it was the excellent work of Crew fan Doug Sershen, but I felt it was worth sharing. With his blessing, I am going to pass along some of his own research as to the Crew's depth. It's stuff I wish I would have though of, but didn't.

One caveat: Doug didn't do league-wide research. He compared the Crew to fellow contenders New England, Chicago, D.C. United and Houston, as well as the league's top offensive team, the Los Angeles Galaxy. I have also added New York to the list. Those are certainly the most interesting comparisons, but I just wanted to make it clear that this isn't a league-wide look. Also, these totals include players who may not still be with that team. (Chad Barrett, formerly of Chicago, I am looking in your direction.)

Doug's first bit of research related to game-winning goals. The Crew have gotten game-winning goals from a league-leading nine different players. Chicago, New England, D.C., and Houston have all gotten them from seven different players, while LA and New York have gotten them from four.

Second, Doug looked at how top-heavy these teams are in terms of goal scoring, calculating how many of a team's goals were scored by its top two goalscorers. Ranked by diversity, here are his findings, which I have updated after this weekend's games:

1. Columbus: 14 of 44 (31.8%)
2. Chicago: 10 of 31 (32.2%)
3. New England: 13 of 36 (36.1%)
4. Houston: 15 of 35 (42.8%)

5. D.C. United: 21 of 41 (51.2)
6. New York: 16 of 31 (51.6%)
7. Los Angeles: 32 of 49 (65.3%)

And to take a singular event out of the equation, here are the teams ranked by the number of players with more than one goal:

1. Columbus: 10
2. Chicago: 9
3. New England: 8

4. Houston: 7
5. D.C. & N.Y.: 6
7. Los Angeles: 4

And finally, Doug points out that in the first seven games, Rogers and Moreno scored 10 of the Crew's 14 goals, and there were a total of five different scorers in that time, plus an own-goal. Then came the shutout streak. But since the shutout streak ended, Rogers and Moreno have scored just five of the Crew's 30 goals, and there have been 13 different scorers in those 14 games.

Again, thanks to Doug Sershen for crunching those numbers. Excellent work!

Sigi's Props For Padula

After another solid defensive effort by his team, Schmid took a moment to single out the performance of everyone's favorite pirate, Gino Padula.

"The defending is something we have been focusing on, and it's because of the usual suspects," the coach said. "But a guy I want to point out is Gino Padula. I think he did a great job in the New England game against Nyassi, and he did a great job tonight against a very dangerous player in Dane Richards. It's tough when you have to mark a guy who is faster than you, but you have to deal with it and not panic. He got some help from Robbie at key times, and we also tried to force New York to play the ball to the right so that Richards couldn't get in behind as much."

Mr. Numbers Nerd: Allow The First Goal Edition

Earlier in the week, the nefarious numbers runner known as Zman emailed me and asked for some historical perspective on the Crew's ability to rally after allowing the first goal. I am sure Z was motivated by some sort of lucrative bookmaking venture, but it piqued my curiosity. So I looked it all up and crunched all the numbers. On Wednesday. Then on Thursday, the Crew forced me to go back and update my calculations.

Please be aware that all calculations are from the "modern" (i.e. post-shootout) era, as it made little sense to invest the time to heavily research game-by-game results in an effort to recalculate history and pretend that shootouts never existed. For apples to apples comparisons, this examination starts in 2000, the first year that draws were possible.

With Thursday's win, the Crew improved to 4-6-4 when allowing the first goal. Their fourth victory set a new team record, breaking the previous record of three, set by the 2001 club that went 3-4-4 when allowing the first goal. The fourth win of 2008 equals the total number of victories from 2005-07 combined.

The fourth win also puts the Crew in an eight-way tie for third in league history. The 2000 Chicago Fire won six games after allowing the first goal, and the 2001 Miami Fusion won five.

The Crew have now collected 16 points when conceding the first goal, which broke the previous club record of 13 set by the 2001 team and temporarily tied by the current team.

The 16 points puts the Crew in a three-way tie for third all-time league-wide. The 2000 Fire (6-7-1) grabbed 19 points, and the 2006 edition of Real Salt Lake (4-9-7) equaled that mark.

The current Crew are now averaging 1.14 points per game when falling behind 1-0. Only seven other teams have averaged a point per game in that circumstance, including the 2001 Crew team that averaged 1.18 points per game.

The league record is held by the 2001 Miami Fusion, who went 5-3-1 to average an astonishing 1.78 points per game!

The last team to average at least a point per game was the 2005 San Jose Earthquakes (4-4-3), who averaged 1.36 points per game.

Here are the seven teams in modern MLS history that have averaged at least a point per game when allowing the first goal:

1. 2001 Miami Fusion (5-3-1): 1.78 ppg
2. 2001 Chicago Fire (4-4-2): 1.40 ppg
3. 2005 San Jose Earthquakes (4-4-3): 1.363 ppg
4. 2000 Chicago Fire (6-7-1): 1.357 ppg
5. 2003 Chicago Fire (3-4-1): 1.25 ppg
6. 2001 Columbus Crew (3-4-4): 1.18 ppg
7. 2002 Los Angeles Galaxy (4-6-2): 1.17 ppg

And for those who want to see how special this group is in Crew history, feast on these Crew numbers, which show the record and points per game when allowing the first goal:

2000: 1-13-1 (0.27)
2001: 3-4-4 (1.18)
2002: 3-10-1 (0.78)
2003: 2-11-2 (0.53)
2004: 1-4-5 (0.80)
2005: 1-12-0 (0.23)
2006: 1-13-4 (0.39)
2007: 2-8-1 (0.64)
2008: 4-6-4 (1.14) [135]

The Kings of the Comeback

Seriously, so what's up with this team and all these comebacks?

"We don't panic," said Danny O'Rourke. "We feel like we can come back from anything. Obviously, we'd rather win 1-0 or 2-0 and keep that shutout, but we have confidence in each other that we can score if we give up a goal."

"We've got strong character," added goalkeeper William Hesmer. "We've proved time and time again this year that we're a resilient group. We've had a troubling past two years and now we don't let things get us

---

[135] The Crew finished the season at 4-7-5, for 17 points and 1.06 points per game. Those numbers are both club records. The total points is 3rd in MLS history and the points per game is 8th in MLS history.

down. We always know we're in the game. One goal, to us, is nothing. If we give up an early goal, we feel that we have the firepower to get it right back and hold a lead."

What a Week

The lead-up the Thursday's match was an eventful one for the Crew. Their flight home from Toronto got caught up in Hurricane Ike-related windstorm that hit in Columbus on Sunday. After many tense and turbulent moments above the city, their flight was diverted to Cleveland, where they caught a bus home to Columbus.

Upon arriving home, they learned firsthand that more than 350,000 American Electric Power customers in central Ohio had lost power, affecting millions of people across the region, including the players themselves. Even Crew Stadium was without power until Tuesday.

In days loaded with easy and understandable distractions, the team focused on their game plan and took care of business Thursday night.

"The guys have been great," said Schmid. "Everyone has stayed on an even keel. They've been tremendous. A lot of the guys like candles anyway, so the power outage didn't bother them. The flight from Toronto was rocky, but luckily I wasn't on the plane or I would have had a barf bag for sure. But they stayed even keeled."

"This is our job," said Rogers. "It's our job to stay focused. Me and my roommate Brad (Evans) don't have much to do anyways, so all we look forward to is training and game days and playing for the fans. We're in first place and we still have a lot to play for, so we can't let anything cause us to lose focus."

"It was a different week for sure," added Hejduk, "but we were able to put that stuff behind us and get our game faces on."

The game faces and the 3-1 result were very important to the coach. "Today we said we wanted to send a message," said Schmid. "This is a team we could run into in the first round of the playoffs[136], so we wanted to make sure they know that if they come into Crew Stadium, they are in for a fight. This is our house, and we are strong here. That was our message before the game, and our guys showed their character and rose to the occasion."

---

[136] Or, inexplicably, MLS Cup.

Heart & Soul

The cover of the Crew's 2007 media guide featured photographs of Frankie Hejduk and Duncan Oughton, who were respectively (and appropriately) labeled "Heart & Soul." One of the more touching scenes from Thursday's game happened during the celebration after Hejduk's goal, when Frankie made a 60-yard dash to the Crew bench and leaped into Oughton's arms. While Frankie said it wasn't premeditated, it was nonetheless a wonderful Black & Gold moment.

"I don't score enough to have planned goal celebrations," said Hejduk. "It was pure adrenaline. I just ran over to the bench, and Duncan was the first guy to run out to meet me. I think Duncan was happier for me than I was."

Robbie's Celebration

Rogers' goal celebration was also of note. After giving the Crew the lead, Rogers sprinted across the field to embrace the fans in the Nordecke.

"Those guys went up to Toronto last week and they have been great all year, so I had to give them a little something after I scored," he said. "I got drenched in beer, but it beats getting bottles thrown at me like in Toronto."

The Bee-YOO-ti-ful Game

"One of the things we have gotten better at as the year has gone on is keeping possession of the ball, stringing passes together, and moving from one side of the field to the other to get the defense off balance." – Sigi Schmid.

About 10 minutes before Eddie Gaven iced the game, the Crew put together another breathtaking display of soccer that will never show up on a score sheet. But these beautiful stretches deserve their due, so here's a timed breakdown:

74:32— Gino Padula heads down an aimless New York clearance on the left side of the Crew's defensive third. The ball bounds to a retreating Robbie Rogers along the left sideline near midfield.

74:40— Rogers crosses midfield, cuts to the middle and drops a ball to Brian Carroll in the middle of the center circle.

74:43— Carroll plays a slightly backward diagonal ball to Hejduk on the right side, just behind the half line.

74:45— Hejduk one-times a back pass to Danny O'Rourke.

74:47— O'Rourke one-times a pass up to Carroll, who is in the center circle again.

74:49— Carroll takes a controlling touch and plays forward to Emmanuel Ekpo, who is in the middle of the park, just ahead of the center circle.

74:53— After taking three dribbling touches forward and to the left, Ekpo lays the ball off to Padula on the left sideline.

74:56— Padula quickly plays the ball up the line to Rogers, who is about 30 yards out.

74:57— Rogers one-times a pass to Ekpo, who is left-center, about 25 yards out.

75:01— After shielding the ball and fighting off a challenge from Andrew Boyens, Ekpo dribbles back and drops a pass to Eddie Gaven, who is right-center, maybe 40 yards out.

75:06— After taking the space he has been given, Gaven squares the ball to Ekpo in the center of the field, about 25 yards out.

75:09— After Gaven pulls a defender out of the way with a run across the top of the box, Ekpo makes an easy pass to Pat Noonan, who has his back to goal at the edge of the 18, near the right corner of the box.

75:10— Noonan one-times a pass back to Ekpo, who had moved over to the right to be in perfect alignment with Noonan.

75:13— After holding the ball for a beat, Ekpo squares the ball to Rogers in the middle, just as Hejduk begins making a backside run from the right flank.

75:15— Rogers pops a delicate right-footed spinner into the New York penalty area as Hejduk angles in from the right side. The ball checks up beautifully and hits Hejduk in stride. Both Hejduk's run and Rogers' pass beat three Red Bull defenders.

75:17— Hejduk's shot is saved by Conway.

75:21— Rogers' rebound shot is also saved by Conway.

75:24— Conway pounces on the trickling ball to snuff out the Crew's threat.

The whole sequence was what makes this game so beautiful. The final tallies: 52 seconds, 15 passes, 8 players, 3 gradual sideline-to-sideline switches, 2 shots, and 2 forced saves.

That's right, only Hesmer, Marshall, and Moreno did not get a touch during that stunning stretch of sexy soccer. Like I said, it will never show up in a box score, and 52 seconds is an awfully long highlight, especially when no goal is involved, but dammit, that sequence deserved some recognition.

(It should be noted that Marshall and Moreno had touches in the Crew's 12-pass sequence that led to Gaven's goal, and we'll let Hesmer off the hook since he's a goalie.)

Where There's a Will, There's a Save

After the Crew came up empty on their 52-second poetry session, the Red Bulls almost equalized moments later when John Wolyniec ran up the middle of the field and was in clear on Hesmer. Woly got stoned by the goalie.

"Will Hesmer made a great save to go down to his right," Schmid said. "It was a big-time save at a key moment in the game. That's what you need out of your defense. Defenders need to step up and make plays, and goalkeepers need to step up and make plays when you need them."

The Stanford Rifle

With Crew dead-ball wizard Guillermo Barros Schelotto resting his hamstring, others had to fill the void on corner kicks and free kicks. When Columbus earned a free kick 30 yards from goal in the 10th minute, the obvious choice to strike the ball was… Chad Marshall? Perhaps being on the receiving end of Schelotto's free kicks allowed the towering center back to learn by osmosis. He struck a shot that was destined for the upper part of the net before it was comfortably snagged by Red Bulls goalkeeper Jon Conway.

"That was the first one I ever took," said Marshall. "I was so nervous, I just wanted to get it over with. At least it was on goal."

Chad Marshall unleashes the first direct free kick shot of his career during a 3-1 victory over the New York Red Bulls on September 18, 2008. Let this photo serve as undeniable proof that his shot was indeed on goal. (Photo by Sam Fahmi.)

The Danny O Goal Watch

Danny O'Rourke has now played 91 career games without a goal. Teammate Brad Evans has predicted that Danny will score a goal in 2012, but Danny has said he is aiming for 2011.

Stoppage time in a 3-1 game rarely brings the kind of excitement that a national television audience witnessed when Danny O made a run up the middle, received a pass from Eddie Gaven, and ripped a shot that traveled mere inches over the crossbar. Just 120 lousy inches over the crossbar. (Andy Iro is not available as I write this, so I cannot have him convert it to centimeters.)

"My fantasy stock watch is rising," Danny joked from his locker. "I keep getting closer and closer. I was excited to play in the midfield for the last 10 minutes of the game. BC obviously does a great job, but through injuries and because we added another defender, I got to move up. I was happy to do whatever it took to help the team out, but it so happened that I made a late run and Eddie played me a great ball. I thought 'why not?' and decided to let it rip."

O'Rourke didn't mind at all that his shot sailed high, adding, "At least it didn't go out for a throw-in."

He Wears No. 2 For a Reason

There's comedy, there's high comedy, and then there's the postgame game scene when deadline-frenzied reporters anxiously waited for Frankie Hejduk to emerge from an interminable treatment session in the trainer's room. As the desperation mounted, the reporters relied on creativity to save the day. The locker room TV started showing Hejduk's postgame interview with ESPN. In an instant, up went the volume as several recorders were held directly in front of the TV's speakers.

While the reporters stood on their tip toes and held their recorders up to the wall-mounted TV, Hejduk emerged from the trainer's room and walked right past the gaggle of TV-taping journalists. Frankie grabbed a drink of water, fiddled with some items in his locker, and seemed to enjoy the surreal scene. It was fitting that his locker's nameplate reads "2 Frankie Hejduk."

"This is awesome," he said. "It's like a have a clone, and I'm just letting my clone do interviews for me."

Once the media stopped recording his clone's TV interview, everyone gathered around the original Frankie, so they ultimately got the quotes they wanted without needing the express written consent of ESPN and Major League Soccer.

Frankie the Fall Guy

Hejduk was an offensive force throughout the game. Not only did he have a goal and an assist, but he could have had multiples of each. Frankie attributed his big game to the cool September evening.

"I told everyone that I wish every game was played in this type of weather," he said. "Hopefully some day we get to play in the winter instead of in the summer heat. The game is faster and the guys are more in tune with the game because they don't have to fight the sun and humidity. I feel like I could run for a second game right now. If you play in the weather that soccer is meant to be played in, it's that much easier. I thought everyone had a lot more energy, I thought the game was more exciting, I thought the fans were more pumped up…and I think all of that had to do with perfect soccer weather."

The marketers, accountants, and public at large might find the concept of winter soccer to be untenable in the United States, but it would certainly play to Hejduk's strengths.

"There's no question that that's my game—running," he said. "It's so much harder to do when it's 90 degrees and humid compared to when it's cooler. I can play my game when it's cooler. I can get up and down, make my runs, and then get back. It was easy to play out there."

Beard Contest Update

When I saw Adam Moffat in the locker room, I noticed that rather than sporting some "sick designs" in his facial hair, he merely displayed the kind of thick stubble that suggested he had probably shaved as recently as halftime. So I asked him about the results of Paco's beard contest.

"It just kind of ended and there were never any rulings," he lamented. "They didn't even hand me a trophy. I'm so distraught that I might never grow a beard again."

By the time our brief conversation had ended, he had in fact grown another beard.

Timing is Everything

Given that the remnants of Hurricane Ike knocked out power to Crew Stadium for two days, MLSnet beat writer Craig Merz couldn't help but feel relieved at how it all worked out.

"We got lucky with the timing of the power outage," said Merz. "In another two weeks, it could have melted our Butter Bruce."

For those who missed our ridiculous conversation in a previous Notebook, Merz has proposed that the Crew carve a giant butter sculpture of Los Angeles head coach Bruce Arena during the Galaxy's visit on October 4.

During his stint with D.C. United, Arena was a frequent critic of the "circus-like" atmosphere of soccer in "Middle America." Merz sought to add a state fair touch this year, since nothing says entertainment to "Middle America" more than butter sculptures.

"If that power outage happened the first weekend of October, all we would have had is a buttery puddle of Bruce," he added.

Duncan's Trip Home

After being called back in to the New Zealand National Team for the World Cup Qualifiers against New Caledonia, Duncan Oughton got to visit with his family and some familiar names. The Kiwis beat the New Caledonians to win the Oceana title and a place in the Confederations Cup. New Zealand will eventually face the fifth-place finisher in Asia for a spot in the 2010 World Cup.

"It was a very fruitful trip," Duncan said. "Two wins, we qualified for the Confederations Cup and now we're 180 minutes from the World Cup. Over there, we won 3-1, and then didn't need to worry much about the second leg since we'd taken care of the business on the road. We are very happy because the Confederations Cup will be a huge cash injection into our country, soccer-wise, and then to be that close to the World Cup is great."

While New Caledonia sounds like a small-town high school, it is actually a series of islands about 750 miles east of Australia. It is a non-self-governing French territory. Let's turn it over to Duncan for more.

"New Caledonia is a French population," he explained. "They speak French there. They have quite a few useful players. They were the best team we played in qualifying, and they have a nice, proper stadium, which isn't the case with some of the other countries, so we were able to knock the ball around.

"We had Ryan Nelsen in from Blackburn and Simon Elliott was there, too, so it was nice to have those guys back in the fold," he continued. "And it was good to get 90 minutes in with the first team. Plus I got to see my mom, dad and brother, so it was a bit of a family reunion. It was a good experience, but then it was good to get back here because we are doing so well. Tonight was a fantastic win for us because it's good to get that separation in the standings again."

Dunc's Pub Thingy

There will be a slight delay in our official focus group naming of Duncan's dreamed-of future pub. I did not do as a good a job as the team did in maintaining focus during a crazy week.

When I first proposed this idea, Dante Washington could not believe I was going to go through with all of it. And really, it is a quite an undertaking for such a stupid joke. But as I told him at the time, "If something isn't worth doing, it's worth overdoing."

It's just not worth overdoing on time, apparently. We'll get the final results for the Crew-Galaxy Notebook, and of course give Duncan his chance to speak his mind about the whole absurd process.

Players Are Fans Too

Remember that game in Kansas City last year when the Crew were victimized by an atrocious stoppage-time penalty call? Remember how angry you were that the game was decided by a deplorable refereeing decision?

Well, Frankie Hejduk feels your pain. I'm not referring to the pain he felt that night, which was a different sort of pain since it was literally his team and his job. But Frankie feels your pain as a fan because in week two of the NFL season, his hometown San Diego Chargers were victimized by a game-deciding referee blunder. Long story short, the Chargers had forced a fumble from the Broncos quarterback with a little over a minute to play. They recovered the ball and should have won the game, 38-31. However, the referee ruled it an incomplete pass, and since he had blown the whistle, the ball got to stay with Denver even though instant replay confirmed it was a fumble. Two plays later, the Broncos scored the winning touchdown and two-point conversion to beat the Chargers, 39-38, dropping San Diego's record to 0-2 on two last-second losses.

"Why have instant replay?" Frankie the Chargers Fan grumbled when Danny O broached the subject. "That's what it's for, right? It was a definite fumble, everyone knew it, the whole league knows it... whatever, dude. The Chargers were 0-2 last year and still won 11 games."

Footballers' Fantasy Football

While Frankie might get a little worked up over the real San Diego Chargers, a group of Crew players reserve that sort of anguish for their fantasy teams. Fantasy football talk is the bane of the office water cooler, but one can't escape it in a professional locker room either.

The Crew's league consists of chief smack spokesman Danny O'Rourke, along with Hesmer, Carroll, Marshall, Miglioranzi, Moreno, Plotkin, Garey, Noonan, and Gruenebaum.

"I have a tough matchup this weekend with Andy Gruenebaum," said O'Rourke. "His team name is something stupid about the Chiefs always losing, since that's all they do. He's a Chiefs fan. He and I just made a blockbuster trade, and if you ask anyone else, they will say he is an idiot. We traded two studs and some crap players, but I got Terrell Owens and he got Michael Turner. I drafted Turner late and was able to sell him high. Our matchup this week could come down to that trade, but I have all the confidence in my team."

(UPDATE: I don't know how their match-up turned out and I don't know how fantasy scoring works, but Turner rushed for 103 yards and 3 TDs, while Owens had 2 catches for 17 yards and no TDs. That doesn't look good for Danny.)

After two weeks, Marshall, Hesmer, and Plotkin lead the league with 2-0 records. "You know who the big surprise is? Chad Marshall," O'Rourke said. "He's a fantasy rookie and on draft day we were all laughing at some of his picks, but his team is shaping up nicely. I am proud of him. Chad actually beat me in week one by three-and-a-half points. He made a big-time move by starting Philip Rivers over Derek Anderson and it paid big dividends for him. I applaud that move. I wouldn't have done it."

Two guys are suffering from tough luck, according to O'Rourke. "BC (Carroll) had a good draft, but he's been hurt by injuries," he said. "Stefani picked Tom Brady, so he's our charity case.[137] I might just give him some of my good players since I can't play them all."

While Danny is confident his team will win the title, he's also geared up to ensure that his bitter rival does not. "As long as Will doesn't win, we'll be okay," he said. "Will knows a lot about fantasy football. We'll come home from practice, and we'll both be reading stuff about players and then looking over to see what the other one is up to. It's a war within a war."

Some might argue that O'Rourke and Hesmer had an unfair research and transaction advantage this week since they never lost power at their place. Danny didn't disagree. "The two best players in the league had power, so it was a case of the rich getting richer."

Sight of the Night

At the player tunnel, two loyal Crew fans proudly dressed head to toe in the Crew's famous banana kit. The thing is, only the shorts were real. These two men had painted the jerseys and socks onto their bare skin. With an astonishing eye for detail, including the Crew logo and the Glidden sponsorship, one guy painted himself into a Frankie Hejduk jersey, while the other painted himself into a Guillermo Barros Schelotto shirt. It was a hilarious sight.

This sort of bodypainted jersey thing works well for stripper soccer tournaments during the World Cup or European Championship, but for two dudes? Not so much. Especially when one of the guys commented, "I'm not shaving everything for just one game."

When Duncan Oughton came out of the tunnel for pregame warm-ups, he took one look at the fellows, paused, leaned up against the fence, and pretended to lose his dinner. And his lunch. And possibly his breakfast.

The rest of the players seemed amused as they jogged past for warmups. Hejduk even offered a hearty "All right, dudes!"

But after the game, Oughton was still scarred by the encounter. "The only thing I have to say is that that one guy was wearing the hairiest Crew shirt that I have ever seen."

Questions? Comments? Reading this internet article by candlelight because you still don't have power? Feel free to write at sirk65@yahoo.com

---

[137] New England Patriots superstar QB Tom Brady blew out his knee in week one.

While some fans made Duncan Oughton lose his lunch over their peculiar mixture of yellow body paint and black body hair (above), fans of all ages (below) enjoyed the Crew's primetime thumping of the Red Bulls on Thursday, September 18, 2008.
(Both photos by Sam Fahmi)

Road Work: Crew 1, New England 0

Match date: Saturday, September 27, 2008
Scoring:
35: CLB Marshall 4 (Rogers 2)
Attendance: 15,035
Crew's record afterward: 15-6-5

RETROACTIVE RECAP

Just three weeks after the 4-0 pasting at Crew Stadium, the Revs got a chance to host the Crew and claw their way back into the Eastern Conference race. Or not. The Crew blew the race wide open, taking an 8-point lead in the East, with a 1-0 victory in rainy Foxboro. Chad Marshall's corner-kick header in the 35th minute was the only goal of the game. The Crew made it hold up despite playing a man down for the final 25+ minutes after Frankie Hejduk got ejected for receiving one of the goofiest second yellows in MLS history. Despite playing with a yellow, Hejduk inexplicably decided to kick the ball from the hands of Revs' goalkeeper Matt Reis as Reis attempted to punt the ball. Sigi Schmid was ejected in stoppage time after protesting a non-call when Revs forward Taylor Twellman undercut Crew goalkeeper William Hesmer. ("I don't know why I was ejected," Schmid told Shawn Mitchell of the Columbus Dispatch. "I didn't start verbally abusing the referees until after I was thrown out." I love that quote.)

QUOTES

Sigi Schmid: "We haven't made the playoffs the last two years, so we're highly motivated and we know that it's not a given. There were so many years that we were out of it, so our team is very focused and trying to take each opportunity for all it's worth, wrap it with two hands, and hold on to it. For the team right now, it's a matter of maintaining first place. We want to get home field in both rounds of the playoffs, and we'd like to grab the Supporters' Shield. It would be just another honor and feather in the cap for how well they've played all season."

Chad Marshall: "We knew it was going to be battle. The last time we played them, we had a favorable result, winning 4-0, so we knew they were going to want this one at home. So we just came out and did what we had to do and got out with three points. It was unfortunate to go down a man the last 30 (minutes), but we battled and did what we had to do and get numbers behind the ball. We didn't really give them anything. It's a credit to our team defense."

The Incidents, Pt. IV:
(Not) Leaving (For) Las Vegas

Just when Crew fans thought it was safe to focus their attention on championship dreams, a third and final off-field incident came along and threatened to blow up the whole thing. Instead of worrying if their team could win that elusive first title, Crew fans began to worry if they would even have a team.

A basic chronology follows…

Monday, September 29, 2008

Tripp Mickle of the Sports Business Journal reported that the group looking to bring an MLS expansion team to Las Vegas, led by California businessman Mark Noorzai, was also negotiating to buy a minority share of the Columbus Crew. "It's pretty close to being in the final stages," Mickle was told by group spokesman Paul Caligiuri. Yes, *that* Paul Caligiuri, who Crew fans associate with backdoor deals to abandon Columbus. Shawn Mitchell's first attempt at getting answers for the newspaper did not yield much in the way of comments, reassuring or otherwise. The Crew Fan Freakout started at code orange.

Tuesday, September 30, 2008

Under normal circumstances, it would be preposterous to call John Wagner an "underling." After all, the man is the President of Hunt Sports Group and oversees the operations of not just the Crew, but FC Dallas as well. Wagner is a big-time sports executive who answers only to Clark Hunt, and normally his presence would carry a lot of weight. But this was the exception to the rule. While it makes perfect sense that Wagner was first on the scene to dispel the rumors of the Crew's rumored relocation, it did little to ease fans' concerns. It didn't matter if Wagner was telling the truth. To anyone possessing an already worried or suspicious mind, Wagner's emergency appearance seemed like nothing more than an "underling" being flown in to do some damage control.

"It's not going to happen," Wagner told Mitchell when asked about the Crew relocating to Las Vegas. "The Crew is staying here. It has a soccer-specific stadium and a great fan base. The team is staying."

Meanwhile, Crew President & General Manager Mark McCullers joined the fray by posting a message on the team's official blog. "I've always believed that actions speak louder than words," it read in part, "so our actions will continue to demonstrate that we intend to build the Crew into a valued and influential community asset – in Columbus. This year, we have seen that the actions of our fans have demonstrated that Columbus can get behind a winning team and deliver a tremendous, authentic soccer atmosphere in our stadium. Let's allow our actions to continue to speak for themselves and build upon the substantial momentum that we have developed this year. Our team and staff are focused on a strong push into the postseason. We need you with us."

Wednesday, October 1, 2008

On Wednesday morning, Crew fans opened their morning papers to find Dispatch columnist Michael Arace on the offensive. As the beat writer for the NHL's Hartford Whalers during their relocation process, Arace had been down this road before. Regarding the Crew's situation, Arace clearly felt it was wisest to shoot first and ask questions later. Arace wrote that the Crew's relocation was a foregone conclusion, then sprayed verbal bullets in every direction.

"The paranoia [of Crew fans] is well-founded," Arace wrote. "Major League Soccer really is after them. By all appearances, the league is going to take their team and move it to Las Vegas."

He warned of verbal smokescreens, a conniving Paul Caligiuri, dispassionate absentee ownership, civic titans eager for revenge on the Hunts over the hockey deal gone wrong and resulting lawsuit, a Trojan Horse minority investor eager to put a team in Vegas, the league's disdain for the Columbus market, and the lack of a Sigi Schmid contract extension and new training facility as proof that the team was not putting down roots. Basically, he took every possible paranoid scenario and ran with it as if it were a done deal.

Some argued that this was sensationalist journalism, but others suggested that Arace's wide swath of machine gun fire was very much intentional and designed to flush out someone who would talk. As one knowledgeable person told me, "Arace is a cagey mother(bleep)er."

Thursday, October 2, 2008

If that was the intent of Arace's blast, it paid off. Wednesday morning, the Dispatch got a call from a local sports brokerage outfit called The Team, LLC. They wished to meet with Mitchell and Arace that afternoon to shed some light on the transaction and to refute the "wild speculation" that was out there. In Thursday's paper, Mitchell revealed that The Team stated that:

- The Noorzai-led Crew group (called Crew Sports Holdings) was different than the Noorzai-led Vegas group.
- Crew Sports Holdings would include local investors with the long-term goal of transitioning to local ownership.
- If Crew Sports Holdings was successful in buying a minority stake, Noorzai would move his family to Columbus.
- Paul Caligiuri was not part of Crew Sports Holdings, only the Vegas group.

One sticking point that still lacked resolution was the multiple-ownership angle. It was believed that MLS was looking to get down to one owner per team. At one point, the Phil Anchutz (5), Lamar Hunt (3), and Robert Kraft (2) owned all 10 of the league's teams. By 2008, including expansion teams, there were 14.5 owners for 16 teams. Anschutz Entertainment group owned the Los Angeles Galaxy and half of the Houston Dynamo, while Hunt Sports Group owned the Crew and FC Dallas.

In his earlier conversation with Mitchell, HSG's Wagner reiterated that it would eventually be one owner, one team. And The Team, LLC, stated that this minority purchase was the first step in transitioning to local ownership. (With the presumption being that Noorzai would be a local owner once he moved to Columbus.)

What made this so perplexing is that if the multiple ownership restrictions were true, the Hunts selling the team to Noorzai would not solve the problem if Noorzai were indeed successful in getting a team for Las Vegas. If the Hunts could not own Columbus and Dallas, and if Noorzai could not own Columbus and Las Vegas, it seemed that the long term implication was that either Noorzai would own the Crew and abandon Vegas, or Noorzai would own the Crew and move them to Vegas.

Friday, October 3, 2008

Arace popped up with a new column that went over the meeting with The Team, LLC. "I want to believe everybody right now ," Arace wrote, "-- Crew general manager Mark McCullers, Hunt Sports Group president John Wagner, Noorzai's agent -- because what they are saying in terms of the Crew's stability is what the team's staunch supporters deserve to hear. But I can't help but maintain some skepticism."

I spoke with Crew PR Director Dave Stephany at training that morning, and he seemed exhausted. All week, people had grasped on to every loose straw and had woven them into a wicker casino and stadium complex.

"But Dave," I said, "you have to understand what you are dealing with here. Ohio is football country. There are only a few states that can rival Ohio's love for the game. There are two professional teams in the state, and as points of reference, neither one is doing you any favors. The majority of the state roots for the Cleveland Browns, and the Browns, one of the NFL's most rabidly supported teams, were stolen away to Baltimore. If it can happen to the Cleveland Effin' Browns, it can happen to *any* team, and it sure as hell can happen to the little ol' Columbus Crew. The rest of the state roots for the Cincinnati Bengals, and Bengals fans are scarred by the concept of the idiot offspring of a great man. Mike Brown has run their franchise into the ground since Paul Brown died. I am not saying that Clark Hunt is the idiot offspring of Lamar Hunt, but the truth is that people don't know Clark, so they are free to assume the worst based on their own experience in this area."

I went on to explain that people felt like they *knew* Lamar Hunt. He was always around, was highly visible, and was as friendly as a man as one could ever hope to meet. On any given game day, a large number of people in that stadium had spoken with Lamar Hunt at one time or another, and he probably introduced himself on many of those occasions. Lamar came across as this saintly, friendly, trustworthy grandfather figure that everybody knew and loved. If Lamar were alive, nobody would have read anything into a minority sale to an out of town investor. But even if it's unfair, people don't feel that they *know* Clark Hunt, so anything's possible. He could be a combination of Mike Brown and Art Modell for all the fans knew.

And then to top it off, not only did the Crew have a fan base comprised of Browns and Bengals fans assuming the worst based on their own scarred experiences, but there was also a little matter of the Columbus Dispatch. Mitchell is a dogged newshound. Arace had an up close and personal look at the shady relocation with the NHL's Hartford Whalers, so his B.S. detector immediately and involuntarily turned up to 11. All in all, a few statements by John Wagner or some local sports brokers would do nothing to either sweep this story under the rug or placate the nervous natives in Crewville.

"The only person who can put this to bed," I said, "is Clark Hunt himself. If he's genuine, people will pick up on that."

Wednesday, October 15, 2008

Noorzai's Las Vegas group failed to submit an expansion application for the 2011 season. Was this due to their focus on Columbus? Or because the Crew became their focus for a Vegas team? It's easy to guess which option Crew fans ran with. Even though he did not submit an expansion application, Noorzai muddied the waters by reaffirming his commitment to bringing a team to Las Vegas. "I have never taken my foot off the pedal," he told the Las Vegas Sun. "We're going strong and working with the league."

Again, if each owner could only one team, and if Noorzai was committed to Vegas but didn't even apply for an expansion team, just what exactly was going on here?

Sunday, October 26, 2008

This was the day that began to put this Vegas thing to bed for me. It was the day that Clark Hunt himself came to town and dispelled the rumors. As you'll see in the D.C. United Notebook, I spoke to Mark McCullers and told him of my theory that people don't know Clark like they did Lamar. And McCullers spoke very authoritatively about Clark's passion for the Crew, and mentioned that the comparisons to Lamar are unfair because Clark is running multiple companies whereas Lamar was at the stage in life where he could focus on the fun of his sports teams.

At the same time I spoke with McCullers, Mitchell and Arace spoke with Clark Hunt himself. Among the things that Hunt told the Dispatch was that HSG would no longer have to divest itself of a team, which substantially altered the playing field. He also stated that HSG had no intention of ceding control of the Crew, and that the Crew would not be leaving town.

"The best way to state it directly," Hunt told the Dispatch reporters, "is that I'm confident the Columbus Crew will be playing in Columbus, Ohio, for at least the next 50 years. Beyond that, I'm not making any predictions."

As for being genuine, Arace wrote the next morning that throughout the interview, Clark sounded like his dad. It was a compliment.

The Nordecke's message was crystal clear on the Vegas matter. (Photo by Sam Fahmi)

Playoffs and Beyond

Circumstances saw to it that Clark Hunt was uncharacteristically visible in the Crew community since October of 2008.[138] The Supporters' Shield ceremony, the playoff games, MLS Cup, the Governor's reception, the unveiling of Championship Row, the 10th anniversary of Crew Stadium, the awarding of the championship rings...Clark has had plenty of ceremonial reasons to interact with the Crew community. And he truly interacted. He's spent time in front of the Nordecke, both in Columbus and at MLS Cup in Carson. He visited tailgating Crew fans in the Home Depot Center parking lot to thank them for making the trip to Los Angeles. He shook hands and posed for pictures after inviting fans to attend the second half of the team's post-game celebration party at the Manhattan Beach Marriott. Watching these interactions, and spending brief periods of time talking to Clark and Dan while in LA, completely eased any fears I may have had.[139]

---

[138] I would like to stress it was the circumstances. As moving as my speech to Dave Stephany may have been, Clark's appearances were completely unrelated.

[139] One can never say never, and I don't know that one can truly hold Clark to his 50 year promise. 50 years is a long time to promise anything, especially in business. But by the time MLS Cup rolled around, I no longer worried about the Crew being sold out from under us in the immediate future. I believed that the Hunts were sincere in their desire to keep the Crew in the family and in Columbus, with no designs on selling the team so it could be relocated to Vegas.

A man actively looking to sell a team for relocation does not open himself up to close and personal interaction with the team's most rabid fans as Clark did. A family actively looking to sell a team for relocation does not repeatedly invoke the name of their beloved patriarch and how much he loved the team and would have loved to be there to see all this, nor do they speak about how the Crew and Crew Stadium is an important part of that patriarch's legacy, as both Clark and Dan did.

The Vegas story was a strange ride. In the end, it went bust. The Crew announced on February 5, 2009, that the negotiations were off. In October, that news would have been greeted by the fans with a Mardi Gras styled celebration. Instead, it was an afterthought.

While the initial news and developments scared an awful lot of people and led to lots of rampant speculation, the Vegas rumors and the team's MLS Cup run combined to create a new bond between Crew fans and the Hunt family. Crew fans got to interact with Clark and Dan while studying their every move, and most came away seeing that Lamar's family does indeed care about the Crew. They got to see it up close and personal, like they did with Lamar.

For the Hunts and the fans alike, I think there was a lot of good in that.

So that's the Vegas side trip that completes The Effed Up Stuff Quartet, following Drunky the YouTube Racist, the West Ham "Brawl.", and the team's near death experience on the way home from Toronto. Any of these things could have distracted the team or taken the wind out of the Nordecke's sails, but everyone pressed on and was handsomely rewarded for their perseverance in the face of adversity and controversy.

Now back to our regularly scheduled programming, when Whatshisface The English Guy came to town…

Sirk's Notebook: Crew 1, Los Angeles 0

Match date: Saturday, October 4, 2008
Scoring:
43: CLB Moreno 9 (O'Rourke 3)
Attendance: 22,685
Crew's record afterward: 16-6-5

The David Beckham Jerseyfest, Shriekapalooza, and Flashbulb Jamboree pulled into Crew Stadium on Saturday night. He came, he saw, and he left with his team's playoff hopes in tatters.

Veni. Vidi. Ouchie.

It was far from a work of art, but the Columbus Crew defeated Beckham's Los Angeles Galaxy, 1-0, on Saturday, delighting an overflow crowd of 22,685 people who all wore black out of respect for the Galaxy's almost flat-lining playoff chances.[140] Meanwhile, the victory ultimately clinched first place in the East for the Massive Bananas, who will have home-field advantage throughout the Eastern Conference playoffs.

Beckham's appearance gave the event a big-game feel, but the crowd was hardly deferential. Sure, camera flashes lit up Crew Stadium like a firefly Woodstock every time Becks lined up for a free kick, took a throw-in, or, um, retreated into his defensive third to get a touch on the ball. But he was also heckled, jeered and mocked. Apart from his introduction, the biggest cheer Beckham earned all night was when he received a yellow card. His preceding hack of Robbie Rogers earned him boos before the booking.

"I was expecting a great atmosphere, and it was a great atmosphere," said Beckham. "There were a lot of people out there and I am sure they enjoyed themselves, especially with the Columbus win. I enjoyed it, apart from losing."

Faces in the Crowd

Part of that atmosphere was created by the Crew's suspended right back, Frankie Hejduk, and suspended head coach, Sigi Schmid. As expected, Hejduk spent part of the game singing and chanting with the rowdy denizens of the Nordecke.

---

[140] At least I am assuming that was the impetus for the Crew's "black out" promotion.

As for Schmid? "I watched from a radio booth while sitting on a table," he explained. "If you stand, you can't see the whole field, so I watched with my face pressed up against the glass. It fogged up a little."

When he made a surprise visit to the media room to deliver his postgame comments, Sigi assured everyone it was perfectly legal. "Believe me, right now I'm wearing an ankle bracelet and there's a beeper on there so the league can track me and know exactly where I am at," he joked. "They are also recording all of my comments."

Although he did not watch the match from the Nordecke like Frankie Hejduk did, Ohio Governor Ted Strickland (center) was in the house for Beckapalooza. To his credit, the Guv usually makes it to a few games per year, even when Beckham is not playing. (Photo by Sam Fahmi)

Deliver It Like Danny

Forget bending it like Beckham, the best service of the night came from secret weapon Danny O'Rourke, who assisted on Alejandro Moreno's 42nd minute goal. O'Rourke collected a weak clearance by the Galaxy defense and then whipped a wicked cross into the box where it found the head of Moreno as he cut in front of Galaxy defender Chris Klein.

"I was playing high because they were only leaving one man up top, so I cheated forward a bit," O'Rourke explained. "I took a touch and saw Brad (Evans), Alejandro, and Robbie making runs. All three made good runs so I put it where one of them could get on the end of it. Alejandro finished it brilliantly."

"(Danny) got his head up and I saw that he was trying to swing the ball in," said Moreno. "As he swung the ball in, I tried to get in between defenders and get in front of Klein and put it into the back of the net."

The goal was Moreno's ninth of the season, setting a new career high. "It's important because before the season started, Sigi set a goal for me of 10-15 goals. Maybe 15 is on the high side, but that's something I can shoot for in the remaining games. More important, and more remarkable, is the season that we are having as a team. At this stage of my career, I know this type of season doesn't come along often, so I am very appreciative."

Pinpoint playmaker Danny O'Rourke is most lethal with the ball at his feet, as seen here against the Galaxy on October 4, 2008. (Photo by Greg Bartram / Columbus Crew)

Where Did The Goals Go?

The Galaxy came in with the league's best offense and the league's worst defense. The Crew came in with the league's second-best offense. Conditions were ripe for one of those crazy goalfests that seem to happen annually at Giants Stadium. (Fun fact: Giants Stadium has hosted a 5-4 game for FOUR consecutive seasons. Seriously. Look it up.) [141]

Instead of a shootout, the Crew's lone tally stood up because the defense put up a goose egg against the goal-getting Galaxy.

"I think the thing about the Galaxy is that they complement each other so well," said Andy Iro, who started in the middle of the back line. "Edson Buddle is a big, bashing guy with a decent touch. Then you complement him with Beckham serving balls, and then you have this little whip-it like Donovan scurrying around, and then you have Eddie Lewis who is going to drop off and hit shots from 20-25 yards out. They have every facet of an attacking lineup. It was good for us, and we played well as a team, and we came up with some blocks at crucial times. It was a good, good, good team defensive effort."

"I thought our defensive effort was very good," said Schmid. "Andy Iro has grown over the course of the season.[142] I thought he came in played very solid, and then Chad Marshall did what we have become accustomed to back there. Danny O'Rourke did a good job at right back, and we keep plugging him into different roles at different times. Gino Padula did a good job on Beckham. He had service from set pieces, but I don't really recall much service from the run of play."

"I had very little to do," admitted goalkeeper William Hesmer. "What can I say? The defense played great against the highest scoring team in the league."

Roughing Robbie Rogers

I think I have used that section heading several times this year, but so be it. It sounds good, and it's accurate.

Tackles on Rogers earned yellow cards in the 29th and 32nd minutes. The latter card was issued to Beckham for a late, leg-swinging slide tackle. The booking earned Beckham a one-game suspension for accumulation.

---

[141] Okay, so you don't have to…9/27/08: COL 5, NY 4.….8/18/07: NY 5, LA 4

5/20/06: NY 5, CHV 4. ….. 9/17/05: NY 5, NE 4

[142] Figuratively. He was not one meter and 99 centimeters by season's end.

"You never want to go into a game thinking about not getting a yellow card, because it throws you off your game and you end up not going into any tackles," Beckham explained. "It was one of those challenges where the referee was handing out cards quite easily tonight."

Did I mention it was a late, leg-swinging slide tackle? And that it occurred just three minutes after another cautioned hacking of Rogers? Hats off to referee Jorge Gonzalez for stopping the Rough-A-Robbie defense early in the game.

David Beckham stands over Robbie Rogers after Beckham's desperate, yellow-card slide tackle on the Crew's young speedster. (Photo by Sam Fahmi)

The two quick yellows got me to wondering how many cards Rogers has drawn this year. Using the play-by-play recaps available on MLSnet.com, I went through the Crew's games and looked it up. Two caveats: First, the play-by-play failed to say who suffered the foul when Kyle Beckerman got a yellow for a reckless tackle against the Crew on July 12. Second, I counted second yellows as yellows, not reds.

The results? Not only does Rogers lead the league with 69 fouls suffered, he has also drawn 15 yellow cards, one straight red, and two penalty kicks. When one contemplates all of the non-calls, it's staggering to think about the amount of violence that comes his way.

How ridiculous are those numbers? The next two Crew players COMBINED would only equal Rogers on reds and penalties, and still fall three yellows short of Rogers' total. Alejandro Moreno is second on the team, drawing 7 yellows and two penalties. Guillermo Barros Schelotto is third, drawing 5 yellows and one straight red.

Crew on the Crowd

Needless to say, the Crew enjoyed playing in front of a packed house.

Robbie Rogers: "It was a great atmosphere and I think that's how it's going to be in the playoffs, so it was good for us to get a game like this where the nerves were a little high, and we found a way to win."

William Hesmer: "The atmosphere again tonight was electric. It's been like that for a handful of games this year. You can't say enough – I know it's cliché to keep saying it – but the crowd gives us that little extra boost to dig in and we really mean it, they've been a huge part of our success."

Andy Iro: "I would look up into the stands and it would be all black. That was a good feeling. And it was really, really loud. There was a time when Bobby (Warzycha) was shouting instructions to me, and he wasn't that far away, and I couldn't hear him. You hope for that atmosphere in the playoffs. When you're playing, you just think, 'I'm all right. I got the crowd behind me.' That's the way it should be. That's when it's fun as a player."

Alejandro Moreno: "We looked at is as though there would maybe be some people here who haven't been here all year, and this was our chance to show them our progress. There were many who have been here all season, but there were others that we hope will come back based on our win tonight. We hope that they will come back and support us in the playoffs."

Bruce on the Crowd

First, let me say that Craig Merz and I should be ashamed of ourselves. After weeks of rehashing Bruce Arena's "circus-like atmosphere" comments from 1997 and joking about the Crew displaying a Butter Bruce on the plaza, neither of us thought to ask Arena about his thoughts on the burgeoning supporter culture in here in Middle America.

But that's where Chris DeVille of Columbus Alive came to the rescue. He asked Arena if he has a different opinion of Columbus now compared to his critical comments in the past.

"When was this? 1996?" Arena asked.

"A long time ago," DeVille confirmed.

Arena then dusted off some of his favorite routines from back in the day. "It has progressed," he said. "This certainly beats playing in the Ohio State football stadium on a 57-yard field with horses running around. This is a fabulous venue. I've been here with the national team for some very important games. But I am pleased that you can recall that from 13 years ago. That's good."

Yes, very good. Well done, Chris. Merz and I owe you one.

MLS Fantasy Spotlight

After joking two weeks ago that his fantasy stock watch was on the upswing after taking a shot not-on-goal, I asked O'Rourke what his MLS fantasy expectations were now that he assisted on the game-winning goal against LA.

"Maybe someone will pick me up off the waiver wire," he replied.

Jersey Switch

Early in the first half, O'Rourke ran to the Crew bench and changed his shirt. I was worried that he had busted his right eye open for the third time in a month. Instead, it was a much more mundane jersey change.

"I wore a long-sleeved jersey and I did a lot of push-ups yesterday, so it was really tight up top," he deadpanned. "No, it was brand new and wasn't broken in yet, so it was really uncomfortable to run in. When Eddie Lewis went down, I went and changed to my other jersey."

Supporters' Shield In Sight

After the weekend's action, only the Houston Dynamo stand between the Crew and their second Supporters' Shield title. Any combination of points earned by the Crew or points dropped by the Dynamo totaling three would clinch the Shield for Columbus. Created and paid for by the league's supporter groups, the Supporters' Shield is awarded annually to the team with the highest point total in MLS, and winning the shield would clinch the Crew a second-round berth in the 2009-10 CONCACAF Champions League.

While the Supporters' Shield admittedly didn't carry as much weight back in 2004, when the Crew rattled off an 18-game unbeaten streak en route to the franchise's first Shield, I have always viewed it as a missed opportunity that the club has not commemorated the '04 team's achievement with an in-stadium banner.[143] (In an overlooked bit of Crew lore, it was none other than

---

[143] This oversight was rectified at the start of the 2009 season.

Duncan Oughton who scored the Crew's lone goal in the Shield-clinching draw in Denver on the final Saturday of the season.) A lot has changed since then, and this year's team seems to be fully aware of the Shield, what it represents, and the benefits of bringing it back to Columbus.

"The Supporters' Shield is arguably hardest thing to win in this league," said goalkeeper William Hesmer. "The MLS Cup is four games, but to win the Shield, you have to prove it over a 30-game season. In most leagues, that is how they determine the champion. It's something that we want to win, and it would also put us in international competition next season."

Media Culpa

Speaking of the Supporters' Shield, many people, myself included, would have been shocked to learn in March that the Crew would be on the verge of running away with it in October. William Hesmer was not one of the doubters.

"I think it was you guys who said we weren't going to do so well, [144] you guys in the media, and that fired us up," he said. "I think we always go into a season saying that we're going for championships. Every year. In the offseason, not making the playoffs for the past few years sat heavy on guys, so there's a little extra incentive. I think now we're pegged to be one of the top teams, but we're a team that's free-spirited and we go out there and play as hard as we can and the results take care of themselves."

Arena on Winning, the Crew, and the Knicks

Bruce Arena knows a thing or two about winning, and when asked what it would take to turn around the Galaxy, he also found a way to work the Crew's turnaround into the discussion.

"Winning is a mentality," he said. "You not only need to have the right players to win, but there's a mentality that goes along with it. That's certainly the coach's responsibility. It's every day and in every experience. When things don't go the way they're supposed to go, and there's reasons for it that you can avoid, then you need to bring the hammer down.

"It's not going to happen overnight, or even week to week, so much as it will happen from season to season. A good example of that would be the

---

[144] While I don't think I publicly said it, I certainly didn't envision this type of season. I figured they'd challenge for a playoff spot—maybe make it, maybe not—but I certainly didn't think they'd be THIS special. So fair enough, William.

Crew, a team that hadn't made the playoffs since I don't know what year.[145] They've had to slowly build, and I know Sigi—he's a detail guy and he has a way of doing things. It's maybe taken him a while to convince guys to do things his way, but they're doing it right now. They don't have many new players, but they've matured and grown. It's a lesson for everyone. You don't always need new players, you just need to let them grow."

In Arena's eyes, the Galaxy's situation is different. "In our case, it's not just the mentality, but the roster," he said. "Managing your roster and salary cap is a part of modern day sports in America. We've had some problems with our roster and salary cap, and that needs to get better for us to improve our team. I like to look at other sports, and if you look at the extreme end of mismanaging a roster and salary cap, there's the New York Knicks in the NBA. I'm not saying we're the Knicks, but we sure are giving it a shot."[146]

Beckham on the Knick-like Galaxy

After the game, Beckham was asked if he was frustrated that the club has not done more to surround him and Landon Donovan with more talent.

"At the end of the day, this team is not about me and Landon," he said. "This organization is not about me and Landon. We're just in a position where maybe we aren't getting a little bit of luck. We look at each other in the dressing room and we want to play with each other[147], and that's the thing. You want to be proud of the team, and proud of your teammates, and to look at your teammates and know everyone is giving 100 percent each game. Sometimes that's happened this year, and sometimes it hasn't. Any other questions are higher up. It has nothing to do with me."

---

[145] Bruce, in the highly unlikely event that you're reading, it was 2004.

[146] What a tremendous quote. Only Bruce Arena would have the stones to take over a high-profile and carefully-polished MLS club and immediately compare them to one of the worst-run franchises in all of American professional sports. (Even though he was right.)

[147] I almost went on the disabled list after pulling every muscle in my stomach, neck, and face while trying to stifle my Beavis & Butthead laughter when he said that.

I have no idea what the heck is going on in this photo, but it makes me laugh every time I see it. Sam snapped the button at exactly the most awkward moment (Photo by Sam Fahmi.)

Buddle-licious Quip of the Week

Former Crew man Edson Buddle, on the horde of media that descended on the Galaxy's training session just to, um, chronicle his return to Columbus: "It's not just here. It's like this everywhere I go, man. They follow me everywhere."

Buddle-licious Baffling Quote of the Week

Edson Buddle, on any differences in his play now compared to his days in Columbus: "As the years go by, you see more, you know? It's like aging."

The Sunny Side of Bruce

Maybe the L.A. life has mellowed out Bruce Arena. Over the years, Arena has been known for being caustically condescending, but at Galaxy training on Friday, he showed his condescendingly comedic side. His exceptionally dry wit was in top form.

As he gave his interviews to the TV and radio reporters, we writers could overhear Arena telling the TV folks, "Our goal is to win the game. The game plan is so complicated that I won't bother telling you about it because you'd never understand it anyway."

We had a chuckle over it, and when Arena came over to meet with the writers, Craig Merz did not hesitate to ask Arena for more detail on his game plan. Arena cracked a smile. "It's very, very sophisticated," he continued with a bemused smirk. "We still haven't completed it. We'll be in the lab until midnight working on this one."

Obetz Decorations

The interior of the Crew's Obetz facility is decorated with many photo spoofs playfully mocking players and staff. Here's one that I feel comfortable sharing. On the door to head trainer Jason Mathews' office, the players posted a spoof of the Real Men of Genius ads. The page features photos of Mathews and assistant trainer Skylar "Paco" Richards. The text reads:

Real Men of Genius: Mr. Athletic Trainer

Here's to you, Mr. Athletic Trainer. Without your undying commitment, your athletes would find themselves swollen, achy, and dehydrated. Sure, most people would take pleasure in a job well done, but no one boasts of a wrinkle-free tape job like you do. You hold you head high while sporting a fanny pack past the year of 1988. For you, your 15 minutes of fame is when the camera lands on you standing behind your star athlete, because you know behind every great athlete is a great athletic trainer. So crack open an ice cold bottle of Gatorade, oh injury preventer-er and caretaker-er, and remember that you put the I.C.E. in R.I.C.E.

At the bottom of the page, in what looks suspiciously like the handwriting of team administrator Tucker Walther, is a note that reads, "Get real! Trainers are people who couldn't be administrators!"

Dunc's Pub Name

After fielding suggestions from the Dante-Dunny Think Tank Foundation, conducting focus groups with fans and media, and then submitting a list of finalists to the Walther Polling Institute for a final vote amongst the players and team staff, we at the Sirk Margeting Group finally have an official market-tested and focus-group-approved name for the pub that Duncan Oughton hopes to open some day in the future.

First, let me say that the Walther Polling Institute took its mission very seriously. Every single member of the team staff, be it players, coaches, technical directors, trainers, doctors, equipment managers, or interns, received a vote. The WPI saw to it that every single person on the team side of the organization received the gift of franchisement in these proceedings.

Now, without further ado, the winning name is......

(do that drum roll thing where you trill your tongue)......

The Muppet Lodge!

Here is the final team voting after the fan and media votes winnowed the original field down to these five finalists:

1. The Muppet Lodge—15
2. Beaker's—13
3. Oughton Inn—9
4. Duncan's Baaaaaar—5
5. The Donkey Touch Pub—3

I have it on good authority from Jason Garey that the reserve team, aka "The Muppet Squad," was the voting bloc that pushed the The Muppet Lodge to the top of the list.

On Sunday night, I placed a call from the SMG world headquarters to the Oughton residence to share the results of this arduous process. Needless to say, Duncan was ecstatic. Or maybe not.

"I don't know that the investors would be happy with the name Muppet Lodge," he said. "Doesn't the name 'lodge' imply 'lodging', meaning there would be rooms with beds for the Muppets to stay in? I don't know if I am comfortable with that idea. I mean, you can pull up a barstool and take a nap for as long as you'd like, as long as I can keep billing drinks to your tab, but I don't know that I want to provide any bed-based lodging. Especially for those Muppets."

Oughton also gave his thoughts on the other finalists:

* Beaker's: "That one was obviously Dante's idea.[148] Very predictable from the big fella."

---

[148] It was.

* Oughton Inn: "The 'man room' in my house is called the Out Inn, which sounds just like 'Oughton', so I've already thought of that one without a so-called think tank."

* Duncan's Baaaaar: "That one's not bad, actually. It's pretty clever for a sheep joke. I'm not surprised at all that Andy Gruenebaum's thoughts immediately turned to animals."

* The Donkey Touch Pub: "Why would Dunseth want me to name my pub after him? He's a very vain man."

The Kiwi was also flabbergasted to hear about the many companies and organizations that were involved in this process.

"The Sirk Marketing Group?" he said. "If I saw the initials SMG, I would think Sirk's Muppet Gang, which probably explains the final result of this bloated process. I would like to thank SMG for their tireless work and thousands of dollars spent on a process that yielded a name that we would have thought of in three sips of beer over the course of 37 seconds. It takes a talented group to make such a big and costly project out of something that could have been accomplished for free in 37 seconds."

"The Dante-Dunny Think Tank Foundation?" he asked with astonishment, upon learning that ex-teammates Dante Washington and Brian Dunseth were in the think tank business. "I believe their motto is 'Two Men – One Brain.' But from my past experiences with Dante and Dunny, I've found that 99.9 percent of what they think up is absolute garbage, so I think they should be commended for coming up with suggestions that were merely less than average, which is a big step up from garbage. I would like to thank Dante and Dunseth for their hours and hours of tireless thinking, even though those two men are about as useful as a smelly fart in an elevator."

Duncan took on a more appreciative tone upon learning that the fans and media served as focus groups that whittled down the original list of names. "I would like to thank the fans and media who voted and, as a result, got rid of a lot of the rubbish put forth by that supposed think tank where each member has a tiny half-brain," he said. "I am thankful for their efforts to negate some of the less-than-average thinking that went into this whole process."

Rather than shock, Duncan found peril behind the existence of the Walther Polling Institute. "I noticed that Tucker was scurrying around the locker room like a little rodent," he said. "It's unusual when he leaves me out of whatever secretive scurrying he's doing, so I knew something was going down.

"It just shows how seriously he takes his non-work responsibilities," he continued, "as well as how much time he has to waste from his real job. The guys are going to be in for a shock when they find out that instead of flying to Chicago, we will have to walk there because Tucker was too busy working his poll[149] to order our plane tickets. Training this week will consist of a five-day jog. We will leave Obetz on Wednesday and then arrive at Bridgeview on Sunday morning for the game. Blisters aside, there are going to be many guys with heavy legs for that game. So thank you, Tucker. There's only one man who could jog from Ohio to Illinois and then immediately play a soccer game, but he'll be away with the U.S. National Team."[150]

I asked one last time if he would consider using the name The Muppet Lodge since it was so thoroughly vetted by time-testing marketing techniques.

"Time will tell," he said. "It will depend on the investors, but maybe we will use part of the name. We might use the word 'the' or the letter 'm' or something, so don't feel that all of this was the big waste of everybody's time that it certainly appears to be."

The Man Behind The Name

The Muppet Lodge was suggested by Scottish beard-growing sensation Adam Moffat, who agreed with my idea that he should be entitled to some sort of reward for choosing the winning name.

"Since I suggested the winning name, Duncan should definitely have to have a weekly Scottish Night at his English-style pub," Moffat said. "There would be an open mic for bagpipe players and you'd have to wear a kilt or you don't get in. I better get Scottish Night for suggesting the winning name for Duncan's pub, because I didn't get a thing for winning that beard contest."

I told Duncan of the Scot's desired reward. "It's a possibility," said the Kiwi, "but the big question will be what will Moffat and his mates wear under their kilts? 'Nothing' is not an option! And I didn't know he played the bagpipes. I thought he played a little hand flute."[151]

---

[149] Duncan excels at the sneaky double entendre.

[150] Frankie Hejduk, of course.

[151] Again, Duncan is the master of sneaking in these little double jokes that are perfectly plausible on their own.

Fantasy Football Update

The Crew's fantasy football league is causing much anguish these days. For example, poor Alejandro Moreno didn't know what hit him in week four. "I had to go against Brett Favre, so that was fun," he said, his voice dripping with sarcasm. (Favre threw six touchdown passes that week.) Meanwhile, Danny O'Rourke suffered what he deemed to be an embarrassing loss to Brian Carroll's previously winless team.

This past weekend featured the much anticipated "Superclassico" between O'Rourke and Hesmer. "The Superclassico is turning into such as we speak," Danny emailed as Monday Night Football kicked off. "Will is leading by 35 points heading into the game tonight, and I have ALL DAY ALL PRO Adrian Peterson and Ryan Longwell, the kicker for the Vikings. If Peterson is truly the player he is tagged to be, then tonight he should perform on this huge platform on MNF and in a must-win game."

Considering it was the last I heard from Danny, I'm guessing that Peterson and Longwell did not do enough to erase Hesmer's 35-point lead.

Jason Garey, who got a big victory over Andy Gruenebaum this week, already called the result in favor of Hesmer before the Monday night game kicked off. "O'Rourke continues his struggles, despite claiming to be Columbus' own fantasy football god, by getting crushed by Mr. Hesmer," he gleefully emailed. "O'Rourke is now 1-4 and has made some of the worst trades in fantasy football history!"

Now that the results are final, I will try to get the league standings and some more comments. If/when that happens, I will publish an update on the Crew's official blog, The Black & Gold Standard.

The New Haircut of the Iro Generation

Generation Iro was sporting a Mohawk during Saturday's game, which prompted the following conversation between me, G.I., and Steven Lenhart.

SS: So what's up with the Mohawk?

GI: It was time for a change-up. I tried it out and we got a big victory, so I have to stick with it.

SS: Are you going to let it grow really high? Or use some hair-straightener to make big spikes?

GI: I'm not going to use any straightener, and it won't grow very high, but I am going to leave it until we lose. We're on a good streak right now.

SS: Has anyone on the team made fun of you for it?

GI: Danny O'Rourke has made fun of me for it, but look at his hair.

SS: Yeah, he likes to do that Fauxhawk thing with the hair gel, but only you have the guts to do a real Mohawk.

GI: Exactly! Danny is an idiot! And then Duncan tries to make fun of me, but all you have to do is look at the way Duncan dresses.

SS: So this wasn't part of a team contest, like that beard contest?

GI: No, I just did it.

(Enter Steven Lenhart.)

SL: But what I don't understand is, where did it come from, dude?

GI: Inspiration.

SL: Inspiration from whom?

GI: The man on high.

SL: What does that even mean? The man on high?

GI: The man on high.

SL: The man on high told you to get a Mohawk? That's ridiculous!

SS: So you don't like the Mohawk?

SL: I am definitely a hater.

SS: So you're not going to grow your own Mohawk and engage Andy in a battle of the Frohawks?

SL: Definitely not. The thing is, I know I can't pull it off. He just hasn't figured it out yet.

Afterward, I mentioned to Danny O that Iro called him an idiot. Danny responded by giving the universal hand signal for buttoning his lip. "I am going to be the bigger man," he said. (This means that Danny will have to metaphorically grow to a height of 198 centimeters.)

Tucker Walther then chimed in with his own suggestion. "I think Andy should dye his Mohawk blonde," he said. "That way he can be black & gold."

Questions? Comments? Hope the Crew never lose again so Andy has to keep his Mohawk and it gets to the point that Andy's Mohawk is so popular that the Crew will have an Andy Iro Mohawk skull cap giveaway for the first 5,000 fans in attendance one night? Feel free to write at sirk65@yahoo.com

Andy Iro's Mohawk against the Galaxy. (Photo by Greg Bartram / Columbus Crew)

Frankie Hejduk: Tailgating Captain

In a move that was even reported overseas, Crew captain Frankie Hejduk decided to serve his one-game suspension in style. Since he couldn't suit up for the Crew's sold-out match with the LA Galaxy, he did the next best thing—he tailgated with the fans. Hejduk made his way out to the Nordecke's massive tailgate party where he sang, danced, shook hands, and shared an "apple juice" or two with the Crew's most fervent supporters. It served as yet another example of the unique bond that had formed between the players and the Nordecke.

Above, Hejduk offers a toast with Hard Hat Mike. Below, Hejduk's surprise tailgate appearance put a smile on every Crew supporter's face. (Photos by Sam Fahmi)

Road Work: Crew 2, Chicago 2

Match date: Sunday, October 12, 2008

Scoring:

13: CHI McBride 3 (Mapp 7)

59: CLB Gaven 3 (unassisted)

61: CLB Schelotto 7 (Rogers 3, O'Rourke 4)

79: CHI McBride 4 (Conde 1, Blanco 9)

Attendance: 14,994

Crew's record afterward: 16-6-6

RETROACTIVE RECAP

The Crew had a chance to capture the Supporters' Shield outright with a victory at Toyota Park. They came tantalizingly close, but were done in by an old friend. The Crew's all-time co-leading goal scorer, Brian McBride, made his first appearance against the team with which he had made his name. From 1996-2003, Brian McBride *was* the Columbus Crew. He was a local celebrity on par with any Buckeye or Blue Jacket. His popularity transcended soccer in Central Ohio.

After 4+ years in the English Premier League, McBride returned to MLS. Citing family reasons, as he and his wife are from the Chicago area, McBride opted to play for the Fire rather than the Crew. Fans in Columbus considered the move treasonous, and McBride further displeased his former followers when his 79th minute equalizer knotted the score and prevented the Crew from clinching the Shield outright. It was his second goal of the game.

Fortunately, Houston's 0-0 draw with D.C. United later that evening meant that the Dynamo could no longer catch the Crew. The Supporters Shield would be coming back to Columbus for the first time since 2004. The bus full of Crew fans that made the trip to Chicago found out that the Shield was theirs during a stop somewhere in Indiana. The celebration was on.

It wouldn't be the last that the Crew heard from McBride & the Fire.

QUOTES

Brian McBride: "Columbus has been a good, consistent team all year. I took today's game like I do every game. I tried to help my teammates win the game."

Guillermo Barros Schelotto: "We came here with the idea of clinching the Supporters' Shield, but getting a tie on the road is not bad, especially since Chicago has always played us hard the last two years since I've been at Columbus."

Road Work: New York 3, Crew 1

Match date: Saturday, October 18, 2008
Scoring:
48: NY Angel 12 (Kandji 2)
62: CLB Lenhart 4 (Schelotto 19)
76: NY Angel 13 (Stammler 4, van den Bergh 4)
83: NY Cepero 1 (unassisted)
Attendance: 18,546
Crew's record afterward: 16-7-6

RETROACTIVE RECAP

With the Supporters' Shield in hand and a road game on the Giants Stadium turf before them, Sigi Schmid opted to roll out a lineup featuring just five regular starters. Since nobody could have imagined that this game was an MLS Cup preview, the game was notable for only three reasons...

First, it was the first and only time all year that the Crew lost a game in which they had scored. They entered the night at 16-0-5 when scoring at least one goal, and would finish the regular season at 17-1-5.

Two, it was the first and only time the Crew would lose all year when Gino Padula was in the lineup. The Crew would finish the regular season at 11-1-2 in such games. (And 14-1-3 including the playoffs.)

Finally, the game will always be remembered as the game in which New York's rookie goalkeeper, Danny Cepero, in his very first MLS appearance, became the first goalkeeper in MLS history to ever score a goal. His 80-yard free kick in the 83rd minute would take a large bounce on the plastic playing surface, soar over Crew backup goalkeeper Andy Gruenebaum, and land in the Crew's net, bewildering one and all.

QUOTES

New York goalkeeper Danny Cepero: "I just put it in the general area with no intention of scoring and kind of hit it somewhere where my teammates could do something with it. I didn't even know it went in until I had to ask Kevin (Goldthwaite) and be like, 'Uh, did that go in?' and he said, 'Yeah.' I go, 'Do I get credit for that?' and he says, 'Absolutely.' It wasn't until right then that I knew. That's crazy to say the least. It's incredible. It's one of those random stats that I guess I can always look up and say, 'Hey, there I am.'"

Sigi Schmid: "I think we eased off a bit this week for sure, but now we want to push for these next five weeks. We need to come out every day and work hard at training."

Sirk's Notebook: Crew 1, D.C. United 0

Match date: Sunday, October 26, 2008
Scoring:
77: CLB Evans 5 (Hejduk 4)
Attendance: 19,591
Crew's record afterward: 17-7-6

So this is how the munchkins felt when Dorothy's house plopped down on the Wicked Witch of the East.

With the Supporters' Shield already in hand and a celebration already planned, the Columbus Crew liberated their fans from a decade of tyranny by defeating D.C. United, 1-0, thereby terminating the playoff hopes of the Crew's longtime nemesis. A 0-0 draw would have knocked United out just the same, but the clamor in the stands made it known that the fans wanted to send their traditional tormentors home as losers. In the 77th minute, Brad Evans obliged with a 30-yard left-footed dagger that kissed the post, hit the net, and mortally pierced the black heart of the Imperial Eagle. From that moment until the final whistle, gleeful chants of "no-more-play-offs!" rained down upon the villainous visitors.

In many ways, it was a game that meant more to the fans than the players. That's not a knock on the guys, but none of them were around when United defeated the Crew in three consecutive conference finals. Those were epic Good versus Evil battles, with the low-key Crew taking on the arrogant and antagonistic army from the Mid-Atlantic. And each year, Evil's triumph was more painful than the year before. Now, a decade later, the shoe was finally on the other foot. And the other foot was finally doing the booting from the MLS Cup party.

"Fans' memories are longer than players' and coaches' memories are," said Crew coach Sigi Schmid, about ending United's season. "For sure, I think the fans were pleased with that. I know our ownership was very happy with it because there is a history with D.C., when Columbus had those very talented teams with McBride, Warzycha, Stern John, and all those people, and D.C. kept knocking them off. Is it payback? No, because it's a different era. But it's certainly something that our guys know about."

And the Crew pulled out all the stops. They even eschewed the usual banana kit in favor of their black alternates, thereby depriving United of their traditionally malevolent black uniforms. It was a subtle gesture appreciated by many. And of course, the Crew were presented with the Supporters' Shield, which had been won by United the two previous seasons. The pregame ceremony, in which the trophy was transferred to members of Crew Union, Hudson Street Hooligans, and La Turbina Amarilla, was another pleasant reminder of where the teams currently stood.

Two hours later, after the sun had set on both Crew Stadium and United's season, the team sponsored by Das Auto got on Das Bus to Das Airport and flew in Das Airplane back to Das Capital where they cleaned out Das Lockers and made Das Tee Times at Das Golf Course. For anyone who worked, played, or cheered for the Crew in the late 1990s, United's solemn postgame trudge-off was a sight to behold. Nearly a decade after repeatedly bearing the brunt of a seltzer bottle to the face, Crewville finally got to laugh at D.C. United as they slipped on a Massive Banana peel.

Schadenfreude is a curious thing in sports. After staking out a good spot in the field to watch the Nordecke officially present the Supporters' Shield to the Crew, I almost abandoned my spot to return to the tunnel. I wanted to observe Crew fans finally getting their chance to meaningfully taunt United's players, especially holdovers like Jaime Moreno and Ben Olsen. I thought it would make good Notebook material.

But then I realized it was stupid. The 2008 Columbus Crew worked too hard and did too well for me to be distracted by D.C.'s demise. It would have been disrespectful to ignore the current team's accomplishments in favor of overhearing a few choice taunts directed at last decade's news. So I stayed put.

As karmic repayment, my friend Mateo later rewarded my decision by sharing this gem he unfurled as the white-clad United players shamefully slunk away…

"We took your colors. We took your Shield. Now get the (bleep) out!"

In the northeast corner of the stadium, a 1,500-strong teeming mass of black & gold awaited the Supporters' Shield winners as they made their way across the pitch for the official presentation. The scene was raucous, deafening, and utterly surreal.

I turned to Crew President & GM Mark McCullers and said that if someone had described this scene to me on March 29, I wouldn't have believed a word of it.

"Me neither," he laughed. (More on that later.)

Soon, my slack-jawed amazement was disrupted by a bear hug from behind. It was Notebook Hall of Famer Dante Washington, who was giddily caught up in the moment. He was so excited, you'd think he was still playing.

Once the team ascended to the stage, the events became a blur. The fans sang Alejandro Moreno's name, bowed for team MVP Guillermo Barros Schelotto, and chanted "We are massive." Frankie Hejduk and Duncan Oughton, heart & soul, kissed the Supporters' Shield and held it high. Pirate Padula, Old Man Ezra, and Danny O took their turns. The fans chanted "Sigi! Sigi! Sigi!" until the Crew's coach made his way up to the stage and received a thunderous ovation. Sigi has never been accused of being the cuddly, emotional type, but he was clearly moved by the occasion. And when the Nordecke chanted "we're not done yet," they were joined in full voice by none other than Crew owner Clark Hunt.

Crew captain Frankie Hejduk raises the Supporters' Shield in front of the Nordecke on October 26, 2008. Looking on to the right, from background to foreground, are Crew owners Clark Hunt and Dan Hunt, as well as Crew President & GM Mark McCullers.
(Photo by Greg Bartram / Columbus Crew)

Not since the birth of the Dawg Pound in the mid-80s have I witnessed such a powerful and organic bond form between the fans and a team. That's not to say that the fans of other teams and other sports don't support their teams, or that players from other teams or other sports don't appreciate their fans, but the relationship between the Nordecke and the 2008

Columbus Crew has taken on a special quality that has brought out the best in both. Neither group quits working for the other.

Once the party moved inside to the locker room, it wasn't as crazy as one might expect. Then again, the silver "V" of the Supporters' Shield isn't exactly as conducive to celebratory drinking as, say, the Stanley Cup.[152] Rather, the team seemed content to ride the buzz from the Nordecke celebration, knowing they had to get back to work the next day.

I will now get out of the way and let Sigi and the players reflect on the emotional presentation in the corner...

Head coach and scarf-wearing reconstruction architect Sigi Schmid:

"It takes a lot to make me emotional, but that was great to see. The Nordecke and the support that we've received all season... You guys that have been around a long time, like Merz, who's been here from the first season... I don't think it's ever been like that, with the emotion and the passion in that corner. And we don't want to ignore the other fans and season-ticket holders that have supported us. One guy came up to me and said he drives up from Kentucky each game, so we don't want to forget those people either. But this was the culmination of a great season.

"It's...it's...really, really believe me...it's...I never try to compare things...it's a little bit like how I felt when I won my first NCAA title with UCLA. I played in three Final Fours and came up short each time, so to win it after rebuilding that program...they weren't even a playoff team when I took them over and then to get them to that stage, that was pretty emotional. Then tonight, when they were chanting and shouting and we were given the Supporters' Shield, and it's like, you know, we've come a long way. We've come a long way, but the real tribute goes to the players. They are the ones who believed and they are the ones who put in the work all the time.

"As a coach, your job is to create an environment where the players can flourish. That's what we've always tried to do. I was talking to (United coach) Tommy Soehn before the game and he said he had six or seven guys out with injuries, and I said, 'I remember my first year here, and we had like nine or 10 guys out with injuries.' It makes you realize how hard it was. So I appreciate the patience of the Hunt organization in allowing us to do this, and

---

[152] Okay, that was an in-joke for certain people. I am not going to name names, but let's just say that with McGyver-like ingenuity involving medical tape, beer cans can be tied to the upper part of the Supporters Shield, making the trophy a suitable drinking apparatus. Only a few people were involved in the pictures I saw, but it was tremendous.

I think we have given the city of Columbus a great reward in how the players have matured and grown together. It's a tribute to them."

One "SS" holds another. Sigi Schmid with the Supporters' Shield in the Crew's locker room on October 26, 2008. (Photo by Greg Bartram / Columbus Crew)

Indefatigable team heartbeat and captain, Frankie Hejduk:

"We play the way our fans are – with passion, energy, emotion and offensiveness. That's how we've been doing it all year, and it's great. Tonight, we were feeling their love and they were feeling our love. The atmosphere that they produce makes us play better. They bring a lot of energy to our locker room before the game, during the game and after the game.

"Nobody could have predicted this. Nobody can predict that type of energy. And it's positive energy, and I think it's been growing bigger and bigger as the season has gone along. Who knows what it could be like five years from now. They've brought a buzz to our locker room and to the fans in the rest of the stadium. They've made a difference in the way we play and the way other teams come into this stadium. It was no secret around the league that this was a visitor-friendly stadium. It's not that way anymore. Other teams know that when they play us, they have to play against 12 men.

"This is the best moment since I've been here. I can't speak for Duncan or Chad, but it's not too hard to figure out for me. The season we've had, the locker room and the fans... It's all been second to none. We still have a job to do, but it's good to carry this momentum into the playoffs. We hope to celebrate with a different cup in a few weeks. We have to take it one game at a time, but it would be a pretty huge celebration if we were to bring the other one back."

Longest-tenured vet and soul of the Crew, Duncan Oughton:

"As long as I've been here, it makes it all the sweeter. The fans deserved this because they have been great all year, and as cliché as it is, they have been our 12th man. Their group has been swelling in size as the year has gone on, but the core of them has been there all year. It was nice to share that with them. It was a special moment and I will always remember it. Winning the Open Cup in 2002 was great, and the 2004 season was very nice... This is definitely up there, but playing alongside Dante Washington many years ago was a very special memory that can never be topped."

(Dante, who was listening in right next to me, then stood on the bench in front of Schelotto's locker and did the Nordecke's "Guillermo" bow at Duncan.)

Duncan Oughton displays his gift HSH jersey on October 26, 2008.
(Photo by Sam Fahmi)

303

Goose egg collecting Goalkeeper of the Year candidate Will "William" Hesmer:

"It was awesome. I have never really been that close to the corner. I don't get to score any goals like the New York keeper, so I never get to run over there to celebrate. I never get to go in there, but to be that close tonight, and to feel that passion, it was inspiring.

"Tonight was great as long as nobody lets complacency set in. But I think it's good if guys are thinking, 'Man, that was cool, and I will do whatever it takes to do that again on a bigger stage in Los Angeles.'"

United-slaying midfielder and mid-season revelation Brad Evans:

"I've never experienced anything like that. UC Irvine doesn't exactly get the biggest crowds. It was great to be a part of it. This is only my second year, so hopefully there is more of that to come in the years to come."

Crew Swiss Army defender and local-meathead-done-good, Danny O'Rourke:

"It was awesome. Getting up on that podium and chanting and jumping up and down with the fans, it was the perfect way to end the regular season and to start the fun of the playoffs. I don't think we're going to need any extra motivation. We're already pumped."

The invaluably invisible Brian "BC" Carroll, who has stealthily anchored the midfield for three consecutive Shield winners:

"It was awesome. Being able to celebrate the Supporters' Shield in the corner with the fans was amazing. The passion, the energy, and the fire that they bring really helps us out. D.C. has some great fans too, but we never had a ceremony like this. The way our fans were able to present us with the trophy this year was really special and it was a great sight to see. It lets you envision, and it whets your appetite to do it again at the MLS Cup final. We were able to attain this goal, and now it's right on to work toward the next one."

As I left the locker room, I flagged down Mark McCullers to follow up on our ultra-brief exchange on the field. I asked him what was going through his mind as he watched the Supporters' Shield presentation at the Nordecke.

"The word that comes to mind is pride," he said. "I am just so proud to be a part of that. I have to say that it was one of the proudest moments of my professional career. Like Sigi said, it's an emotional moment. To see the passion of the fans, it's a feeling you can't describe. It's why we're all in this business. It's what we all work for."

I then asked Mark to expound on our exchange about how neither of us would have believed tonight's postgame scene if someone from the future had told us about it on March 29.

"There's just no way," he said. "I would love to be able to say that it was exactly like we wrote the script, but everybody would know I was not being honest. It just all came together. One of the things we did talk about at the beginning of the year was becoming closer as a club. We wanted to make sure the competition side of the club and the front office side were working with each other and working for each other. I think that manifested itself on the field, but also off the field. That philosophy also took hold with our fans. They worked hard for us, and the team worked hard for them. But while we had that philosophy, I never in my wildest dreams could have imagined a night like tonight." [153]

Given recent news events[154], one of the most heartening sights of the night was the presence of Crew owner Clark Hunt. Not only were he and the Hunt family in attendance, but he was delightedly whooping it up on stage with the team. I mentioned that it seemed to carry added weight since Clark isn't nearly as visible to Crew fans as Lamar was during the Crew's formative years.

"To be fair, Clark's situation is much different than Lamar's," McCullers explained. "Clark is overseeing a number of companies, whereas Lamar had the luxury of being able to focus on his love of soccer. Nobody should think for a second that Clark doesn't love soccer or the Crew as much as Lamar did, even if he can't be as visible as Lamar was able to be. Clark loves it. So does Dan, and so does Norma, Lamar's widow, who also was here tonight. They really care about this club and they wouldn't have missed this for the world. They wanted to be a part of it tonight, and to share in the moment, and I certainly can't blame them. What a night."

---

[153] You know, I give Mark props for being honest. It's very fashionable to play the "nobody believed in us" card, and while I think the Crew felt they would do better than most expected, this was a dream season by any standard. (And looking back a few pages, even Frankie said nobody could have expected this, so props to the captain as well.)

[154] Las Vegas MLS franchise seeker Mark Noorzai's interest in buying a minority share of the Crew.

What a night indeed.

Questions? Comments? Can't wait until the Crew evens the score by ending United's season is 2009 and 2010 as well? Feel free to write at sirk65@yahoo.com

"Hard Hat Mike" became "Hardware Mike" after accepting the Supporters' Shield from the D.C. United supporters' groups on October 26, 2008. (Photo by Sam Fahmi)

Bonus Crew-D.C. Notebook Blog
October 31, 2008

Hey gang,

Sirk here. Greetings from sunny Cleveland. (No, seriously. It's actually sunny here.)

A death in the family[155] left me with little time to devote to this week's Notebook, so I banged one out in pretty short order, focusing on the most important aspects of Sunday night's game. I had a fair amount of leftover quotes that I didn't have a chance to get to, nor could figure out how to shoehorn into what I had written, and it seems a shame to let them go to waste. So I am now sitting in the spare bedroom at my brothers' house, preposterously hunched over the keyboard and monitor that they have set up on a Fisher Price kiddie table. I am not kidding. The best part is that my youngest brother, Chris, HAS a computer desk, but it's sitting empty in the den downstairs. Ohio State gave the kid a degree this spring, but his brain cannot link the concept "computer" with the concept "computer desk." I am now convinced that if it weren't for the popular football team, many of you would have worthless diplomas.

Anyway, I am sending a few random bits to the Crew office so they can put them up on the blog. Nothing earth-shattering, but I figured I'd share. There's no rhyme or reason to this…I am just going to blurt out a few bits and leave it at that.

Pronouncing Schelotto

With as much time as the players spend with one another, you'd think they'd have already had every inane conversation imaginable by this point of the season. Or at least know how to pronounce each other's names. Yet, when I walked into the locker room, I immediately stumbled into a

---

[155] My maternal grandmother, Doris Gray (1930-2008.) She was an artist—drawings, paintings, and woodcarvings. One of my favorite "toys" when visiting my grandparents was a blank sheet of paper and a pencil. She would doodle awesome drawings, and I would…well…I wasn't that good. She secretly kept my inept childhood scribbles anyway, and began showing them to me a year or so before she passed. Funny stuff. I used to lament that I did not inherit her artistic abilities, but I finally realized something on the drive back to Columbus after my deathbed visit with her just before she died. What I realized is that she instilled in me the wonder and possibilities of a blank page. From a young age, I was exposed to the joy of creating. As I grew up, I adapted to my own strengths and weaknesses, and began using words instead of pencils, paintbrushes, or carving tools. Although she left us in October, I will always see her in every blank page.

conversation between locker neighbors Duncan Oughton and Guillermo Barros Schelotto about how exactly to pronounce the latter's name.

The radio was blasting and the locker room was noisy with dozens of simultaneous conversations, so I could only pick out bits and pieces, but I did hear Duncan ask the very popular question, "But then why do some of the announcers on television say 'Es Schelotto'?"

Although I couldn't hear his reply, Guille gave an explanation and even used his locker's nameplate as an illustrative aid. Satisfied that they had ironed everything out, the two Crew legends started making goofy faces and hand signals at one another until they each busted up laughing. I'm not sure what that was all about, but it was amusing.

The Post Giveth and the Post Taketh Away (But Not in That Order)

In the first half, D.C. United fruitlessly hit the left post of the north goal on two occasions. Bryan Namoff was denied in the 13th minute, and Luciano Emilio was rejected in the first minute of stoppage time. Poetically, in the 77th minute, Brad Evans drilled the same post, except his shot caromed into the net to give the Crew the 1-0 victory.

Crew coach Sigi Schmid had a theory on why that particular post was so accommodating for both Evans and Crew goalkeeper William Hesmer. "I think Will took some sandpaper out there and roughed it up so that their shots would bounce away, and then our grounds crew went out at halftime and painted it so it would be nice and smooth when Evans hit it."

I told Hesmer of Sigi's theory. "I like to say you're living right and that somebody is looking after you," he said. "You're living life the right way. That's how I like to look at it at least. Or at least that somebody on our team is living right. I'd like to think it's me, but we'll let that judgment come down hopefully a long time from now."

Crew goalkeeper William Hesmer was all smiles on October 26, 2008, because he, or possibly one of his teammates, was living a good life, thus making the goalpost the Crew's friend during the season-ending 1-0 win over D.C. United. (Photo by Sam Fahmi)

Sizzling Symmetry

The Crew scored the first and last goals of the 2008 MLS regular season. And those goals were both game-winners. And they were both absolute freakin' bombs.

On March 29, Adam Moffat launched his first Moffat Rocket, a low missile that hit the side netting of the south goal. On October 26, Evans lasered a 30-yarder off the goalpost and into the north goal. And if all that weren't symmetrical enough, Evans is the player who replaced Moffat when the Scot went down with a season-ending knee injury. Spooky, huh?

"I didn't think of that," Evans said from his locker. "Adam opened the season with the Goal of the Week, so hopefully we can end it that way." (Actually, Moffat's goal only earned a nomination, but Evans did in fact earn the season's final Goal of the Week award.)

In the tent, I told Moffat it was strange that the season began with a Moffat Rocket – "and then ended with an Evans Rocket," he interrupted. "That's a good observation. I taught him how do that, and he executed it perfectly."

There's no doubting that Evans was delighted with the strike. "It was the goal of a lifetime," he said. "Gino (Padula) scored his goal of a lifetime in training this week and I saved mine for the game."

The Shield—Then and Now

The Crew's two Supporters' Shield titles (2004 and 2008) feel completely different from one another. The 2004 team had more ties than victories and captured the Shield with the lowest point total of any Shield winner in league history. The 2008 team ran away with the honor.

"Obviously, it feels good," said Schmid. "I don't think there's anyone in that locker room that would say it doesn't feel good to come up with 57 points. But the most important thing is that we finished strong. We won 8 of our last 11 games. Not to draw comparisons because I wasn't here in 2004 per se — although I got fired after the Crew tied us in LA, and it was a game we thoroughly dominated – but I don't think that team finished as strongly or as convincingly. Talking to Robert and Lapper, that team sort of backed into some ties. I don't think this team backed into anything. We've found different ways to win, and I think that's what separates this team from them."

Not Done Yet

The Crew had every reason to celebrate on Sunday considering that most people in and around the league didn't give them much chance back in March. But they are not content with just one trophy.

"It feels good when you're lying in bed, and in the back of your head you can think, 'Screw you guys, we knew we were better than what you all thought,'" said Hesmer. "But at the same time, we still have a lot of work to do. Houston's still the top dog. They've won it two years in a row and they are the team to beat. But we can't look to November 23 right now. On Saturday, we have to go into Kansas City, and they are feeling really good about themselves right now, so we have work to do."

When Schmid was asked to name his favorite part of the Shield ceremony, he pinpointed the "we're-not-done-yet" chant. "That was really important," he said. "We're not done yet. Alejandro has a saying that he says to the guys before every game, 'Do what you do.' Just go out there and do what you do. So I thought 'we're not done yet' was very apropos because we still want more. The last time (the Supporters' Shield and MLS Cup) was done in the same year was in 2002, so I'm a little bit familiar with that. (Schmid's Galaxy did the honors.) It's now 2008, so we want to do that. It's the 13th year of MLS and 13 was my mom's lucky number, so maybe there's a good omen going on there." [156]

Danny O's Mad Skills

The Danny O Goal Watch is expected to produce a Danny O'Rourke goal by 2011 or 2012, depending on who you ask. As if to prove that he is taking this project seriously, Danny O has been showing his offensive skills lately. First came the shot somewhat near goal last month. It was way high, but Danny proved he knew where the opponents' goal was located, more or less. Then came the pinpoint cross to assist on the Crew's winning goal against the Galaxy, revealing Danny's inner Schelotto.

On Sunday, another piece of the puzzle fell into place when Danny showed wizardry in the open field. I just about fell down when Danny did The Ol' Inside/Outside on a guy. I don't have the video at my disposal at the moment, but dribbling with a full head of steam in the latter stages of the match, Danny played the ball around a United player one way while sprinting around the player the other way, then met the ball up-field and continued with his dribble. Seriously. Danny O.

"What can I say?" he said with a shrug. "I was feeling good, you know?"

---

[156] Sigi is always looking for omens. Whether it was wearing the bar scarf, visiting Ruby Tuesday two days before every home game, or looking for lucky numbers, Sigi is a superstitious man. But like they say, never (bleep) with a streak.

Fantasy Football

The week eight results weren't in when I chatted with Danny, and I haven't had a chance to follow up with him this week, but after a 1-5 start, Danny's team knocked off Jason Garey's team one week after Garey talked smack about Danny in the Notebook. The victory has resuscitated O'Rourke's season thanks to a generous MLS-circa-1996 playoff system.

"Two and five, still alive!" Danny excitedly proclaimed. "That's what my players were chanting. I actually had a pregame pep talk with my players the day before. I have all the best players but they are not playing up to their standards, but they went out and pounded Garey's team. I scored 163 points, which is the highest ever."

Through seven weeks, Chad Marshall sat atop the Crew's league, but Danny thinks the center back's good scheduling fortune is about to run out. "Chad is in first place, but he might have lost (in week eight) because the team he was playing against this week might have actually scored more than 70 points. His streak of playing (bleep) teams is over."

Thus endeth the leftovers. I will be returning to Columbus this week and will definitely be at the second leg against the Wizards.

First came the in-joke in the D.C. Notebook, then came the footnote about the in-joke, and now (with his permission) comes photographic proof. Team administrator Tucker Walther was one of several folks involved with improvising a way to take a celebratory drink from the thoroughly un-cup-like Supporters' Shield. (Photo by Jason Mathews)

2008 Columbus Crew Team Award Winners

NOTE: I missed the team awards ceremony on Monday, October 27, 2008, as I drove up to Cleveland that night to be with my grandmother. While I could not be at the awards ceremony, I can retroactively preserve the basics of what went down. The award ceremony presentation text that makes up the rest of this section is all courtesy of the Columbus Crew.

Guillermo Barros Schelotto – Crew Most Valuable Player

This year, the Crew MVP honor once again went to Guillermo Barros Schelotto, who collected seven goals and 19 assists in 27 games, finishing first in the league in assists by a wide margin. Schelotto also set a new Crew record for most assists in a season, eclipsing John Wilmar Perez's 15 in 2001, and finished the season tied for second in MLS history for most assists in a single season. Five of his assists led to game-winners and his extraordinary performances were recognized with four MLS Player of the Week selections, MLS Player of the Month honors for August and inclusion on the MLS inactive All-Star roster.

Chad Marshall – Crew Defender of the Year

A big, athletic defender, Chad Marshall has consistently frustrated the efforts of the opposition's attack in 2008 – thanks to his aerial dominance and well-timed tackles – while only earning two yellow card cautions all season. This season has also seen Marshall utilize his size and leaping ability to get on the end of set pieces, as he has registered a career-high four goals (three of which were game-winners) – good for second in the league among defenders – giving the Crew another dangerous offensive weapon.

Alejandro Moreno – Crew Budweiser Golden Boot

The Budweiser Golden Boot Award is presented to the player who, over the course of the regular season, scored the most goals for his team. The Crew's leading scorer for 2008 is forward Alejandro Moreno, who found the back of the net nine times – a career high – while also adding four assists, in 27 games. Moreno has also worked his way back into the Venezuelan National Team picture this season and has scored twice for his country, as well, including the game-winner against Ecuador on Oct. 15 in FIFA World Cup Qualifying action.

Frankie Hejduk – Glidden Man of the Year

The Glidden Man of the Year award is presented annually to the player who embodies an exceptional sense of leadership, civic pride, family values and community service. Frankie Hejduk continued to lead the Crew both on and off the field in 2008. The Crew captain once again put in a stellar campaign on the pitch this season, earning his sixth MLS All-Star selection, while also continuing to be a key call-up for the U.S. Men's National Team. He tirelessly patrols the right side of the Crew defense, while also providing a dangerous element on the offensive end with his timely overlapping runs. Hejduk continues to be a fan favorite and has steadfastly recognized and acknowledged impact and importance of the newly-formed Nordecke supporters' section in Crew Stadium's northeast corner.

Glidden Man of the Year Frankie Hejduk delivers an "apple juice" toast at the Crew's team awards ceremony on October 27, 2008. (Photo by Sam Fahmi)

Brian Carroll & Alejandro Moreno – Crew Coaches Award

Selected by the Crew coaching staff, the Coaches Award is presented to the player or players they considered to be the most coachable and to possess all of the characteristics of a true team player, including attitude and work ethic.

Brian Carroll has proven to be one of the top offseason acquisitions in the league in 2008. One of the best holding midfielders in MLS, Carroll has produced at a consistent level all season while playing in all but eight minutes of the Crew's MLS matches. Carroll contributed a goal and two assists, along with his diligent work rate, two-way play in the midfield and a winning mentality.

Not only was Alejandro Moreno the Crew's goal-scoring leader, notching a career-high nine, his tireless work ethic and willingness to sacrifice his body allowed the Crew to consistently earn scoring opportunities in the opponent's defensive third, while his professionalism is an example to the team.

Gino Padula – Newcomer of the Year

A mature presence at left back, whose calm confidence with the ball has added yet another dimension to the Crew attack, veteran Argentine defender Gino Padula signed with the Crew on March 24 after previous successful stints in Argentina, Spain and England. Padula made his Crew debut in a win at home on April 12 vs. Chivas USA and started two more games, both Crew wins, for the Black & Gold before going down with hamstring and knee injuries that sidelined him for several months. Padula returned to the starting lineup on Aug. 16 and the Crew compiled an impressive 11-1-2 record when he was in the lineup this season.

Robbie Rogers – Crew Sierra Mist Goal of the Year

On ESPN2 Primetime Thursday on Sept. 18, Robbie Rogers broke a 1-1 tie and put the Crew ahead for good with a dazzling effort from distance just seconds after the halftime restart. Rogers took a short scoop pass from Gino Padula near the left sideline and went to work from there. Rogers raced past two defenders, juked a third and, with plenty of space, struck a game-winning 30-yard blast that left goalkeeper Jon Conway with no chance.

Chad Marshall – Crew OhioHealth Comeback Player of the Year

Defender Chad Marshall returned in stunning fashion this season, after a series of concussions forced him to miss 17 games in 2007 and left his career in jeopardy. On the eve of the 2007 season, Marshall suffered a concussion in a preseason match, which caused him to miss significant time on the field, including the first eight games of the 2007 MLS campaign. Marshall returned from his prolonged absence for the Crew's June 3 match at Chicago, helping to spark the club's best run of play in 2007. Over the next 11 games, all of which Marshall started, the Crew compiled a record of 5-3-3 that included a six-game unbeaten streak and five of the club's eight shutouts on the season. Unfortunately for Marshall and the Crew, his return would be short-lived, as he suffered another concussion in mid-August and it was determined that it was best for his long-term health and safety to sit out the remainder of the season. He was placed on season-ending injured reserve on Aug. 31.

The 2008 season has been a different story and a new beginning for Marshall. Refocused and renewed by his forced time away from the game, he returned with vigor to his regular spot on the backline and was the only member of a stingy Crew defense to start in 29 of the club's 30 games this season, while also registering a career-high four goals.

Eddie Gaven – U.S. Soccer Foundation Humanitarian of the Year

Eddie has been a visible community ambassador for the Crew and Major League Soccer this year and throughout his career. The Hamilton, N.J., native is now in his sixth MLS season, having entered the league with the MetroStars in 2003 at the tender age of 16.

Along with his on-field credentials, which include 28 career goals, 25 career assists and multiple caps with the U.S. National Team, Eddie brings an impressive off-the-field passion for community service to the Columbus area. He has participated in the Crew's School Assembly program, speaking to hundreds of elementary-age children about the importance of making healthy choices, staying in school and displaying good character. He has also visited with pediatric hospital patients on numerous occasions, bringing a smile to the faces of youngsters facing serious medical conditions. In addition, Eddie has volunteered to assist with Habitat for Humanity building projects in Columbus for the past two seasons. As an instrumental part of the Crew's clean-up efforts with Keep Columbus Beautiful and the United Way, Eddie and several teammates volunteered to pick up litter in and around Driving Park Recreation Center on Community Care Day.

Eddie not only gives of his time, he has also been a generous supporter of worthy causes in the area. He was the first to donate to the St. Stephen's House Community Food and Toy Drive, an effort to help needy community residents during the holiday season. In addition, Eddie donated one of his U.S. National Team jerseys to the Crew Soccer Foundation's sports memorabilia fundraising auction to assist in funding programming for youth in Central Ohio.

315

Brian Carroll – CSF Crew Chiefs Hardest Working Man of the Year

In his first season in the Black & Gold, Brian Carroll has made a noticeable impact for the Crew, both on and off the field. Carroll's constant work rate in the Crew midfield has helped the Crew's counterattack to become one of the most feared in the league. In addition to his incredible engine, his experience and quiet leadership in the locker room have also been important factors in the Crew's impressive turnaround this season. He's been a stalwart in Coach Sigi Schmid's lineup since arriving in Columbus and played all but eight minutes in every game for the Crew in the 2008 MLS regular season.

Brian Carroll was the co-winner of the Coaches Award and the outright winner of the Hardest Working Man of the Year Award. (Photo by Tucker Walther)

Guillermo Barros Schelotto – Crew Fans' Choice

For the second straight year, team MVP Guillermo Barros Schelotto was also the fans' selection in on-line balloting for the Fans' Choice award.

Crew Union, Hudson Street Hooligans & La Turbina Amarilla of the Nordecke – Jim Nelson Fan of the Year Award

Renamed this year to honor the memory of longtime Crew fan Jim Nelson, who passed away just prior to the 2008 season, the Crew Fan of the Year award has, in years past, been presented to one particularly dedicated supporter. This season, however, the award belongs to not just one devoted person, but to hundreds of devoted people, the Crew's most rabid supporters – Crew Union, Hudson Street Hooligans and La Turbina Amarilla of Crew Stadium's Nordecke. Following the construction of the permanent stage in Crew Stadium's north end, the Crew's three primary supporter groups banded together in the northeast corner. The energy and excitement that has emanated from the new location has become one of the stories of this season – both locally and league-wide. Their drumbeats, chants and unbridled enthusiasm have become a hallmark of Crew Stadium in 2008, and Crew players and coaches have repeatedly cited the Nordecke as a significant reason for the team's unmatched success at home this season.

Representatives from all three supporters' groups in the Nordecke accepted the Jim Nelson Fan of the Year Award. (Photo by Sam Fahmi)

SECTION III

*

THE PLAYOFFS

*

Road Work: Crew 1, Kansas City 1

Match date: Saturday, November 1, 2008
Match note: First leg of Eastern Conference semifinal
Scoring:
53: KC Arnaud 1 (Lopez 1)
92+: CLB Lenhart 1 (Moreno 1)
Attendance: 10,385
Crew's playoff status: Series tied 1-1 on aggregate

RETROACTIVE RECAP

The Crew's first playoff appearance since 2004 seemed to take the same kind of disastrous tone that undid that year's Supporters' Shield-winning team. Despite having the better of the play, the Crew coughed up the lead in 53rd minute when a Brad Evans turnover resulted in a Kansas City counterattack. It culminated in a Davy Arnaud header off a Claudio Lopez cross to put the Wizards up 1-0.

Undaunted as always, the Massive Bananas pressed on. In the 75th minute, Kansas City's Hercules Gomez was ejected for a tackle from behind on Gino Padula.

Just when it appeared the Wizards would survive the Crew's onslaught, super sub Steven Lenhart once again came to the rescue. Danny O'Rourke's long-range shot caromed off of KC defender Tyson Wahl to the chest of Alejandro Moreno. The Venezuelan chested the ball into the path of Lenhart, whose one-time volley looped inside the left post to level the score in the second minute of stoppage time. The Crew were headed home on level terms.

QUOTES

Sigi Schmid: "At that point we were playing a man up and we wanted to bring in another forward, and Steve's a big guy. We figured he could get in the box and get on the end of some crosses. The team sometimes calls him 'magnet' because the ball just seems to find him."

Frankie Hejduk: "It was a typical playoff game. Both teams were battling back and forth. I thought we did what we needed to do in the first half; I thought we dominated and we had a couple of chances. In the second half, they came out with a lot of energy and brought the game to us. Obviously, the red card killed them. That made it a whole different game. We had a never say die attitude, but that's not a shock. We've been doing it all year and w e knew we were going to come back."

321

Sirk's Notebook: Crew 2, Kansas City 0

Match date: Saturday, November 8, 2008

Match note: Second leg of Eastern Conference semifinal

Scoring:

7: CLB Evans 1 (Carroll 1)

58: CLB Rogers 1 (Moreno 2, Schelotto 1)

Attendance: 11,153

Crew's playoff status: Winner of conference semifinal, 3-1 on aggregate.

Shortly after the Crew booted the Kansas City Wizards from the 2008 playoffs, the Crew's longest-tenured vet, Duncan Oughton, couldn't help but smile.

"It's nice to throw the Curse of '04 off of our shoulders," he said. Oughton was too polite to use the more popular, player-specific name[157] for the bad mojo that had been hanging over his beloved club ever since that fateful Halloween night in 2004, but the Crew's 2-0 victory on Saturday shed yet another piece of excess baggage. The 2008 Supporters' Shield winners had overcome the taint of the 2004 Supporters' Shield winners' first-round flameout.

"It's good to get rid of that," he went on, "but we still have a lot of work to do."

Next up in the therapeutic baggage-toss spree is a primetime Thursday date with Brian McBride and the Chicago Fire in the Eastern Conference Final. But first, a look back at random notes from Saturday…

A Fine How-Do-You-Do

After Steven Lenhart's stoppage-time equalizer in K.C. allowed Columbus to bring the series home on the level, the Crew wasted no time in jumping on the Wizards in the crazed confines of Crew Stadium. In just the seventh minute, Brian Carroll floated a ball over the Wizards' defense, into the path of the streaking Brad Evans. The bouncing ball left charging K.C. goalkeeper Kevin Hartman in no-man's land near the edge of the penalty area. From 19 yards out, Evans looped the ball over Hartman and watched it bounce into the empty net.[158]

---

[157] The Curse of Tony Sanneh.

[158] That was the third time in 2008 that the Crew scored on Hartman while he was stranded in no man's land. Rogers' goal on May 3 and Moreno's goal on June 14 followed similar scripts.

"I saw Brad running in the middle so I tried to get the ball to him," said Carroll. "It worked out. It was a great finish."

"It happened so fast that I didn't even see how BC got the ball," said Evans. "I just called for it, and Brian put a nice ball over Jimmy Conrad, and kind of got him turned around a little bit and as soon as the ball hit the ground, I saw Hartman in the corner of my eye and my only option was to put it up high, and luckily it took a good bounce. At first I thought it was going wide to be honest, but it took a fortunate bounce, bounced really high and into the back of the net, so I was relieved at that point, for sure. BC's ball took a big bounce, so chipping it like I did was automatic. It was the only option going through my mind at the time."

The Limits of Limiting the Seemingly Limitless

Kansas City coach Curt Onalfo was very gracious in defeat. He spoke very highly of the Crew and the challenges that Columbus posed to his club.

"We knew it was going to be tough playing against the team that had been the best in Major League Soccer all year," Onalfo said. "It's an interesting thing when you prepare your team to face this Crew team. You spend an awful lot of time telling your players what they need to limit. And that's the sign of a good team. The Crew are good on attacking restarts, they are very, very good on the counter, Alejandro Moreno does an outstanding job up top in terms of work ethic and holding the ball, Schelotto finds great little seams and makes excellent decisions, and Robbie Rogers is an exciting young player. So that's just to name a few things. They have a lot of strengths. They are a very, very good team. We knew going in that we would have to play pretty much a perfect game."

Listening to Onalfo, one couldn't help but marvel at the thought that "we need to limit the lethal Carroll-to-Evans goalscoring connection" was nowhere on the coach's very long list of things to limit. Naturally, the two holding mids jumpstarted the Crew's victory.

"It's been one of our staples all season," said Crew defender Danny O'Rourke. "Whether it's the 11 guys who start on the field or the guys who come off the bench, we know that whoever's in there, somebody is going to step up big. And tonight, right off the bat, we get a great ball from BC and a great run by Brad and we we're up 1-0. We know that somebody is going to step up and you can't focus on everybody."

Redemption-ish

There was certainly an uplifting quality to Evans' goal, since his turnover in the first leg led to Kansas City's goal that put the Crew in a 1-0 hole in the two-game aggregate goals series. A week later, his goal gave the Crew a 2-1 aggregate lead.

"It was good for some redemption," he said, before immediately quibbling with his own choice of words. "Not really redemption, but it was good to give something back to us. I kind of gave it up last week, so it was good for our confidence to get an early lead."

Abe Thompson's Tap-In

What Tony Sanneh's 2004 penalty kick dribbler is to Crew fans, Abe Thompson's 15th minute tap-in travesty may become to Wizards fans.[159] After Davy Arnaud got behind the Crew midfield, he played a ball wide right to Kevin Souter. Souter sent a low ball into the Crew's penalty area, where an unmarked Thompson had the opportunity to tap the ball into the net from three yards away. Instead, he flubbed the tap-in, which initially went backwards before spinning right back in front of him. He blasted his second attempt right at Crew goalkeeper William Hesmer, who amazingly recovered to smother the play.

"I'm out there and I'm flying across the goal," Hesmer recalled. "I'm about to dive down to my right because I think that's where he's about to hit it. Then I see him hold up. Maybe he thinks that I am going to have it covered, so then he tries to go across my body. When he did that, I think it hit off his ankle and just kind of spun there. Luckily, I didn't go down yet, so I was able to hold my ground. He still got to it first and hit it well, but it went right to my hands. We dodged a bullet on that one, for sure. When something like that happens, you certainly hope it's going to be your day. You say, 'We got out of that one, now let's sharpen it up.'"

It was a legendary miss at a crucial moment. A goal would have knotted the series again. Instead, the flub left the Wiz deflated. If there had been a drain installed in the goal area,[160] the Kansas City season would have circled right down it. Except for one wide, long-range shot by Jimmy Conrad, Kansas City would never seriously threaten Hesmer again.

---

[159] Seriously, how many times did I mention Tony Sanneh in 2008? In retrospect, even I didn't realize the full extent of how that 2004 game had seeped into my tortured Cleveland fan soul.

[160] This was an inside joke for sideline reporter Katie Witham, who, in one of her blondest moments ever, mistook the penalty spot for a drain during our pregame walk of the field. She pawed at it with her foot for a sec, then I laughed at her. She's a good sport about such things.

The Dagger

The goal that put the game/series away was a beauty. It started with an ever-dangerous throw-in at midfield, which I'd wager was another item pretty low on Onalfo's "things to limit" list. Hejduk threw the ball in to Eddie Gaven, who knocked it back to Hejduk. Frankie then played the ball up the line to a triple-teamed Guillermo Barros Schelotto.

What happened next was magic. Pinned against the sideline in a sea of blue, Schelotto, with a surgeon's precision, passed the ball right through the legs of K.C. defender Michael Harrington. Schelotto's perfectly-weighted nutmeg pass beat three defenders and found Alejandro Moreno in stride on the right side of the penalty box. Moreno rolled a low cross through the box, and it found Robbie Rogers, who pounded the ball inside the near post with his left boot.

"I don't think Guillermo got into the flow of the game much," said Crew coach Sigi Schmid, "but at the end of the day, a player like him makes the incisive pass that sets up the second goal, and that's why he's out there."

The goal was instructive in that Rogers spent most of the game being hounded by 2-3 defenders, and while he drew a lot of attention, he struggled to break through it on the dribble. Schelotto showed how a crafty veteran can pass his way out of those situations. At the same time, the goal was somewhat ironic in the sense that Rogers had drawn a crowd of blue shirts all night, yet on this particular play, he was left wide open and made the Wizards pay the price for their negligence.

"I think I was just following the play," Rogers said. "I knew that if Ale was out wide, someone else would have to fill the middle. (Brad Evans) was near post and the ball came to me at the far post. I was just thinking, 'I better put this on target or they are going to kill me.' I struck it pretty well and it went in."

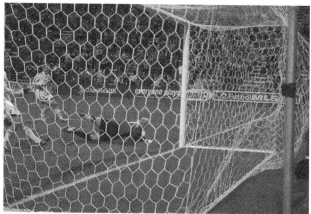

Robbie Rogers' shot hits the back of the net. (Photo by Sam Fahmi)

Once the ball hit the net, Rogers hopped on over to the Nordecke to celebrate. They were happy to see him.

Oh No, It's Arnaud

The Crew were very wary of K.C. midfielder Davy Arnaud. He led the counterattack that produced the Wizards' goal in the first leg, and he also sprung the counterattack that produced Abe Thompson's near tap-in at the beginning of the second leg. The man tasked with tracking Arnaud was (who else?) Brian Carroll.

"I thought Brian played very well," said Schmid. "Early in the first half, Davy Arnaud got behind our midfield a couple of times in the first 10-15 minutes. That was something I pulled Evans over about, and then had him relay the message to BC, and after that, I don't think Arnaud got behind us the rest of the night."

"He's a tricky player," Carroll said of Arnaud. "He makes a lot of good, deep runs out of the midfield and keeps the ball well for them. He had a few runs early, and Will made a good save on the one chance (by Thompson), and then we were able to keep him at bay after that. I'm glad we were able to limit his touches and limit his chances."

Between the assist on the first goal and the hounding of Arnaud, Schmid was pleased with Carroll's play. "He played an excellent game, but then again, that's what I have come to expect out of him."

Postseason Imitates Regular Season

It seemed to me that this series was the Crew's season in a nutshell. They fell behind on the road in the first leg, yet somehow mustered the goal they needed to come back and earn the draw. Then at home, they jumped on their opponent and kept a clean sheet. It all seemed very familiar.

"I think the way the season has gone gave us the confidence to come back in the first game, and then we carried that momentum into this game," said Carroll. "So yeah, I'd say that is an accurate statement."

"It's just us doing what we've been doing all year," said captain Frankie Hejduk. "We're confident in our play and we're confident in ourselves. That confidence has bred a winning attitude, and a winning attitude has bred winning."

Sight & Sound of the Night

Sight of the Night was seeing Clark and Dan Hunt in the house for the second straight game. They were on the sidelines late in the game and in the locker room afterward.

Sound of the Night belongs to a familiar chant that started in the Nordecke, but quickly spread across the stage and over to the west side of the stadium. It happened late in the game, and it was an anticipatory chant for Thursday's match-up with the Chicago Fire. I'm not sure if I can print it here, but the chant was the traditional one that demands that people extinguish the fire in an all-natural, strictly biological fashion.[161] It was fun to see the whole stadium so alive and getting pumped up for the conference final.

Baffled by the Bubbly

As reporters stood around waiting for more players to interview, Shawn Mitchell of the Columbus Dispatch nodded toward a tub and asked me what was with the champagne. With my keen powers of observation suddenly activated by Shawn's query, I looked down and realized that I was in fact standing mere inches away from a tub filled with iced champagne bottles. "I dunno," I replied.

Given that I didn't even notice the champagne in the first place, it goes without saying that this wasn't the put-on-the-goggles-and-cover-the-lockers-with-sheets-of-plastic type of bubbly bath commonly seen when hauling in hardware. The champagne tub was pretty much full, although the lid did look like it caught a brief spray. Team manager Tucker Walther carried a bottle around like a wino in need of a paper bag, but the players were very low-key. One easily got the sense that they know they're not done yet.

Still, some appreciated the gesture and what it represented. "I think those champagne bottles have been on ice for six years, so it's good to get them out," said Danny O'Rourke, referencing either the Crew's last payoff victory or the time since the Crew's 2002 U.S. Open Cup triumph, when there was indeed a champagne shower in the locker room. "We're excited, but we know we haven't won anything yet."

One front office person commented that the champagne was intended to celebrate both the Supporters' Shield (which had been clinched while the Crew was at Midway Airport preparing to return from Chicago) and the Crew's first playoff advancement in a half-dozen years.

---

[161] "Piss on the Fire!"

It was then that the light bulb went on in my head. The champagne may have seemed out of place, but we as a nation just spent a month watching one champagne celebration after another in our National Pastime. In baseball, teams do the all-out champagne celebration when clinching a playoff spot and then again after each and every victorious playoff series. By the time the Philadelphia Phillies won the 2008 World Series, they had participated in *four* cork-popping, clothes-soaking, ultra-expensive drench-fests.

So in the end, maybe the champagne wasn't so strange after all. Either way, in celebrating a first-round playoff victory, the Crew's locker room barely qualified as a quaint cocktail party when compared to the Dom-spouting delirium of any baseball clubhouse at the same stage of the postseason journey.

Field of Dreams

Most grounds crews would struggle to have a grass playing surface in pristine condition in preparation for a rainy November weekend, but Brett Tanner and his crew had to get Crew Stadium looking pristine after five (5) (FIVE!) high school championship soccer matches in the span of 27.5 hours. The games started Friday at noon and ended Saturday at 3:30, a mere four hours before the Crew and Wizards kicked off. ONN sideline reporter Katie Witham and I walked the field before the game, and we could not believe what excellent shape it was in.

When we spoke with V.P. of Operations Scott DeBolt, Katie asked what the grounds crew did to make the field as incredible as it was. "Prayed," he deadpanned.

DeBolt went on to reveal that after the conclusion of Friday's matches, the grounds crew rolled the field with their steamroller-like flattening device. That helped squish out any of the divots and cleat marks from Friday's games. After Saturday morning's game, the grounds crew mowed the field, and at the conclusion of the afternoon game, they repainted all of the lines. "And then they prayed some more," he added.

Well, their prayers were certainly answered. Against all odds, the field was magnificent. Sometimes it's easy to take Crew Stadium's immaculate pitch for granted, but Tanner and his crew deserve extra credit for Saturday's surface. What an amazing job they did. The only person who could possibly be displeased would be Abe Thompson, who lost the "bad bounce" excuse for his goalmouth flub.

The Wayback Machine

In his "Flick Ons" blog, my good buddy Flick noted that there had been a mere 2,233 days between Crew playoff victories. With his kind permission, I am reprinting a few tidbits that he dug up while looking through the wayback machine.

The last time the Crew won a playoff game...

...the price of gas was $1.31 per gallon.

..."Dilemma" by Nelly, featuring Kelly Rowland, was the country's #1 song according to Billboard.

...Robbie Rogers, who scored the Crew's second goal Saturday night, couldn't legally get into an R-rated movie by himself. That's OK, though, since he also wasn't old enough to drive himself to the theater. He was 15.

...Barack Obama was a state legislator in Illinois. I think he's been in the news lately, but I can't remember why.

...the national debt was about $6.2 trillion. Now it stands at around $10.4 trillion.

...Wikipedia was about one year old, and hadn't quite realized its place as the message board and high school kid go-to source for information.*

...the Cincinnati Bengals finished 2-14. Hey, wait a minute.

...a German-born gentleman named Sigi Schmid was busy coaching the Supporters' Shield winners to an MLS Cup victory. Hmm...

[* Notebook footnote: Since Flick mentioned Wikipedia as a go-to source for message board posters and high school kids, I figure it's worth mentioning that the highly-amusing Dan Loney, whose blog resides at BigSoccer.com, once decreed Wikipedia to be one of "The Four Pillars of Internet Scholarship", along with Google, Babelfish, and IMDB. Just thought I'd share in case any budding scholars are missing a pillar or two in their bookmarks.]

Mr. Numbers Nerd: Playoff Oddities Edition

Here's an oddity I found last offseason, but couldn't find an immediate use for. As luck would have it, this weekend provided the perfect window of opportunity to use this tidbit in a relevant manner.

When Michael Kraus entered Saturday's game for the Wizards, he became part of a very unique fraternity. By making his professional debut in a playoff game, he has joined, at least temporarily, the short list of MLS players who have played more career postseason minutes than career regular season minutes.

The list...

* +21 minutes: Khari Stephenson (K.C. 2004-05)
[190 RS minutes, 211 PS minutes]

* +31 minutes: Michael Kraus (K.C. 2008)
[0 RS minutes, 31 PS minutes]

* +32 minutes: Hamisi Amani-Dove (DAL 2001-02)
[101 RS minutes, 133 PS minutes]

* +300 minutes: Ian Woan (CLB/MIA 2001)
[107 RS minutes, 407 PS minutes]

Two more notes of interest:

First, like Kraus, Hamisi Amani-Dove made his MLS debut in the playoffs. All of his career playoff minutes were earned in 2001, whereas all of his career regular-season minutes were earned in 2002.

Second, amazingly enough, this group is going to grow again this coming weekend. New York Red Bulls goalkeeper Danny Cepero has 180 career regular season minutes and 180 career playoff minutes. Saturday's Western Conference final will put Cepero over the top and give him more career playoff minutes than regular season minutes.

Of course, both Kraus and Cepero will have the opportunity to remove themselves from this bizarre list during the 2009 regular season. Stephenson, Amani-Dove, and Woan are oddities etched in stone.

Celebrity Lookalike?

Before the game, I was chatting with Crew PR Director Dave Stephany when Duncan Oughton walked over to us. Duncs sported a mustache/soul-patch combination that had Dave convinced that Duncan looked like Matthew McConaughey in some movie. Dave couldn't pinpoint the film, and Duncan and I were stumped.

"Are you sure it's from a movie?" Duncan finally asked. "Or are you just thinking of something from real life where he's, like, smoked up and sitting on the beach naked while playing the bongos?"

That must have been it, because Dave never thought of the movie, though he later concluded it was probably some random Letterman appearance that he was thinking of.

And for the record, at the time of this conversation, Duncan was lucid, clothed, and non-percussive.

Fantasy Football Update

In addition to the Supporters' Shield and the Visa MLS Defender of the Year trophy, Chad Marshall is looking to add an MLS Cup and a Columbus Crew Fantasy Football League title to his 2008 haul. Entering this past weekend, Marshall led the league with an 8-1 record.

His opponent this past weekend was Danny O'Rourke. "I am hoping to do some giant-killing this week," O'Rourke said. "I don't even want to talk about last week."

O'Rourke then proceeded to talk at length about his previous week's loss to Alejandro Moreno, which came down to the penultimate offensive play by the Washington Redskins in their blowout loss to Pittsburgh. A meaningless completion to Moreno's Chris Cooley at the end of the game allowed the Venezuelan to best O'Rourke by a half-point. "I don't want to talk about it," he once again muttered after talking about it.

The loss dropped Danny O's team to 3-6, which caused O'Rourke to update his team's motto. It is now "Three and six, still in the mix!"

I asked what a loss to Marshall would do to his team's motto. "I think I would go from 'Three and five, still alive' to 'Three and six, still in the mix' to 'Three and seven, I'm-going-to-trade-all-my-players.'"

Sigi the Salesman

Sigi made his case for a sellout for Thursday's Eastern Conference final. His plea has already been relayed in a few print and online articles, but all of them left out Sigi's silly postscript.

"I'd like to see us fill this place on Thursday night," he said. "I'd really like to see it packed. As far as I know, there are not a lot of pro sports in Columbus. I know Ohio State is probably close to pro football, but I don't think there are a lot of other pro sports here. It has been a long time since there has been a professional team on the verge of winning a title. There's no reason why we can't pack this place with all the people in Columbus who say they watch soccer."

After letting his words sink in for a moment, he chuckled and added, "That's my marketing pitch, so if we sell out, I expect a bonus from (Crew President/GM Mark) McCullers."

Salesman Sigi fires up the ticket-buying public on November 8, 2008.
(Photo by Greg Bartram / Columbus Crew)

So to help the 2008 MLS Coach of the Year hit his ad hoc sales targets, do your part and drag as many people to the game as you can. Talk it up to anyone who will listen. If you get home from work on Thursday and see that your neighbor has keeled over dead on his driveway, bring him along "Weekend at Bernie's" style. (Besides, it's Novemeber. Everyone in attendance will be cold to the touch anyway.)

Thursday night will be the most monumental home game in Crew history. It is the club's fifth conference final(s) appearance, but they did not have home field advantage against D.C. United in 1997, 1998, and 1999, nor did they have home field advantage against New England in 2002. This is the very first time that the Crew can clinch an MLS Cup berth at home.

In addition to that, the game has many obvious subplots…

* Can Columbus finally knock off Chicago in a knock-out game? The teams have never met in the playoffs, but the Fire have won all three U.S. Open Cup matchups.

* Can Mexican National Team legend Cuauhtemoc Blanco get over the psychological hurdle of playing a high stakes cold-weather game in Crew Stadium? Or will he be haunted by chants of "dos a cero"?

* Will University of Dayton alum and Kettering native Chris Rolfe finally give his "I score pretty much whenever I set foot in Crew Stadium" routine a rest? And will the Crew's defense give him any choice in the matter?

* While both parties will say that Jon Busch's acrimonious departure from Schmid's Crew team is no longer an issue, one of these proud, talented and competitive men, whether they want it or not, will be accorded with some measure of vindication when the final whistle blows. Which man will it be?

* And then there is the elephant in the room: Brian McBride. With a trip to the MLS Cup final on the line, the most accomplished player in Crew history will be wearing the wrong shirt while lining up against the most accomplished team in Crew history. How (messed) up is that?

The Massive Bananas have spent seven-and-a-half months methodically stripping away the black & gold baggage of yesteryear. Over the course of 32 games, they have proven to be different from every Crew team of the past. On Thursday, as if it were scripted, they will come face to face with that past at both ends of the field.

For the citizens of Crew Nation, there is only one word to describe the tangible and intangible stakes:

<u>Massive.</u>

Questions? Comments? Completely incapable of concentrating on anything between now and Thursday? Feel free to write at sirk65@yahoo.com

Guillermo = John Rambo. Yes, John, we **DO** get to win this time! (Photo by Sam Fahmi)

Sirk's ECF Notebook: Crew 2, Chicago 1

Match date: Thursday, November 13, 2008
Match note: Eastern Conference Final
Scoring:
29: CHI McBride 1 (Mapp 2)
49: CLB Marshall 1 (Schelotto 2)
55: CLB Gaven 1 (Moreno 3, Schelotto 3)
Attendance: 14,688
Crew's playoff status: 2008 Eastern Conference champions

Prior to Thursday's 2-1 victory in the Eastern Conference Final, the last time the Columbus Crew had defeated the Chicago Fire in Crew Stadium was over the 4th of July weekend in 2004. Funny, that. Because in Crew Nation, November 13 is now Independence Day, for that is the day that Columbus Crew emancipated themselves from the suffocating tyranny of failures past. In three consecutive home games, the Massive Bananas exorcised the D.C. demons, reversed the Curse of Tony Sanneh, and eradicated Chi-town's Promethean pestilence while breaking through the previously impenetrable Conference Final barrier. And as the mantra goes, they're not done yet.

As usual, here's a collection of notes, quotes and hazy recollections from the game...

The Cleveland Moment

Being from Cleveland, and also growing up a Toronto Maple Leafs fan, conference finals have not been kind to me. Counting the Crew and teams that are bigger than or approximately as big as the Crew (meaning the original, inexplicably huge MISL Cleveland Force is included, but not the less popular Crunch or Force II), my teams had been a combined 4-20 at this exact stage of the postseason. That's a .167 winning percentage. As we all know, the Crew contributed four of those losses. The 1988 Force[162], 1995 & 1997 Indians, and 2007 Cavaliers had been the only teams to advance.

So being from Cleveland, it's in my DNA to be on the lookout for the Cleveland Moment. And the day that the Chicago Fire signed Brian McBride, I just knew that the Crew's season would come down to a showdown with the former face of the franchise. What could be more in line

---

[162] Featuring a rookie named Brian Bliss. Yes, the same Brian Bliss that is the Crew's technical director. Brian LOVES it when people say they remember him playing for the Force when they were kids. Try it sometime, even if you have to lie.

with my personal sporting history than having Brian McBride come to Columbus and score against the Crew in a conference final?

Three months later, it came to be. Here was Brian McBride, Crew legend, being booed with every touch, getting repeatedly serenaded with the word "traitor," and looking at his illustrated visage adorning a large sign that read, "Wanted: McBride. Treason."

Crew legend Brian McBride did not receive a warm welcome from the Nordecke when he showed up for the Eastern Conference Final wearing the baboon-butt colors of the rival Chicago Fire. (Photo by Greg Bartram / Columbus Crew)

And there was Brian McBride, leaping for a Justin Mapp cross, towering over a helplessly outsized Danny O'Rourke, bonking the ball with his head, and floating it over the desperate swat of Crew goalkeeper William Hesmer.

The Drive. The Fumble. The McHead. Our downtrodden destiny had been delivered. It was every bit the gut-punch I imagined it would be. My mind was already writing "So this is what it's going to feel like when LeBron stomps the Cavs in three years" material.

But then, in the midst of all that internal wallowing, I remembered one vitally important fact: The Massive Bananas don't care about any of that. They just do what they do.[163]

---

[163] I can't explain it, but the Massive Bananas completely took me out of character. Re-reading all of this material a year later, it blows my mind how continually optimistic this team made me feel, and how often I dared to put it into writing. It is completely against my sports fan nature, but this team kept me believing.

Brian McBride celebrates what could have been the "Cleveland Moment" that I had grown accustomed to over the course of my 34 years. (Photo by Sam Fahmi)

Halftime

Given that the Crew came out firing on all cylinders in the second half, one might assume that coach Sigi Schmid lit into his team for their lackluster opening 30 minutes, but that was not the case. The Crew took the upper hand late in the half, so it was pretty much business as usual, with only a few minor adjustments.

"I think this game was the first time they were maybe a little bit anxious, so I tried to be calmer than normal," said Schmid. "In fact, we were done with our halftime talk with like four minutes left. I didn't want to burden them a bunch of stuff because sometimes you talk too much at halftime. And then if you start going, 'Oh, and one more thing and one more thing and one more thing', they start to think, 'He's all concerned.' So we kept it short and kept it in check that way."

So what did he tell his team? "We talked about trying to get in behind their defense," he explained. "We felt we were getting close on set pieces, so maybe we could get something there, but we really wanted Rogers and Gaven to push forward a little bit higher so that instead of playing balls to their feet and having them run at them, we could get them in behind the defenders."

Captain Frankie Hejduk said the locker room was serene at the half. "We just kept our heads up," he said. "We came in at halftime and just knew. There's an aura about this team that we know we are going to come back.

There's a lot of positive energy in this room. Sigi knew it. We knew it. It was going to come. We just needed to put away or chances. We knew it was going to happen."[164]

It Happened, Part One: Marshall Over Bake

So, just like Sigi drew it up, the Crew earned a restart in the 48th minute by springing Eddie Gaven behind the Chicago defense. Frankie Hejduk took a quick restart deep in the Columbus end. He played the ball to Brad Evans, who quickly played a ball up the right side to Alejandro Moreno, who then flicked the ball into the right channel for a sprinting Gaven. Fire defender Gonzalo Segares earned a yellow card for sending Gaven to the turf.

Crew MVP Guillermo Barros Schelotto hovered over the ball, 18 yards out and off to the right side of the penalty area. The Nordecke, and much of the rest of the stadium, as well, bowed in his direction while chanting "Guilleeeerrrrmo! Guilleeeerrrrmo! Guilleeeerrrrmo!" With Chicago's hulking defense, there was only one viable target—Chad Marshall. It's a target that Schelotto rarely misses.

As the clocked ticked into the 49th minute, Schelotto raised his hand and approached the ball. He struck it true, swerving a service to the edge of the six yard box. At the other end of the play, Chad Marshall and Brian McBride, the two most proficient aerial players in Crew history, began their dance. Marshall zigged, McBride zigged. Marshall zagged, McBride zagged. Marshall leaped...but McBride couldn't leap fast enough or high enough. The MLS Defender of the Year towered over the former Crew legend, powering his header off the bottom of the crossbar and into the net.

The crowd erupted. Chad Marshall erupted. Teammates tried to corral him with a congratulatory hug, but it was to no avail. They bounced off of him like 1950s linebackers trying to tackle Jim Brown. As he watched the replay in the radio booth, Crew Technical Director Brian Bliss's jaw nearly hit the floor when he saw how far Marshall skied over McBride. "It's like he dunked on him," Bliss marveled.[165]

---

[164] This attitude seemed to create a self-fulfilling prophecy over and over again. Not only did the Crew "know" they would come back, but I think opponents came to "know" they were in trouble. The only thing I have ever seen like it was during the 1995 Indians season. In a strike-shortened season, the Indians racked up an astonishing 48 come-from-behind victories and won a mind-boggling 27 games in their last at-bat. After a while, the comebacks became a fait accompli. I think the same became true of the 2008 Crew and their opponents.

[165] This is one of my favorite lines ever. Bliss was not talking smack...he was as incredulous as anyone else. It was a magical play. While Marshall's goal did not win the game, and while Marshall would go on to score the game-winner in MLS Cup, THIS is the goal that will go down in Crew legend.

"It was a great ball and I timed it right," said Marshall. "Thank God it hit the bottom of the post and went in. I probably would have cried and walked off the field if it had hit the post and come out. That was huge for us."

Not just huge. Massive. It was an iconic goal, dripping with drama and symbolism. After that magical moment, the only people in the stadium who felt that Chicago was going to recover to win that game were probably wearing red…and lying to themselves.

As play resumed, I thought about Dispatch reporter Shawn Mitchell, who had spent the previous Thursday night up in Cleveland, covering the Browns-Broncos game. Faced with a tight deadline and a back-and-forth shootout, Shawn told me he spent the night simultaneously working on two stories—one with Cleveland winning, the other with Denver winning. Anytime anything happened, he worked the new facts into each story. I laughed and told him that he could have saved himself a lot of bother by just working on the story where the Browns blow it at the end.

So from the other side of the stadium, I wondered if Shawn was working on two stories again. I was hoping he saved himself a lot of bother by focusing on the one where Columbus prevails. Then again, he'd watched this team all year. He surely knew. No need to send him a text.

Book Bonus Section: Photo Sequence of Marshall's Goal

This section wasn't part of the original Notebook, but Marshall's goal was so epic it deserves photographic treatment. Greg Bartram had an incredible photo of Marshall and McBride as the ball had just come off Marshall's head. I don't have the rights to that photo, though, as it had been sent to Getty Images. Likewise, Jay LaPrete of the Associated Press had an excellent photo from the other end of the field in which you could see how far over McBride that Marshall had skied. Of course, that photo's not mine either.

Thankfully, Sam Fahmi has a sequence of photos from that legendary goal. They are from behind the goal, looking through the net. I am publishing all four pictures, and if you look closely, you can see the ball on its way in the first photo, almost at the bar in the second, half-way through the goal in the third, and bulging the back of the net (to the right of the pole) in the fourth.

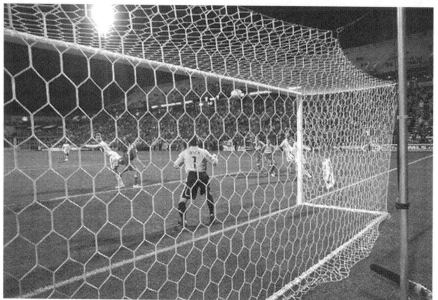

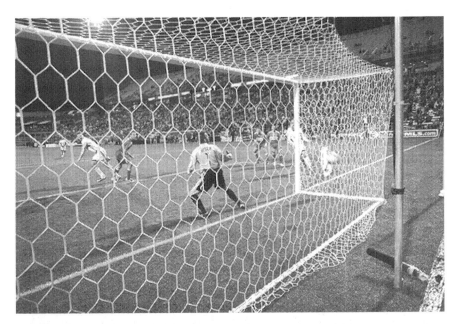

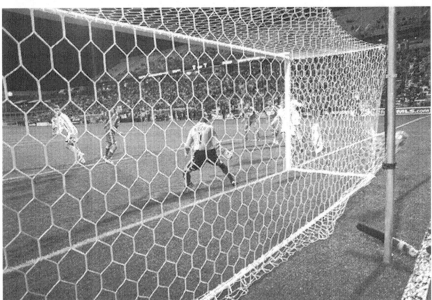

Four-photo sequence Chad Marshall's legendary goal over Brian McBride, which leveled the 2008 Eastern Conference final at 1-1 in the 49th minute.
(Photos by Sam Fahmi)

It Happened, Part Two: Gaven's Game-winner

As they have done so many times this year, the Crew quickly followed the equalizer with the go-ahead goal. It took just six minutes.

It's funny that Bliss had made a basketball reference regarding Marshall's goal, because in the 55th minute, Schelotto posted up, basketball-style, on the much taller Bakary Soumare. Alejandro Moreno floated a header in Schelotto's direction. The Argentine knocked the ball down with his back to Soumare and, when the ball bounced up in the air again, he held off Soumare to pop a header in Moreno's direction as he ran up the right side. Moreno immediately popped another header behind Soumare and into the perfectly timed run of Eddie Gaven.

After watching Guille and Moreno emulating sea lions frolicking with a beach ball at Sea World, the young midfielder took one controlling touch of the bouncing ball, and then hammered his shot downward and into the far left corner of the goal.

"Somebody was closing in on my left, so I had to get the shot off quick," Gaven said. "Luckily it went in the corner."

When the ball hit the net, Gaven sprinted into the open arms of the Nordecke. Perhaps he also rewarded Schelotto and Moreno by tossing a sardine into each of their mouths, although that was not caught on camera and is therefore pure conjecture on my part.

Eddie Gaven is mobbed by teammates in front of the Nordecke after scoring what would be the game-winning goal in the 2008 Eastern Conference Final.
(Photo by Sam Fahmi)

The Rest of the Game

The longer the second half went on, the less I remember. I have a pretty solid recollection of the Robbie Rogers laser beam that Busch saved in the 59th minute, but as the minutes ticked away, my brains drained from my head like sands through an hourglass. I remember Ekpo dancing around the Fire... I remember Chicago having a couple of near misses, including Hesmer smothering a close shot by McBride... I remember Rogers not going to the corner flag like she should have, and then getting it right the next time he got the ball.

Basically, I just remember being really antsy. It was like watching some sort of thriller movie where you knew the main character was going to prevail in the end, but you still got worked up with every scary plot twist. Or something.[166]

Dwight's Call

No man has personally witnessed more Crew soccer with his own eyes than has Dwight Burgess. That's a fact. As the game moved into the second minute of stoppage time, Crew radio play-by-play man Neil Sika told the listening audience, "I can think of no better man to bring you home than the Voice of the Crew, Dwight Burgess." And with that classy comment, Sika zipped his lip and deferred to the man who has called all but a handful of Crew games since April 13, 1996.

For posterity's sake, here is Dwight's historic call of the closing moments:

"Ball played forward...Hejduk doesn't get to that one, but Evans cleans it up and goes to Moreno, who is well back. He goes to the far side; open there is Rogers. Robbie Rogers just does a 360-degree dribble and now accelerates toward the corner flag...the balance of this one is on the wristwatch of the man in the middle...Columbus closing in on their very first trip ever to MLS Cup...Terry Vaughn checks his wristwatch...the ball is driven forward...Marshall is there!...the defender of the year clears long...near the Crew bench THAT'LL DO IT! THE COLUMBUS CREW ARE GOING TO THE 2008 MLS CUP! THEY ARE ON THEIR WAY TO LA! FOR THE

---

[166] Seriously...what happened to me? Historically, in terms of horror movie analogies, my teams of been the randy teenagers looking for a quiet spot at the secluded lakeside camp, or the random ill-defined minority character who volunteers to go outside and see what made that noise in the yard...and suddenly I let myself think of my team as the "guaranteed to survive" smoking hot chick whose name is above the title on the slasher flick movie poster? It's unreal.

FIRST TIME IN CLUB HISTORY....And as they have done ALL season long....WhatEVER it takes, just DO what you DO!....Could you have written a better script, Neil?....Brian McBride comes back and gets the first goal of the game, but Columbus responds...early in the second half....they stand up tall when they must...and they are on their way to the Cup!"

Dwight gutted out the latter half of that call while being crushed in the center of a congratulatory group hug as Neil, Crew V.P. of Corporate Sales & Broadcasting Chad Schroeder, and I piled onto the beloved bald broadcaster. Ever the pro, he just kept talking. He did what he does.

The Trophy and the Stage

For the second time in a month, the Crew collected a trophy that is impossible to drink out of. However, had they used a blow torch to remove the lid from the Eastern Conference Championship Trophy, it only would have been good for shots. That is one tiny trophy. It's as if it were commissioned from a Nigel Tufnel napkin sketch.[167] Then again, unlike Stonehenge, it's supposed to be tiny. The conference trophies are a mere appetizer for the big hardware that's up for grabs in Los Angeles.

As the team milled about at midfield in their 2008 Eastern Conference Champions t-shirts and ball caps, Dante Washington and I were almost speechless. Every now and then, I would say something intelligent, along the lines of, "The Columbus Crew. Seriously. The Columbus (bleepin') Crew." Dante would respond by staring forward, slightly shaking his head in amazement.

Commissioner Don Garber presented the trophy to Crew owners Clark and Dan Hunt, who then handed it over to Frankie Hejduk and Sigi Schmid. Then the whole team climbed up on the stage and started bouncing up and down until the stage began to buckle from the Massiveness of it all. The players hopped off before there was a total collapse.

"We knew it was coming, and it was kinda uh-oh, but we had to get everybody up there, you know?" said Hejduk. "This doesn't happen often. Like Sigi said before the game, you never know when it's going to come, so seize the moment and seize the opportunity. We did that today."

Nobody was injured in the celebration mishap, but even if the worst would have happened, the Crew would have had the services of Alejandro

---

[167] "This is Spinal Tap" is a classic movie. It's even better on DVD since they do the commentary track in character as the band watching the film 20 years later. Tremendous.

Moreno in California. "I didn't get up there," Moreno said. "I was chasing my kid around, and I am getting too old to climb up and jump around. I will save getting up on stage for if we win MLS Cup."

Crew on the Crowd

Starting in the northwest corner by the tunnel, Crew players took the Eastern Conference Championship Trophy on a counterclockwise tour of the stadium, stopping for a long while in front of the Nordecke, which was still packed the gills nearly a half hour after the final whistle. Here's what the Crew had to say about the crowd...

Sigi Schmid: "I believe we were going to win it anyway but certainly the energy – it goes hand-in-hand. The energy the fans have gives the energy to the team. In the second half we came out with good energy and that inspired the fans. Then when they (the Fire) were starting to pound on us, obviously their energy kept us going. It's a lot easier to chase or to make that one run when somebody is screaming for you and chanting for you and all of those things."

Frankie Hejduk: "The atmosphere was second-to-none. They've been behind us the whole year. We really challenged Columbus to come out. I would have liked to have seen more but it was loud. It was crazy. The Nordecke was more packed than it has ever been and they were behind us more than they have ever been. They've helped us."

Chad Marshall: "It helped that we were at home and had the fans behind us for 90 minutes. It was awesome. We fed off the crowd's energy and I'm glad we got a win for them."

Eddie Gaven: "The fans were awesome. They gave us so much energy and we fed off of it tonight. It's definitely great to have them on our side."

William Hesmer: "The crowd scene has spread all over. You see it everywhere now. It was fun to see everyone around the stadium bowing toward Guillermo."

Danny O'Rourke: "Look at the fans tonight. The crowd was unbelievable."

Brian McBride (Fire): "It's good to see that the team has that kind of support. The Fire has it with Section 8. It's strong, get-behind-the-team support and it's great for any team or organization."

McBridesmaid

In nine MLS seasons, Brian McBride's teams are now 0-5 in conference finals. This prompted Nordecke denizen Jonathan Smith to dub him "McBridesmaid." [168] It's a strange world when Brian McBride is scoring goals against the Crew and Columbus fans are thinking of cleverly cruel nicknames for the Black & Gold legend. But both sides know that business is business, and each side has to do what they need to do. Even if it's weird.

"It was pretty strange," McBride said of being an enemy combatant at Crew Stadium. "I didn't think there was going to be much of a strange feeling or anything. I just thought it was going to be a normal game. I got to spend some time with my best friend yesterday, and I got to visit with Duncan and Dante today and, yeah, it was strange. Come game time, it was about the game, but there was a little weirdness in the beginning."

Crew fans parsed McBride's words throughout the week, seeming to think he was dismissing Columbus in some way, particularly when he said that his ties to Columbus were "a sidebar" to the story of the big game. He felt the game was the story, not himself versus the Crew, but emotions were running high leading up to the game, and it seemed to pour fuel on the fans' fired-up psyches.

It would be a mistake to think that McBride has anything but fondness for the Crew and central Ohio. After the game, a crushed McBride was asked if part of him felt pride that the club he had helped build had reached its first MLS Cup.

"I'll always be a supporter of the Crew," he said. "When the Fire's playing them, I won't be. Of course I'm excited for them to do well. You can't spend this many years here and all of a sudden wish ill will on anybody. The Hunts are great. I got a chance to get to know them and have the utmost respect for them. The organization itself is a great one. I'm with the Fire now. My heart's here because I'm playing here with the Fire, but yeah, I'll always support the Crew when we're not playing them."

McBride wasn't sure if he would watch MLS Cup, but said he probably would. Would he be rooting for the Crew?

"Of course," he said. "There's no ill will. I wish them the best. Just right now there's a sore feeling (from the Fire's loss) because it's still fresh. I'm disappointed; I'm bummed; I'm down."

---

[168] That is everything a good fan taunt should be—clever and cutting.

Crew Players on the Thrill of Victory

Here are what some Crew players had to say about their emotions at the final whistle or during the postgame celebration…

Duncan Oughton: "This is awesome. This club has waited so long for an Eastern Conference championship. We're obviously ecstatic, but we're not done yet. I'm obviously very happy and can't explain it too much, but I've been around a long time and it means a lot."

Eddie Gaven: "It feels good. For everyone in this room, for the fans, for everyone in the organization who has put in a lot of work this year, it feels good."

Danny O'Rourke: "Coming back home to play for the Crew was exciting, but to play for a team going to MLS Cup and with a chance to win MLS Cup is beyond words. When you fight hard for your team and your city…we do it for each other, we do it for the city, and we do it for the organization. I'm happy to be a part of it."

William Hesmer: "When the final whistle blew, I think I just ran straight to Danny and gave him a big hug, and then he jumped on top of me. I wanted to give everybody a hug for the effort they put in tonight."

Frankie Hejduk: "I felt excitement, relief, positive vibrations… everything all at once. It was emotional, and you could see it in everyone's faces. It's been an amazing run, but we still have one thing left to do."

Alejandro Moreno: "We're very excited. When you see the fans and see the support, and you know that you can provide this sort of emotion for them with the victory, it is special. This is a great moment for the Crew organization, the city of Columbus, and all the fans who have shown up in numbers to support us."

Sigi Schmid: "We're obviously very proud. The crowd was tremendous. We didn't sell it out, but anyone who watched this game on TV or was here saw something that they'll remember for a long time. I know it means a lot to Robert (Warzycha) and Mike Lapper because they were there all those years when they kept stubbing their toe on D.C. United and didn't get there. I know it means a lot to them and they're very happy. I think they were a lot more nervous before the game than I was. It's something that's great for this city, great for this franchise to get over this hurdle. Now we've got the opportunity to take one more step."

Chad Marshall's Night

There were a lot of happy people in the Crew's champagne-soaked locker room, but none seemed happier than Chad Marshall. Not normally the most talkative member of the team when microphones are around, Marshall gleefully babbled a stream of pure elation to the ring of reporters that surrounded his locker.

"I was the happiest I've ever been," he said, about hearing the final whistle. "I just told somebody that. I just started running. I don't know why. It was awesome. It's been fun for me. I just started running around. I don't even know what I was doing. It was awesome. This has been a fun year for me. To go through all of that concussion stuff last year and then to come back and help the team this year, it's been awesome."

Marshall had every right to be elated. Not only did he come back in 2008 when his career appeared to be in jeopardy...and not only did he win the 2008 Defender of the Year award...but in the biggest game in club history, Marshall took his game to an even higher level. At BOTH ends of the field. He scored the biggest goal of his life and physically dominated his matchup with McBride.

"Chad Marshall was a man amongst boys tonight," said Hesmer. "Brian McBride is a legend of U.S. soccer and has played on the biggest stage, and tonight Chad showed how good HE is."

Chad Marshall also had a dominant game on the defensive end of the field.
(Photo by Sam Fahmi)

McBride's Goal Revisited

While I recoiled at the thought of McBride's goal being a Cleveland Moment, Schmid thought nothing of it in that sense. "It was a goal," Schmid said. "I just thought it was 1-0 Chicago. I didn't think, 'Aw, McBride scored it' or anything like that. I just thought it was 1-0 Chicago, and that we had to come back from that."

Hesmer explained what happened on the goal. "They caught us with a quick throw-in, and then it was a good ball (from Mapp)," Hesmer said. "It was McBride on Danny, and Brian is going to win that aerial matchup any time. I'm trying to get out there because I see the mismatch and need to get off my line to get to it, but I don't get there in time and I am caught in the middle. I didn't help our defense on that play."

O'Rourke shrugged off Hesmer's attempt to pin the goal on himself. "I could have made that play if I was as tall as Chad Marshall," O'Rourke said. "And Will helped our defense out with some big saves in the second half."

Crew on Comebacks

McBride's goal set up yet another Crew comeback. Counting the playoffs, the Crew improved to an astonishing 5-7-6 when allowing the first goal. Here's what more Crew players had to say about the team's comeback ability...

Alejandro Moreno: "You don't want to be in that position, but this team has done an excellent job of maintaining order and understanding that there is enough talent on the field to score goals. After falling behind 1-0, most teams would panic. Most teams would try to get people forward and really expose themselves in the back. We didn't do that."

Chad Marshall: "I'd like to stop doing it. I'd like to stop digging that 1-0 hole. But we just know what we're capable of. We don't put our heads down. We have great players on this team and we know we can get goals."

Eddie Gaven: "This team has been awesome all year. We have faith in the way we go out and play ever single game that we would be able to get it back. Thankfully, we did."

William Hesmer: "If it takes allowing a goal to piss us off and get us playing, I'm not happy about it, but I'll do it. When we go down a goal, I think it motivates our attack players more. Sometimes they don't come out and control the game like they are capable of. I think they are too modest in their abilities, to be quite honest, and that they are much better than they give themselves credit for."

Danny O'Rourke: "It's habit, I think. When you have that same mentality all year, it becomes second nature. When we fell behind, we didn't panic. We knew we've been in the scenario before, and when we came out in the second half, we came out flying."

Lamar

Team administrator Tucker Walther approached me in the jubilant locker room. He reached into his pocket and pulled out the commemorative Lamar Hunt gold coin that the Crew introduced on opening day in 2007. Tucker smiled and said, "We won because we had the 13th man out there with us today."

Maybe an hour later, I bumped into Mark McCullers. I had watched the first half next to him in the radio booth, but he never came back for the second half. Given that the Crew took the lead while he was gone, I told him I was prepared to boot him out if he had tried to come back. He then relayed the following story.

"I left at halftime because there were people I wanted to see and visit with," he said. "On my way back to the radio booth, I stopped by the Lamar Hunt Suite. I am not kidding that the moment I stepped into Lamar's suite, Chad scored the tying goal. The thing is, the TVs in the suites are on a slight delay, which I forgot about. So I heard everyone going crazy, and I looked at the TV and saw Guillermo standing over the ball and wondered why everyone was so excited. Then I saw the goal. And then Eddie scored to make it 2-1, and that settled it. There was no way I was leaving the Lamar Hunt Suite for the rest of the night."

So there are two completely independent stories of good Lamar mojo. Coincidence? I think not.

BC's Beard

As another week went by, the disparity in the team's playoff beards has really begun reveal itself. At one end of the spectrum, you have a guy like the bushy-faced Eddie Gaven. At the other end of the spectrum, you have a guy like Brian Carroll, who has mustered a tiny patch of hair midway up his jaw line, as well as a few random strands in the vicinity of his mouth.

I didn't get a chance to talk to BC about his playoff beard, but I did seek out the Crew's beard-growing champion, Adam Moffat, to see what advice he might have for his fellow midfielder during the lead up to MLS Cup.

"In these nine days," said Moffat, "I think Brian can catch Eddie Gaven if he starts applying Miracle Grow right now."

Official team spokesman for all things manly, Danny "Meathead" O'Rourke, revealed that a lot is at stake in the MLS Cup final.

"The goal is to win MLS Cup so BC can start working on his playoff beard for next year," O'Rourke explained. "We hope to get him up to Eddie Gaven's level by then. The chances are he won't be able to, but he's trying at least. BC's got like seven years on Robbie, and I think Robbie has beat him out in the Junior Miss division of the playoff beard competition. It is what it is."

It is what it is, unless it is what it isn't. Leave it to Duncan Oughton to offer the secret truth behind BC's playoff beard.

"BC isn't growing a beard," Oughton revealed. "There are only a few hairs on his face, and they are going to grow really long. That's because they are whiskers. BC is a little rat. Those are his real rat whiskers that are coming in."

Fantasy Football Update

How pervasive is fantasy football in our culture? Imagine standing in the middle of a jubilant locker room, only to have a player say, "Let's talk fantasy football."

That player, of course, would be O'Rourke, who was excited that his team had knocked off Chad Marshall's first-place juggernaut. "Four and six, still in the mix!" O'Rourke crowed. "And this week I have Stefani's (crappy) 1-9 team. Chad and Pat Noonan are tied for first at 8-2, but I am making a run for it."

Stat of the Night

The Crew are 9-0-2 at home against MLS competition since Craig Merz was hired by MLSnet. "The June 7 loss to San Jose doesn't count, because I was filling in for the AP that day," Merz clarified. He was hired by MLSnet the following week, and it wasn't until then that Craig started magically influencing games for the better.

Fun Moreno Moment

Alejandro Moreno's postgame interview session was briefly interrupted by his four-year-old son, Alejandro, Jr. Here is the transcript:

Junior: "Papi! Papi!"

Senior: "Hold on, buddy."

Junior: "I am going to fight"!

Senior: "You are going to fight?"

(Senior quickly and quizzically looked down at Junior, who was waving around one of those inflatable yellow thunder sticks as if he were a swashbuckling pirate about to do battle with Gino Padula. Senior flashed a bemused smile.)

Senior: "Okay, that's good."

Then, without missing a beat, Senior resumed answering the question he was in the middle of answering, while Junior continued to slay imaginary dragons or whatever. It was a fun little moment.

Fun McBride Moment

It was a somber scene around McBride's locker as he glumly answered questions after the Fire's loss. He softly replied to each inquiry until he heard a familiar voice lob a question from his right. McBride instantly picked up his head, turned to the side, and let a smile cross his face. "Hey Craig!" he said, the volume of his voice shooting up. "How ya doin'?" Merz was yet another old friend that Bake was happy to see upon his surreal return to Columbus.

What a Night

November 13, 2008, was quite a night. It was a night for unabashed man-hugs. It was a night for celebratory singing, dancing, and jumping about. It was a night for champagne.

It was a night for a woman to ask a friend to shoot a photo of her and her husband, so there'd be a permanent record of their bliss that night. So the friend snapped a photo of husband and wife, cheek to cheek, their smiles beaming. And then Dante Washington handed the camera back to Carly Oughton.

And it was a night of reflection.

I thought about Lamar Hunt, Tom Fitzgerald and Jim Nelson, and how the ravages of time, an inattentive driver and a seemingly innocuous slip on the ice, respectively, kept them from being here in the flesh for that special night. I thanked Lamar, poured some victory beer on the Fitz memorial boulder, and smiled at a Crewzer for Jim.

I thought about my earliest days covering the team, which began with years two and three of the great D.C. torment. It made me think of so many people. I thought of the four guys I interviewed this year for the Where Are They Now segments for the game program: Brian Maisonneuve, Mike Clark, Todd Yeagley, and Ansil Elcock. All professed to being Crew fans to this day, so I hoped they were watching. I hoped ALL of those 1997-99 Crew players were watching, even if they didn't have a primo bench seat like Robert Warzycha and Mike Lapper. I thought of Jamey Rootes, Jim Smith, Jeff Wuerth, Shane Murphy and other colleagues from that era, and hoped that they were watching too.

I thought about all of the near-misses and not-so-near misses over the years, and how, without them, Thursday would not have been so sweet. Winning a conference final means more after you've lost four of them. Beating Chicago in the most important meeting ever means more when they've owned you for the better part of a decade.[169]

I thought about this year's team: skillful, exciting, and unflappable. I thought about what a long, strange, delightfully unexpected journey it has been from the Adam Moffat Show on March 29 against the Hosers, to the Biggest Win In Club History (For Now) on November 13 against the Fire.

I thought about how they're not done yet.

So I thought about lots of stuff on the way home, including what I needed to pack for LA. I will be arriving on Thursday, and the plan is to blog on The Black & Gold Standard in the days leading up to the game, so be sure to check out the team's official blog starting Thursday evening-ish. I will then have the usual Notebook on TheCrew.com. MLSnet is sending Merz, so be sure to check out Craig's articles before and after the big game. And the Dispatch is sending Shawn Mitchell and Michael Arace, so I am positive that they will have plenty of awesome coverage, as usual.

Maybe when I get to LA, it will truly sink in....the Columbus Crew are in MLS Cup.

Before I go, I thought I'd turn it over to Frankie Hejduk for a few final words...

"It's been a lot of hard work – a lot of ups and a lot of downs – but this city deserves a championship. We're going there to win it. We are going to California with no other goal than to bring an MLS Cup championship back to Columbus."

---

[169] Heading into conference final, the Crew were 10-17-10 against the Fire in MLS play, plus 0-3 in the U.S. Open Cup, for a total of 10-20-10. Ouch. It's amazing how one game can trump the frustration of 40.

Questions? Comments? Have strange marks on your arms from pinching yourself? Feel free to write at sirk65@yahoo.com

Andy Iro was all smiles while sporting his 2008 Eastern Conference Champions gear in front of the Nordecke on November 13, 2008. (Photo by Sam Fahmi)

The Awkwardness Amidst the Joy

The Crew's victory in the 2008 Eastern Conference Final was undeniably the club's biggest win on its home field. After coming so close so many times, the team finally broke through the conference final barrier and would get a chance to play in MLS Cup. The game that the 2008 Eastern Conference final supplanted was the 2002 Lamar Hunt U.S. Open Cup final.

To me, there are three enduring images from October 24, 2002. The first, of course, is Lamar Hunt celebrating with the team on the podium. Lamar got to see his beloved Crew win the tournament that bears his name. It doesn't get much cooler than that. But the other two images that stand out both involved Crew players who wanted it so badly and had left so much of themselves on the field that all they could do was collapse to their knees at the final whistle. The first picture depicted Brian McBride, hands over his mouth, as Eric Denton rushed to congratulate him. The other picture depicted Jon Busch as Brian Dunseth bent down, grabbed each side of the goalkeeper's head, and deliriously rattled the loose screws therein.

There are many players who loved playing for the Columbus Crew every bit as much as Brian McBride and Jon Busch did, but it would be hard to argue that there is anyone who loved it more.

Jon Busch was a minor league journeyman, perennially deemed to be too small, until Greg Andrulis gave him a chance. Busch grabbed that chance with both hands in 2002, and he finished the year backstopping the Crew's first title of any kind. I will never forget talking to him postgame. He was extremely emotional, and rather than talk about his amazing run, he kept going out of his way to talk about his then-girlfriend (now wife) Nicole. He wanted the world to know that she believed him and kept encouraging him to follow his dream, and so that title was for her. It was a very touching scene. Crew fans embraced Jon Busch because it's easy to root for the unshakably driven "little guy" who makes it against the odds, and in the case of a goalkeeper, it is literally a little guy that makes it against the odds.

And then there's Brian McBride. He was the face of the franchise. With no disrespect to any other Crew players, past or present, McBride has been the Crew's one transcendent star who *everyone* in town knew by both name and sight. Love or hate soccer, if you lived in Columbus, you recognized and respected Brian McBride. Due to the perfect combination of timing, talent, good looks, and classy personality, he had an entirely different level of soccer fame in this town, and with that platform, he always did the Crew proud.

And the truth is that a lot of the values that we enjoyed about the 2008 team were instilled by McBride and his teammates. We all applaud Duncan Oughton for being the soul of the team, and while Duncan is a great guy in his own right, he will be the first to tell you that guys like McBride instilled in him what it meant to be a professional and what it meant to play for the Columbus Crew. Before leaving for the Olympics, Robbie Rogers said he was excited to play with McBride because he is a Crew legend and that the current players still hear a lot about him. Even while playing in England, Brian McBride cast an influential shadow on the rebirth of the Columbus Crew.

To me, the Eastern Conference final was a cruel construct. On one hand, it was very symbolic. The Massive Bananas were slaying the demons of yesteryear, and what could be more symbolic than defeating a Chicago Fire team led by two beloved Crew alumni representing the near misses of yesteryear? On the other hand, it felt awkward and sad that Busch and McBride were to be sacrificed at the Altar of Massiveness. If I could have, I certainly would have written a different script than having to torture those two guys by seeing the Crew finally break through while they trudged off the field in enemy colors.

Don't get me wrong— it sure as hell beats the alternative, which was to see the two of them break every Columbus fan's heart by prematurely ending the Massive Season while celebrating with the frickin' *Fire*. But at the same time, it's not how I would have drawn it up. Neither man deserved to have their noses rubbed in our dream season. Busch was playing with the Fire because that was the only team that would give him a chance after two blown knees. And true to his career, he prevailed against the odds and claimed the 2008 MLS Goalkeeper of the Year Award. And while McBride signed with the Fire of his own volition, it's hard to hold too much animosity toward a man who wants to wind down his career with his hometown team in an effort to put his family first. As he had stated, they moved to another continent for him, and now it was his time to put them first. It was time to be near extended family and to not worry about making the kids change schools multiple times. Fair enough.

That's not to say that McBride and Busch didn't deserve every bit of heckling that got from Nordecke during the Eastern Conference final. It's not like McBride signed a pact not to score goals and Busch signed one not save shots against the Crew. They were playing to win, and they stood between the Crew and unprecedented glory, so the Nordecke had every right to play to win as well. So the chants of "Columbus reject" and "traitor" were well within the bounds of fair play. But it still seemed bizarre. McBride scored one of the most potentially devastating goals ever scored *against* the Crew. McBride and Busch were thoroughly heckled by *Columbus* fans. While playing for the *Chicago Fire*.

Again, not how I would have drawn it up. But some day in the future, I hope both sides let it go and understand that it's just business. The fans have every bit as much of a right to boo and heckle in support of their team as the player has the right to perform at his best, no matter the opposition. And vice versa. Some time down the road, once these awkward encounters cease, Jon Busch will hopefully be a proud and beloved Crew alum once more. And the day he hangs it up, Brian McBride should consider himself Crew and should be regarded by fans as nothing less than the Crew legend that he is.

That's what I hope, at least. For all of us. And let's face it, the Crew's victory in the Eastern Conference Final has kept that dream very much alive. Had McBride scored the only goal and Busch pitched the shutout, it would have been a heartache that probably couldn't be forgiven by an emotionally-scarred fan base.

With their 2-1 comeback victory, the Massive Bananas not only *made* history, but they may have indirectly *preserved* history as well.

On a personal note, I also have a hard time hating on McBride because he once did me an incredibly meaningful favor.

I didn't really know Brian very well during his time here. He wasn't a Notebook regular, mostly because he was as highly polished off the field as he was on it. He wasn't one to fill up a recorder with crazy quotes. It was much more fun for me to joke around with those who would.

But when my mom was diagnosed with terminal cancer in 2002, Brian was one of many people with the Crew who kindly stepped up and gave her a very special day. PR Director Jeff Wuerth and GM Jim Smith arranged for her to watch a game from the VIP pavilion outside of Smith's office. Tucker Walther made her a personalized jersey. And her very favorite player in the whole wide world, Brian McBride, met with her before the game, offered some words of encouragement, signed the jersey, and presented it to her. Then he went out and scored a goal. I mean, it wasn't Babe Ruth promising to hit a home run for a sick kid in a hospital, but it was a nice touch nonetheless.

For the next few months, she brought up that day every time we talked. A photo of their meet-up sat framed in her living room.[170] And to top it off, until he left for England, Brian would occasionally ask me how she was doing. When I'd tell her Brian asked about her, she would turn positively giddy, no matter how ill she felt.

My mom was a sports fan, but in addition to her teams, she had favorite players that she would root for no matter where they played. Her personal Mount Rushmore consisted of football's Troy Aikman, baseball's Mike Piazza, hockey's Brendan Shanahan, and soccer's Brian McBride.

When McBride scored that goal to go up 1-0 against the Crew in the Eastern Conference final, not only did I wince at the Cleveland Moment, but I also shook my head, thinking of my mom clapping for Brian. She would have been happy for him, even though she would have wanted the Crew to win. In the end, once the Crew's comeback was complete, it would have been a perfect night for her.

So whenever I think about how much the sports fan in me should hate on McBride for playing for the loathsome Fire, the son in me finds it impossible, even when he's scoring big goals against the Crew. My mind always goes back to that special day, when Brian graciously made a little sliver of time for my mom during a very difficult time in her life. Granted, I had connections, but the truth is that Brian quietly did that sort of thing for a lot of people when he was in Columbus. It's just the type of person he is.

I hope Brian and the fans know and feel that the respective booing and goal-scoring are only business. Awkward business, but business nonetheless. Fair is fair. But I hope it is only a temporary arrangement that ends the second he retires, because at that precise moment, Brian McBride will always be Crew to me.

---

[170] Also in her living room was a "totally authentic" Brian McBride bobblehead constructed by my friend Stephanie. When the Crew ran out of McBride bobbleheads before I could get my hands on one, Steph brilliantly performed plastic surgery on a Crew Cat bobblehead. She cut out McBride's black and white headshot and affixed it over Crew Cat's face with a piece of string that went around the feline's skull, like one of those cheap plastic Halloween masks. Then she plastered a new nameplate on the bottom that read "Makbride" with a backward "k". Steph assured my mom that it was "totally authentic." My mom loved it, and it sat right next to the framed photo of her meeting with Brian.

My mother, Jeanne, holds up her personalized Crew jersey after Brian McBride autographed it and presented it to her on July 6, 2002. My mom would surely stress my obligation to point out that she was suffering from "chemo bloat" and that she was wearing a ridiculous wig to cover her bald head, so let those two facts be noted in the official record. Regardless, it was one of her favorite pictures, and it was happily displayed in her living room until she passed away from cancer on June 19, 2006.[171]
(Photo by Greg Bartram)

---

[171] Ghana eliminated the U.S. from the 2006 World Cup later that morning. Good times.

Playoff Beards: BC vs. Gaven

In that Eastern Conference Final Notebook, there were plenty of cracks about Brian Carroll's playoff beard and how it paled in comparison to that of Eddie Gaven. To provide some visual perspective, here's a pair of photos taken by Andy Mead. These pictures were shot at Crew training on November 21. Since this was a full eight days after the conference final, Gaven probably expanded his lead a little. Nevertheless, here's what Moffat, Duncan, and Danny O were talking about...

Brian Carroll after nearly a month without shaving. (Photo by Andy Mead / YCJ)

Eddie Gaven, apparently after typing a manifesto in a remote Montana cabin.
(Photo by Andy Mead / YCJ)

LA Blog: Greetings from the Golden State

November 20, 2008

Hey gang,

Greetings from the Golden State. Thanks to the Shawn Mitchell Rental Car Taxi Cab Express, I am writing to you from the Hyatt, where it is anticipated that, in couple of hours, Guillermo Barros Schelotto will be named Major League Soccer's 2008 Volkswagen Most Valuable Player. If he's not, I'm stealing trophy and holding it hostage. Shawn can hop back behind the wheel of the Grand Marquis and drive me down the 405, Al Cowlings-style. [172]

Unlike Craig Merz, who flew from Phoenix to LAX with Ted Danson, I had no celebrities on my flight. But that's okay. This is my fourth trip to Los Angeles, and I am excited that this one will last longer than 48 hours, which is my previous LA record. My previous trips...

* 1998 (approximately 48 hours):

Matt Bernhardt and I flew out for MLS Cup '98, just for the heck of it. We went to the first-ever MLS Supporters' Summit. We also saw Chicago defeat D.C. United, 2-0, to become the first non-D.C. champion of MLS. We were rooting for the Fire because we didn't yet know that we should have been rooting for a center circle blimp crash or something.

I also went for a tour of LA with a fan of another team who had a rental car. We saw the Hollywood sign, witnessed a long line of black-clad bat-munchers waiting for Black Sabbath's autograph on Sunset Boulevard, and met a woman who played "Blonde-haired-chick-at-the-bar-who-is-shown-a-photo-by-the-cops-and-shakes-her-head-no" in the then soon to be released Nicolas Cage film, "8MM." (I can't begin to tell you how excited I was to verify her claim when the movie came out a few months later.[173]) This woman was a dancer at this dance club that the guy with the car suddenly announced that we were stopping at, despite it never coming up when we discussed our sightseeing itinerary. It wasn't the type of dance club where we did any of the dancing. There's a much longer story there that involves the guy with the car being asked to leave the establishment, but there's no need to

---

[172] I forgot to mention Shawn's response: "I should have rented a white Bronco."

[173] Actually, she went into much greater detail about her part and her dialogue, but in the final edit, all she ended up being was a chick who looks at a photo and shakes her head no during a montage sequence. I enjoyed her performance nonetheless.

get into that here, other than to say that I was so incredibly happy to get back to the safety of the hotel. It was a night that could have gone (and almost did go) very, very wrong.

I learned my lesson, though. Shawn was thoroughly vetted before I let him drive me from the airport to the Hyatt.

* 1999 (approximately 20 hours)

On that Thursday, Bernhardt and I made the impromptu decision to fly to LA that weekend for Sunday's Women's World Cup final. On Saturday's flight out, we sat next to a woman who was dating a guy who used to play keyboards for Debbie Gibson. Seriously. For a good portion of the trip, it's what she talked about to anyone who would listen.

We arranged to buy our tickets from the sister of a guy who was selling tickets on BigSoccer. After arriving in LA after 11:00pm on Saturday, Matt and I drove to Fullerton, placed a call from a gas station pay phone at midnight, and told her we were waiting there with the promised sum of $200 cash for the pair of tickets. ("Safety first", that's our motto.)

After procuring the tickets without getting beaten, murdered, and/or robbed, we had to find a hotel since we never bothered to make reservations anywhere. We eventually found one vacancy at a motel on Colorado Boulevard in Pasadena. I could tell you about the purple-ish shag carpeting, the 1970s brown-yellow-red patterned drapes, or the ancient television that actually had a lineup of channel-specific pushbuttons for changing the channel. But instead, I will tell you about the two most awesome features of our room.

1. We were told that the room had two beds, but we could only see one when we walked in. Matt opened a door to what we thought was a closet, but turned out to be a larger walk-in type closet....with a small bed stashed inside. Seriously. They turned a walk-in closet into a second, claustrophobic bedroom. Matt insisted on sleeping in there. I was happy to oblige.

2. By far the most stupendously awesome feature of the room was the narrow mirror attached to the wall that ran along the length of my bed. "There's only one way to use that mirror," Matt shuddered.

So, um, yeah. If you're planning a last minute trip out here to see the Crew, great rooms will surely be available in Pasadena!

Anyway, after a few hours of creepy sleep, we went to the WWC final the next day. Our seats were about 30 rows from the field and about 40 rows from, apparently, the sun. Afraid of missing a goal if I got up to get some water, I sat through two games and 210 minutes of scoreless soccer as the sun sapped the life from my body. By the time Brandi Chastain famously ripped off her shirt, I was long since woozy and incoherent from heat exhaustion. But I was there, darn it.

BOOK UPDATE: I have found photos of our 1999 hotel accommodations!!!

As if those brown, red and yellow curtains weren't sweet enough, imagine that those chairs are a very bright blue, which they were. Also, that doorway off to the right was Bernhardt's closet/bedroom. (Photo by Steve Sirk)

My bed was to the left and cannot be seen in this picture...unless you look at the horizontal bedside mirror on the right. (Photo by Steve Sirk)

*2004 (Approximately 48 hours)

Flick, Fid, and I flew out to MLS Cup "to see the Eastern Conference champions take on the Western Conference champions." That's what we told ourselves when we booked our flights, hotel, and rental car. We did not wish to jinx the Crew. Tony Sanneh had other plans. As a result, we got stuck watching D.C. United win it again. Yuck.

The trip was not without its highlights. We cruised up and down Rodeo Drive in our rented Buick Century, which became even funnier when a red light stopped us right next to a Rolls Royce Phantom. We had dinner in Hermosa Beach with Dunny and Tucker, at which time Flick, Fid, and I walked out on the pier to see a Pacific sunset. In the ensuing years, Dunny would later describe our group sunset-viewing as "cute." Oh, and we ate breakfast at the Carson Denny's in the vicinity of a decked-out-in-denim Troy Dayak. I'm talking denim vest with no sleeves underneath. It was truly a sight to behold. But not quite like the sight of a late night gangsta-gangsta donut shop in Long Beach. Although I would have enjoyed a donut at that juncture of our unplanned and aimless tour of Wherethe(bleep)arewe, I adhered to that time-tested gangland safety rhyme, "If you're not sure which colors, don't stop for crullers."

So, um, yeah. Here I am again. But this time I will be here for more than 48 hours, so who knows what will transpire between now and Monday? I am looking forward to it, especially the parts that involve sleeping and/or food, both of which have been virtually nonexistent in the last 24+ hours.

I will be blogging when I can for the next few days. I'll probably slap another update up here after the MVP announcement. Then again, I've told Shawn to keep the Grand Marquis running. If Guille doesn't win, forget the Black & Gold Standard and turn on CNN.

Cheers,
Sirk

PS- Oops. It already leaked out. Guille won the award. I'm not rewriting this, but I will tell Shawn it's safe to park the car.

LA Blog: Friday Morning Notes

November 21, 2008

Random Friday morning notes after ten glorious hours of sleep-deprivation recovery...

Guille

So, as everyone already knows, Guillermo Barros Schelotto was named the 2008 Volkswagen MLS MVP award winner. This is the part where I would chime in with some quotes and stuff if it weren't for the fact that I need to file an Amber alert on my recorder. I seem to have misplaced it. Either that, or I hurled it in anger in traffic. (When it's gridlocked, people here like to use off-ramps as passing lanes before forcefully merging back onto the gridlocked highway. It's fantastic.)

There was a ceremony at the Hyatt featuring a roped off stage with framed Schelotto photos propped up on easels at either end of the stage. Add a bunch of flowers and an urn, and it would have looked like a memorial service. But add a shiny trophy, and voila, it's an awards ceremony. (Or a memorial service with a very impressive urn.)

I don't have exact quotes since my recorder is MIA, but Guillermo said, as he frequently has, that the MVP is nice, but he is here to win MLS Cup. He credited his coaches and teammates with the team's turnaround and for making his transition to MLS easier. He said he wants to be back in Columbus for "one or two" more seasons, and that contract talks had been put on the back burner due to the focus placed on winning the championship. He said Columbus is where he wanted to play, and had no designs on playing in New York, Chicago, LA etc. When asked what he liked about Columbus, he said the security, the tranquility, the people, that it's a pretty city, "and Easton." [174]

Crew President & GM Mark McCullers said that signing a big foreign name is always a gamble, because you never know how they will adapt. He said that the Crew had high hopes for Guillermo based on Schelotto's full trophy case, as well as what they gleaned of Guille's personality during the time spent with Guillermo and his family down in Argentina. McCullers said that Guille's MVP season and the Crew's resulting MLS Cup run is "certainly

---

[174] That was great, as it threw all of the national writers for a loop.

on the high end of what we thought could be possible when we brought Guillermo here. It says a lot about the type of person and competitor he is."

I doubt there is anyone reading this who hasn't read Shawn Mitchell's excellent Guille profile in Wednesday's Dispatch, but if you haven't, you really should.[175]

I love this picture of Guille. MVP SchmemVP. The Great Guillermo was in LA on a business trip, and his business is winning team trophies, not personal trinkets.
(Photo by Wade Jackson / YCJ)

Mistaken Identity

A half hour after the awards ceremony, McCullers and I encountered Schelotto outside the Hyatt. He was wearing jeans and a t-shirt.

We commented that Guille wasted no time in getting comfortable after the ceremony.

"It's Gustavo," said Schelotto. Said *Gustavo* Schelotto, Guillermo's twin brother. Sure enough, Guille was in the lobby, still dressed up, talking with his parents.

Frye's

Since I suddenly found myself without a recorder, Craig Merz took me over to Frye's (a popular electronics retailer here in LA) to get a new one. What a

---

[175] I obviously can't reprint Shawn's story here. It was really good, though. I suppose you could always go to the library and look it up on microfilm if you're THAT curious about it.

strange store. It's basically done up in a tropical grass hut motif. There are actual grass huts inside the building. Seriously. Nothing says "the latest high-end electronic gadgetry" like wandering into the hut of a Vanuatu coconut merchant.

Chillin'

Apart from training and league commitments, the team isn't under any sort of lockdown. This week is being treated like any other road trip. Alas, don't expect to find paparazzi shots of Crew players partying with Snoop Dogg or Lindsay Lohan or whoever you're supposed to party with when you're in LA. Rather, the guys seem to be passing the time by draining the batteries on their iPods and laptop computers, often simultaneously.

Swag

As a welcoming gift, players were given black vests with the MLS logo on the back up near the neck. Andy Iro commented that he wouldn't need a vest this winter because he was going to spend his offseason on the beach.

"I think you should wear the vest to the beach," said Danny O'Rourke. "Swimming trunks and this vest. And then when women come up to you, you can say, 'Wanna know who I work for?', and then spin around so they can see the back."

Andy and Danny then simultaneously laughed and recited some rap lyric that I am too old and out of touch to have any clue what it was. It wasn't a line from the Humpty Dance. I would have known it if it was from the Humpty Dance.[176]

That's all for now… Merz and I are heading out to training. More later.

---

[176] Or "Parents Just Don't Understand" by DJ Jazzy Jeff & the Fresh Prince.

LA Blog: Friday Afternoon Notes

November 21, 2008

Some quick afternoon notes before heading to Garber's press conference…

MLS Cup Support

The Crew's supporters will be seated in the Home Depot Center's northeast corner on Sunday. Hey, that's where the Nordecke is located at Crew Stadium! What a serendipitous coincidence!

"That's perfect,"said midfielder Brad Evans. "That's awesome. I heard that for the first time yesterday. If we can replicate (the Nordecke) as much as possible, it would be awesome."

"I think we have a good support system, both in Columbus and California," said striker Steven Lenhart. "It definitely helps, playing-wise, knowing that the people who love and support you are in the stands."

Lenhart Ticket Domination

Lenhart is up to 96 tickets for the game, which leads the team. "My mom is making the list, and it keeps getting bigger," he said. "I don't even know how many people I will know out of the 96. I look forward to seeing who's there."

Adam Moffat shook his head. "I only know like 15 people, and he's got *96* that want to come to this game," said the Scot. "If Steve gets in, we'll know who those 96 people are. It will be quite clear."

"Yeah, you'll see them," said Lenhart. "I think they just bought 96 yellow shirts."

Robbie on His Season

Robbie Rogers drew a lot of media attention after training. He was asked if he felt he expected to have such an excellent season.

"I felt like I was capable of this, but I still have a lot to learn and can keep improving," he said. "I mean, I guess I'm happy with how it's gone since we're in MLS Cup, but I still have a lot to learn."

Literal Answer

A reporter asked Rogers to compare the feeling in the locker room now compared to this time last year. Robbie consulted his mental calendar and answered the question literally, as asked.

"At this time last year, we weren't playing games," he said. "We were just doing training camp. That was kind of a bummer."

Scouting Report

Lenhart's assessment of Rogers' game: "Robbie is *sooooo* fast. It pisses me off."

Frankie on the Red Bulls' Counter Attack

Captain Frankie Hejduk doesn't think the Red Bulls will bunker and counter as much as some might expect, and if they do, the Crew will approach the game the same way they have all year.

"We've played against teams that have tried to bunker in and counter against us, so we are ready whenever we play those teams," he said. "I don't think they'll do that as much. It's a one-off game, so I think it will be both sides battling back and forth. They had to play that way because they were on the road in the playoffs. That's how teams sometimes play when they are away. But this is a one-off game. We are just going to go out and play our game. We're worried about ourselves. We need to make sure we go out and execute our game plan like we have all year."

A Pair of MLS Cup Newcomers

Hejduk finds it compelling that the Crew and Red Bulls are both making their inaugural visits to the league's title match.

"I think it's exciting," he said. "It gives the game more of a buzz, you know? For a while there, it was the same teams making it to the final, and it got a bit stale. I think this is a good thing for the league, the Crew, and the Red Bulls. These are two teams that have been there from the beginning and have never won a cup. It's a great story and it's diversified the league a little bit. Now every team can look at this game and think, 'Hey, we're okay. If they can do it, we can do it.' I think two fresh faces are good for everyone."

Actual Guille Quotes!

Armed with my new recorder, here are some actual Guille quotes!

On MLS Cup: "It's going to be a big game with a lot of expectations. There is a lot of media, so hopefully all games in the future will get more interest from the media."

On why he has succeed where other foreign imports have failed: "I worked hard to understand the soccer from here, and to adapt to my teammates. I also tried to share my own experiences for the benefit of the team."

368

On the leadership he has brought to the team and winning the MVP: "It's not that I am a leader— it's just that the team has done well. Given my position, people highlight the goals and assists, but it is about the team, not a leader. The MVP award is not for me, but for the team."

On his fans watching Crew games on television back in Argentina: "It's very important that people watch the soccer here. It's not important that they see me, but it's important that they see the league so the league can be more important."

Ale's Game

Alejandro Moreno was asked about his role as a front-line pummel horse for the team. "I do what I do, and I do it to the best of the ability," he said. "I think my teammates appreciate it, and I think Sigi appreciates it, and that's all that matters to me. It's my job, and I don't think anything about it. It's what I've done for seven years in this league. It hasn't gotten any prettier, and it probably won't get any prettier, so it is what it is."

LA Traffic

As we drove down the road from the HDC, Merz wanted to write something down before he forgot it. I told him I could help out and reach into the back seat for his notebook so he could focus on driving.

"Never mind," he said. "I will just wait until we get on the 405. Then I will have plenty of time to take out my laptop and write the whole article."

Frye's, Part II

I told Lenhart about my experience at Frye's, what with the grass huts and all. He seemed perplexed.

"Really?" he said. "I've never seen grass huts before. The one by my house has a space shuttle."

Seriously, I am even more baffled than before.

LA Blog: Dwight

November 22, 2008

After the Crew clinched the Eastern Conference title, I rattled off a few questions to the Voice of the Crew, Dwight Burgess. My hope was to include his responses in the section of the Notebook where I transcribed his historic radio call, but alas, computer problems on Dwight's end prevented him from responding before my deadline.

Since I'm out here blogging this week, I figured I'd take a moment to share Dwight's thoughts on that night.

First off, Burgess was surprised when current radio man Neil Sika figuratively passed the mic to him for the historic call. "I did not know that was coming," said Burgess. "The gesture was very much appreciated."

As someone who has personally witnessed more Columbus Crew soccer than anyone, living or dead, I asked him for his thoughts when the final whistle blew and he got to call it live on the radio.

"When the match ended, I was numb" he said. "It's just been so long, so many close calls, and, well, you know. I then began to think about Fitz, Lamar, and the others who have come and gone; those that gave so much to the organization. I hope those that are still out there are enjoying 2008 with the rest of us!"

Dwight also felt a bit of relief when the Crew finally got over the conference final hump. "As the only original Crew employee left, I am glad to know it wasn't because of me!"

Postscript

Dwight is sometimes my chauffeur on road trips. Due to flight times and hotel arrangements in Los Angeles, that particular duty has largely fallen upon Craig Merz, Shawn Mitchell, and my good buddy Flick. I should be somewhat thankful, because car rides with Dwight can be maddening. By popular demand (from Dwight), I am reprinting this anecdote from a March 2005 notebook about our pre-season trip to Virginia Beach…

Among his many talents, Dwight is a master of Making Conversations More Difficult Than They Need To Be. To wit, on our drive to the airport, I told Dwight that my layover is in Philadelphia. Dwight

370

suggested that I go see the Liberty Bell. (As if I'd have time.) Then the following conversation took place:

SS: I've already seen the Liberty Bell. We had to stand in line for two hours.

DB: You did not have to stand in line for two hours.

SS: Yes we did.

DB: I beg to differ.

SS: Okay, fine. If we wanted to see the Liberty Bell, we had to stand in line for two hours.

DB: That is also incorrect. You could have seen the Liberty Bell some other time when the line was shorter.

SS: We were only in Philadelphia for the afternoon.

DB: So? That doesn't mean anything. You could visit Philadelphia some other time. What you meant to say is that because you wanted to see the Liberty Bell on *that* day and at *that* time, you willingly *chose* to stand in line for two hours.

SS: (Bleep.)

DB: All I'm asking is that if you're going to tell a story, tell it honestly.

SS: (Bleep.)

Ahh, memories. Anyway, there's a Burgess-themed blog entry for you guys.[177] Off to training. I'm still waiting on a photograph from Moffat or Lenhart so I can post about their exciting celebrity sighting.

---

[177] This has nothing to do with anything, other than it is a great Dwight story. Years ago, I joked that I wanted to personally sponsor something on the broadcasts, like fake injuries or something stupid. Well, during a dubious late-game injury, Dwight announced, "This bit of time wasting is brought to you by Sirk. When you think 'waste of time', think 'Sirk!'"

LA Blog:
Moffat & Lenhart's Celebrity Sighting

November 22, 2008

As I mentioned in my first blog entry, Merz flew to LA with Ted Danson. Not to be outdone, Steven Lenhart and Adam Moffat had an LAX encounter with tennis superstar Serena Williams.

"It was awesome," said Moffat. "Ezra Hendrickson spotted her first, then Andy Iro saw her. We were about to get on the bus, but then I decided I needed to get my picture taken with her. My friend back home is a big tennis player, so I figured I'd send the picture to him to see if he enjoys it."

And how exactly did Ms. Williams react to being accosted by two goofballs like Moffat and Lenhart?

"She was a bit shy at first," Moffat said. "Steve made sure I spoke. He said, 'You have to speak because of your accent.'"

Ahh, so there was a gameplan. Chicks love accents, even if it's from Glasgow and renders the words undecipherable. With the accent getting them in the door, the conversation began to flow.

"She asked what we do, and I said 'play soccer,'" Moffat recounted. "She said, 'Are you here to play against the Galaxy?' I said, 'No, we're here to play in the MLS Cup at the Home Depot Center,' and then she said, 'What's that?'"

Whew. With the heavily-accented chitchat out of the way, the guys got their photos taken with her.

Having witnessed the entire scene, midfielder Stefani Miglioranzi insists that it was Serena who rushed up to Moffat and Lenhart and asked to he photographed with them. Also, Stefani noted that "her legs are stronger than both of theirs put together."

Anyway, both Moffat and Lenhart enjoy playing tennis. As luck would have it, the Home Depot Center is replete with many top-notch tennis courts. "We've been eyeing the courts here, honestly," Lenhart said, as he and Moffat are eager to see if tennis greatness is contagious.

Alas, the guys are more concerned about soccer greatness at the moment, so that will have to wait. And since the winter will make tennis tough when they return to Columbus, they will instead focus on sports at which they already excel, such as corn hole.

"We are much better at corn hole than at tennis, for sure," Moffat said.

"We will not be beat," Lenhart declared.

But wait...corn hole is an outdoor sport too.

"Well, we tried to play indoor corn hole back in Columbus," Moffat said. "It's a bit harder with a roof. Seven foot ceilings make it not so easy. You can't throw it that high."

"Yeah," added Lenhart. "You need a different strategy."

Moffat (left) and Lenhart (right) flank Serena Williams.
(Photo courtesy of Adam Moffat)

LA Blog: A Brief Chat with Dan Hunt

November 22, 2008

On Saturday morning, I had a friendly chat with the youngest Hunt brother, Daniel, who has been spotted with increased frequency at Crew events. Then again, maybe it's just because I know who he is now. An affable guy, Dan was bubbling with excitement over the Crew's first MLS Cup appearance.

"The Crew is one of the last few teams that hadn't been to the final, so to be here is great," he said. "We wish our dad was here, because he loved the Crew just like Clark and I do. We miss him, but hopefully we can win one for him tomorrow."

Although he is based out of Dallas, Dan says the Crew are never far from his thoughts.

"I very rarely miss a match," he said. "I have the MLS package, so I see them all. When my travel schedule allows, I love coming to Crew games in Columbus. It's a great stadium and the fans are passionate. Sometimes I get to a road game, and of course I get to see them when they come to Dallas."

Whether it be in person or on TV, Dan has fallen head over heels for this group of players.

"What a wonderful team they've turned out to be this year," he said. "Sigi's done an awesome job. This year's Crew team has played some of the prettiest soccer in this league's history. Not only do they score goals, but more often than not, they are beautiful goals. And I have never seen a locker room like this one. They love playing the game and playing for each other, and they are all willing to do whatever they have to do. They know their responsibilities to their teammates, and there's accountability in that room to meet those responsibilities, but they still make it fun. They're a joy to watch and a joy to be around. It's a special group. It makes you want to root for them even more."

And so, like their father before them, Clark and Dan Hunt are skipping Sunday's Kansas City Chiefs game to be at MLS Cup.

"Championship opportunities come around so rarely, you just can't miss a championship," Dan said. "The funny thing is, it doesn't matter what it is. My parents would have missed a Chiefs game for a championship game for Clark or I in whatever sport we were playing. That carries forward. Championship opportunities are so rare in life that I definitely want to be here to cheer on the Crew."

LA Blog: Gibberish about Saturday

November 23, 2008

Crew training was rather uneventful. The players seemed ready to get on with it. Also, Danny O'Rourke and Frankie Hejduk assured me that despite Sunday being Will Hesmer's birthday, the team will not be gorging on ice cream and birthday cake before taking the field. So if you were worried about that, worry no more.

The grass at the HDC was immaculate, but long. However, I am happy to report that I was back at the HDC after sunset, and the grounds crew had given the pitch a fresh mowing.

After training, I spent much of my afternoon at Hollywood United's charity match. Notebook Hall of Famer Brian Dunseth took the field along with such diverse jugadors as Golden Globe and Emmy Award-winning actor Anthony LaPaglia, World Cup champion Frank LeBouef, Good Charlotte singer/guitarist Benji Madden, and many others.

Perhaps the biggest crowd-pleaser of them all was Gilles Marini, who starred in the movie version of "Sex and the City." Flick, Dante, and I were told by several swooning female sources that Gilles did a scene containing full frontal nudity. During the game, Flick and I referred to Gilles as "Full Frontal Nudity" until Flick came up with shorter, catchier nickname: "Mr. Junk." Mr. Junk scored a few goals, most of which were almost onside.

A player of particular interest to Flick was Eric Braeden, who plays "ruthless kingpin" Victor Newman on The Young & The Restless. Flick is a huge fan of that show, so he was all aflutter. Actually, his wife is a huge fan of that show, so Flick got to make the obligatory "guess who I'm standing 10 feet away from?" call home to his wife. (I'm not sure if Flick made a similar call when chatting with Jimmy Jean-Louis of the TV show "Heroes" because I wasn't there for that.)

As the game went along, and Flick and I proved to be nowhere near competently knowledgeable about celebrity affairs, we came to rely on Dunny's 21-year-old sister, Whitney, and her group of friends. This support system came to be known as "Whitneypedia."

When the referee blows the final whistle, it is customary to see an on-field jersey swap or prayer circle. On this day, however, the musicians involved in this match introduced the world to the concept of the postgame on-field cigarette circle. As veteran Crew observers, Flick and I probably haven't seen anything like that since the glory days of Silvio Rudman.

The best part of the evening came when Dunny brought Mr. Junk over and introduced him to everyone. Mr. Junk greeted Dunny's wife, mom, and sister with a peck on each cheek. Then Dunny gave the following classic introduction: "Gilles, this is Flick. He likes three kisses." And Flick promptly received three kisses, although he would later taunt, "I got 50% more kisses than Whitney."

Oh, and for those who remember Dunny talking about his stepdad back in those 2003 Notebooks, I got to meet the infamous Roger. He told me that now that he's hit his 50s, his pimp hand isn't as strong as it used to be. I think he was just trying to set me at ease. Or to get me to lower my guard.

Apart from Mr. Junk, I didn't meet or talk to any of the actual celebrities. But I did meet and talk with a soccer blogging celebrity, Bruce McGuire of du Nord. If you haven't already bookmarked his blog, do so. It's a tremendous one-stop shop with links to all of the vital soccer stories of the day. Bruce is an enthusiastically friendly man, and it was a pleasure to meet him after all this time.

I met Bruce on the way to the HUFC afterparty at the HDC's stadium club. I have a feeling that most anything Dunny does in life is followed by an afterparty. It was fun to spend time BSing with Dante and Dunny like the old days.

On our way to drop Dunny off at home afterward, he let loose with the following zinger from the back seat: "Hey Flick, are the cookies done baking yet, or can we turn down the heat in here?"

Once we dropped Dunny off, Flick and I headed to In 'N Out Burger for some burgers. Although Whitneypedia informed us about the top-secret menu that apparently everybody who's cool already knows about, we just stuck to the normal menu posted on the wall. (I believe one of the secret menu items that Whitneypedia told us about was called "Animal Style", and if you order your combo Animal Style, they will just throw all the burger ingredients and fries into a mountainous glop of random food. Perhaps they even pour your Coke on top of the whole mess, like carbonated gravy. We don't know though, because we ordered our meals Human Style.)

Wow...this blog entry is petering out in a hurry. I am tired. I can't believe MLS Cup is just hours away. Guess I'll try to get some sleep, although it may be tough to come by.

Dunny (left) with actor Donal Logue after the Hollywood United charity match.
(Photo courtesy of Brian Dunseth / TheOriginalWinger.com)

Meanwhile, Dunny was kind enough to provide photographic evidence of an "Animal Style" meal at In-N-Out Burger. Whitneypedia wasn't lying.
(Photo by Brian Dunseth)

A "Flick-On" About MLS Cup Eve

In my blogging about that Saturday before MLS Cup, I overlooked one very pertinent scene regarding my mood heading into MLS Cup Sunday. Thankfully, my good buddy Flick captured the moment in his own blog.

Flick wrote:

"The moment I realized that the nervousness and excitement was greater than expected was when Sirk and I went to In-N-Out after the postgame party on Saturday night. Whether it be a serious discussion of the game's events or me dicking on somebody or something, Sirk and I always easily slip into conversation. In-N-Out, though, was a completely different story. The conversation was a series of starts and stops with most stops leading to some variation of, 'I can't believe that the Crew are playing in MLS Cup tomorrow.'

"We tried to discuss the game, how we thought it would play out, what we thought the Crew needed to do to win the title. But really, in the end, the only thing we could say was, 'I can't believe that the Crew are playing in MLS Cup tomorrow.'

"It was like two kids talking on Christmas Eve, trying to discuss the newest Star Wars toy, but really just filling dead air as they think about the next day."

The Redondo Beach In-N-Out Burger probably deserves some sort of historical marker plaque for being the place where Flick and I struggled to converse for the first and only time in almost a decade of friendship. (Photo by Stefani Miglioranzi)

LA Blog: It's Here

November 23, 2008

Today is MLS Cup. And the Crew are playing in it.

I've known that for a while now, and have actually been quite immersed in that fact since Thursday, but this morning it suddenly feels *real*.

The skies in Manhattan Beach are cloudy, but that's not stopping golfers from taking their whacks at the course outside my hotel window. And it's not going to stop the Massive Bananas from playing the game *they* love at the Home Depot Center. Today, the men of the Columbus Crew can make their own sunshine.

A few random MVP notes...

Crew radio man and undercover Broadway talent agent Neil Sika wanted to know if Guillermo Barros Schelotto was the only league MVP not to make the All-Star team.

Amazingly, the answer is no. Just last year, D.C. United's Luciano Emilio was the league's MVP and not only did not make the All-Star team, but he didn't even get one of those fake, collective bargaining mandated "inactive All-Star" slots that Guille was awarded.

All other league MVPs started that year's All-Star game, except for the Dallas Burn's Jason Kreis in 1999. He came off the bench and played 45 minutes.

Well. I have to meet Merz for breakfast, so we'll just wrap this one up now. I will try not to confuse Craig at breakfast, like I did with this conversation yesterday morning while watching OSU-Michigan...

Graphic shows OSU has 81 yards of offense, while Michigan has minus-1 yard.

SS: Wow, OSU has minus-81 times the offense of Michigan.

CM: (Staring at me.)

SS: Minus-1 times minus-81 equals 81. So, technically, OSU has minus-81 times the yardage that Michigan does.

CM: Don't ever do that to me again this early in the morning.

Well, off to breakfast, and then the HDC. May it be a glorious day in Crew history.

Wyatt's Winning Ways

I don't recall melting Craig's mind at breakfast. There was no math involved this time, other than me mentally calculating how much money I had been saving by mooching off of his hotel's free breakfast each morning. Mostly we discussed how strange it was that a team on which we have invested so much time and effort, and so many thoughts and words, was on the cusp of winning a title. Who wouldn't feel good about being along for that ride? What writer wouldn't want the opportunity to tell that story? And with this particular group, how could you help but want for them to finish the job? Journalistic objectivity applies to the printed page, not what's held in the heart.

After breakfast, we went back up to Merz's room so he could get ready. As I sat on the couch watching TV, I received a text message from the nefarious numbers runner known as Z-man. As big a Crew fan as there is, Z could not make the trip to Los Angeles for MLS Cup. He and his wife Janice had recently welcomed their first child into the world on September 10, and in the early days of parenthood, Z felt he could not shirk is fatherly and husbandly duties in order to make a cross-country trek, even for the Crew's first MLS Cup appearance. I found his devotion to family to be every bit as admirable as his baby-making schedule was ill-timed. (Then again, at that point, who in Columbus had ever realistically plotted childbirth around MLS Cup?)

While Z could not be there in person, he was certainly there in spirit. As was his son. My phone displayed a photograph of Wyatt Coakley Zartman, on the 74th day of his life, cloaked in his father's Crew scarf, awaiting MLS Cup as if it were his birthright.

(Photo by Andy Zartman)

Sirk's MLS Cup Notebook:
Columbus Crew 3, New York Red Bulls 1

Match date: Sunday, November 23, 2008

Match note: MLS Cup 2008

Scoring:

31: CLB Moreno 1 (Schelotto 4)

51: NY Wolyniec 2 (Richards 2)

53: CLB Marshall 2 (Schelotto 5)

82: CLB Hejduk 1 (Schelotto 6, Gaven 1)

Attendance: 27,000

Crew's playoff status: 2008 MLS Cup champions

At about 11:30 p.m. Sunday night, I sat on a couch outside the entrance to the Manhattan Beach Marriott, second-hand smoking Mark McCullers' victory cigar. As the Crew's president & general manager proudly puffed away, technical director Brian Bliss and V.P. of corporate sales & broadcasting Chad Schroeder delivered punchline after punchline, while PR Director Dave Stephany and I served as a giddy laugh track. Team photographer Greg Bartram was moved to bouts of I-love-you-man sentimentality.

During a rare quiet moment, Dave turned to me and said, "Sirk, I don't want to alarm you, but the hat on your head says 'Champions.'"

It's easy to make fun of the Cleveland guy. For good measure, I looked at my hat anyway. It did, in fact, say "MLS Cup 2008 Champions" directly above a Columbus Crew logo. I don't know that I was alarmed so much as confused. As a Clevelander, I am not used to this sort of thing. Seasons end with a burst of profanity, a despairing lament, or an apathetic shrug, not giddiness. Couches are kicked rather than lounged upon. Drinks are for drowning sorrows, not lubricating laughter. Any smoke clouds wafting through the air are emitted from the ears and nostrils, not by special-occasion stogies.

But this was different. I was a stranger in a strange land.

I had two very interesting conversations in the days leading up to the game. After witnessing the tail end of the Crew's laugh-filled practice and media session on Friday, a Los Angeles Galaxy staffer asked me if the team was always this hyper. I was taken aback for a second because it never occurred to me that the Crew's behavior was anything but normal. I had to explain that the Crew are a very loose bunch and this was nothing out of the ordinary for them. Rather than a team flipping out on the big stage, what he was witnessing was a team not tightening up on the big stage.

The other conversation happened Saturday, when a reporter asked me if the Crew were overconfident.

"It's only overconfidence if they lose," I said.

But the reporter offered some seemingly valid points. There was a lot of talk about "when" the Crew win on Sunday, not "if" they win. Questions about the Red Bulls were often dismissed with an explanation that the Crew were focused on their own game and if they play as they are capable, they would win.

"But that's how they've been all year," I countered. "They never think they are going to lose. Some call it arrogance, although Sigi's favorite euphemism is 'being confident in your abilities.' How do you think they come back as often as they do? Nothing bothers them because they honestly think they are going to win every game, and that the result is totally up to them."

The reporter agreed, but just wanted to double check. It was a weird build up to the game. It seemed that everyone was grasping for some sort of reason that the game would or could be close. The "New York is a Cinderella team of destiny" angle had been played for all it was worth, so people were feeling out alternatives. The theory of "Crew hubris" was starting to float around, but it never gained much traction.

In my informal, unscientific survey in the day or two leading up to the match, I found only one person who predicted that the Crew would score fewer than three goals.[178] And that journalist had the Crew winning 2-1.

But the New York Giants were heavier underdogs in January's Super Bowl.[179] That's why they play the games. And as the Red Bulls' previous victims could attest, soccer is the cruelest game of them all.

---

[178] And people think reporters don't know what they are talking about.

[179] The wild-card Giants stunned the 18-0 New England Patriots, 17-14.

Chad Marshall exits the team bus in the bowels of the Home Depot Center, prepared for the biggest game of his Crew career. (Photo by Greg Bartram / Columbus Crew)

Meanwhile, Crew owner Clark Hunt stops by tailgate parties to thank Crew fans for making the trip to Los Angeles to support the team. (Photo by Mike Flickinger)

It's a funny thing when that first whistle blows. Suddenly, it's just a soccer match. The week's worth of hype and over-analysis instantly dissolves, and it's just two teams kicking a ball back and forth, just like it has been all year. I think it's different when watching on TV. On TV, you KNOW it's MLS Cup and that it's a big deal. But in person, the start of the game is almost anticlimactic. The game starts and it's just... a game.

That's how it felt to me, at least. Well, until things really got going. But in those first few minutes, it felt strangely humdrum. Just another game. Then again, that was the Crew's approach all week. Maybe it rubbed off on me.

Then I was hit with a dose of the unexpected. Although Frankie Hejduk warned it wasn't going to play out that way, everyone assumed New York would follow the game plan that got them here: absorb enormous amounts of pressure and attempt to capitalize with their lethal counterattack. Then absorb more pressure and let the goalposts work their late-game magic.[180]

Instead, New York came out and attacked. They controlled possession. They won nearly every loose ball. They kept the Crew pinned in their own end.

According to Crew coach Sigi Schmid, the Crew's objective was to lure New York out of their tried and true game plan, but it backfired because it went too far. "I think we gave New York a little too much space in the first half," he said. "That was partly by design because we wanted to bring them out of their shell a little bit, so they couldn't sit back and counter. But we dropped back too much. They did a good job of spreading the game around, and we let the field get too big which left too much space for Brad Evans and Brian Carroll to cover."

Fortunately for the Crew, the Red Bulls never put a shot on goal, although William Hesmer was forced to command his box on corners and crosses, which he did with the utmost conviction. Still, the Red Bulls had their chances, such as John Wolyniec's 20-yarder, Kevin Goldthwaite's glancing header, and Juan Pablo Angel's 14-yard half-volley, but none of their attempts were on frame.

And then the Red Bulls got a taste of their own medicine.

---

[180] New York surrendered 24 shots, including three that hit the post and stayed out, in their 1-0 victory over Real Salt Lake in the Western Conference final.

Danny O'Rourke marks New York's star striker, Juan Pablo Angel. Despite the Red Bulls' chances, the Crew's defense did not yield a shot on goal in the first half.
(Photo by Andy Mead / YCJ)

"Goldthwaite, toss in....Angel posting up on the left of the six...cleared out, Evans 30 yards from the Crew goal, but New York still finds the possession....van den Bergh battles with Gaven and Schelotto. Schelotto dispossesses on the sideline, leads it up to Moreno. He doesn't have the numbers, so he will try to outpace Jimenez here...running right at him...into the area...his right-footed shot...HE'S GOT A GOAL! IT SLIPPED BY CEPERO! ONE-OH TO THE CREW IN THE THIRTY-FIRST!" – **Neil Sika, 610 WTVN**

Two individual efforts. All it took was two phenomenal individual efforts to turn the game on its ear.

The first effort came from Guillermo Barros Schelotto, whose wizardry somehow kept the ball alive along the right sideline. As Dave van den Bergh attempted to shepherd the ball over the line for a New York throw-in, Schelotto snuck up from behind, reached his right leg between van den Bergh's, stopped the ball on the line, and pulled it back into the field of play. As the Red Bulls all raised their hands lobbying for a throw-in, Guille played a seemingly harmless ball up the sideline to Alejandro Moreno.

Moreno did the rest. Alejandro Moreno brings a lot of things to the table, but nobody has ever accused the Venezuelan of being a speedy, open-field, face-to-face, attack-dribbling menace. Yet he attacked Jimenez on the dribble and was able to get into the box. And while Jimenez routed Moreno wide for a poorly-angled shot, Moreno set a low drive that ticked off the fingertips of the overcommitted Cepero, then trickled an inch inside the far post.

"I was trying to give Guillermo an option," Moreno said. "When the defender allowed me to turn and go at him, I was thinking I could beat him full speed toward the end line. Then I saw Cepero was shaded to the near post, so I thought I could get the far post and I was able to do that."

Soccer is a game of inches and, with mere inches to work with, Schelotto and Moreno reminded us all that soccer is also a game of precision.

Coming out after halftime, the Red Bulls were in an unenviable position. Time and time again, it has been proven that scoring a goal against the Massive Bananas is akin to rolling up the Sunday paper and swatting at a beehive.

In the 51st minute, John Wolyniec thumped the honeycomb piñata. Dane Richards, whose dazzling dribbling ability is one of New York's scariest weapons, wove some magic amidst four Crew defenders at the edge of the penalty area. He then slotted a perfect little pass into the path of Wolyniec, who fought off Frankie Hejduk, slid to the ground, and redirected the ball under the paw of Hesmer. It was the type of gritty, goalmouth battle that has been Wolyniec's forte in his 10 MLS seasons, and it resulted in the biggest goal of his career.

"It could have been a deflating moment," said Crew defender Danny O'Rourke, "but we didn't let that happen all year, so… I mean, we were a little bit pissed off that it happened, but we are so confident in our abilities that we knew we would get it back."

So therein lays the ironic futility of the moment. What was needed to give the Red Bulls life all but sealed their doom.

"53rd minute….ball-in…HEADER! TWO-ONE! …MARSHALL!" – **Dwight Burgess, 610 WTVN**

In the northwest corner of the Home Depot Center, the New York fans jubilantly celebrated their team's equalizing goal, as oblivious as a group of frisky summer campers in a horror flick.[181] At the exact same time, in the northeast corner, the SoCal Nordecke was bowing and chanting "Guillermo" as the great Schelotto hovered over a corner kick.

Cue the chainsaw music.

What happened next was textbook. Schelotto's swerving cross met Chad Marshall in stride, nailed Mashall in the temple, and rocketed past Cepero and into the back of the net.

"Right after they scored, Chad scored that header, which stopped the gray hairs from growing in a bit," Duncan Oughton mused.

"I asked Chad, 'Which one you want?'" said Brad Evans, regarding which runs the players would make, "and he just said, 'I got this.' I don't know that he called his goal, but he definitely called his intent to win that ball and get his shot."

"We seem to have a knack for scoring goals in bunches or after the other team scores, so I thought I'd keep that going," said Marshall. "Guillermo served a great ball and I made the right run… it's pretty much the same as always. I am surprised it got through all those people. I didn't even see it until the last second, and luckily it stayed on frame and didn't hit the goalkeeper."

The goal would prove to be the game-winner, capping a miraculous season for Marshall. One year removed from potentially career-ending concussion headaches, Marshall not only won Defender of the Year, but scored an iconic equalizer over Brian McBride in the Eastern Conference final, then headed home the deciding goal in MLS Cup.

"Chad has grown by leaps and bounds," said Schmid. "I don't see how Bob Bradley can look past him anymore with the national team. He's a guy that definitely deserves a solid look. He's matured as a player and, on the offensive end, on set pieces, there's obviously not a player who's a better target in the league than Chad Marshall is right now."

---

[181] Sweet! When footnoting the Eastern Conference Final Notebook, I apparently recycled this analogy from the MLS Cup Notebook. It's like time-warp self-plagiarism. The one you read first was the rip-off of the one you read just now.

Chad Marshall unleashes a roar after scoring what would be the game-winning goal.
(Photo by Andy Mead / YCJ)

Marshall and teammates celebrate in front of a delirious SoCal Nordecke.
(Photo by Wade Jackson / YCJ)

Watching the game in the radio booth poses the occasional challenge, such as trying to afford several people a view of the action at all times. Neil and Dwight were obviously seated at the very front, so they had the undisturbed view that their job requires. But when standing a few feet behind the announcers, the booth's side walls cut off end views. So Mark McCullers, Brian Bliss, Chad Schroeder and I developed an elaborate movement scheme designed to let everyone follow the match. As the action moved from one end of the field to the other, some of us would clear space so that others could overlap to fill that space and acquire a clear view. Our system soon became second nature, and it was as precise and fluid as any world-renowned ballet.

I am even prouder of the fact that we adapted when Bill McDermott joined us in the second half. Within minutes, we adjusted to a five-man shuffle. This really has nothing to do with anything, but I just wanted it to be known that the Crew organization is capable of holding its shape, moving in tandem, and making smart tactical adjustments even while watching the game in the radio booth.

The highlight of the booth experience happened in the 78th minute, when Schelotto collected a pass from Moreno at the top of the 18, held the ball for what seemed like an eternity while picking his spot, and then sent the game-clinching shot toward the upper corner of the goal... where it clanged off the crossbar.

Bliss leaped high into the air and let loose with an extremely loud expletive. The rest of us immediately doubled over in laughter and starting cracking jokes about how close we might have come to incurring the wrath of the FCC.[182]

"Aw, it was just some crazy fan," Bliss said with a dismissive wave of his hand.

For the record, Bliss's outburst wasn't captured by either of the booth mics, so it was a moot point.[183] Also soon to be a moot point was Bliss's despair over a clinching goal.

---

[182] "Blissy just cost WTVN $500,000!"

[183] I cannot tell you how crushed I was upon listening to the tape. I was hoping that since I was looking for it, I would at least be able to catch the slightest bit of Bliss's four-syllable outburst in the background. Alas, I could not. So disappointing.

"Rogers, a beautiful ball over the defense to the weak side, 1-v-1. It's Moreno, now working with Gaven. It's a bad pass, but Moreno wins it back....Gaven plays it to Schelotto...HEJDUK!...HEADERRRRRRRRR... IT'S IN! THREE-ONE!" –
Dwight Burgess, 610 WTVN

In the 82nd minute, the Crew wrote their own Hollywood ending. Their MVP saved his best for last and stamped the game with a jaw-dropping display of creative vision. At the other end of the scoop pass was the Heart of the Crew, the captain and the man who gleefully tailgated with the fans in October. While holding the ball outside the edge of the box, Schelotto found the improbable and sharp-angled run of Hejduk, and Frankie nodded the ball past a hard-charging Cepero. The ball bounced into the net as Hejduk rushed to the corner to celebrate with the reserves who were warming up on the sideline.[184]

"I don't know what Frankie was doing up there, to be fair, but Frankie has a knack for that sort of thing and Guillermo can find anyone," said Evans. "Frankie did a good job to finish that goal. It took guts. I thought Cepero was going to crush him, but Frankie got to it first. That was huge."

Frankie Hejduk celebrates the clinching goal. (Photo by Wade Jackson / YCJ)

---

[184] Some had misinterpreted this as Frankie rushing to celebrate in front of New York's fans. This was not the case. Frankie doesn't score often, but when he does, he tends to rush to the reserves to celebrate with them since they are part of the team too.

It's not that common to find a team's right back making runs into the opposing penalty area while protecting a one-goal lead with nine minutes to play in the championship final, but that's why it's been so much fun watching players like Guille and the Dude.

"Fortunately, Guillermo has eyes in the back of his head and he saw me make that run," said Hejduk. "I've made that run before and people are like, 'What in the hell is he making that run for? What is he doing up there?' Well, now you know. When you have a guy who can see those runs, it makes me look good, because half the time even I don't know why I make those runs. But he made me look good on that one. It was an incredible ball. That third goal took the wind out of their sails."

"Frankie scored an amazing header," said Oughton. "It was a perfect ending. He's the captain and he's the guy banging it in at the end? Amazing."

After the Hejduk goal, it was all over except the shouting. And that shouting came from the proud members of the Big Nasty Fan Club. The 96 friends and family of Steven "Big Nasty" Lenhart started chanting "We want Lenhart!" in the game's waning moments. Sigi was happy to oblige, running the big forward out there in the 90th minute. Lenhart promptly won a header at midfield, making it worth Schmid's while.

"Whether it's one minute or 90 minutes, I got to be out there," Lenhart said with his ever-present smile. "I even touched the ball once! The fan support has been tremendous all year and it was awesome to get out there in front of my family and the people I love. It meant so much to me."

And if it meant more to him than his clutch goals have meant to the Crew, that would be saying something. The goofy, fro-haired kid from the college that nobody heard of quickly made a name for himself in his rookie campaign. In limited playing time, he banged home four goals, including a game-winner and a pair of last-gasp equalizers. And then he scored a series-altering equalizer in the Crew's opening playoff game.

There's no doubting that Steven Lenhart earned his golden moment in the California sun.

Earlier this month, longtime Cleveland Indians broadcaster Herb Score passed away. Though I never met the man, Herb was like an extra grandfather to me. He was the voice of Indians baseball and I spent most of the summer evenings of my youth listening to Herb lovingly bumble his way through broadcasts.

As has often been said, in his 30-plus years as a broadcaster, Herb Score watched more bad baseball than anyone. It took until the final three years of his broadcast career before the Indians even contended. They won two American League pennants, but lost the World Series each time. Herb's final broadcast was the infamous Game 7 loss to the Florida Marlins in the 1997 World Series. I have never forgiven Jose Mesa, not because he blew the World Series for Cleveland, but because he didn't give Herb Score a chance to make that championship call.

Herb was on my mind as the clock ticked down at the Home Depot Center. I was standing directly behind Dwight Burgess, the Voice of the Crew. Dwight hasn't been around nearly as long as Herb had, and the soccer over the years has been nowhere near as awful as early-60s to early-90s Indians baseball, but I didn't want the Crew to be playing in MLS Cup 2033, while everyone was rooting for Dwight as much as the Crew.

Neil Sika (left) and Dwight Burgess (right) got to call history. (Photo by Steve Sirk)

The last of the original Crew employees, Dwight has personally seen more Crew soccer than anyone. Through radio or television, he has been in our cars or living rooms week after week for 13 seasons. On April 13, 1996, he called the Crew's inaugural 4-0 victory over D.C. United. And now, on November 23, 2008, he called history…

"After the goal kick, Lenhart heads the ball down for Alejandro Moreno. Ale accelerates toward the corner flag and holds the ball there. Knocked out of bounds. Throw-in Columbus. The Hunt Sports Group is gathering behind the Crew bench. Clark Hunt, who referenced his father, Lamar, prior to kickoff, is about to accept the championship trophy. The balance of this one is on the wristwatch of the referee AND THERE IT IS!...THE COLUMBUS CREW ARE CHAMPIONS OF MAJOR LEAGUE SOCCER!........(long stretch of crowd noise, letting the cheers tell the story)… Thirteen long years, the Crew faithful have stood by their team…. At the start of the 2008 season, head coach Sigi Schmid said, 'Our goal is to make the playoffs.' Sigi, you did it! You made the playoffs!...You won the Supporters' Shield!...And you are the champions of Major League Soccer!"

At the final whistle, **Danny O'Rourke** leaps into the arms of **William Hesmer** as teammates rush off the bench to join the celebration. (Photo by Wade Jackson / YCJ)

The players mobbed the field. Black and gold confetti filled the air. The Crew's captain was misidentified by the commissioner of Major League Soccer, Ivan Gadzidis*.

(* For people reading this years from now, the MLS Commisioner in 2008 is actually Don Garber. He's the guy who incorrectly named Guillermo Barros Schelotto as the Crew's captain, instead of Frankie Hejduk. In the words of John Harkes during the ABC telecast, "Poor Frankie.")

Schelotto may not have been captain, but he became the third player in MLS history to collect the regular-season and MLS Cup MVP awards in the same season. Tony Meola accomplished the feat with the Kansas City Wizards in 2000, while Carlos Ruiz did it with Schmid's LA Galaxy in 2002.

"He's the MVP," said Brad Evans. "That's the bottom line. If you had to pick one player from our team, it would be him because he can see the whole field and knows exactly what to do in every situation. Whenever he touches the ball, he knows exactly what he's going to do. That's something I can learn from him, and it's something the whole team can cherish about having him play for us."

Guillermo Barros Schelotto accepts the MLS Cup MVP trophy from MLS Commissioner Don Garber. Guille became the third player to capture the regular season and MLS Cup MVPs in the same year. (Photo by Wade Jackson / YCJ)

Captain Frankie Hejduk shows off the big prize, the newly minted Anschutz Trophy, awarded to the MLS Cup champions for the very first time.
(Photo by Andy Mead / YCJ)

As the players bounced up and down on the podium, which was anchored more securely than the one that started sinking in Columbus 10 days earlier, Schelotto waved his arms like a conductor, attempting to lead his teammates in a rousing rendition of the Nordecke's "We Love You" song.

Then the team made its way to the SoCal Nordecke to show the fans their newest prize. Frankie Hejduk and Duncan Oughton, Heart & Soul, held the trophy together and kissed it in front of the fans. After weeks of chanting "we're not done yet," the diehards squinted in the reflection of the shiny trophy and chanted "we're all done now."

Hedjuk and Oughton, Heart & Soul, kiss the Cup. (Photo by Andy Mead / YCJ)

Frankie Hejduk and Duncan Oughton lift the Cup in front of the SoCal Nordecke. In the lower right corner, Nesta Hejduk, Frankie's 10-year-old son, raises his fist in triumph. (Photo by Andy Mead / YCJ)

And then came the chants for the scarf-wearing architect of the Massive Bananas. "Sigi! Sigi! Sigi!" Schmid ambled over and took his turn hoisting the trophy.

"It was special," he said of the moment. "I think we formed a very special bond with the Nordecke and all three supporters' groups. It was great to hear that from them, but I am happy for the fans, happy for the city and happy for Warzycha, Lapper, Dante Washington, Yeagley, Clark and all those guys. I know this meant a lot to them."

It meant a lot to a lot of people.

Duncan Oughton is the longest-tenured Crew player. He fought back from a potentially career-ending knee injury that needed experimental surgery, just so he could do his part for the club he loves. Unfortunately, his part didn't involve much playing time in 2008, but to a man, the players insist that he is an irreplaceable ingredient to the Crew's locker room, bringing both leadership and laughter. And now he's a champion.

"It's amazing," he said while wandering the field in his championship hat and t-shirt. "I've been waiting for it for so long. I mean, look at it. It's amazing. The organization has been waiting for so long and I feel like a big part of the organization, so it's an amazing feeling. It's everything I thought and more."

As the one player whose career has bridged the gap between the Crew originals and the Massive Bananas, Oughton knew that the former Crew men would be watching intently. "Those guys will be happiest guys in the world," he said of the Crew's former players. "It's always been a tight organization full of good, good people, so I think this is a little bit for them."

One of those former players was assistant coach Mike Lapper.

"I was just talking to Dante and we said it's surreal," Lapper said. "I've been here since 1997 and we never made it to the big dance. It's been a great privilege for me to learn under Sigi and Robert. I couldn't get it done as player, but it's finally happened as a coach. I am so proud to be a part of this group. The funny thing is, we're a real family. You see everybody out here with their kids. Team bonding has been great since day one. It's not just the guys that are on the field. You need a core group of players that are going to show up and play hard at practice every day, even if they know they probably won't see the field. And those guys brought it, which made the first team better."

Pat Noonan took part in his fourth consecutive MLS Cup final. He was on the losing end of the previous three with the New England Revolution. At long last, he can ditch the simian backpack.[185]

"It feels a little different," Noonan said while clutching his gold medal. "It's a lot heavier. It's a great feeling to celebrate with your teammates and the organization. I've only been here for half a year, but I could immediately tell what this team was about and what this organization was about. It's well deserved."

Noonan was an established star in MLS when he left for Europe last winter. When he came to Columbus, he found himself in the position of not only having to integrate himself into a winning team, but doing so as a bench

---

[185] Someone later commented that Simian Backpack would be a good name for a rock band. I think Dave Barry would agree.

player. It takes a special kind of person to pull that off with grace, and Noonan did it.

"It was great to come into a team that was in the midst of a playoff run," he said. "Obviously it would have been nice to be starting more, but I was able to put my minutes in and contribute when called upon, and I couldn't be happier with how it all turned out. I supported these guys the way they would have supported me. The great thing about this team is that no matter if you were a starter, a reserve, or one of the guys who didn't dress, we all worked hard together and it's great to have this type of group atmosphere as we celebrate the victory."

Danny O'Rourke is a champion. He won a high school state championship at Crew Stadium. He won an NCAA national championship at Crew Stadium. And now he's won an MLS Cup championship while playing for his hometown Crew. What was he thinking as he celebrated on the field?

"I'm thinking that I'm up by 40 on Andy Gruenebaum, but I'm a bit nervous because he's still got two guys left," he said.

You. Have. Got. To. Be. Effin'. Kidding. Me. He hasn't even left the confetti-strewn field and he's already got his fantasy football updates? [186]

"Of course," he said. "Terrell Owens got 30½ points for me today, so that's just icing on the cake."

So, um, OK. Once Danny received and digested his fantasy football updates, what was he thinking in terms of the Crew's championship?

"You always talk about it, and winning the title is obviously the ultimate goal, but when we started, our goal was to make the playoffs," he said. "And we did that, let alone win the Supporters' Shield, set a record for Columbus, and win MLS Cup. It hasn't sunk in yet, but we have the rest of our lives to reflect on it.

"This is for guys like Mike Lapper, Robert Warzycha and my old college coach Todd Yeagley," O'Rourke continued. "It's been great talking to guys like that. This is for everybody. This is for the city, the organization, and all the players that have ever come through. We're just fortunate to be the

---

[186] This is seriously one of the most dumbfounding things I have ever experienced as a reporter. It's so....Danny. He actually had one of the reserves (I think he said it was Brian Plotkin) keeping track of his fantasy team for him while he was on the field trying to win an MLS Cup.

team to win it for the Crew, but this is for everyone back home in Columbus and for anyone who has ever cared about the Crew."

Walking off the field, reserve midfielder Cory Elenio looked at his gold medal, smiled, and said, "I'm one for one!"

You sure are, kid. And while you entire career lies before you, I'm glad you're savoring the moment. If he hasn't already, I'm sure Frankie could tell you a thing or two about that.

Schmid told the following story of his postgame encounter with Hejduk:

"Frankie said, 'We got it! We got it!' I said, 'No, you got it,' He said, 'We wouldn't have gotten it without you.' It means a lot. I've known Frankie since he was 17 years old and I recruited him out of high school. He's the same dude, as he would say. He's always going to bring you a lot of energy. For him to win the championship is tremendous, as it is for all the guys in this room. Alejandro broke down in tears when we hugged, because we won the championship again. But for Frankie, it's special. When you get to that age, you want to win that title and you want to know what that tastes like."

Hejduk spoke excitedly when asked about winning his first pro championship at the age of 34. "It's one of the best feelings because it ended in a championship," he said. "Making the World Cup quarterfinals when nobody expected us to was awesome, but winning a championship is second to none.

"This has been a long time coming for the Hunts," he continued. "Their family believed in soccer in America when there were times when people weren't sure which way it was going to go. They kept it alive, so to give them a championship, and to bring it back to Columbus, where they built the first soccer-specific stadium, is incredible. It's great for the city too. They've always believed in us, and they have been waiting for us to get over that hump and into the final. And now that we got into the final and won it, it's unbelievable."

Speaking of the Hunts, Clark and Dan Hunt were in fine spirits, as one might expect.

"Being in the sports business gives you an appreciation for championships," Clark said. "They're very hard to get. We have been in this business a very long time, and the key is that when you have the chance to play in a championship game, to go out there and get it. There are teams that may get to the championship but never win one. Nobody remembers who finishes second. For example, in the first eight or so years of the Crew, we went to four conference finals, which is actually a very good record. But we never made that next step. Today, they took it. They capped off one of the finest seasons in MLS history, in terms of both regular season and playoffs. We got the double, and we're thrilled."

Reporters asked what his father, Lamar, would say if he were alive to see this moment. "He would definitely give the credit to the players and coaches," Clark said. "It was never about him. It was always about the organization, and the people that made it up. That's not only the guys on the field, but the front office. He would tip his cap to both groups."

"I am overwhelmed with joy," said Dan Hunt. "This is for our dad. We miss him so much. This is for him. He always dreamed of seeing the Crew win a championship."

Dan then leaned in and dropped this tidbit on me. "I hinted at this when we talked yesterday, but I kept a lid on it. But I was in those Chicago Bulls' locker rooms in the 1990s, and this team is every bit as special as those Bulls teams were. I have never seen a group of guys fight for each other like this team has. We are all so proud of them."

So how about that special locker room? Sigi talked about what he was looking for when rebuilding the Crew into a champion.

"What you look for are different components," he explained. "Once we got Alejandro, who could hold it up top, we knew where Guillermo would fit in. Then we knew we needed some wingers who could play with pace and pizzazz, which meant we needed two holding midfielders. But the main key to building a team is that you have to build a locker room. You need a locker room where guys enjoy playing with each other and for each other, and they enjoy coming to work every day.

"You've got to have a good locker room and players who buy into what you're doing and guys that are all on the same page," he said. "My last year in LA, that locker room ended up being destroyed, and not by my choice. You need that. Our locker room in Columbus is tremendous. Guys have fun and they come to work with a smile."

When building a locker room, the coach obviously needs his star players to get it. For example, Guillermo Barros Schelotto came in as an Argentine legend, but quickly adapted to his new league, club, and teammates.

"Guillermo's a different type of guy and he trains a little different," said Schmid. "I remember the week after he got here, Robert Warzycha looked at me and said, 'Are you sure?' [187] And I said, 'Yeah, I'm sure.' It's all about character. A good friend of mine knew Guillermo and vouched for his character. Somebody I knew also knew Guillermo and his family, so he vouched for my character, and it sort of became a marriage that way. One person was saying, 'Guillermo, this is a guy you will love playing for,' and another person was saying, 'Sigi, trust me, this is a guy you will enjoy having play for you.' It's been everything we hoped for. He's a great personality."

Just as importantly, Schmid said that the character of the team needs to extend well beyond the starting 11. "That's what I mean about this team," he said. "Guys like Duncan Oughton, or Jason Garey, or Stefani Miglioranzi…guys who either weren't on the field or even in the 18…they were always there for the guys. They always came and trained equally hard. I'm just so happy for a guy like Duncan, who has toiled so long for this club, to get the championship, the ring, and the trophy. It's just as much his as anyone else's."

Winning never gets old to Guillermo Barros Schelotto. He's an incurable hoarder of hardware. He humbly accepts individual accolades, as it is his duty to accept them, but he understands that legends are forged from the glory of team triumphs. Thus, it seems that his legend never stops expanding. The guy has won so many trophies that you'd half expect to wander into his house and find that he uses championship cups as wastepaper baskets. But that's not how Guillermo rolls. Every title is sacred.

---

[187] I get so angry when people twist this quote around to make it sound like Robert didn't want Guillermo here, or that he thought Guillermo was a terrible player, or anything else of that sort. Guillermo and the Crew were from two totally different worlds. In those first few days or weeks, I think it was natural to wonder if those two worlds would be able to blend together. But as Sigi said in the rest of his quote, the trust enabled each side to find common ground for the betterment of everyone. Guillermo readily adapted to the ways of his new team, and his new team adapted to his way of doing things. Unlike David Beckham, who seemed to exist in a separate universe from his Galaxy teammates, Schmid knew that given time, Schelotto would integrate himself into the team. And he did.

As Schelotto walked off the Home Depot Center pitch, Dave Stephany dusted off his limited Spanish and said, "Numero dieciocho!"

Schelotto gave him a quizzical look.

"That's 18, right?" Stephany asked. "18 championships?"

"19," Schelotto replied, without missing a beat.

Dave started running through the list. "One with Gimnasia, 16 with Boca (Juniors) and now this one…"

"One with national team," Schelotto interjected. "19."

Indeed, Schelotto was a member of Argentina's gold medal-winning team at the 1995 Pan American Games. And while Dave was referring to club titles, it's never wise to short-count a proud title junkie.

Earlier in the week, Stephany had some news for Schelotto. Dave had learned that Carlos Bianchi, Schelotto's famed coach during Guille's historic stint with Boca Juniors, planned to divert his family's vacation to Los Angeles so that he could personally watch Schelotto's attempt to conquer MLS. Bianchi was coach for nine of Schelotto's 16 Boca titles and the two hold each other in high esteem.

Dave informed Guillermo that Bianchi hoped to say hello to him either before or after the game and wanted to make sure that would be OK. Guille enthusiastically said it would be.

Bianchi's pending appearance was kept secret so as to avoid a crush of South American media and fans. He was furtively escorted into a private suite, and when the game was over, he was transported to an undisclosed location in the bowels of the Home Depot Center, where he and Guille could meet.

After meeting with Bianchi, Schelotto said, "I felt that we couldn't lose with him in the stands."

The scoreboard offered no evidence to the contrary.[188]

---

[188] I am sticking this random note here because I have some room at the bottom of the page. At 5:50pm EST, as I wandered the confetti-strewn field, I received the following text from my delirious friend Scot Sedley. I quote: "Ha! Holy shit! Holy shit! Yessprsprsprs!" I just feel that those triumphant words need to be preserved, excitable text typos and all.

Speaking of Argentines, let's not forget the fact that, including the playoffs, the Crew were 14-1-3 when Gino Padula patrolled the left side of the Crew's back line. While Padula begged Schelotto to win a title for him, it's not like he's accepting Schelotto's sloppy seconds.[189]

Schmid had a lot to say about Padula's performance in the title match. Padula was tasked with shutting down the speedy Dane Richards, one of New York's most dangerous weapons.

"I thought Gino did a good job with Dane Richards for the most part," Schmid said. "Dane's a dangerous player with good speed, but Gino's an experienced fullback who can play against guys with more pace than him. He knows how to get into the right positions. Sometimes people think speed has to match speed, but sometimes the fastest guys aren't the best defenders because they may not be the most aware or the most disciplined. Gino is very tactically disciplined. His positional play is very good. That helped him defend Dane today.

"He hurt himself early in the game, but there was no way he wanted to come out. He basically soldiered through. There was a little break in the first half and he came over and said, 'Don't take me out!'"

Gino Padula did well to defend New York's speedy Dane Richards (right).
(Photo by Andy Mead / YCJ)

---

[189] "Sloppy seconds" was a classic gaffe. I was really going for "hand me downs", but at the time I was writing this, NHL player Sean Avery was suspended for making a comment about how NHL players fall in love with his ex-girlfriends. Or, as he dubbed them, "sloppy seconds." Since I wrote this while recovering from the California Death Flu, my mind was a little foggy and I accidently garbled terms with the newsworthy events of the day. Oops.

William Hesmer caught me off guard. His on-field comments started out normal enough.

"It's a great feeling to see all your hard work come to fruition," he said. "To actually raise the trophy is kind of surreal." The birthday boy even said that the MLS Cup trophy was the best birthday present ever, trumping even those "sweet Batman and Superman costumes that I used to rock back in the day."

But after a brief moment of contemplation, he slipped this one in on me. "Honestly, I've got a little bit of sadness right now," he said. "There's no way this whole team stays together and it's been such a special year that I don't want it to end. The way MLS works, we are not going to be able to keep everybody together, so I am trying to soak it in, but there's some sadness knowing that some guys are going to end up going separate ways."

It's a universal truth of professional sports, but it seemed like a distant concern. But the truth is that it wasn't a distant concern. The reserve league had been discontinued, an expansion draft was days away, and the league's MVP, Coach of the Year and Defender of the Year all faced uncertain contract situations. While the core of the team will be back in 2009, the MLS Cup was truly the end of the line for that unique and special group known as the 2008 MLS Cup Champion Columbus Crew.

Moments later, I got an unexpected lump in my throat when Brad Evans told me, "This is the best feeling I've ever had, for sure. I never had a playoff experience at Irvine, so if this is what it feels like, I'd like to have a few more years of this, know what I mean?"

Ugh. For some time, based on roster composition and salary levels, I had assumed that Evans would be the player the Crew would most likely lose in the expansion draft. Suddenly, that draft was just three days away. And as it turned out, Evans was indeed the player selected by the Seattle Sounders. The lump in my throat was justified.

Once the Crew locker room was opened, it was party time. I had barely made it into the room when Jason Garey informed me, in no uncertain terms, that I needed a beer. Moments later, he returned and slapped an ice-cold can into my hand. At first I told him not to be insulted if I held on to it for a bit while I did interviews, but after watching most of the players drinking, I decided it would only be fair if I started drinking too, just to maintain the player/reporter relative-sobriety equilibrium.

Being free to rationalize on-the-job drinking is one of the major advantages of working for the team. Who was going to yell at me? My boss, who was drinking? My boss's boss, who was drinking? My boss's boss's bosses, who were drinking?

So I wandered around with a beer in one hand and a recorder in the other. I was in Walt Wheeler's idea of paradise.[190]

After mic-dropping on some of Hejduk's comments, I moved in to ask some questions of my own. The Crew's captain looked up at me with exhausted, puppy dog eyes.

"Dude, can I be done now?" he pleaded. "I'm really sorry, but I've been doing this since the game ended, and I just want to be done. Can I be done?"

I told him he's a champion, and that champions can be done whenever the hell they want.

"Thanks, dude," said the Heart of the Crew, with a quick clink of our beer cans. And with that, Hejduk walked across the room, collected his oldest son, and sat down in front of his locker. He wrapped his arms around Nesta and said some words into the 10-year-old's ear. And then father and son surveyed the joyous room from their embrace, soaking in every last detail of the moment. Together.

Nothing Frankie could have said into my recorder would have been as lasting or important as that.[191]

----

[190] Walt was a longtime media colleague who was known, on occasion, to have a few beers in the stands before heading to the postgame press conference. Good times. Walt moved out of Columbus, but is a Nordecke legend, making it back when he can. He was part of the SoCal Nordecke on MLS Cup Sunday, and I could have easily pictured him walking from locker to locker with a beer in his hand as I was that day.

[191] In a day filled with great and memorable moments, that may have been my favorite.

Nesta Hejduk produced an amusingly unique sign for his dad. Hours later, father and son would celebrate the Crew's championship together. (Photo by Mike Flickinger)

Boxes of iced champagne sat in the middle of the room, curiously untouched. Players were coming and going, getting their pictures formally taken with the Anschutz Trophy, so the champagne waited.

The players took the opportunity to shave off their playoff beards, but it wasn't as simple as removing them outright. Rather, the guys left Fu Manchus, porn 'staches and other ridiculous remnants on their faces.

Gaven and Moffat sport new facial hair. (Photo by Greg Bartram / Columbus Crew)

Somewhere between 60 and 90 minutes after the final whistle, the Crew finally convened in the center of the locker room and reach for the bubbly. Corks popped. Ice-cold champagne erupted in every direction, each bottle a mini vino Vesuvius. The players hopped up and down, singing the wordless "whoa-oa-oa-oa-oa" part of the Nordecke's "We Love You" song. Random screams of triumph filled in the gaps, as did giggled profanities when a few unlucky people found out how much champagne stings when it hits the eyes. (That's why team administrator Tucker Walther wore ridiculously oversized goggles that made him look like a hard-partying hornet.)

After the initial blasts of champagne had subsided, the team chanted "Speech! Speech! Speech!" until head coach Sigi Schmid made his way to the center of the room to address his men.

"No practice tomorrow!" he bellowed to a round of rambunctious cheers.

"I am very proud of you guys, not only for your effort, but for putting up with me," he continued. "I know what it means to the guys that were out there, but you don't know what this means to guys like Robert Warzycha, Mike Lapper...a guy like Dante Washington, who came all the way out here...and all the guys that played for the Crew in the past."

The team gave Robert, Lapper and Dante a huge ovation, while some players poured a little champagne in honor of those who had come before.

"You were all tremendous," Schmid went on. "Whether you were in the lineup or not in the lineup, you guys were great. Your attitude was super, and it was exemplified by Duncan Oughton the whole way through."

And with that, Oughton, the longest-tenured vet and Soul of the Crew, was surrounded by teammates who cheered wildly and honored him with his very own champagne shower.

Once that commotion died down, Sigi wrapped it up.

"Make sure you find guys with a little bit of design in them so they design you a nice (bleeping) ring!"

More wild applause.

"And since the Hunts are here, make sure they throw a few diamonds in there!"

Even more wild applause.

"From the bottom of my heart, and from the whole staff, I love you all. I love the effort that you put in. Congratulations to all of you!"

And then it was Sigi's turn to get soaked.

Scenes from the wild champagne celebration. Above, **Robbie Rogers** gets a good spray going. Below, it looks like **Greg's** camera took a few direct hits.
(Both photos by Greg Bartram / Columbus Crew)

Above, Stefani Miglioranzi tests the absorbency of Steven Lenhart's blond afro. Below, Jason Mathews, Frankie Hejduk, Mike Lapper, Duncan Oughton, and Ezra Hendrickson are soaked to the bone. (Both photos by Greg Bartram / Columbus Crew)

After the game, Schmid fielded so many questions about his future, it was almost as if he were standing in front of LeBron's locker when the Cleveland Cavaliers visit Madison Square Garden.

"I don't know where I'll be next season, to be honest," he said. "My contract expires at the end of this month. I didn't want to talk about it during the playoffs. The last offer came in two days before the playoffs, and I felt that was too late. I just wanted to get through the playoffs. Then I will make a decision that is best for my family and my future. For sure, the fans of Columbus will always have a very special place in my heart, and this team will always be special. It's a team I built. Yeah, there are some old guys there and the old guys stepped up today, but there are also a lot of young guys. If you look at that team, there are a lot of guys between 22 and 28 that are good players."

One thing is for certain—his rapid rebuilding of the Crew into a championship team increases his value to both the Crew and his most likely outside suitor, the expansion Seattle Sounders.

"I think a big thing for me over the years at UCLA is that we were so successful that people forgot that at one point, I had to build that UCLA program," he said. "When I came to the Galaxy, there were a lot of good players here, so it was like, 'Sigi took a good team and moved them on.' After that, I think people doubted that I could build a team. So now it's nice to be able to say that I can build a team, and that I remember how to do that." [192]

Clark Hunt was fully aware that there are some big issues on his plate. "Today is for the Cup, and tomorrow is the day we start worrying about 2009," he said. "We've got a great core of young players, and we're in good shape from a salary cap standpoint so that we can keep the core of the team together, so we're definitely thinking about repeating in 2009."

As for Schmid, Marshall and Schelotto, Hunt said, "It's our goal to have all three of them back. It's not easy to keep championship teams together, but I think all three of them want to be back in Columbus, and we have the financial resources to make it happen. We'll enjoy the victory tonight, and then 2009 starts tomorrow."

---

[192] It was this part that convinced me that Sigi was going to Seattle. If he hadn't already made up his mind, his subconscious was clearly steering him that way.

I reminded him that the fans had a message for him when he and his family visited the SoCal Nordecke before the game. (The fans chanted "Re-sign Sigi!")

Hunt chuckled. "It just shows that we have very smart fans."

Meanwhile, the locker room celebration continued. Schelotto is not much of a reveler, and it soon became apparent that he had hid in the fringes of the initial champagne celebration. Oughton and Padula would have none of that. They popped fresh bottles and rushed into the back locker room, where Schelotto was hiding out. "MVP! MVP! MVP!" screamed the Kiwi as he and Pirate Padula soaked the Most Valuable Player.

Soon after, the team began a rather strange chant: "Na-ked-cart-wheel!" They directed this chant at Chad Marshall, who immediately obliged his teammates' request.

"It's something I do sometimes to lighten up our spirits, so I am glad I could do it today in front of all the media," Marshall said, sardonically. "I can't wait to see how many internet sites it pops up on."

And just when it couldn't get any stranger, out came the clippers. There was Oughton, chasing down Schelotto. He cornered the legend and buzzed a lock of Guille's hair. Duncan then handed the clippers to Guillermo and instructed him to take his shot. Guille had obviously never worked clippers before, as he made a few tentative attempts at removing some of the Kiwi's hair, except the clippers were upside-down, or he moved the clippers in the wrong direction. Fortunately, teammates were willing to assist Guillermo, and soon he was politely removing chunks of hair from the Kiwi's head while everyone cheered.

Duncan then took control of the clippers and turned his eye toward the Holy Grail of hirsute perfection: Gino Padula. Spewing every Spanish swear word he could think of, Oughton raced after Padula as the Pirate screamed for mercy, throwing anyone and anything into the Kiwi's path. Padula may rely on guile, but had Dane Richards been brandishing clippers, the Pirate could have outrun him.

Oughton let Padula off the hook and soon the players took the beard concept one step further and started giving each other ridiculous haircuts. Oughton ended up with a terrific mullet, including an inch-deep bald divot on his hairline. Jason Garey was soon sporting a terrific Sling Blade hillbilly bowl-buzzcut. And strength and conditioning coach Steve Tashjian used the opportunity to reintroduce The Legend, his looped-around Mohawk-muttonchop-mustache combination.

Above, Duncan Oughton takes the clippers to Guillermo Barros Schelotto. Below, Guille politely and delicately returns the favor. (Both photos by Greg Bartram / Crew)

When the commotion finally wound down and the locker room began to clear out, I caught up with Crew President and GM Mark McCullers.

"I know it's a cliché, but it's hard to put it into words," he said. "My 10-year anniversary with this club will be Monday, as a matter of fact. I guess the 10-year anniversary is the trophy anniversary, but I hope it doesn't take 10 more for the next one.

"My satisfaction comes from seeing everybody else achieving the success," he continued. "It's so rewarding for me to see these guys. It's something that they are going to remember for the rest of their lives. I'm going to remember it as well, but one of the reasons I got into this business is the feelings of people at the stadium, and to know that you are delivering that experience and making them happy. Now I get a chance to do it not only with the fans, but also with the players and the rest of the organization. There's nothing like it. There's nothing like creating this type of experience and satisfaction for other people. It's great."

In a moment of sheer serendipity, I looked across the room and caught a glimpse of Dante Washington. He was standing in an inch-deep pool of champagne and ice that had collected on the floor. The "2008 MLS Cup Champions" hat on his head was nearly as crooked as the grin on his face.

Indeed, there's nothing like it.

McCullers told me that his daughter was obsessed with the idea of touching the Cup while they were out on the field. He told her that she would be able to touch it later.

She wanted to touch it right then, so he explained to her, "It's ours. We won it. We can touch it whenever we want."

"It's ours?" she asked, seeking clarification.

"Yes, we get to take it home with us," he said.

She thought for a moment, then asked, "How will we get it through security?"

A more pressing question might have been, "How will the Crew get it out of the stadium?"

As he prepared to leave the empty locker room, Dave Stephany wondered if anyone had grabbed the trophy, so he made his way to the room where the portraits with it were taken. There it still sat, so he went to collect the Crew's prize. But there was some uncertainty amongst its handlers as to whether the Crew could just take it. A flurry of cell phone and walkie talkie activity ensued.

Dave insisted that it should go with the team and explained that, on top of that, the club was hosting a victory reception at the hotel that evening and wanted to have the trophy at that celebration, as well. And, he stressed, the bus was ready to leave, so unless somebody actually stopped him, he was taking the trophy to the hotel, where it could be picked up later if need be.

And with that, Dave lugged the Anschutz Trophy out to the team bus, where it rightfully rode to the hotel with the champions.

If you talk to enough people around the Crew, they ultimately throw around the words, "the Crew family."

Sunday night, at the Manhattan Beach Marriott, the Crew held a massive family reunion. The Hunts threw a private dinner celebration for the players, coaches and staff... and everyone's spouses, children, parents, best friends, and...like...third-uncles-once-removed. It was literally every available member of the extended Crew Family. And everyone was excited to meet everyone. A very poplar phrase was "I've heard so much about you."

And then at 8:00, the celebration was opened to the fans, who got to pose for pictures not only with their favorite champion players, but the Anschutz Trophy itself.

"How cool is this?" said my good buddy Flick. "These guys go out and win a trophy, then they let clowns like me hold it and pose for pictures with it, as if I did anything."

But that's the thing. The Massive Bananas are not glory hogs. All season long, they have openly talked of the fans' influence on their play. Whether you sit in the Nordecke, the club seats, the upper deck, or in Section 107 like Flick, the team honestly feels that you earned a piece of that trophy. So pose away.

I suppose Flick's larger point still stands: how cool was that? Could you imagine getting within 100 feet of the Lombardi Trophy at a party at the team hotel on Super Bowl Sunday?

Flick didn't get to hold the World Series trophy when his Cincinnati Reds won it in '90.
(Photo by Steve Sirk)

For all the previous talk of 2009 starting on Monday, the truth is that it couldn't wait that long. It started Sunday night. The Hunts and McCullers had an impromptu meeting in the hotel kitchen about the expansion draft, and then Bliss and McCullers set up an 8:30 a.m. meeting since the list was due at 10 a.m. the next morning. It seemed almost cruel to have that quick of a turnaround, especially with Monday being a travel day. Would it have killed anyone to do the expansion lists and expansion draft the week after Thanksgiving?

I'm sure the organization had a fairly firm grasp of who would be protected, but it's the human element that got pinched by the quick turnaround. One obviously can't have "the talk" before the MLS Cup final. As a result, everyone had barely washed the champagne out of their hair, and guys like Bliss and McCullers were scrambling to find the time to break the expansion list news to their players on Monday. There is never a good time to say, "Brad, thanks for scoring the series-winner against Kansas City, but we're

415

exposing you." Or, "Eddie, thanks for scoring the conference-winning goal against the Fire, but we're letting Seattle take you if they want."

That conversation is never going to be easy. But does it have to happen within a day of MLS Cup? What would be the harm in letting the players, coaches and staff enjoy their title for a week? I realize that this has probably happened with every expansion draft ever, but I never really thought about it until I had to see it firsthand. It just seemed cruel.

Of course, it beats missing the playoffs and having a month to let all of the players know, and then none of them get picked because they aren't good enough to ride the pine for an expansion team. That's the sort of thing that the D.C. Uniteds of the world are dealing with.[193] But still... in future expansion years, I think that there should be a one-week grace period. The champs should get to enjoy Thanksgiving as champions.

Throughout my time in LA, I heard a few variations of the following sentence: "The shame about something big like this is that guys like Rusty and Tucker don't get to enjoy it as much as everyone else."

On the team side of the organization, equipment manager Rusty Wummel and administrator Tucker Walther are a study in constant motion. In Los Angeles, it was rare to see Rusty without a bag, box, or trunk in tow. And Tucker is the guy who will do anything for anyone, and then spends 25 hours per day doing it. At the team hotel, Tucker could barely blink in the lobby without someone tapping his shoulder and seeking assistance with some want or need.

So on Sunday night, I was happy to see Rusty and Tucker with beers in hand, celebrating with everyone. Later in the night, Tucker sat back in a lobby chair and barely uttered a word. I asked him if he was about to pass out. Instead, it seems that his near-coma was not alcohol-induced, but contemplative in nature.

"I'm just thinking about this year," he said. "I'm just replaying the whole season in my head. I am thinking about all of the people and all of the things that have happened along the way. "

It took eight months to get from the Moffat Rocket against the Hosers on March 29 to the triumphant trophy-hoisting on November 23. And 10 months, if you count the pre-season. What massive trip it has been.

---

[193] Ah, that felt good.

Tucker thinking about things got me to thinking about the time Tucker and I last sat back and thought about things.[194] It was sometime in September and Tucker asked me when I knew that this was a special team. I told him there were a few things that stood out to me.

The first was hearing a preseason tale about the Crew's trip to England. Manchester United was hosting a Champions League quarterfinal, and some members of the Crew wanted to go to the game. Tickets were ridiculously expensive and well out of the price range of some of the team's support staff. The plan was that some guys would go to the game, while others would seek out a pub near Old Trafford. However, Guillermo Barros Schelotto asked some of the staffers if they wanted to go. They said yes, but they could not afford tickets. "No problem," said Guille. With one Schelotto phone call, the staffers were soon watching the game from Man U. star Carlos Tevez's luxury box.

Years ago, Brian Dunseth told me that you can learn a lot of about players by watching how they treat the support staff. The fact that an Argentine legend was looking out for "the little people" was a sign that this was a special team.

The second was Danny O'Rourke's early season penalty travails. Danny had been asked to learn a completely new position as a center back, and it took him a while to shed some of his seek-and-destroy midfield tendencies. He conceded penalty kicks at an alarming rate early in the season, but I never saw or heard of teammates tearing him down, and Danny himself had the amazing ability to not only shake it off, but make fun himself. The confidence shown in him by his coaches and teammates, and the internal strength Danny showed in the face of such adversity, were signs that this was a special team.

Another, and perhaps my favorite, came after the infamous 1-0 loss to New England. Ezra Hendrickson had been called for a soft but necessary penalty in closing minutes. Hesmer saved the PK, but the Revs knocked in the rebound for an 89th minute decision. I was struck by how Ezra made no excuses and accepted full responsibility for the penalty. I was struck by how O'Rourke told Ezra not to worry, because Hendrickson still needed a few more penalties to catch up to him – again, Danny cracking on his own misfortune, this time to lift the spirits of a disappointed teammate. And then I was struck by how Frankie Hejduk tore into the referee's decision, sticking up

---

[194] That was a fun and ridiculous sentence to write.

for his guy like a captain should. Three guys, all doing the right and honorable thing by their teammates.

Yet another clue came on June 7 after the Crew's 2-0 home loss to the expansion San Jose Earthquakes. The Crew's scoreless drought in league play had ballooned to 367 minutes, including a club-record four straight shutouts. After that loss, Robbie Rogers spoke of how the media was going to make a big deal about the slump and scoreless streak, but he wasn't worried at all because this team was too good and too talented to stay down for long. He didn't mumble these words while staring at the floor. He looked me dead in the eye. He meant every last word of it. Then his confidence was rewarded when the Crew scored three goals the next week and they never looked back.

When replaying the season in his mind, or thinking of defining moments, I am sure Tucker thought of many different things since he is around the team 24/7. But in my limited exposure, these were the things that jumped out at me in September when Tucker asked me when I knew that this team was special. These few incidents displayed the resiliency, the toughness, the accountability, the camaraderie and the confidence that shone through on the field as the results began to pile up in the second half of the season.

Tucker and I didn't get to discuss this any further on Sunday. He soon departed for his room and some well-deserved sleep.

Maybe it's kind of cheesy, but it's impossible to talk about everyone, so I want to do a roll call. Some of these players are legends. Some never saw the field. Some may go on to have long Crew careers, while others are already gone. Some may provide you with future thrills and others may be the center of future heartache in this or another uniform. But none of that matters now.

What matters now is that every single one of these men did what they do, and served as a vital ingredient in that magical soup that makes up a championship squad.

Ladies and gentlemen, the 2008 MLS Cup Champion Columbus Crew:

#1 William Hesmer

#2 Frankie Hejduk

#3 Brad Evans

#4 Gino Padula

#5 Danny O'Rourke

#6 Andy Iro

#7 Guillermo Barros Schelotto

#8 Duncan Oughton

#9 Jason Garey

#10 Alejandro Moreno

#11 Pat Noonan

#12 Eddie Gaven

#13 Andrew Peterson

#14 Chad Marshall

#15 Stefani Miglioranzi

#16 Brian Carroll

#17 Emmanuel Ekpo

#18 Kenny Schoeni

#19 Robbie Rogers

#20 Brian Plotkin

#22 Adam Moffat

#23 Ezra Hendrickson

#24 Jed Zayner

#25 George Josten

#26 Cory Elenio

#27 Ryan Junge

#29 Ricardo Pierre-Louis

#30 Andy Gruenebaum

#31 Kevin Burns

#32 Steven Lenhart

#37 Stanley Nyazamba

They are champions, every last one of them, and they are Massive forevermore.

On the flight back to Columbus, I peered out the window and gazed down upon the marshmallow mattress of clouds that sprawled out to the horizon. Somewhere down below, people glumly went about their business in the gloomy grayscale, hoping for brighter days.

The thing is, on those rare occasions when you get a chance to soar above the cloud base, you realize that the sun is always shining.

Such is the view from the top.

Questions? Comments? Think it's more than a coincidence that in the year "aught 8", "Ought 8" won his championship with the Crew? Feel free to write at sirk65@yahoo.com

This really happened. Seriously. It did. The Crew won it all. (Photo by Andy Mead / YCJ)

A close-up of the MLS Cup 2008 gold medal, as hand-modeled by Tracey Tashjian.
(Photo by Mike Flickinger)

Crew Blog: The Big Nasty Fan Club

November 26, 2008

As was widely reported while we were out in LA, rookie Steven Lenhart led the Crew with 96 MLS Cup tickets for friends and family….and friends of family…and family of friends…and whatever other groups of people are needed to bump up that number to the ridiculous total of 96.

Like Adam Moffat predicted, the Lenhart group was easy to spot. Not only were they loud and boisterous, but they all wore yellow t-shirts. (If you recorded the game, they are the swath of yellow that took up a few rows on the far side, maybe a few sections up the sideline from Nordecke LA.)

My good buddy Flick told me that not only was the Lenhart group wearing yellow, but they were wearing incredible t-shirts that said "Proud member of the Big Nasty Fan Club." ("Big Nasty" was Lenhart's nickname in college.)

But the best part of the shirts, according to Flick, was the graphic, which consisted of Lenhart's head superimposed on top of the neckline of a catalog shot of a Crew jersey.

I am happy to report that Big Nasty himself has been kind enough to pass along the graphic so that we can all enjoy it, even those of us who never saw the actual t-shirts.

With that, I now present the official t-shirt graphic of the Big Nasty Fan Club:

(Graphic courtesy of Steven Lenhart / The Big Nasty Fan Club)

421

Crew Blog: Goggles & Haircuts

November 29, 2008

I thought I would check in with a few goofy postgame photos. When I referenced things such as Tucker's champagne goggles or the celebratory haircut mutilations that took place in the locker room, here's what I was talking about.

Tucker's awesome champagne goggles...

(Photo by Steve Sirk)

GM Mark McCullers posing with a bottle tilted over Tucker's be-goggled noggin...

(Photo by Steve Sirk)

Later that night, at the team hotel, Jason Garey kindly posed for this wonderful photo of his hillbilly bowl-buzzcut & trailer 'stache...

(Blurry photo by Steve Sirk)

And then there is The Legend. Earlier this year, strength & conditioning coach Steve Tashjian had a surefire winner in the team's beard competition, but he shaved it off before taking it public. I did my best to describe the video footage I had seen, but now I am happy to report that Tashjian recreated the look and posed for a photo-in-the-round at the team's hotel reception later that night. "Now you can bring The Legend to life, and prove that it exists" Tashjian said, as radio man Neil Sika snapped these four photos for me...

Front side:

(Photo by Neil Sika)

Left side:

(Photo by Neil Sika)

Back side:

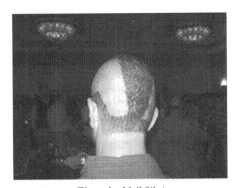

(Photo by Neil Sika)

Right side:

(Photo by Neil Sika)

Two More Awesome MLS Cup Photos

I came across these photos a little bit later after the other pages were already formatted, but they were too good to leave out. So what the heck, they now get their own random page.

Duncan's sensational post-Cup mullet and mustache combo, complete with the missing chunk of hair from the locker room hair clipper wars. (Photo by Janet Handler)

Tucker Walther holds the Cup with the three holdovers from the Crew team that won 2004 Supporters' Shield: Marshall, Oughton, and Hejduk.
(Photo courtesy of Tucker Walther)

2008 Major League Soccer Standings

EASTERN CONFERENCE

	W	L	T	PTS	GF	GA
Columbus Crew	17	7	6	57	50	36
Chicago Fire	13	10	7	46	44	33
New England Revolution	12	11	7	43	40	43
Kansas City Wizards	11	10	9	42	37	39
New York Red Bulls	10	11	9	39	42	48
D.C. United	11	15	4	37	43	51
Toronto FC	9	13	8	35	34	43

WESTERN CONFERENCE

	W	L	T	PTS	GF	GA
Houston Dynamo	13	5	12	51	45	32
CD Chivas USA	12	11	7	43	40	41
Real Salt Lake	10	10	10	40	40	39
Colorado Rapids	11	14	5	38	44	45
FC Dallas	8	10	12	36	45	41
Los Angeles Galaxy	8	13	9	33	55	62
San Jose Earthquakes	8	13	9	33	32	38

PLAYOFFS

Eastern Conference Semifinals
Columbus def. Kansas City, 3-1, on aggregate. (1-1 / 2-0)
Chicago def. New England, 3-0, on aggregate. (0-0 / 3-0)

Western Conference Semifinals
New York def. Houston, 4-1, on aggregate. (1-1 / 0-3)
Salt Lake def. Chivas USA, 3-2, on aggregate. (0-1 / 2-2)

Eastern Conference Final
Columbus 2, Chicago 1

Western Conference Final
New York 1, Salt Lake 0

MLS Cup 2008
Columbus 3, New York 1

2008 Columbus Crew Final Stats

Regular season, playoffs, and U.S. Open Cup

#	Name	GP	GS	Goals	Assists	Points
7	Guillermo Barros Schelotto	31	31	7	25	39
9	Alejandro Moreno	33	33	10	7	27
19	Robbie Rogers	33	31	8	4	20
14	Chad Marshall	34	34	6	2	14
3	Brad Evans	32	23	6	1	13
12	Eddie Gaven	30	27	4	4	12
32	Steven Lenhart	14	5	6	0	12
2	Frankie Hejduk	28	28	2	4	8
9	Jason Garey	11	0	4	0	8
17	Emmanuel Ekpo	22	9	3	1	7
16	Brian Carroll	36	36	1	3	5
5	Danny O'Rourke	34	34	0	4	4
11	Pat Noonan	11	6	1	2	4
22	Adam Moffat	8	7	2	0	4
6	Andy Iro	22	12	1	0	2
15	Stefani Miglioranzi	14	7	0	1	1
1	William Hesmer	34	34	0	0	0
4	Gino Padula	18	18	0	0	0
23	Ezra Hendrickson	14	7	0	0	0
24	Jed Zayner	8	4	0	0	0
27	Ryan Junge	7	5	0	0	0
8	Duncan Oughton	6	1	0	0	0
13	Andrew Peterson	3	1	0	0	0
30	Andy Gruenebaum	2	2	0	0	0
26	Cory Elenio	1	0	0	0	0
25	George Josten	1	0	0	0	0
31	Kevin Burns	0	0	0	0	0
37	Stanley Nyazamba	0	0	0	0	0
29	Ricardo Pierre-Louis	0	0	0	0	0
20	Brian Plotkin	0	0	0	0	0
18	Kenny Schoeni	0	0	0	0	0

2008 Columbus Crew Individual MLS Honors

MLS Most Valuable Player:
Guillermo Barros Schelotto

MLS Cup Most Valuable Player:
Guillermo Barros Schelotto

MLS Coach of the Year:
Sigi Schmid

MLS Defender of the Year:
Chad Marshall

MLS Best XI:
Guillermo Barros Schelotto
Chad Marshall
Robbie Rogers

MLS All-Stars:
Frankie Hejduk
Robbie Rogers
Guillermo Barros Schelotto *(inactive)*

MLS Player of the Week:
Guillermo Barros Schelotto- 5X (4/14, 7/22, 8/25, 9/8, 11/17)
Robbie Rogers (5/12)

MLS Player of the Month:
Guillermo Barros Schelotto (August)

MLS Goal of the Week:
Brian Carroll *(Week 21: One-timer off of a GBS knockdown header vs. Dallas)*
Robbie Rogers *(Week 26: Long distance laser to the upper reaches of the far post in the opening seconds of the second half vs. New York)*
Brad Evans *(Week 31: Long range blast off the post and in vs. D.C. United)*

SECTION IV

*

THE JOYOUS AFTERMATH

*

Airport Adulation

On Monday, November 24, the Crew arrived at Port Columbus Airport at approximately 10:50 P.M. They arrived about an hour before I did, which Danny O'Rourke assured me was on purpose. As a result, I missed all of the fanfare when hundreds upon hundreds of Crew fans clogged the concourses in order to welcome their champions home in style. Thankfully, Sam Fahmi was there to snap some photos of the Crew's hometown coronation.

Assistant coach Robert Warzycha and Columbus Mayor Michael Coleman lift the Cup as the team descends the escalator to baggage claim. (Photo by Sam Fahmi)

Some fans espoused simple truths via homemade signs. (Photo by Sam Fahmi)

I'm sure the TSA just loves frenzied airport mobs like this one! (Photo by Sam Fahmi)

And most importantly, fans that couldn't make it to LA were also given the chance to hold the Cup and pose for pictures with it locally. (Photo by Sam Fahmi)

Crew Blog: Meeting with the Guv

November 26, 2008

On Tuesday night, Ohio Governor Ted Strickland honored the Crew at a Statehouse rally. Merz already has the write-up on what went down publicly. But what happened privately, when the team gathered in Governor Strickland's office?

"What happens behind closed doors stays behind closed doors," said Danny O'Rourke. "But all my parking tickets? Goodbye!"

"Danny gets away with murder anyway," said Andy Gruenebaum. "For the record, I'm clean. I've never, ever done anything wrong in my life. I've never gotten so much as a speeding ticket. In Ohio at least. So I'm set."

"Lots of guys are trying to get stuff wiped off their record," said Adam Moffat. "Duncan was in there for a while. I don't want to get into what all that was about, but it all got wiped away."

"Yeah, I got a few pardons myself," Oughton confirmed. "And then Brad Evans... I mean look at the guy...he needs more than a pardon."

"Adam Moffat got a pardon," revealed Steven Lenhart. "Indecent exposure. He was wearing a British man-thong underneath, but they still busted him when he lifted his kilt. It's all taken care of now, though."

According to William Hesmer, some players may have been seeking proactive amnesty. "Frankie's probably looking for some get-out-of-jail-free cards," he said.

It turns out that Frankie had no such thoughts on his mind.

"Nah, I wanted to sleep here tonight," said Hejduk. "Maybe you have to win two championships before you can do that."

If that's the case, here's hoping that 2009 will be the year that Frankie earns a gubernatorial slumber party.

Above: "We have called this team an asset to our community, but now we also call them national champions!" exclaimed Ohio Governor Ted Strickland on the State House steps before an adoring throng of Crew fans on Tuesday, November 25, 2008.

Previous page: The Crew pose with Strickland (over the Cup, between the Hunts) inside the State House.

Below: Clark Hunt, Governor Strickland, and Dan Hunt pose with the Anschutz Trophy during the Crew's visit to the Ohio State House.

(All three photos by Greg Bartram / Columbus Crew)

Champions Way & Championship Row

At Media Day on March 25, 2009, Columbus Mayor Michael Coleman (above) announced that the road that wraps around Crew Stadium would be renamed MLS Champions Way. Three days later, the Crew unveiled Championship Row (below) on the northeast facade of the upper deck. Championship Row honors the Crew's four domestic championships: 2002 U.S. Open Cup, 2004 Supporters' Shield, 2008 Supporters' Shield, and 2008 MLS Cup. (Both photos by Greg Bartram / Columbus Crew)

Championship Bling

On June 27, 2009, Guillermo Barros Schelotto accepts his 2008 MLS Cup championship ring from Dan Hunt, while Clark Hunt proudly observes. (Photo by Sam Fahmi)

A close-up of Robert Warzycha's diamond-encrusted championship ring.
(Photo by Greg Bartram / Columbus Crew)

The left side of the ring (above) features the person's name and title. It also has the team's regular season record engraved on the Supporters' Shield, as well as two stars to recognize that it was the Crew's second Supporters' Shield title. The right side of the ring (below) lists the score and date of the 2008 MLS Cup final, with the Anschutz Trophy sandwiched in between. Although nearly impossible to photograph, the inside of the ring is inscribed with the Lamar Hunt "LH" memorial insignia, as well as Alejandro Moreno's popular mantra: "Do what you do!" (Both photos by Greg Bartram / Columbus Crew)

The Champs Visit the White House

On Monday, July 13, 2009, the Crew were invited to the White House where they were honored by President Barack Obama for their 2008 MLS Cup championship.

The team took a lengthy and in-depth tour of the White House, participated in a Rose Garden ceremony with the President, and then ran a soccer clinic at a local Washington, D.C., school. (Clearly, you don't want these children learning from non-playoff teams like D.C. United, so you invite the champs instead.)

The team had a great time at the White House. "We were treated like royalty," said Crew President & GM Mark McCullers.

"Congratulations to all the rowdy fans who were with you every step of the way," said the President of the United States of America, Barack Obama. "I hear that Crew Stadium was one of the toughest places for visiting teams." Below, the President congratulates Gino Padula. (Photos by Greg Bartram / Columbus Crew)

Above, Clark Hunt presents the President with a personalized "Obama 44" Crew jersey. Below, the President poses for a picture with the MLS Cup champs.
(Both photos by Greg Bartram / Columbus Crew)

The President, however, was not the only one holding ceremonies. The Crew held a ceremony of their own outside the White House gates. There, McCullers presented former head coach Sigi Schmid and former players Brad Evans, Pat Noonan, and Ezra Hendrickson with their championship rings.

Above, Sigi Schmid accepts his 2008 championship ring from Mark McCullers. Below, Ezra Hendrickson shows off his championship bling.
(Both photos by Greg Bartram / Columbus Crew)

From Those Who Had Come Before...

Throughout the Crew's run to the Supporters' Shield and MLS Cup, Sigi and the players kept making reference as to how this was for the men who had come before. This team seemed to have a good grasp of Crew history and the near-misses that have haunted the club through the years. Surely, having longtime Crew stalwarts like Robert Warzycha and Mike Lapper as assistant coaches, and Dante Washington in the broadcast booth, played a big role in that. Those are three walking, talking history lessons right there. But in interviews, the team seemed to take pride in that. They knew they were playing for the old guys as much as themselves.

In light of that, I thought I would track down some of "the guys who had come before" to get their thoughts on the Massive Bananas breaking through and finally bringing an MLS Cup home to Columbus. This was a last-minute brainstorm, and I couldn't track down every last player, but here are the people I successfully connected with on short notice, in alphabetical order...

NELSON AKWARI
(Defender 2003-2004 / 2004 Supporters' Shield winner / 2004 Crew team Humanitarian of the Year)

Congrats on the great year! Throughout the regular season and into the playoffs, it was clear that the Crew were the most consistent team. You all deserved the Supporter's Shield and MLS Cup. Congrats to the loyal fans and supporters of Columbus! It was an honor to wear the Crew shirt.

GREG ANDRULIS
(Head coach 2001-2005, assistant coach 1996-2001 / 2002 U.S. Open Cup champion and 2004 Supporters' Shield winner / 2004 MLS Coach of the Year)

Lamar Hunt was a great man. What he did for the game of soccer in this country as a visionary, financier and motivator may never be completely understood. Today's players and teams benefitted tremendously from his courage, conviction and determination to see this great sport succeed in this country. There would be no MLS with out him it is really that simple.

When the Crew won the US Open Cup, I was fortunate to be part of that team. The memory I will have forever is seeing Lamar Hunt, Clark Hunt, Jim Smith and the team jumping up and down on the podium at Crew Stadium shortly after the victory. What an incredible night for the man who was responsible for the event, the team, the stadium and the success of the franchise. Our sole goal from that night on was to win an MLS Cup for Lamar.

Watching MLS Cup 2008, cheering wildly for the Crew and enjoying a great result led to a moment of melancholy. I wished that Lamar could be on that podium with Frankie, Sigi, Clark Hunt and the rest of the team, jumping for joy again. What a moment that would have been for him. There is no greater tribute that the Crew could have given to the founder of the franchise than to win an MLS Cup. It was great for the fans, players, coaches and the supporters of the Crew, but especially for the memory of the man responsible—Lamar Hunt.

MARCELO CARRERA
(Midfielder 1996-1998, assistant coach 2000, plus Spanish-language radio through July 2008 / Crew Original)

I watched the MLS Cup and it was a great feeling for me to see Columbus win the championship. I spent many years with the Crew as a player, a part-time assistant, and then on Spanish radio, so I am very happy that the fans and the city got to experience this great excitement.

I remember sitting at a table with Sigi, Robert, Mike Lapper, and Mark McCullers during preseason in 2007, and they asked me if I knew Guillermo Barros Schelotto because they were interested in signing him. I said, "Yeah, I know the guy, and he is a winner." So I am very glad that Guillermo and his talented teammates were winners in 2008. It is something that the city, the club, and the fans needed, and I am proud of how these guys represented the Columbus Crew. I also know it was very important for the Hunt family and the memory of Lamar Hunt, so it made me really happy.

MIKE CLARK
(Defender 1996-2003 / 2002 U.S. Open Cup champion / MLS All-Star: 2000, 2001 / Crew team Man of the Year in 1998, Defender of the Year in 2000, and Humanitarian of the Year in 2003 / Crew Original)

Let me start off by saying congratulations on an awesome season in 2008. As a past player and member of the inaugural Columbus Crew team, I

442

found myself flooded with memories as the Crew marched through the 2008 playoffs. I thought that some of these memories were worth sharing and hopefully those that haven't followed the Crew since its inception will get an even clearer picture why bringing home the championship touched so many people.

The first year for anything is bound to include many mishaps and screw ups, and 1996 was no different. From the front office asking the team to model underwear in a downtown Structure store, where Todd Yeagley was seen doing pushups prior to mingling with the crowd, to "Sneaky" Pete Marino choosing to pick some boxer briefs that were barely legal in hopes that he might land his next date, the public appearances always seemed to be a bit of an adventure.

Before the practice facility was built in Obetz, we initially trained at a high school on the south side of C-Bus where we were forced to change and mingle with students as they prepared to play dodgeball for their 2nd period gym class. We then moved on to OSU, where we did our best while bouncing around from various locker rooms. One thing was certain throughout all of this, though, and that was that we were pumped that we were playing for the best franchise in Major League Soccer and actually getting PAID to PLAY!

The Crew Clinics that we put on throughout Ohio were instrumental in bringing the Crew to towns that may have never heard of soccer otherwise. At the time, it was sometimes a huge inconvenience to travel to parts unknown, but looking back, I wouldn't trade those experiences for anything. Much of the first few years was just that— selling a brand/league. Because of the community outreach that all of the MLS teams participated in, MLS grew in stature every year.

As the years progressed, so did the talent. The Crew had a number of players come and go through the years, and as a member of the Crew for 8 seasons, there are a number that stand out. Ansil Elcock – I never saw him without a smile, and if you invited him over to your home, he always brought some Trinidadian rum that would make your throat bleed. Robert Warzycha - the only player I ever saw who warmed up by ripping 25 yard bombs on goal. He also had a nice tradition of bringing over meat, cheese, and honey-infused vodka when entertaining, but I won't go into detail on that....

McBride, Yeags, Mais, Smitty, David Winner, Timo, Baer (both Amy and Chris), Jim Schmidtke, Lapper, Segna, Sneaky Pete, Dante, Bo, Doc Edwards, Diggity Doctor Khumalo, Stern "The Turn" John, Naps, DeBrito, and many others are names that should resonate with the people who were around the Crew from the very beginning.

There have only been a few coaches through the years, and on the day that Frankie held that championship trophy over his head, I know that Tom Fitzgerald was smiling down on the Crew. Fitzy was the face of the Crew for many years. He always represented himself and the organization with class and had a great relationship with the media, which helped because we were always battling to get face time with the news outlets.

I know that I have rambled a bit, but in a fraction of a second, these and many other thoughts literally shot through my head during the closing seconds of MLS Cup. I do want to say a special thanks to Lamar Hunt and his entire family, for without his dedication and commitment to the Crew and soccer in general, I would never had a chance to realize my dream of playing professionally. I also want to thank Tucker, who took a lot of crap over the years, but there is nobody better at what they do than he is. (And despite what he says, he loves what he does.) And congrats to D-Nuts, the 2nd hardest Crew player ever. I promised Duncan that I would never tell anybody the secret to his longevity....so I won't, but there is a reason that at the start of every preseason with the Crew while I was there, there were often a number of defensive midfielders, but by the end of training camp, the number of healthy d-mids left were minimal at best! That, plus Duncan is a QUALITY player and an even better individual. Congrats on a championship much deserved!

Finally, to the entire 2008 team...your storybook season has had made every Crew fan— which is what I now and forever consider myself— realize the fruits of 12 years of HARD work. Congratulations to every one of you, and I hope the future will bring you even more success.

JEFF CUNNINGHAM
(Forward 1998-2004 / 2002 U.S. Open Cup champion and 2004 Supporters' Shield winner / 2002 MLS Best XI / 2002 Crew team MVP, 2001 & 2002 Crew team scoring champion)

Congratulations, Columbus! Those guys were truly the hardest working team. For the team and for the fans, it was a well-deserved championship.

BRIAN DUNSETH
(Defender 2002-2003 / 2002 U.S. Open Cup champion / 2002 Crew team Humanitarian of the Year)

I want to congratulate the Crew players, coaches, and staff on a championship season, but most of all, I want to congratulate the fans. The fans have been a big part of the Crew from beginning, and I saw it firsthand as an opponent and then with my time in Columbus. Their support is why I will always treasure my time with the Crew, so I was very happy to be in the stadium when their support was finally rewarded with an MLS Cup championship.

Frankie and Duncan are two of the greatest guys you'll meet in MLS, and they are definitely fan favorites, so one couldn't ask for anything better than for those two guys to finally lift the cup for Columbus. And I also felt a lot of joy for Robert Warzycha. He has been with the Crew since the very start in 1996, and I don't know if there has ever been a more ideal foreign acquisition in terms of the long-term building of an organization. As a human being, athlete, and coach, he has proudly represented the Crew through all the highs and lows over the years. When a guy has been in one place for 13 years and nobody can say a bad thing about him, that's really saying something. I'm happy he got to experience a well-deserved championship with the Crew.

ANSIL ELCOCK
(Midfielder 1997-2001 / Crew team Coaches Award 1998)

I certainly watched the Crew as they won MLS Cup. It was a proud moment for me because I still consider myself a part of the Crew. I spent five years in Columbus and have a lot of love and respect for the organization and the fans. Everyone treated me so well. I remember when I first got there, Brian McBride took me under his wing and Tom Fitzgerald was like a father figure to me. He and his wife were so kind to me, and the fans were great. How could you ever forget a place that was so friendly and welcoming? I consider Columbus to be my professional home and I will always do anything I can to help the Crew.

When I watched the 2008 Crew, I couldn't believe the team that Sigi Schmid, Robert Warzycha, and Mike Lapper had assembled. I was very impressed with Guillermo Barros Schelotto and was glad that the coaches believed in him. Some coaches don't believe in older players, but he has great fitness and he showed great skill and leadership.

I called Stern[195] after the championship game. I told him the Crew won the championship and he said, "Yeah, I know!" He was really excited because Columbus means a lot to both of us. There are still many Crew fans in Trinidad. After the game, my phone was ringing like crazy because people wanted to say congratulations to me.

So I want to congratulate everybody for winning a championship for the great city of Columbus. One of Lamar Hunt's dreams was to see the Columbus Crew win a championship, so I am also very happy for the Lamar Hunt family.

DEBI FITZGERALD
(Wife of the late Tom Fitzgerald—head coach 1996-2001, assistant coach 1996 / Crew Original)

Firstly, CONGRATULATIONS to the Columbus Crew, the hardest working team in MLS!

Tom loved and thought very highly of the boys, the Hunt organization, and the fans of the Columbus area. Coaching the Crew was the pinnacle of Tom's career and a magical time for us. Tom was really honored to be a part of the Columbus Crew and their history.

The names of the players may change over the years, but their teamwork and dedication to their fans remains the same. The Columbus Crew are not only champions on the field, but off the field as well. And now they have the hardware to prove it!

ROBIN FRASER
(Defender 2004-2005 / 2004 Supporters' Shield winner / 2004 MLS All-Star, Defender of the Year, and Best XI / Crew team Defender of the Year in 2004 and Man of the Year in 2005)

MLS Cup 2008 was a great moment for many in Columbus. In the two years that I spent there, I got to know the fans, and appreciated their dedication. Playing in front of them was a wonderful experience, and I only

---

[195] Stern John, Ansil's cousin, who scored 55 goals in 70 Crew appearances spanning all competitions in 1998 & 1999. John is the Crew's all-time single-season goal leader with 26, and also holds the Crew record for hat-tricks (5 in the regular season plus the only playoff hat-trick in Crew history.)

regret that we couldn't turn our 2004 Supporters' Shield winning effort into something more.

The greatest thing about playing in Columbus, however, was the team. There were some great players, and some fantastic characters. The combination of older, more experienced players, and younger, talented individuals, really came together in a very special way.

Getting to watch Bobby W be a part of a championship team, was truly special. He is such an integrity filled gentleman that it was a pleasure to see him reap the benefits of years of hard work for that team...since 1996.

The other holdovers from my time there were Frankie, Duncan, and Chad. I had known Frankie for years, and really enjoyed my opportunity to play with him on a daily basis. Duncan is pure class, and like Frankie, one of the most honest and hardworking players that I have ever met. And then there's Chad. What an odd paring we must have seemed like— a 37-year-old playing next to a 19-year-old! I was blown away, back then, by how good he was, and I am even more impressed with how he has matured to this point. We had a great partnership. I would love to take credit for how good Chad is, but the fact of the matter is that he's just that good.

I would be remiss in not mentioning Tucker Walther, the long time team administrator. A great man who really cares about the team and the players. To see him involved in a championship team was also gratifying.

For those guys that I had gotten to know in the winter of my career, I was truly happy to see them win. They are classy people who work hard, and earned their championship. They say good things happen to good people....case in point!

For the fans of Columbus...you waited a long time, and were finally rewarded for your loyalty.

BRIAN MAISONNEUVE
(Midfielder 1996-2004 / 2002 U.S. Open Cup champion and 2004 Supporters' Shield winner / MLS All-Star: 1998, 1999, 2002 / Crew team Man of the Year & Goal of the Year in 2001, Coaches Award in 2003, and Comeback Player of the Year in 2004 /Crew Original)

I want to thank the Crew and the entire city for a wonderful 2008 season! I like to consider myself the biggest Crew fan, and last year was such an unbelievable ride. For me, last year was a fitting tribute to an organization and a city that deserves the BEST. It was an honor for me to wear the black and gold for so many years and to play in front of the best fans in the entire league. My time in Columbus was so special for me and my entire family- we love Columbus!

To watch the way everything came together, and to see the team perform so well from the beginning to the end of the season, was very special for every Crew fan and for every player that was lucky enough to wear the jersey. I want to thank Sigi, Bobby, Laps and the entire coaching staff for putting together such quality on the field. I want to thank the players for such an unbelievable effort week in and week out for the entire season. I want to thank the Hunts, Mark, Brian, Tucker, and the entire organization for always doing things first class. And lastly, I want to thank all the fans and the entire city for making it such an HONOR for every player, past and present, to call Columbus home. Thanks and congratulations to all!

ROSS PAULE
(Midfielder 2003-2005 / 2004 Supporters' Shield champion / 2003 Crew team MVP)

It was a great feeling to see the Crew win their first league title. I absolutely loved playing for the Crew and being a part of such a great organization. The team, Crew organization and fans deserved this one, and I hope more are to come for us all. Congratulations to everyone who has ever been a part of building the Crew to what they are today, and congratulations to the team who brought the title home. Awesome season!

JAMEY ROOTES
(President & General Manager 1995-1999 / 1996 MLS Executive of the Year and 1999 MLS Marketing Executive of the Year / Crew Original)

For me, it was magical to see the Columbus Crew finally reach that pinnacle at MLS Cup 2008. There comes a time in an organization's life where you might start to doubt that you will ever get there. We had knocked on the door so many times before, and I know that when I left, there was a sense of unfinished business. I am thankful that the 2008 team finished the job. There may be new faces, and the names on the back of the shirt may change, but the crest on the front is still the same.

I am happy for a lot of people, but I am most gratified for Clark Hunt and the Hunt family, who finally earned a title for their beloved Crew. Having worked closely with the Hunts, I know they deserved it. As I saw

448

them celebrate on the podium, I couldn't help but think that Lamar was smiling down in that mild-mannered way of his. He would have been proud.

I was also happy for assistant coaches Robert Warzycha and Mike Lapper, who played for the Crew in my time. Robert goes back to 1996. I remember watching tapes of him with then-coach Timo Liekoski, and we thought, "If only we could get this guy to Columbus." Luckily, we did, and he brought an entirely new level of professionalism to the Crew with his playing experience at the club and international levels. Mike Lapper was a U.S. National Team player who was both a great player and a great person. I think it's telling and fortunate that both of these men have been with the organization for as long as they have, and I congratulate them.

I am also thrilled for Mark McCullers, who we brought in a decade earlier to oversee Crew Stadium. He has been a rock for the Crew organization ever since, and it was great to see him get to the mountaintop.

And, of course, I am excited for the fans. When we first started, nobody thought Columbus would make it as a soccer market. I think back to the 25,000 fans we had for our very first game, and how many of those people have lived and died with every pass for 13 seasons until they finally got to cheer for a champion. Congratulations Columbus!

JIM SMITH
(President & General Manager 2000-2004 / 2002 U.S. Open Cup champion / 2001 MLS Executive of the Year)

What an incredible run during the 2008 season! The intensity and determination the Crew displayed during the 2008 season was an inspiration to all those who have played for or represented the Crew organization in the past. It was great to see Robert, Mike and Duncan celebrating and representing all the former Crew players of the past, as they are the links between the "old guard's" 2002 U.S. Open Cup championship and the 2008 team that brought the Crew their very first MLS Cup.

I couldn't be happier for the Hunt Family, who are the unsung heroes of professional soccer in this country. They finally got a well deserved a MLS Cup championship for their Columbus Crew.

Finally, I can't describe how great it was to watch that yellow mass of Crew fans in the corner in LA celebrating a convincing MLS Cup victory. The Crew's championship was for all those fans, as it is the greatest thank you an organization can give to its fans. Congratulations to all.

DAVID "CHUCKY" WINNER
(Goalkeeper 1996-1998 / Crew Original)

With as many teams that I was associated with in my time in Major League Soccer, I always had a special place in my heart for Columbus. I was absolutely thrilled when the Crew won their first MLS Cup championship in 2008. I was at a tournament and watched the game in my hotel room. I was so happy when Frankie scored the game clincher. I texted Lapp and Sigi to congratulate them.

I was fortunate enough to be a part of the inaugural team in 1996 and was with the club for three years. I kinda felt a part of it last fall, even though it has been many years since I was with the Crew. It has been amazing to see how the club has gotten to where it is today, from playing in the Horseshoe to the building of the first soccer specific training ground in Obetz and then Crew Stadium in 1999.

I have many fond memories of my old teammates and friends and coaches over those years. I was fortunate to play for Fitz, who was my coach at the University of Tampa, and Greg Andrulis, who I had as a coach at Clemson Soccer Camp when I was 12, and Timo, who gave me my first chance as a pro. I remember playing in the new stadium when I was with Kansas City and when I came out to warm up the fans on one side all got up to cheer for me. That all changed when the game started and Clarkie slid into my chest. And when the ball went out for a goal kick and a fan poured a beer on me.

But out of all the teams I played with, I loved Columbus the most. It is an awesome city with great supporters. I want to give a special shout out to the supporters from the Shadowbox & the Wrecking Crew.

Ironically enough, my wife, Ashlee, is from Ohio and played soccer at Ohio State, so every year we go home to Ohio for the holidays and I get very nostalgic when we drive past the stadium on 71.

Now that I am in coaching, it is kinda neat to see everything come full circle with the whole staff that I was teammates with. I am the goalkeeper coach for the Austin Aztex now, and we played the Crew in pre-season, so it was great to see Robert Warzycha, Mike Lapper, Ricardo Iribarren, and Brian Bliss for a couple days.

One thing that really put the Crew's success in perspective for me was when I was in Buenos Aires, Argentina, with the Region III ODP team in February 2009. We went to a Boca Juniors game and there were fans with Crew jerseys on with "Schellotto" on the back!

I am hoping for Columbus to repeat this year and for years to come. It has been a long time coming and it has been awesome to see the progress over the years. All the best in '09 and beyond. ~David Winner (Affectionately nicknamed "Chucky" by Adrian Paz.)

TODD YEAGLEY
(Midfielder 1996-2002 / Crew team Man of the Year in 1996 and Humanitarian of the Year in 2001 / Crew Original)

Congratulations to all the players and staff! It was fantastic watching the Crew raise the MLS Cup! The 2008 Crew team played with passion and pride in the uniform. This team embodied the Crew motto: Hard working and honest.

The loyal Crew fans, past players and coaches, and the city of Columbus all share in this wonderful achievement. Thank you for giving all of us a moment that we will always cherish.

A Picture is Worth a Lifetime of Words

Two worlds collide. (Photo by Dave Stephany)

In my own heart and mind, nothing sums up the 2008 Columbus Crew season as well as the photo on the opposite page. That is the Phillip Anschutz Trophy, awarded to the MLS Cup champions, sitting atop a rickety old seat from Cleveland Municipal Stadium. Crew PR Director Dave Stephany snapped the photo while Danny O'Rourke brought the trophy to the CD 101 studios during a post –Cup media blitz in late November.

That photo is dripping with meaning for me. My childhood was spent wandering Cleveland Municipal Stadium, that cavernous behemoth known as "The Mistake on the Lake." It was built as part of Cleveland's bid to host the 1932 Summer Olympics. Oops.

In her early years, Municipal Stadium hosted her share of glorious moments. There were those five National Football League champions and four All-American Football Conference champions that called the place home. The 1948 World Series champions played there, as did the 1954 American League pennant winners. All-time greats graced her field while wearing the home team's colors. Bob Feller's fastball flustered baseball's finest, then Jim Brown spent his Sundays steamrolling mortified mortals. Joe DiMaggio's 56-game hitting streak died there, and Monday Night Football was born there.

But that's not the Municipal Stadium I knew. Heck, it's barely the Municipal Stadium that my *dad* knew. He was 11 years old when the Browns beat the Baltimore Colts, 27-0, to win the 1964 NFL title. While he did not go to the championship game, he attended his first Browns game earlier that season, a 33-33 tie against the St. Louis Cardinals. His first stadium event more or less coincided with the end of the structure's glory years. Shortly thereafter, Art Modell fired Paul Brown, Jim Brown went Hollywood, and the Browns were relegated to mediocrity. Concurrently, the Indians made consistent headway in their 35-year odyssey of ineptitude.

By the time I came of age and my dad could take me down to the lakeshore to watch our teams play, a generation's worth of incompetence had battered the building until it was every bit the worse for wear, as if the bumbling begat the crumbling. To say that the Indians beat fans away from the turnstiles with a stick would give the mistaken impression that they were capable of making contact. The team was so consistently bad that when the 1986 team finished in fifth place with an 84-78 record, my 12-year-old self regarded it as the dream baseball season to which all others would be compared. The next spring, Sports Illustrated put Joe Carter and Cory Snyder on the cover and predicted that the Indians would win the World Series. They lost 101 games.

The Browns, meanwhile, enjoyed a brief renaissance during my formative years. From 1985-1989, they shook off the Modell Malaise and became a playoff staple. Bernie Kosar came home to be the franchise savior, the Dawg Pound was born, and the radio was filled with Browns-related songs with a Super Bowl theme. Unlike the Tribe, the Browns gave fans hope. In a downtrodden sports town, hope is a necessary ingredient in the crushing of souls.

The Browns specialized in the crushing of souls. During their five-year playoff run, the first four seasons ended in horrific playoff losses, two of which were so horrific that they were given names: "The Drive" and "The Fumble." The fifth loss was a blowout defeat in Denver, which was Cleveland's third conference championship loss to John Elway's Broncos in a four year span. Unlike the first two nightmares, it didn't warrant a nickname. Thank goodness for small favors.

But that was my childhood. I went to Cleveland Municipal Stadium to cheer for one team that exemplified incompetence, and another that delivered heartache.

If those Browns and Indians teams had somehow mated and passed their combined genes on to a new sports team, that sports team would have resembled the Columbus Crew.

In their early years, the Crew were eerily similar to the Browns teams of my youth. They had a charismatic leader in Brian McBride, and were loaded with solid and popular stalwarts such as Mike Clark, Brian Maisonneuve, Robert Wazrycha, and Mike Lapper. But like those 1980s Browns teams, those Crew teams of the 1990s were good, but not good enough. Eerily, they even had their own unbeatable nemesis. D.C. United were the Crew's Denver Broncos, defeating Columbus three consecutive years in the conference championship. Not only did the Crew provide heartache in the MLS Cup playoffs, but they suffered some gut-wrenching losses in the U.S. Open Cup, such as the overtime loss to Chicago in the 1998 final, and 1999's 3-2 semifinal loss to the minor league Rochester Rhinos, when the Crew led 2-1 with just minutes to play. (To add insult to injury, the Rhinos beat Colorado to win 1999 trophy…in Crew Stadium.)

For the first half of the new decade, the Crew became schizophrenic, ably mixing headaches with heartbreaks. They had some bad seasons (2000, 2003), some good seasons gone bad (2001, 2004), and a mediocre season with a happy ending (2002.)

Oddly, despite being far less satisfying than the 1990s, this era produced the first two pieces of hardware in club history, as the 2002 team won the U.S. Open Cup and the 2004 team claimed the Supporters Shield, annually awarded to the team with the best record in MLS. In the larger scheme of things, these triumphs brought about less joy than one might imagine. The 2002 team finished with a losing record and still somehow managed to advance to the club's fourth conference final, before losing yet again. The 2004 team played unimaginative, tie-riffic soccer, making them the least fearsome Shield winner in history, with the lowest point total to match. The team flamed out miserably in the first round of the playoffs, including a gruesome Halloween affair known as "The Penalty Kicks", when both Ross Paule and, much more infamously, Tony Sanneh failed to convert from the spot during regulation time, preventing the Crew from advancing past fourth-place New England.

By 2005, the Columbus Crew fully entered 1980s Cleveland Indians mode. On and off the field, they were a wreck. The fan exodus was underway, and a vocal portion of the dwindling fan base became openly hostile toward the organization, the coach, and the team itself, which was a mishmash of non-complementary parts. Crew games ceased being fun for anyone but the opposition.

The Crew attempted to rectify the situation in 2006 by hiring Sigi Schmid to oversee the team's reconstruction. Schmid came to Columbus with a championship resume forged at both UCLA and with the Los Angeles Galaxy. Schmid quickly gutted the roster, which was obviously necessary, yet it also increased the alienation between the fans and the team. As players came and went through the revolving door while Sigi looked for the right parts, the fans had very little to latch on to. Three popular holdovers— Frankie Hejduk, Duncan Oughton, and Chad Marshall— missed significant time with injuries, leaving a team that was every bit as anonymous as it was unsuccessful. This was business as usual for one of my teams.

Schmid was convinced that he was assembling the right pieces. All he needed was a little more time and a run of good health. By the time the 2008 season rolled around, Schmid was on a short leash. If his team didn't blossom out of the gate, the Crew were staring at another rebuilding project. One shudders to think what consequences it would have had on the organization and the fan base. This also would have been business as usual for one of my teams.

I was used to my teams having plans. Marty Schottenheimer had a plan. So did Bill Belichick. And Butch Davis. And Romeo Crennel. And John Hart & Mike Hargrove. And Mark Shapiro & Eric Wedge. And Wayne Embry & Lenny Wilkens. And Doug MacLean. Some of these plans have worked better than others, but none of those plans ever produced a championship. (Well, except for Belichick after he went to New England.)

A MASSIVE SEASON: The Joyous Aftermath

In my world, successful plans are hatched and executed to perfection by other clubs. It's how teams like the Kansas City Wizards, Baltimore Ravens, Arizona Diamondbacks, Tampa Bay Buccaneers, Florida Marlins, Tampa Bay Lightning, Chicago White Sox, and Carolina Hurricanes, etc., have come out of nowhere and win random championships this decade.

But it's not what my teams do. Never ever never ever never ever do they do that. Ever. When you grow up in Cleveland, you learn that from a very young age. No matter how successful the coach, no matter how talented the players, and no matter how good the plan, it's going to fall short somehow, usually in excruciating fashion. It is inconceivable that a plan could work so flawlessly that the team would storm out of the gate, run roughshod over the competition all year long while playing in an attractive and crowd-pleasing manner, then gut-check its way through the postseason and walk away as one of the greatest championship squads the league has ever seen. That's now how I was raised.

Part of me still thinks it didn't happen in Columbus in 2008. But then I look at that photo. I love that photo. It makes me smile. For the fan in me, it's a Massive moment of glory triumphantly perched atop a lifetime of sports fan futility.

So I put this book together so that I (and hopefully you) would never forget the details of that special journey through A Massive Season.

3742770